LOGIC

Puzzles

CHARTWELL
BOOKS, INC.

This edition printed in 2006 for

CHARTWELL BOOKS, INC.
A Division of **BOOK SALES, INC.**
114 Northfield Avenue
Edison, New Jersey 08837

This collection © Arcturus Publishing Limited 2004
26/27 Bickels Yard, 151–153 Bermondsey Street
London SE1 3HA

Individual puzzles © Puzzler Media Ltd 2004
www.puzzler.co.uk

ISBN - 13: 978-0-7858-1995-0
ISBN - 10: 0-7858-1995-9

Printed in China

Cover designer: Alex Ingr

INTRODUCTION

Logic Puzzles contains over 300 cracking conundrums to tease and stimulate. Each has been designed to develop your powers of logical thinking, not to frustrate you and prove how clever the compilers are. To facilitate this learning process, the compilation includes charts for the standard problems to enable you to assess the possibilities and note down the information you gather from the clues. For some of the more difficult puzzles we have also provided useful tips to get you started. The solutions section provided at the end of the book is intended to help you see where you have gone wrong or, much more likely, confirm your brilliance!

We hope you get as much out of these puzzles as we did creating them for you.

AT THE RACES

Three friends went to the races one afternoon, and each backed the winner in a different race. From the clues given below, can you identify the three, work out in which race each picked the winner, and name the horse involved in each?

Clues

1 John backed the winner in an earlier race on the card than the horse chosen by his friend whose surname is Richmond.

2 Horseshoe Falls was Mr Watson's inspired choice.

3 Ben's surname is Farley.

4 Lucky Jim was the winner of the 3.30 race.

	Farley	Richmond	Watson	3.30	4.00	4.30	Four-leafed Clover	Horseshoe Falls	Lucky Jim
Ben									
John									
Leo									
Four-leafed Clover									
Horseshoe Falls									
Lucky Jim									
3.30									
4.00									
4.30									

Forename	Surname	Race	Horse

NURSES

Three nurses have just started work at Storbury's Willowtree Hospital, having previously worked elsewhere. From the clues given below, can you work out where and in which year each woman qualified as a nurse, and which ward at Willowtree she'll be working on?

Clues

1 Ann Bowles has been assigned to Nightingale Ward.

2 One of the nurses qualified in London in 1996.

3 The nurse assigned to Blackwood Ward didn't qualify in 1998, nor is she the one who trained in Cardiff whose name isn't Gail Hart.

4 The nurse assigned to Anderson Ward qualified in 2000; Pam Raynes qualified later than the woman who trained in Glasgow.

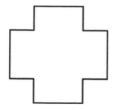

	Cardiff	Glasgow	London	1996	1998	2000	Anderson	Blackwood	Nightingale
Ann Bowles									
Gail Hart									
Pam Raynes									
Anderson									
Blackwood									
Nightingale									
1996									
1998									
2000									

Nurse	College	Year	Ward

SONS OF STORBURY

During the reign of Queen Elizabeth I, the little town of Storbury produced four men who found fame in their particular fields. Their birthplaces in the town are marked by plaques, but all of them died and were buried abroad. From the clues given below, can you work out each man's full name, his profession and where his grave can be seen?

Clues

1 Lambkin, the famous cartographer (that's somebody who makes maps, of course), is not the man buried in Alexandria, Egypt.

2 The painter's first name began with a vowel; Christopher wasn't the ship's captain who commanded the ship Woodbine in the fighting against the Spanish Armada, and Saward wasn't the soldier.

3 Catchpole, who wasn't Edmund, lies buried in Dublin, while the grave of the soldier, an early settler in the New World, can be seen on Cape Cod, Massachusetts.

4 Abel died and was buried in the French town of St Malo.

	Catchpole	Lambkin	Parfitt	Saward	Cartographer	Painter	Ship's captain	Soldier	Alexandria	Cape Cod	Dublin	St Malo
Abel												
Christopher												
Edmund												
Gilbert												
Alexandria												
Cape Cod												
Dublin												
St Malo												
Cartographer												
Painter												
Ship's captain												
Soldier												

Forename	Surname	Profession	Buried at

FOUR CARD GAMBLE

My friend Victor Lentine always sends a few cards through the internal mail to the most attractive young ladies on the staff at the shop in which he works, hoping, as he puts it, that his luck's going to change. Last year, for instance, he sent four cards; from the clues given below, can you work out to whom each went, the department in which each woman works, what picture was on the front of the card and how he signed it?

Clues

1 Victor's card to Ann Brown was signed 'Mr X'; after all, signing 'Valentine' would hardly be preserving his anonymity, would it?

2 Kay Jones was working in Kitchenware; the card with the picture of a dozen red roses went to the assistant in the Shoe Department.

3 The card which went to the girl in the Sports Department was signed 'Your secret lover', causing her rugby-playing fiancé from the Security Department to express a desire to hospitalise the sender; Victor hid from him for a week.

4 The card showing two glasses and a bottle of champagne and signed 'Mystery Man' went to one of the Brown sisters.

5 The card with the picture of two hearts wasn't the one that Victor signed as 'Your secret admirer'.

	Kitchenware	Lingerie	Shoes	Sports	Champagne	Hearts	Roses	Lovebirds	'Mr X'	'Mystery Man'	'Your secret admirer'	'Your secret lover'
Ann Brown												
Kay Jones												
Sue Smith												
Zoë Brown												
'Mr X'												
'Mystery Man'												
'Your secret admirer'												
'Your secret lover'												
Champagne												
Hearts												
Roses												
Lovebirds												

Girl	Department	Picture	Signature

MEETING THE PEOPLE

Yesterday, Ava Goatter, Junior Minister at the Department of Communications, visited a rural area of the East of England and spoke about the latest government policies to four different groups of concerned citizens at different locations. From the clues given below, can you work out the village and location where Ava spoke at each of the listed times, and say to which group of people she spoke?

Clues

1 At the historic Tithe Barn, Ava spoke to a group of parents worried about their children's education.

2 The unruly group of farmers, who were so angry about the latest changes in agricultural policy that they threw tomatoes at poor Ava, were in the tiny village of Luce End, which has no school.

3 Two hours after what turned out to be a rather ill-tempered confrontation with a group of parish councillors, Ava addressed another group of people at the Village Hall in Touchwood.

4 Ava's last speech of the day was, appropriately, in Farewell; her midday talk wasn't given in Runndown.

	Farewell	Luce End	Runndown	Touchwood	Church Hall	St Mark's School	Tithe Barn	Village Hall	Farmers	Parents	Parish councillors	Shop owners
10.00am												
12.00 noon												
2.00pm												
4.00pm												
Farmers								
Parents								
Parish councillors								
Shop owners								
Church Hall				
St Mark's School				
Tithe Barn				
Village Hall				

Times	Village	Venue	Audience

EYEWITNESSES

It's a busy day for the 78th Precinct of a big American city's Police Department, and in the Detective Squad office six officers are taking down statements over the phone from people who witnessed different crimes. From the clues given below, can you fill in on the drawing the name of the detective at each desk, the name of the witness he or she is getting a statement from, and what crime they're talking about?

Clues

1 Detective Grant isn't taking the statement from Jane Murphy.

2 Detective Tucci is seated at desk F.

3 Detective McManus is talking to whoever witnessed the theft of a luxury car and is seated at a desk on the opposite side of the squadroom to the ones being used by Detective Sorvino, who's talking to Elmer Smith, and by the detective who's getting Sam Dominici's account of an assault outside the Broadway Bar.

4 The desk used by the detective taking the statement about the bank robbery is indicated by a letter later in the alphabet than that which marks the one where the witness to the mugging is speaking; the former is next to and left of Detective Kravitz's desk.

5 Jack Fernandez is at the desk next to the one used by the cop dealing with the fraud case.

6 The detective at desk D taking a statement about the arson case isn't Detective Eckler.

7 Alma LaFarge is at desk B.

Detectives:
Eckler; Grant; Kravitz; McManus; Sorvino; Tucci

Witnesses:
Alma LaFarge; Elmer Smith; Jack Fernandez; Jane Murphy; Ned Ogorzov; Sam Dominici

Crimes:
Arson; assault; bank robbery; car theft; fraud; mugging

 A
 B
 C
 D
 E
 F

Desk	Detective	Witness	Crime

Starting tip: Work out the name of the bank robbery witness.

DEEP PHIL

The owner of the service station has just placed an order with Deep Phil's Sandwich Company for snacks to fill her chiller cabinet. From the following information, can you work out how many of each snack she has ordered, the type of bread used for each, and the two combined fillings?

Clues

1 After the wholemeal sandwiches, the next higher quantities are for the ones containing cucumber, then those containing eggs.

2 The owner of the service station has ordered two more of the soft rolls with smoked salmon than the ones with the chutney.

3 The six snacks containing avocado are not on crusty white bread.

4 She has ordered ten of the ham snacks.

5 There's tomato in the malted multi-grain sandwiches, but not a meat.

6 There's lettuce with the tuna.

	Baguette	Crusty white	Multi-grain	Soft roll	Wholemeal	Chicken	Egg	Ham	Smoked salmon	Tuna	Avocado	Chutney	Cucumber	Lettuce	Tomato
6															
8															
10															
12															
14															
Avocado															
Chutney															
Cucumber															
Lettuce															
Tomato															
Chicken															
Egg															
Ham															
Salmon															
Tuna															

Quantity	Bread	First filling	Second filling

ON THE SCENT

In five High Street department stores, five young women are inviting customers to sample five expensive perfumes. From the following information, can you discover which demonstrator is working in which store, and the manufacturer and name of the perfume in each case?

Clues

1 Maggie is working in Harridges, but Ingrid is not in John Harvey or Lewishams.

2 The perfume promoted in John Harvey is neither by D Klein, nor is it 'Time'.

3 Rachel is brandishing a bottle of 'Dawn'. Neither 'Dawn', 'Spirit' or Impetuous' is made by Bacque D'Or. The Bacque D'Or perfume is not being demonstrated in Lewishams.

4 'Impetuous', which is not by Villa Roma, is the perfume being sampled in Rackworths store.

5 'Sapphire' is by D Klein.

6 The Fray Grant product is being promoted in Mark Evans' department store. Carla is demonstrating Shamelle's scent.

	Harridges	John Harvey	Lewishams	Mark Evans	Rackworths	Bacque D'Or	D Klein	Fray Grant	Shamelle	Villa Roma	'Dawn'	'Impetuous'	'Sapphire'	'Spirit'	'Time'
Carla															
Ingrid															
Jan															
Maggie															
Rachel															
'Dawn'															
'Impetuous'															
'Sapphire'															
'Spirit'															
'Time'															
Bacque D'Or															
D Klein															
Fray Grant															
Shamelle															
Villa Roma															

Demonstrator	Store	Manufacturer	Perfume

I'M A CELEBRITY

The success of the recent Australian TV escapade for the group of 'celebrities' has seen many former A-list names begging for airtime, and next year five more celebs from yesteryear will be back on our screens in a variety of second-rate shows. From the information given below, can you work out in what fields they were formerly well-known, what kind of show each will be hosting, and in which month?

Clues

1 Warren Asbean was once a well-known footballer, and Willy Cwmbach, who is not the former magician, will be back on our screens in April.

2 Neither Willy Cwmbach nor Stella Eusterby is the one-time TV cook who will be hosting the new chat show.

3 Neither Hugh Wozzey nor the new presenter of the celebrity secrets show will be on TV from next May; the latter isn't the former newsreader.

4 Miles Older is to humiliate the public in a zany new prank show.

5 The makeover show will be screened in January.

6 The former DJ will be on TV from February.

	Hugh Wozzey	Miles Older	Stella Eusterby	Warren Asbean	Willy Cwmbach	DJ	Footballer	Magician	Newsreader	TV cook	Celeb secrets	Chat show	Game show	Makeover show	Prank show
January															
February															
March															
April															
May															
Celeb secrets															
Chat show															
Game show															
Makeover show															
Prank show															
DJ															
Footballer															
Magician															
Newsreader															
TV cook															

Month	Former celeb	Occupation	New show

CONSERVAT-IVE ESTIMATES

Five neighbours have recently ordered conservatories, and below are details of the size and cost of each, varying according to the quality, size and nature of the site. From the information given, can you discover which design of conservatory each person has ordered, its size, and the cost?

Clues

1 The Eatons have ordered a Buckingham conservatory, but not 8 feet by 10; Mr Deacon's is the 8 x 11.

2 The Griffins are paying £9,000 for their conservatory; the 8 x 12 is the most expensive.

3 Mrs Clifton's conservatory will be 8 feet wide, but the cost isn't £7,000; the £8,000 Ashridge conservatory will not be 10 feet long.

4 The smallest conservatory has been ordered by a woman.

5 The Aurora is not the cheapest conservatory.

6 The Florida conservatory will be the largest.

	Ashridge	Aurora	Buckingham	Florida	Goldcrest	6x10	8x10	8x11	8x12	9x14	£6,000	£7,000	£8,000	£9,000	£10,000
Mrs Clifton															
Mr Deacon															
Mr Eaton															
Mr Griffin															
Mrs Knox															
£6,000															
£7,000															
£8,000															
£9,000															
£10,000															
6x10															
8x10															
8x11															
8x12															
9x14															

Neighbour	Design	Size	Cost

SOMETHING ABOUT A SAILOR

Actually, as far as Jakki Tarr is concerned, it's not so much 'a sailor' as 'sailors' - which is why, on St Valentine's Day, she received five parcels each sent by a member of Her Majesty's Royal Navy and containing a declaration of undying love and a rather nice present. The picture shows the five open parcels. Who sent each, on which ship is he serving, and what gift did he send?

Clues

1 Two packages separate the parcel containing the incredibly expensive silk lingerie from the one holding the diamond earrings; the ship on which the sender of the former is serving has a longer name than the one to whose crew the sender of the latter belongs.

2 Archie sent parcel D, which is standing next to that from the man serving on HMS Osprey.

3 Parcel C contains a bottle of one of the world's most famous – and expensive – perfumes.

4 Parcel B was sent to Jakki by a seaman from HMS Adamant.

5 The chocolates Jakki received from the man on HMS Greyhound are in the parcel immediately left of the one containing Tony's gift to her.

6 Glen's gift of a bracelet and Jim's present are in adjacent packages.

7 Parcel E is not the one Jakki got from Ray, a torpedoman on Her Majesty's Submarine Sentinel.

Sailors:
Archie; Glen; Jim; Ray; Tony

Ships:
Adamant; Greyhound; Osprey; Pendragon; Sentinel

Gifts:
Bracelet; chocolate; earrings; lingerie; perfume

| A | B | C | D | E |

Parcel	Sailor	Ship	Gift

Starting tip:

Work out who sent parcel E.

THE LIKELY LAIRDS

Below are details of five Scottish Highland estates – from the information given, can you discover who is the titled owner of each, the acreage, and its chief source of income?

Clues

1 The Earl of Kilbrae is laird of the estate of the same name, while the Duke of Carndale has the largest estate.

2 The Earl of Brora does not own the Glenkinnon estate, and neither he nor Lord Roskill owns the 12,000-acre deer-farming estate.

3 Lord Roskill owns neither the 14,000-acre estate nor the one that derives most of its income from forestry.

4 The Glenkinnon estate is smaller than Balnaloch, the latter being chiefly an agricultural estate.

5 Lord Calvie's estate is 4,000 acres larger than the one specialising in salmon-fishing.

6 Invercarn covers 16,000 acres.

	Earl of Brora	Lord Calvie	Duke of Carndale	Earl of Kilbrae	Lord Roskill	12,000	14,000	16,000	18,000	20,000	Agriculture	Deer-farming	Forestry	Salmon-fishing	Tourism
Balnaloch															
Glenkinnon															
Invercarn															
Kilbrae															
Strathbeag															
Agriculture															
Deer-farming															
Forestry															
Salmon-fishing															
Tourism															
12,000															
14,000															
16,000															
18,000															
20,000															

Estate	Owner	Acreage	Income

SURPRISE

Five landmark birthdays are approaching, and the subject of each is being given a surprise treat by another family member. From the information given below, can you discover who is celebrating which birthday in each case, the surprise, and who is providing it?

Clues

1 Margaret's daughter is aiming to surprise her mother, who is 30 years older than the person being taken for a family meal.

2 Charles is not the person who will be enjoying a 40th birthday surprise courtesy of his or her mother.

3 Eileen is being taken for a hot-air balloon flight.

4 Somebody's brother is not marking his sibling's 50th or 70th birthday; the sibling is 10 years younger than the person being treated to a West End show.

5 Somebody's nephew has booked a flight on Concorde, but not to celebrate a 50th birthday.

6 Barry will be 60.

	Barry	Charles	Eileen	Margaret	Mike	Balloon flight	Family meal	Concorde flight	Loco driving	West End show	40	50	60	70	100
Brother															
Daughter															
Husband															
Mother															
Nephew															
40															
50															
60															
70															
100															
Balloon flight															
Family meal															
Concorde flight															
Loco driving															
West End show															

Organiser	Subject	Event	Birthday

REASSIGNED

When it was built in the 1950s, Kittlebell House was some miles south of London, and was intended as a secure and secret government HQ in the event of nuclear war, etc. Now it houses the offices of the Ministry of Administration, but some rooms in the basement still serve a valuable purpose! Who was originally intended to occupy each of the rooms, who occupies it today, and what is that person's vital responsibilities?

Clues

1 The room assigned to the person in charge of light bulbs is numbered one higher than that intended for the Minister of Supply (now occupied by Mr Edkins).

2 Mrs Bullamy has responsibility for all washrooms throughout the building.

3 The office which still bears the proud inscription 'Prime Minister' painted on its door has a lower number than that currently used by Mr Rugg.

4 The Minister of Defence's assigned accommodation is now used by the civil servant in charge of first-aid kits. Both this room and the one Mr Trott uses have odd numbers.

5 Room 107 is not used by the person responsible for the drinks machines.

6 Room 103 was originally intended to provide emergency quarters for the Foreign Secretary.

	Foreign Secretary	Home Secretary	Minister of Defence	Minister of Supply	Prime Minister	Mrs Bullamy	Mr Edkins	Miss Lobbs	Mr Rugg	Mr Trott	Cleaning equipment	Drinks machines	First-aid kits	Light bulbs	Washrooms
Room 101															
Room 103															
Room 104															
Room 107															
Room 108															
Cleaning equipt															
Drinks machines															
First-aid kits															
Light bulbs															
Washrooms															
Mrs Bullamy															
Mr Edkins															
Miss Lobbs															
Mr Rugg															
Mr Trott															

Room	Originally	Now	Responsibility

VALENTINE 2500

In the 25th Century, Valentine's Day is still celebrated, and the five female members of the A-shift bridge crew of the starship USS Cupid each found some cards waiting for them when they reported to their duty-station on the February 14th equivalent. From the clues given below, can you work out from which planet each woman comes, her rôle on the bridge of the Cupid and the number of cards she received?

Clues

1 The Science Officer, who received only one card (from her husband), isn't Lieutenant Brown, who comes from Terra, formerly known as Earth.

2 Lieutenant Vanaya's home world isn't New Hope.

3 The Pilot, who was born on the mysterious, mist-shrouded world of Qaid, received fewer cards than Ensign Lolo.

4 Ensign Ruppet (the Astrogator) was not the bridge officer who received five cards.

5 Lieutenant Grigik got nine cards.

6 The young woman from the planet Andros got the most cards, which, if you know about young women from Andros, is hardly surprising.

7 The Communications Officer didn't get as many cards as the Armaments Officer.

	Andros	Beulah	New Hope	Qaid	Terra	Armaments Officer	Astrogator	Comms Officer	Pilot	Science Officer	1 card	5 cards	7 cards	9 cards	12 cards
Lt Brown															
Lt Grigik															
Ensign Lolo															
Ensign Ruppet															
Lt Vanaya															
1 card															
5 cards															
7 cards															
9 cards															
12 cards															
Armaments															
Astrogator															
Comms Officer															
Pilot															
Science Officer															

Name	Home world	Bridge rôle	No of cards

GOING AIRSIDE

The drawing below shows six people going through the last security barrier at London's Heathwick Airport as they prepare to fly to New York City, where they will board internal flights to take them on to their final destinations in the USA. From the clues given, can you fill in each traveller's full name and say where they're going on to from New York?

Clues

1 Arnold, who is on his way home to Boston, Massachusetts, is standing immediately ahead of Mr Fisher, who isn't Paul or Dennis.

2 Dennis is not carrying any hand-baggage.

3 The person en route for Cleveland, Ohio isn't Paul, who is figure 3 in the drawing and whose surname does not begin with an S.

4 Patrick Collins, who isn't figure 2 or figure 6, isn't standing next to Clive.

5 The person surnamed Stevens is travelling to Detroit, Michigan, to conclude a lucrative business deal.

6 Figure 4's surname is Wilson.

7 Figure 5 is going to Pittsburgh, Pennsylvania, to get married.

8 The Elvis fanatic who is making a pilgrimage to Memphis, Tennessee, to visit Gracelands is standing further back in the queue than Joshua.

Forenames:
Arnold; Clive; Dennis; Joshua; Patrick; Paul

Surnames:
Collins; Fisher; Hill; Smith; Stevens; Wilson

Final destinations:
Boston; Cleveland; Detroit; Memphis; Pittsburgh; Syracuse

Passenger No	Forename	Surname	Destination

Starting tip:

Work out Paul's surname.

KNIGHTS OFF

One summer the knock-kneed knights of the Round Table each took a week's annual leave in successive weeks, spending his holiday in a cottage he owned, all in different locations. From the clues given below, can you work out which knight had which week off, say where he spent it, and work out the name he had given to his cottage there, showing, in spite of his pusillanimity, that each still retained a vestigial sense of humour?

Clues

1 The knight who stayed at The Lair in Mousehole was away the week before Sir Spyneless de Feete.

2 Sir Coward de Custarde named his cottage Shivery Nook, in reference to the state he was normally in when he arrived there (or, indeed, simply the state he was normally in).

3 Sir Timid de Shayke took his annual leave entitlement from 3rd to 9th August.

4 The holiday in Tintagel was later than Sir Poltroon à Ghaste's, but earlier than the one spent in the Yellow Cottage.

5 The holiday in Glastonbury began on 10th August.

6 The cottage belonging to Sir Sorely à Frayde was in Marazion.

7 It was some time in August that one knight stayed at the Chicken Run the week after one of his colleagues relaxed in Brittany.

	Sir Coward	Sir Poltroon	Sir Sorely	Sir Spyneless	Sir Timid	Brittany	Glastonbury	Marazion	Mousehole	Tintagel	Chicken Run	Shivery Nook	The Lair	White Feathers	Yellow Cottage
20th July															
27th July															
3rd August															
10th August															
17th August															
Chicken Run															
Shivery Nook															
The Lair															
White Feathers															
Yellow Cottage															
Brittany															
Glastonbury															
Marazion															
Mousehole															
Tintagel															

Holiday	Knight	Location	Cottage

IN THE VAN

Four delivery drivers were sent off in their vans from the country town at the centre of the plan to deliver loads to villages lying in the directions indicated. From the clues given below, can you name the village lying in each direction and the driver who delivered there, and work out the colour of the van each man was driving?

Clues

1 Bryan's red van took him in a direction at ninety degrees to the road to Broxton.

2 The white van did not go to Weirhead.

3 The green van, which headed south with its load, was not driven by Malcolm.

4 Dennis delivered his load in Heatherford, which is in the direction diametrically opposite that taken by the blue van.

5 Cyril drove due north with his fully-laden van.

6 Fernlea is not the village due east of the country town.

Villages: Broxton; Fernlea; Heatherford; Weirhead

Drivers:
Bryan; Cyril; Dennis; Malcolm

Vans:
Blue; green; red; white

N

W ← → E

S

Destination: _____
Driver: _____
Van: _____

Destination: _____
Driver: _____
Van: _____

Destination: _____
Driver: _____
Van: _____

Destination: _____
Driver: _____
Van: _____

Starting tip:

Start by naming the green van's driver.

BAR ATTENDERS

Four friends were seated at their usual table in the corner of the bar of the Dog and Ferret, each drinking a pint of his favourite beverage to wash down a packet of his favourite flavoured crisps. From the clues given below, can you work out the name and tastes of the man in each of the seats numbered 1 to 4?

Clues

1 The salt and vinegar crisps are the favourite flavour of the man in seat 3.

2 The plain crisps are always the choice of the man who orders a pint of mild, who bears a lower number in the diagram than Ernie.

3 Steve is immediately anticlockwise round the table from the man eating the smoky bacon flavoured crisps, but next clockwise from the cider drinker, who is not in seat 4.

4 Jack's favourite tipple is a pint of Guinness.

5 As you walk round the table, Lawrie is sitting two places away from the man eating cheese and onion crisps.

Names:
Ernie; Jack; Lawrie; Steve

Drinks:
Bitter; cider; Guinness; mild

Crisps:
Cheese and onion; plain; salt and vinegar; smoky bacon

Name: _____ _____ _____ _____

Drink: _____ _____ _____ _____

Crisps: _____ _____ _____ _____

Starting tip: Start by naming the man in seat 1.

HOME FROM HOME

Archie Edmonds, a music hall comedian, was booked in at five of those establishments in different towns in successive weeks during a certain year in the late 1940s. From the clues given below, can you name the theatre and town he was playing in each of the weeks beginning with the listed dates, and name the theatrical landlady with whom he stayed for his week in each town?

Clues

1 Archie was booked to perform in Radbury in a later week than the one when he played the Alhambra and stayed with Mrs Knaggs.

2 The name Archie Edmonds was inscribed in Mrs Bossey's Visitors' Book at the end of the week beginning 2nd May.

3 When Archie left Mrs Rule's establishment he was on his way to play the Locarno in Gladwell, which was not his booking for the week beginning 18th April.

4 The spot Archie's agent had booked for him in the last week in April was at the Palace.

5 The stay in Steepleigh was a later one than the week with Mrs Draggon, who does not live in Twistleton.

6 Mrs Tumbrill operated a theatrical boarding house in Listerby, which is not the town where the Tivoli is situated.

	Alhambra	Continental	Locarno	Palace	Tivoli	Gladwell	Listerby	Radbury	Steepleigh	Twistleton	Mrs Bossey	Mrs Draggon	Mrs Knaggs	Mrs Rule	Mrs Tumbrill
11th April															
18th April															
25th April															
2nd May															
9th May															
Mrs Bossey															
Mrs Draggon															
Mrs Knaggs															
Mrs Rule															
Mrs Tumbrill															
Gladwell															
Listerby															
Radbury															
Steepleigh															
Twistleton															

Date	Theatre	Town	Landlady

DIGGING IN

In each of the theatrical digs where Archie stayed, another person on the bill in the same week also had a room. From the clues given below, plus the information obtained by solving the previous problem, can you work out the real name of each landlady's second theatrical guest, describe his act, and name the street in which her house is situated?

Clues

1 Ken Thomas appeared on the same bill as Archie the week after the latter had lodgings in Murdoch Road, Twistleton.

2 Alf Marshall was not sharing digs with Archie during the month of May.

3 The juggler did not share digs with Archie at the house in Handley Lane.

4 It was in Askey Street that Archie and the ventriloquist could chat over old times.

5 Billy Lawton stayed in Handley Lane with Archie the week after the latter appeared at the Tivoli.

6 Arthur Wright was the dapper song and dance man.

7 The magician appeared at the Continental the same week as Archie.

8 Flanagan Terrace is not in Gladwell.

	Alf Marshall	Arthur Wright	Billy Lawton	Dennis Green	Ken Thomas	Ballad singer	Juggler	Magician	Song/dance man	Ventriloquist	Askey Street	Flanagan Terrace	Handley Lane	Miller Drive	Murdoch Road
Mrs Bossey															
Mrs Draggon															
Mrs Knaggs															
Mrs Rule															
Mrs Tumbrill															
Askey Street															
Flanagan Terrace															
Handley Lane															
Miller Drive															
Murdoch Road															
Ballad singer															
Juggler															
Magician															
Song/dance man															
Ventriloquist															

Landlady	Name	Act	Address

MEN ABOUT TOWN

Five men parked their cars in a city centre car park the other morning, in the positions numbered 1 to 5 in the diagram. Each had come into town for a particular purpose that morning. From the clues given below, can you identify the make of each car, fully identify its driver, and say why he was visiting town?

Clues

1 Marvin had parked his Citroen alongside Mr Hall's car on one side, and that of the man who was applying for a bank loan on the other.

2 The driver of the BMW had a civic duty to perform by giving evidence in a court case.

3 Anthony's car is separated from Mr Godber's by one other.

4 The man who parked car 4 was in town to assess a major insurance claim.

5 Jeremy's car is parked next to and left of the Volvo.

6 Roland, whose car occupies an odd-numbered spot, had come to town to purchase an engagement ring for his fiancée.

7 Car 2 in the line is the Jaguar, whose driver was not the man visiting his solicitor to make a will.

8 Mr Walker's car is further right than the Mercedes. Lloyd's surname is not Levitt.

Cars:
BMW; Citroen; Jaguar; Mercedes; Volvo

Forenames:
Anthony; Jeremy; Lloyd; Marvin; Roland

Surnames:
Frankish; Godber; Hall; Levitt; Walker

Reasons for visit:
Apply for bank loan; assess insurance claim; make will; purchase engagement ring; witness in court case

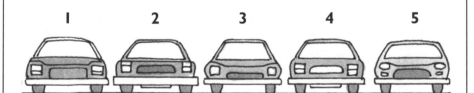

No	Car	Forename	Surname	Reason

WHAT WAS THEIR LINE?

Last summer, five students at Goatsferry University each signed up for a vacation job in their respective home-towns in order to boost their flagging finances. From the clues given below, can you match each name with a town, a degree subject and a holiday job?

Clues

1 The waitress obtained holiday employment in a café in Norwich.

2 The temporary filing clerk is not the same sex as the student from Grimsby, whose degree subject is not German.

3 The history student's family lives in Romford.

4 The subject being studied by the student who gained holiday employment as a delivery van driver is geography; this person is not Philip.

5 Melanie's vacation job enjoys the impressive title of data inputter.

6 Rhyl is Gemma's home-town; John is studying chemistry but is not working at a call centre.

	Grimsby	Norwich	Rhyl	Romford	Tavistock	Chemistry	Geography	German	History	Maths	Call centre clerk	Data inputter	Delivery van driver	Filing clerk	Waitress
Anna															
Gemma															
John															
Melanie															
Philip															
Call cent clerk															
Data inputter															
Del van driver															
Filing clerk															
Waitress															
Chemistry															
Geography															
German															
History															
Maths															

Student	Subject	Home-town	Holiday job

A-TRACTION ENGINE

Among many steam engines appearing in this summer's rally were the following five, each of which was giving a demonstration of some bygone steam-powered activity. From the information given, can you work out the year in which each engine was built, its name and that of its owner, and the work it was doing at the rally?

Clues

1 Samson was two years older that the engine doing the road-rolling demonstration, while Victoria was doing some heavy haulage.

2 Leviathan was built the year after Hugh Jimney's engine; Goliath dated from 1906, but wasn't the showman's engine powering the roundabout.

3 Bill Large brought his Lady Patricia to the rally.

4 Guy Chuffin's engine was built in 1909.

5 Bernie Cole's engine was driving the threshing machine.

6 The engine driving the circular saw dated from 1907.

	Goliath	Lady Patricia	Leviathan	Samson	Victoria	Bernie Cole	Bill Large	Guy Chuffin	Hugh Jimney	Matt Black	Circular saw	Heavy haulage	Road-rolling	Roundabout	Threshing machine
1906															
1907															
1909															
1910															
1911															
Circular saw															
Heavy haulage															
Road-rolling															
Roundabout															
Threshing machine															
Bernie Cole															
Bill Large															
Guy Chuffin															
Hugh Jimney															
Matt Black															

Year	Engine	Owner	Demonstration

RADIO ROMANCE

For the last couple of weeks, Radio Eastland presenter Vee Aitcheff's been running an on-air Valentine's Day competition to win a meal for two in the most romantic location in the world. Last night the five finalists (all women) were selected. All that remains is for the panel of 'expert judges' to choose the winner. Can you work out the name of each finalist's partner, where they live and which romantic location they've nominated?

Clues

1 Wendy's partner is Bill; Maggie and her partner, whose first name begins with a vowel, aren't the couple from Thetbury.

2 Alan and his partner both live in Stowburgh; it's Ian's girlfriend who has nominated Venice as the most romantic location in the world.

3 Aileen's partner isn't called Keith; neither Helen nor the finalist who has nominated the Orient Express as the most romantic place in the world (and therefore assured herself of victory, since the railway company which operates an excursion train of that name agreed to donate the prize three months ago) is either Keith's partner or a resident of Thetbury.

4 Trevor and his partner don't live in Mannbridge or Thetbury.

5 The finalist from Mannbridge has nominated an unspecified and uninhabited South Sea island as her most romantic location.

6 Rachel, who comes from Kessworth, isn't the finalist who dreams of a romantic meal in the Serengeti National Park.

	Alan	Bill	Ian	Keith	Trevor	Kessworth	Mannbridge	Stowburgh	Thetbury	Wyndfield	Casablanca	Orient Express	Serengeti Park	South Sea island	Venice
Aileen															
Helen															
Maggie															
Rachel															
Wendy															

Finalist	Partner	Home-town	Nomination

MURDER IN MIND

Inspector Greymattre is a detective created by novelist Simone Georges. In Murder in Mind, the great man investigates the murder of a business tycoon, Monsieur Boniface. Five individuals each come under suspicion before being eliminated prior to the dénouement. Who became the leading suspect in each of the listed chapters, what is his/her connection with Monsieur Boniface, and what motive was he/she suspected of having?

Clues

1 Greymattre suspected Boniface's business rival of killing him in an attempt to corner the market; this person was the next suspect to materialise before Juliette.

2 Revenge was the motive attributed to one of the two female suspects.

3 Jean-Pierre was Monsieur Boniface's junior partner.

4 It was in chapter 8 that spite was thought to be a possible motive for murder.

5 Jealousy was the presumed motive of a character who fell under suspicion some time before Gaspard.

6 Henri was the Inspector's leading suspect in chapter 9.

7 Monsieur Boniface's mistress became a strong suspect in chapter 6.

8 Véronique was suspected in a chapter numbered one lower than that in which Greymattre's attention centred on the chauffeur.

	Gaspard	Henri	Jean-Pierre	Juliette	Véronique	Business rival	Chauffeur	Junior partner	Mistress	Secretary	Corner market	Financial gain	Jealousy	Revenge	Spite
Chapter 2															
Chapter 5															
Chapter 6															
Chapter 8															
Chapter 9															
Corner market															
Financial gain															
Jealousy															
Revenge															
Spite															
Business rival															
Chauffeur															
Junior partner															
Mistress															
Secretary															

Chapter	Suspect	Connection	Motive

ON PARADE

The squad of twelve soldiers was lined up in front of the saluting base occupied by brass hats at an army parade. From the clues given below, can you name the soldier in each of positions 1 to 4 in each of rows A to C, as perceived from the platform?
All of the soldier's names are mentioned in the clues below.

Clues

1 Charles is immediately behind William. William's immediate right-hand neighbour is Edward.

2 As viewed from the saluting base, Robin is somewhere to the left of Alan in the same row, which is not row C.

3 Norris is in a column somewhere to the right of Miles, and somewhere to the left of Shaun, none being in the same row. Miles is further to the rear than Shaun.

4 Brian is on parade in position 2 of row C.

5 Paul is in the front row of the parade, in which two other men separate him from the man who is immediately in front of Shaun.

6 Ian is Donald's right-hand neighbour in their row of the parade.

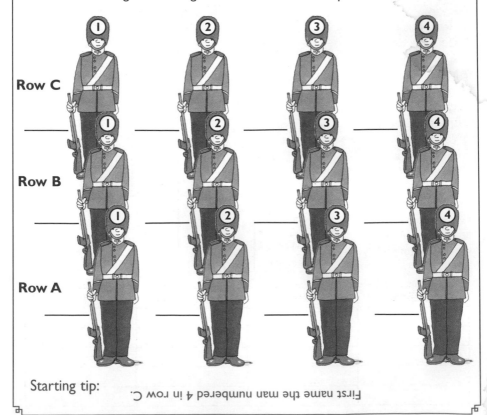

Row C

Row B

Row A

Starting tip:

First name the man numbered 4 in row C.

CAFE REGULARS

During a recent business visit to Cornchester I lunched each day at the Black Cat café, where I shared a different table with someone who I gathered, from the conversation I struck up, was a regular diner there, always eating at that same table. From the clues given below, can you name the person I ate with each day, work out at which table he eats, and say what job he does in Cornchester?

Clues

1 I ate with Terry Jones later in the week than the day I shared the bank clerk's regular table.

2 On Wednesday lunchtime I sat at table 2.

3 Jim Smart always eats at table 15 at the Black Cat cafe; I met him earlier in the week than the shoe shop manager.

4 The lawyer is not Simon Benson. I did not eat on Monday with the lawyer, who always has lunch at table 6.

5 I had an interesting conversation with post office clerk Dominic Taylor the day before I ate at table 12.

6 Thursday was the day I lunched with Raymond Grey.

7 My Friday luncheon companion was the pharmacist.

	Dominic Taylor	Jim Smart	Raymond Grey	Simon Benson	Terry Jones	Table 2	Table 6	Table 8	Table 12	Table 15	Bank clerk	Lawyer	Pharmacist	Post office clerk	Shoe shop manager
Monday															
Tuesday															
Wednesday															
Thursday															
Friday															
Bank clerk															
Lawyer															
Pharmacist															
Post office clerk															
Shoe shop manager															
Table 2															
Table 6															
Table 8															
Table 12															
Table 15															

Day	Regular	Table No	Occupation

SUNNY SHINGLETHORPE

This year's tourist brochure has just been issued by the seaside resort of Shinglethorpe. The attractions described therein include five events which have become regular features over the years. From the clues given below, can you work out which event takes place in which month, say how many days it lasts, and work out how many years in succession it has been staged in the town?

Clues

1 The balloon fiesta, which has been held for a longer period than the event staged in May, is one day shorter.

2 The longest-lasting event takes place every June.

3 The event of ten years standing will take place some time after the two-day celebration.

4 The classic car rally takes place the month before that with the longest history.

5 The three-day event has been staged for eleven years now; and takes place the month after the Folk Festival (not lasting two days).

6 The Carnival is a one-day event and will take place the month after the event with a twelve-year history.

7 The Jazz Festival has a longer track record than the event staged regularly in April.

	Balloon fiesta	Carnival	Classic car rally	Folk Festival	Jazz Festival	1 day	2 days	3 days	4 days	5 days	9 years	10 years	11 years	12 years	15 years
April															
May															
June															
July															
August															
9 years															
10 years															
11 years															
12 years															
15 years															
1 day															
2 days															
3 days															
4 days															
5 days															

Month	Event	Duration	No of years

IN THE SWIM

Five teenagers are members of our local swimming club. Each specialises in a different stroke or activity, and each is a different age. From the clues given below, can you fully identify the five, name their respective events, and work out their ages?

Clues

1 Glyn Scales is a year older than the butterfly swimmer.

2 Stephanie is younger than the club member named Finn.

3 Jacqueline's stroke is the crawl.

4 The swimming club member named Damon is 16; his speciality is not the breaststroke.

5 The diving expert is called Fish.

6 The backstroke swimmer is 14, while Anna is not 15.

7 The person called Dorsell is 17 years old.

	Dorsell	Finn	Fish	Gill	Scales	Backstroke	Breaststroke	Butterfly	Crawl	Diving	13	14	15	16	17
Anna															
Damon															
Glyn															
Jacqueline															
Stephanie															
13															
14															
15															
16															
17															
Backstroke															
Breaststroke															
Butterfly															
Crawl															
Diving															

Swimmer	Surname	Stroke	Age

FAMILY PETS

The families living at numbers 1 to 8 in Fauna Road each have a different pet or pets. From the clues given below, can you name the family living at each address, and describe their pet?

Clues

1 The tropical fish have their aquarium in the lower-numbered half of a semi-detached pair of houses; the Keiths live in the other half.

2 The python, which does not share a semi with the tortoise, lives on the other side of Fauna Road to the Ansons, the python in the right-hand house of a pair as you look at the diagram, and the Ansons in the left-hand house of another, whose other half is not where the Gardners live.

3 The surname of the family at number 1 appears next in the list after that of that at number 4.

4 The Olivers of 5 Fauna Road do not own a bird; the Morgans live on the other side of the street.

5 The family with the parrot is directly across the road from the Coleman family.

6 The stick insects live at number 2, but the goldfish are not at number 6.

7 The Iggledens live next door but one to (and on the same side of the street as) the tortoise.

8 The Evans' hamster lives at a house numbered one lower than the budgerigar's.

Families:
Anson; Coleman; Evans; Gardner; Iggleden; Keith; Morgan; Oliver

Pets:
Budgerigar; goldfish; hamster; parrot; python; stick insects; tortoise; tropical fish

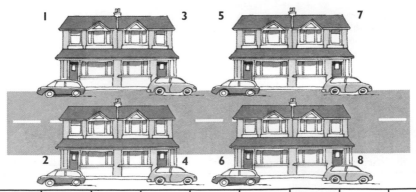

No	1	2	3	4	5	6	7	8
Family								
Pet								

Starting tip:

First name the family which lives at number 1.

ON ESCORT DUTY

My friend Don G Varney runs – indeed, is – a one-man escort agency, and, being of a very smooth disposition, attracts plenty of custom. In a busy spell last summer, he partnered a different lady on a different social occasion on successive weeks. From the clues given below, can you work out which event took place on which date, name the client Don escorted to each, and say what coloured dress she wore for the outing?

Clues

1 Marjorie wore the green dress to a function which took place a week after the Licensed Victuallers' get-together.

2 The date of the Women's Institute dance was June 25th.

3 The film premiere was the event Don attended the week before he escorted the lady in the white dress.

4 The Hunt Ball and the function to which Don took the wearer of the scarlet dress were held in the same month.

5 The blue dress adorned the client Don escorted on July 9th.

6 Corinne engaged the services of Don G Varney when she received an invitation to the mayor's reception, which took place some time before Enid's outing.

7 The pink dress was not worn by Vanessa, who did not employ the services of Don G Varney on June 18th.

	Film première	Hunt Ball	Licensed Victuallers	Mayor's reception	WI dance	Corinne	Enid	Marjorie	Vanessa	Yvonne	Blue	Green	Pink	Scarlet	White
June 11th															
June 18th															
June 25th															
July 2nd															
July 9th															
Blue															
Green															
Pink															
Scarlet															
White															
Corinne															
Enid															
Marjorie															
Vanessa															
Yvonne															

Date	Function	Escort	Dress

THE GOOD DOCTOR

In Regency times, Dr John Middleton, MD, had two things which made him popular – a big house adjacent to Paddington Green (a venue popular for early morning duels) and the ability to keep quiet. In one particular week, he attended a different duel soon after dawn every morning, although his services weren't always required. Who was the challenger and offender on each occasion and what was the result of their duel?

Clues

1 The challenger in Monday's duel, who required treatment for a wound in the left shoulder, didn't meet with the Hon Miles Martin.

2 The duel in which the offender received a pistol-ball in the right side took place the day before the Hon Toby Ward's, but the day after the one in which Major Steele was the offender.

3 Lord Tilney's duel with Captain Ferrars took place the day after the one in which both participants fired but missed.

4 Sir Darcy Croft and the man who had challenged him because of a family feud (who was not a 'Sir') both sustained identical wounds to the lower left arm.

5 Sir Henry Hurst duelled on Wednesday.

6 Colonel Vernon and his opponent both chose to 'delope', firing into the air to make it obvious they intended no harm.

	Colonel Vernon	Hon Toby Ward	Lord Tilney	Sir Henry Hurst	Sir Nick Price	Captain Ferrars	Hon Miles Martin	Lord Osborne	Major Steele	Sir Darcy Croft	Both deloped	Both missed	Both wounded	Challenger wounded	Offender wounded
Monday															
Tuesday															
Wednesday															
Thursday															
Friday															
Both deloped															
Both missed															
Both wounded															
Chall wounded															
Off'r wounded															
Captain Ferrars															
Hon M Martin															
Lord Osborne															
Major Steele															
Sir Darcy Croft															

Duel day	Challenger	Offender	Result

MISS RAFFLES' REVENGE

When Prinz Adelbert von Zuchenberg-Grollwitz made certain slighting remarks about the intelligence of British criminals following an attempt by associates of Miss Raffles to rob his palace in Zuchenberg City in 1899, she took offence and within a year had robbed not only Prinz Adelbert but also his four sons of valuable jewels. What did Miss Raffles take from each Prinz, in which month and in which European capital?

Clues

1 The theft of the sapphires from a hotel in Rome didn't take place in January or November of 1900.

2 It was in April that Miss Raffles purloined the peerless pearls.

3 The rubies belonging to one of Prinz Adelbert's sons were not the first of the family jewels to go missing.

4 When Prinz Patrizius invited a beautiful stranger back to admire the etchings at his family mansion in Berlin, he didn't realise that he was about to lose his precious jewels.

5 Prinz Constantin was robbed of diamonds, but not in June.

6 The member of the Von Zuchenberg-Grollwitz family robbed in London in June was not Prinz Siegfried.

7 The theft of the emeralds was Miss Raffles' next raid on the family after her theft of Prinz Hugebert's jewels, which were not those she took from the safe of the German Ambassador to Austria in Vienna.

	Diamonds	Emeralds	Pearls	Rubies	Sapphires	January	April	June	August	November	Berlin	London	Paris	Rome	Vienna
Adelbert															
Constantin															
Hugebert															
Patrizius															
Siegfried															
Berlin															
London															
Paris															
Rome															
Vienna															
January															
April															
June															
August															
November															

Prinz	Jewels	Month	Capital

WELL-WISHERS

After many years appearing in TV shows and 'B' films, Sue Brett was cast in a leading rôle in a new Broadway show. On the opening night she received a number of supportive telegrams from people with whom she had previously worked; and she pinned these on her dressing table mirror, as shown below. Can you discover the message on each, the name of its sender and the TV show or film in which that person appeared with Sue?

Clues

1 The telegram wishing Sue 'All the best!', from the star of Outlaw, isn't in line, vertically or horizontally, with the one sent by Wayne.

2 The message from Pat, who worked with Sue in Blue Eyes, has an even number and isn't next to the one signed 'GG', which is separated by one other by the cable from whoever played Sue's older sibling in the series Green Valley.

3 A woman sent the telegram with a number two higher than that from the star of the murder mystery film, Dead on Time.

Messages:
'All the best!'; 'Break a leg!'; 'Good luck!'; 'I knew you'd make it!'; 'Knock 'em dead!'; 'You're a star!'

Senders:
GG; Joanne; Larry; Pat; Shari; Wayne

Shows/Films:
Blue Eyes; BMP; Dead on Time; Green Valley; Nurses; Outlaw

4 Telegram 2 says 'Break a leg!'
5 No 6 is from the co-star of BMP.
6 Telegram 5 is signed by Larry and doesn't say 'You're a star!'.
7 The message from whoever worked with Sue in Nurses has a number one higher than that (not No 1) saying 'I knew you'd make it!'.
8 Shari's wishes Sue 'Good luck!'.
9 Joanne didn't send telegram 3.

	1	2	3	4	5	6
Message						
Sender						
Show						

Starting tip:

PARTNERS

The Police Department in the American city of Oppida assigns its detectives in pairs (just like all those you see on TV), and the cosmopolitan nature of the city's population makes for some very mixed pairs! From the clues given below, can you work out the names of the male and female partners in each of these pairs, and say which district of the city they cover and how long they've been working together?

Clues

1 Detective Sergeant Rick Salinas, who was born in Puerto Rico, and his partner operate in Stenburg; Detective Joe Murphy and his partner have been working together successfully for six years.

2 Armenian-descended Detective Robyn Petrosian and her partner are the newest of the teams, but still have five successful years behind them.

3 The detectives who cover Kingsland have worked together for seven years.

4 Detective Erika Fahmy, who has an Egyptian-born father, has worked with her present partner for longer than the pair from the West River precinct.

5 Sarah Thorson and her partner (assigned to the Parkstown precinct) have worked together for two years longer than Greek-American Vince Zaimis and his partner.

6. Detective Andy Chen, whose ancestry is 100% Chinese, works with Detective Sergeant Angel Boncour, who goes to visit her grandparents in Haiti every year.

	Angel Boncour	Erika Fahmy	Leah Kravchuk	Robyn Petrosian	Sarah Thorson	Haven Point	Kingsland	Parkstown	Stenburg	West River	5 years	6 years	7 years	8 years	9 years
Andy Chen															
Floyd Gibowitz															
Joe Murphy															
Rick Salinas															
Vince Zaimis															
5 years										
6 years										
7 years										
8 years										
9 years										
Haven Point					
Kingsland					
Parkstown					
Stenburg					
West River					

Male	Female	Precinct	No of years

ARDLUCK STORIES

Sir Jonah Ardluck, Bt, had five sons, all jolly good chaps but – well, slightly prone to misfortune; each of them was accused of something he hadn't done and had to flee the country and make a new life elsewhere under an assumed name. From the clues given below, can you work out what each brother was unjustly accused of having done, where he fled to, and in which year all this happened?

Clues

1 The brother accused of murdering a bookmaker to whom he owed a lot of money (it was an accident – he only pushed him into the river for a joke!) managed to get away to Canada, where he became a lumberjack.

2 Eustace (accused of forging cheques) fled London in a later year than the man who joined the French Foreign Legion.

3 One brother went into exile (not in 1891) after being accused of stealing a valuable diamond.

4 Ambrose left England six years after whoever travelled to Tibet.

5 One of the Ardlucks left for Australia in 1888.

6 The man accused of cheating at cards fled the country earlier than Desmond.

7 Cuthbert settled on the South Sea island of Pingo-Pingo and managed to become its king after the previous ruler mysteriously vanished.

	Cheating at cards	Forging cheques	Murder	Seducing friend's wife	Stealing jewel	Australia	Canada	Foreign Legion	Pingo-Pingo	Tibet	1888	1891	1894	1897	1900
Ambrose															
Bernard															
Cuthbert															
Desmond															
Eustace															
1888															
1891															
1894															
1897															
1900															
Australia															
Canada															
Foreign Legion															
Pingo-Pingo															
Tibet															

Brother	Accusation	Fled to	Year

REVOLUTIONARY

The Latin American republic of Bananaria has always had a high turnover in Presidents, but even for the Bananarians last month was something special, with five Presidents leaving office in one way or another. From the clues below, can you work out the name of each of these men, what he did before he became President, the day of the month on which his Presidency came to an end, and how it ended?

Clues

1 The former diplomat was not the first to leave office but did do so four days before Kevin O'Malley; neither was imprisoned at the end of his Presidency and O'Malley was not an Air Force General before taking office.

2 President Carlos Borracho was neither the first to be overthrown nor the one-time General of Bananaria's Air Force; each of these three men fled the country.

3 President Felipe Horrendo decided to flee to Brazil when it became obvious that his stint as Head of State was about to end; the man whose Presidency came to an end on the 15th didn't flee to Switzerland.

4 The former Cabinet Minister ceased to be President on the 11th; Pablo Torcido was ousted on the 23rd by a coup.

5 The former Admiral was assassinated before he could flee.

6 Jaime Indigno never had served in the Army.

	Admiral	Cabinet Minister	Diplomat	General (Air Force)	General (Army)	3rd	11th	15th	19th	23rd	Assassinated	Fled to Brazil	Fled to Switzerland	Fled to USA	Imprisoned
Carlos Borracho															
Felipe Horrendo															
Jaime Indigno															
Kevin O'Malley															
Pablo Torcido															
Assassinated															
Fled to Brazil															
Fled to Switz															
Fled to USA															
Imprisoned															
3rd															
11th															
15th															
19th															
23rd															

President	Occupation	Leaving date	Method

SONIA'S BOOKS

Sonia is a rather untidy young lady, and the table in her bedroom on which she does her homework currently bears a miscellany of exercise books devoted to different subjects. From the clues give below, can you identify the subject to which each of the books numbered 1 to 7 belongs, and work out the distinctive colour of its cover?

Clues

1 Sonia's history book is partly covering the one which has a red cover.

2 The grey book is next right on the table from the one issued by the English teacher.

3 The home economics book is further left (as you see it) on the table than the blue one (which isn't No 7).

4 Sonia's brown Geography book is somewhere to the left of the green-covered book, which is not her science book.

5 Book number 2 on the table has a pink cover.

6 The French exercise book is next right from the mauve-coloured one, while at least two other books separate the French book from that with a green cover.

7 Sonia's maths book is in position 4 on the table.

Subjects:
English; French; geography; history; home economics; maths; science

Covers:
Blue; brown; green; grey; mauve; pink; red

Book	1	2	3	4	5	6	7
Subject							
Cover							

Starting tip:

Begin by placing Sonia's history book.

PICTURE STORY

Three young couples went to the cinema on successive evenings. From the clues given below, can you name the pair who went out on each evening, and say what type of film each couple saw?

Clues

1 Adam took his girlfriend out some time after another couple watched the space epic.

2 Jacqueline was taken to the pictures on Wednesday.

3 Christopher and Karen had a night at the cinema later in the week than the pair who went to see the romance.

4 Sophie did not go out on Friday evening.

	Adam	Christopher	Dean	Jacqueline	Karen	Sophie	Action movie	Romance	Space epic
Wednesday									
Thursday									
Friday									
Action movie									
Romance									
Space epic									
Jacqueline									
Karen									
Sophie									

Evening	Boyfriend	Girlfriend	Type of film

ON AN EXPEDITION

Mrs Dee's three young sons wanted to go on an expedition (nominally to the Amazon rainforest, but actually to the end of the garden) and they asked her to provide provisions for them. From the clues below, can you work out each boy's age, and what fruit drink and sandwich their mum provided to sustain them on their expedition?

Clues

1 The boy who had the strawberry drink and the boiled egg sandwich is younger than Adam.

2 The 5-year-old had an apple drink, but his sandwich didn't contain ham.

3 Chris Dee is just 6 years old.

	5	6	7	Apple	Orange	Strawberry	Cheese	Egg	Ham
Adam									
Billy									
Chris									
Cheese										
Egg									
Ham									
Apple									
Orange									
Strawberry									

Child	Age	Juice	Sandwich

FARM PRODUCE

Over the last few years, several farmers in the Storbury area have turned up small archaeological finds consisting of one largish item and a few coins dating from the Iron Age. From the clues below, can you work out the name of each farmer and his farm and say what item and what number of coins he found?

Clues

1 It wasn't Sam Straw who found a silver plate and a small hoard of coins in a field on Pond Farm.

2 Hugh Holt, who runs Chapel Farm, found ten fewer coins than were dug up with the pewter bowl on one of the other farms.

3 It wasn't on Grove Farm that a hoard of ten gold and silver coins was found.

4 The largest hoard of coins was discovered by the owner of Holly Farm while he was making good a ditch damaged by flooding.

5 The Iron Age sword (made, logically enough, from iron) was discovered along with a hoard of thirty small coins, some from as far away as Greece.

6 Ben Barns found the silver-gilt cup on his farm.

	Chapel Farm	Grove Farm	Holly Farm	Pond Farm	Bowl	Cup	Plate	Sword	10 coins	20 coins	30 coins	40 coins
Ben Barns												
Hugh Holt												
Luke Lamb												
Sam Straw												
10 coins												
20 coins												
30 coins												
40 coins												
Bowl												
Cup												
Plate												
Sword												

Farmer	Farm	Item found	No of coins

THE FOUR SISTERS

In an attempt to prove that they can produce quality drama, Albion-TV is putting on a production of The Four Sisters, by the Russian playwright Tartanov, in which four sisters who have pursued very different courses in life gather at the family's country estate, where their father is on his deathbed. Can you work out the name and rôle in life of each sister, and the forename and surname of the actress who will be playing her?

Clues

1 Cressida's surname has fewer letters than that of the actress who has been cast as Ludmilla.

2 Natasha (who is being played by Miss Duckson) is not the sister who has become a teacher and political activist in the slums of Moscow.

3 Helen will be taking the rôle of Anastasia, the youngest of the four sisters.

4 Neither the woman playing Feodosia (the sister who has made a career as an actress and lives an immoral life in St Petersburg) nor and Ms Bluegrave (who is taking the rôle of the invalid sister who has never seen anything of life outside the family estates) is called Esther.

5 Marcia Sowright comes to Albion-TV's production of The Four Sisters fresh from her fantastic West End success in The Elephant Woman.

	Actress	General's wife	Invalid	Teacher	Cressida	Esther	Helen	Marcia	Bluegrave	Duckson	Sowright	Wyelor
Anastasia												
Feodosia												
Ludmilla												
Natasha												
Bluegrave												
Duckson												
Sowright												
Wyelor												
Cressida												
Esther												
Helen												
Marcia												

Character	Rôle	Forename	Surname

LOCOMOTIVES

In the Northchester Museum of Transport are four locomotives of the Victorian era, each restored to pristine condition, painted in the livery of the company which originally owned it and coupled to one of the carriages it would have pulled in the old days. From the clues below, can you work out each loco's name, which company it belonged to, what colour it is and what type of carriage it is displayed with?

Clues

1 The East of England Railway (EER) locomotive has a name one letter longer than that of the one in the vermilion livery, which isn't coupled to a restaurant car.

2 The North British Railway (NBR) was famous for the chartreuse shade in which its rolling stock and locomotives were painted.

3 Moorcock was built for the Midland and Welsh Railway (MWR).

4 The name of the lavender-painted locomotive coupled to the royal coach used by Queen Victoria contains an even number of letters.

5 The locomotive coupled to a sleeping car has a shorter name than the one which was operated by the London and South-Western Railway (LSWR).

	EER	LSWR	MWR	NBR	Chartreuse	Lavender	Russet	Vermilion	1st class carriage	Restaurant car	Royal coach	Sleeping car
Argus												
Duncan												
Granada												
Moorcock												
1st class carriage												
Restaurant car												
Royal coach												
Sleeping car												
Chartreuse												
Lavender												
Russet												
Vermilion												

Locomotive	Company	Colour	Carriage

BACK LANES

The diagram shows eight swimmers ready for the start of a women's backstroke event. From the clues given below, can you fully identify the swimmer in each of lanes 1 to 8?

Clues

1 Anna is in a lane numbered two lower than Powell's and two higher than Edwards'.
2 Precious is in the lane numbered next higher than Delia's, which itself bears a higher number than Willis'; the latter is not Chloë.
3 Leeanne Calvert is one of the swimmers.
4 Edwina has been given an odd-numbered lane.
5 Lane 6 is occupied by Ms Overton, whose forename is next but one after that of the swimmer in lane 8 in the alphabetical list.
6 Briony's lane number is one higher than Vicky's.
7 Sally will swim in lane 3.
8 The swimmer named Mavity is not in lane 4.

Forenames:
Anna; Briony; Chloë; Delia; Edwina; Leeanne; Sally; Vicky

Surnames:
Burrows; Calvert; Edwards; Mavity; Overton; Powell; Precious; Willis

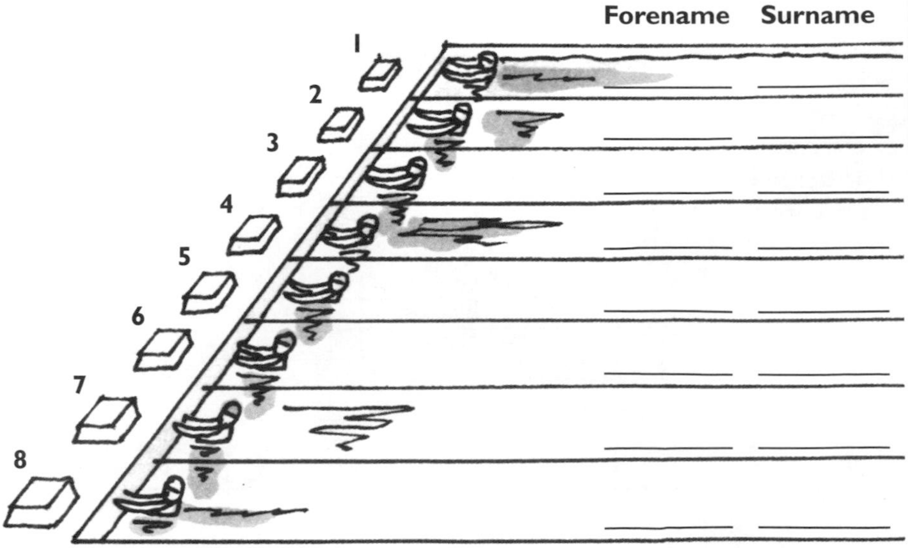

Forename   Surname

Starting tip:
Begin by working out the number of Anna's lane.

UNDER THE HAMMER

Several bargains were snapped up at our local auction house, including the five items described below. From the information given, can you work out the lot number and description of each item, the name of the highest bidder, and the price paid?

Clues

1 Both Lot 17 and the porcelain figurine were sold to male bidders, and both went for less than Biddy Hyer paid for her piece.

2 Biddy Hyer's item is the next lowest lot number below that successfully bid for by Warren I Pryce.

3 The first edition was Lot 42, a higher number than that attached to the item for which Rosa Mount paid £1,600.

4 The Victorian painting fetched a higher price than was paid by Job Lott.

5 Lot 30 went for £1,250, while the highest price was paid for the Art Deco bookcase.

6 Mr Upton-Pademoor acquired the Georgian table.

	Biddy Hyer	Job Lott	Mr Upton-Pademoor	Rosa Mount	Warren I Pryce	Art Deco bookcase	First edition	Georgian table	Porcelain figurine	Victorian painting	£1,250	£1,600	£1,900	£2,250	£3,000
17															
23															
30															
42															
56															
£1,250															
£1,600															
£1,900															
£2,250															
£3,000															
Art Deco bookcase															
First edition															
Georgian table															
Porcelain figure															
Victorian painting															

Lot No	Highest bidder	Item	Price

LITTLE ARROWS

Cupid was especially busy last night, flitting about with his little bow and arrow piercing lovers' hearts. Every ten minutes he caused a new couple to fall hopelessly in love – from the following information, can you work out the time and venue of each amorous encounter, and the names of the boy and girl involved?

Clues

1 At 8.30pm Elaine felt the effects of Cupid's arrow, but not in a restaurant.

2 Twenty minutes later it was Matt's turn, and at 9 o'clock Cupid visited the fairground, but not with an arrow directed at Paul.

3 Cupid was doing his stuff in the cinema ten minutes after he helped Scott to fall in love, and ten minutes before Gail did likewise.

4 Jeff was in the pub when Cupid's arrow struck.

5 Paul and Gina did not become a couple...

6 ...but Kevin and Natasha became an item thanks to Cupid's intervention.

	Cinema	Disco	Fairground	Pub	Restaurant	Jeff	Kevin	Matt	Paul	Scott	Elaine	Gail	Gina	Liz	Natasha
8.30															
8.40															
8.50															
9.00															
9.10															
Elaine															
Gail															
Gina															
Liz															
Natasha															
Jeff															
Kevin															
Matt															
Paul															
Scott															

Time	Venue	Boy	Girl

HIDDEN TALENTS

This problem features five people who started their working lives in fairly humdrum occupations, but, following a twist of fate, discovered an unsuspected talent, and became leading figures in various fields. From the clues given below, can you fully identify the five, and work out the details of their early and subsequent careers?

Clues

I One of the men gave up working in insurance to become a top-ranking jockey.

2 The former bank clerk named Nicholls is not Quentin, whose talent for sculpture led to a massive change of life-style.

3 The top model did not work for the post office before being 'discovered'.

4 Noel's surname is not Minto.

5 Charmian Smith was not the person who became a much sought-after artist.

6 Franklyn started his adult life by selling shoes for a living.

7 The surname of the famous fashion designer is Green.

	Davis	Green	Minto	Nicholls	Smith	Bank clerk	Cook	Insurance clerk	Postal worker	Shoe salesperson	Artist	Fashion designer	Jockey	Sculptor	Top model
Charmian															
Franklyn															
Leonora															
Noel															
Quentin															
Artist															
Fashion designer															
Jockey															
Sculptor															
Top model															
Bank clerk															
Cook															
Insurance clerk															
Postal worker															
Shoe salesperson															

Forename	Surname	Early career	Current career

WHITE VAN MEN

Spinning around the M25 are the following five white delivery vans. From the information given below, can you discover who is driving which make of van, his load, and his eventual destination?

Clues

1 The Ford is en route to Maidstone, but neither it nor the Leyland is carrying boxes of shoes.

2 Neither Nigel's van nor Terry's is the one carrying car parts and none of these three vans is going to St Albans, nor is Terry driving a Leyland.

3 Colin is delivering electrical domestic appliances, but is not at the wheel of a Leyland.

4 The TVs are destined for Guildford, while the Mercedes is full of washing machines.

5 Sam and his Fiat are not on their way to Redhill.

6 Dean is delivering food.

	Fiat	Ford	Leyland	Mercedes	Renault	Car parts	Food	Shoes	TVs	Washing machines	Guildford	Maidstone	Redhill	St Albans	Slough
Colin															
Dean															
Nigel															
Sam															
Terry															
Guildford															
Maidstone															
Redhill															
St Albans															
Slough															
Car parts															
Food															
Shoes															
TVs															
Washing machines															

Driver	Make of van	Load	Destination

CAROUSEL

The diagram below shows the cases of seven passengers who have just completed their return flight stacked up on the carousel at the airport. From the clues given below, can you name the person to whom each case belongs, and say where he or she lives?

Clues

1 Norma's case is two to the right of the one belonging to the passenger from Stoke.

2 The case of the woman from Portsmouth is at one end of the line.

3 The man who owns case 6 does not live in Lincoln.

4 The Carlisle resident's case occupies an odd-numbered spot on the carousel.

5 The owner of case 3 is Keith.

6 Holly lives in Colchester; her case is somewhere to the right of Ray's.

7 Case 5 belongs to the inhabitant of Swansea.

8 Olga's case is immediately next to that of Dean, who is not from Norwich.

Passengers:
Bernice; Dean; Holly; Keith; Norma; Olga; Ray

Towns:
Carlisle; Colchester; Lincoln; Norwich; Portsmouth; Stoke; Swansea

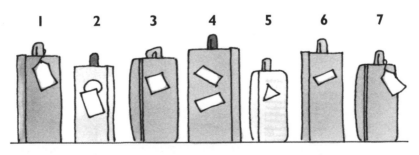

	1	2	3	4	5	6	7
Name:							
Town:							

Starting tip: First work out the home-town of the owner of case 6.

HIGH FLYER

Captain Stan Stead works for Anglian Airways, and has five international flights booked for next week. From the information given, can you discover his destination on each date, which terminal he will be departing from at Gatrow Airport, and the flight number?

Clues

1 On the 10th he will be departing from Terminal 2, but not at the controls of flight AA84 and not bound for Helsinki.

2 Two days later he is flying to Milan, and on the 16th he will be captaining flight AA129 to a German destination.

3 The flight from Terminal 4 departs four days after AA182.

4 The flight to Stockholm, numbered more than 100, will depart from Terminal 1.

5 The Frankfurt flight will not be leaving from Terminal 3.

6 Flight AA143 will leave from Terminal 5 next week.

	Berlin	Frankfurt	Helsinki	Milan	Stockholm	Terminal 1	Terminal 2	Terminal 3	Terminal 4	Terminal 5	AA84	AA97	AA129	AA143	AA182
10th															
12th															
14th															
16th															
18th															
AA84															
AA97															
AA129															
AA143															
AA182															
Terminal 1															
Terminal 2															
Terminal 3															
Terminal 4															
Terminal 5															

Date	Destination	Terminal	Flight No

NOTHING LIKE A DAME

Every year Luvisholme Amateur Dramatic Group put on a pantomime for the village. Below are details of their last five productions – from the information given, can you discover which pantomime they staged each year, the actor who played the dame in each case, and the total number of tickets sold?

Clues

1 Their least successful panto in terms of ticket sales was in 1998, but in the following year they did better with Robin Hood.

2 Will Hammett's performance was seen by 450 people, but not in 1997.

3 Fewer than 500 tickets were sold overall when Rory Lynes played the Wicked Stepmother in Cinderella.

4 500 tickets were sold for Dick Whittington.

5 Bill Topper played the dame in the 2001 panto, which wasn't Aladdin.

6 The group put on Jack and the Beanstalk the year before Noel Season played the dame; on the latter occasion more tickets were sold than for Aladdin.

	Aladdin	Cinderella	Dick Whittington	Jack and the Beanstalk	Robin Hood	Bill Topper	Noel Season	Phil Hall	Rory Lynes	Will Hammett	350	400	450	500	550
1997															
1998															
1999															
2000															
2001															
350															
400															
450															
500															
550															
Bill Topper															
Noel Season															
Phil Hall															
Rory Lynes															
Will Hammett															

Year	Pantomime	Dame	Tickets sold

GONE FISHING

As dawn breaks, five fishing-boats are putting out from Seahaven harbour. From the following information, can you discover the name and registration number of each vessel, the name of the captain, and the type of catch each is after?

Clues

1 The Marina is SH18, while the Seagull is under the command of Capt Bulwark.

2 The crew of the Jenny are fishing for crabs, but the Ocean Queen is not looking for mackerel, and her captain is not Capt Windlass.

3 Neither the crew of the Neptune nor Capt Binnacle and his crew will be emptying lobster pots.

4 Capt Helm's boat, SH60, has neither the shortest nor the longest name of the five.

5 Capt Futtock is hoping to make a catch of prawns, in a boat whose name is one letter shorter than that of SH42.

6 SH34 is a herring boat.

	SH18	SH34	SH42	SH56	SH60	Capt Binnacle	Capt Bulwark	Capt Futtock	Capt Helm	Capt Windlass	Crabs	Herring	Lobsters	Mackerel	Prawns
Jenny															
Marina															
Neptune															
Ocean Queen															
Seagull															
Crabs															
Herring															
Lobsters															
Mackerel															
Prawns															
Capt Binnacle																
Capt Bulwark																
Capt Futtock																
Capt Helm																
Capt Windlass																

Name	Registered No	Captain	Catch

DRONES BEHAVING...

...cautiously! During one memorable week, each of the five members of the Drones Club were being very careful not to meet a certain gentleman from out of town who was trying to contact them. From the clues below, can you work out who each Drone was avoiding, that person's home-town and the reason he was looking for the Drone in question?

Clues

1 Archie Fotheringhay was avoiding the irate father of a young lady with whom he had shared a brief dalliance while visiting a distant relation.

2 Mr Tripp was in fact Sergeant Tripp of the CID, investigating a case involving car theft – though the Drone he was looking for told the others it was only a jape!

3 Mr Fox, who was looking for Gerald Huntington, wasn't the journalist from a provincial paper who was trying to track down one 'man about town'.

4 The solicitor who wanted to talk to one Drone about a breach of promise case was not from Bristol.

5 The man hunting for Edward Tanqueray had a surname two letters shorter than that of the bookmaker from Runcorn.

6 Mr Milton was from Dover.

7 The man making efforts to get in touch with Rupert De Grey came from Leeds.

	Mr Bell	Mr Fox	Mr Milton	Mr Tripp	Mr Westley	Bristol	Dover	Leeds	Norwich	Runcorn	Bookmaker	CID officer	Irate father	Journalist	Solicitor
Archie Fotheringhay															
Edward Tanqueray															
Gerald Huntington															
Montague Ffolliott															
Rupert De Grey															
Bookmaker															
CID officer															
Irate father															
Journalist															
Solicitor															
Bristol															
Dover															
Leeds															
Norwich															
Runcorn															

Drone	Out-of-towner	Town	Description

CHIEF CONSTABLE'S

Last week, the Chief Constable of the Eastshire Constabulary presented awards to half a dozen officers who had distinguished themselves in various ways during the previous year. The picture below is the one that accompanied the press release about the awards; from the clues given, can you fill in the name of each award-winner and say what the award was given for?

Clues

1 No award-winner has a surname initial the same as that of his position in the picture.

2 Officer C's surname appears in the alphabetical list immediately after Officer B's, and immediately before that of whoever won the annual marathon.

3 The officer who got an award for charity work is shown standing immediately left of PC French.

4 The officer who received an award for arresting an armed man has a surname which, in the list, immediately follows that of man D and immediately precedes that of whoever was given an award for working out a new way to deal with police records.

5 Officer A's surname features in the list immediately before that of the man who received an award for foiling a payroll robbery and immediately after Officer F's.

6 PC Abbot did not get his award for rescuing a swimmer from drowning.

PCs' names:
Abbot; Brennan; Campbell; Dodds; Ellis; French

Awards for:
Arresting armed man; charity work; foiling robbery; records improvement; rescuing swimmer; winning marathon

Name: _____ _____ _____ _____ _____ _____
Award for: _____ _____ _____ _____ _____ _____

Starting tip: First position PC French.

NO BUSINESS LIKE IT

This is the heartwarming story of five little girls from Northchester who desperately wanted to be in showbusiness, and when they grew up all fulfilled their ambitions – sort of – by getting a job at the city's famous Variety Theatre. From the clues below, can you work out each young lady's full name, what she originally wanted to be and her job at the Variety Theatre?

Clues

1 Judy, who wanted to be a pop singer, doesn't have an on-stage job at the Variety.

2 Ms Hayes' original ambition was to be a concert pianist.

3 The Variety Theatre's usherette (who had wanted to be an actress) has a surname beginning with a consonant.

4 The girl who has grown up to become producer of the new show at the Variety has an odd number of letters in her forename and an even number of letters in her surname, which is the same as that of the theatre's owner.

5 Paula Edison never had any ambition to be a ballerina.

6 Ms Miller (a dancer in the chorus of the Variety's latest show) has a forename which appears in the alphabetical list before Miss Smith's but after that of the girl employed as the comedian's stooge in the show, losing her skirt and getting a custard pie in the face six evenings a week plus a matinee on Saturday.

	Edison	Hayes	Miller	Oates	Smith	Actress	Ballerina	Comedienne	Pianist	Pop singer	Barmaid	Chorus dancer	Producer	Stooge	Usherette
Anita															
Denise															
Gillian															
Judy															
Paula															
Barmaid															
Chorus dancer															
Producer															
Stooge															
Usherette															
Actress															
Ballerina															
Comedienne															
Pianist															
Pop singer															

Forename	Surname	Ambition	Job

GUARDING THE GATES

During the English Civil War, a walled town with four entrance gates was held by a Parliamentary garrison. From the clues given below, can you name each of gates 1 to 4, and work out the full name of the Roundhead guard on duty at each?

Clues

1 Ezekiel was on guard at the next gate clockwise round the walls from Stonegate, whose protector is not Wise.

2 Marketgate is not the town's south gate.

3 The western gate of the town is the responsibility of Jeremiah, whose surname is not Lamb.

4 Fletcher is guarding the gate directly across the town from the one named Castlegate.

5 Watergate is the exit to the east of the town.

6 Moses is the Roundhead soldier named Kettley.

Gates:
Castlegate;
Marketgate; Stonegate;
Watergate

Forenames:
Ezekiel; Jeremiah;
Moses; Nathaniel

Surnames:
Fletcher; Kettley;
Lamb; Wise

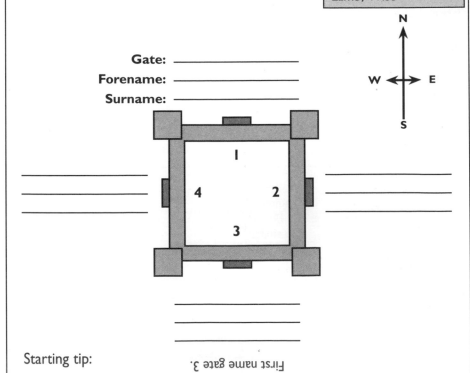

Gate: _____
Forename: _____
Surname: _____

Starting tip: First name gate 3.

PHILIP PHIBBS

Philip Phibbs, perhaps because of his unusual surname, has always modelled himself on Billy Liar, the 'hero' of book and film. Last week, a different acquaintance or family member tried to keep a record of the number of fibs he told on each consecutive day, giving up after finally losing count. Can you work out who assessed his output of porkies on which day, name their connection with Philip, and say what number they reached?

Clues

1 Shaun totted up over a hundred lies on a later day of the week than the one when it was Philip's brother who attempted the count.

2 Phibbs' boss carried out his survey later in the week than Desmond, whose total was higher than the one reached on Tuesday.

3 On Wednesday, 87 untruths were recorded, but not by Philip's workmate.

4 The Monday total of fibs by Phibbs was not 101.

5 Peter carried out the Friday count, which was abandoned at the immediately lower figure than the previous day's.

6 Darren threw his hand in when a total of 96 porkies had been reached.

7 The largest total was arrived at by Philip's friend, who went out with him the evening after the day when Robert was the self-appointed lie-detector.

	Darren	Desmond	Peter	Robert	Shaun	Boss	Brother	Father	Friend	Workmate	87	96	101	138	145
Monday															
Tuesday															
Wednesday															
Thursday															
Friday															
87															
96															
101															
138															
145															
Boss															
Brother															
Father															
Friend															
Workmate															

Day	Name	Connection	No counted

CHAMBER OF HORRORS

Nemzetigyarmat Castle was for centuries the home of oppressive noblemen, but today it's a theme park, with attractions using ideas from its own history. The old gatehouse now houses a waxworks, and in an underground chamber are models of four notorious villains formerly associated with Nemzetigyarmat Castle. Can you fill in on the drawing the full name of each villain represented, and say what form his villainy took?

Clues

1 The figure representing the man named Arpad is standing immediately between those of the werewolf allegedly responsible for hundreds of deaths in the mid-18th Century and the model of Wekesits, which is not figure 3.

2 The feared 16th Century sorcerer, whose surname was not Szakanky, stands immediately left of Istvan.

3 Figure 2 represents the man surnamed Bardonyes.

4 The model of Ferenc is immediately right of the one depicting the vampire.

5 One of the four villains was named Laszlo Hederadam.

Forenames:
Arpad; Ferenc; Istvan; Laszlo

Surnames:
Bardonyes; Hederadam; Szakanky; Wekesits

Villainies:
Murderer; sorcerer; vampire; werewolf

Forename: _____ _____ _____ _____

Surname: _____ _____ _____ _____

Villainy: _____ _____ _____ _____

Starting tip:

First name figure 1.

WE WUZ ROBBED

Jack Moanwell is the manager of a poorly performing football team which has lost each of its last five matches by varying scores. Each time Jack has come up with a different excuse at the after-match press conference. From the clues given below, can you name the opposing team on each of the given dates, work out the score, and say what excuse Moanwell gave on each occasion?

Clues

1 Moanwell blamed his goalkeeper's error for the 0-1 defeat the week after the game with Boxford United.

2 The referee in the match against Dorquay was blamed for appalling errors of judgment.

3 The state of the pitch on 25th January gave Jack a ready-made excuse for his team's failure to score.

4 The 2-5 defeat was not inflicted by Hacklesfield.

5 The 0-2 drubbing was incurred in the team's latest game of their unfortunate sequence, which was not blamed by Jack on a run of injuries to key players.

6 The match on 1st February was against Glumthorpe.

7 Dartlepool ran out 3-1 winners against Moanwell, but not in the week before the latter complained of intimidation by over-physical opponents.

	Boxford United	Dartlepool	Dorquay	Glumthorpe	Hacklesfield	0-1	0-2	0-4	1-3	2-5	Appalling referee	G'keeping error	Injuries	Intimidation	State of pitch
18th January															
25th January															
1st February															
8th February															
15th February															
Appalling ref															
G'keeping error															
Injuries															
Intimidation															
State of pitch															
0-1															
0-2															
0-4															
1-3															
2-5															

Date	Opponents	Score	Excuse

UNLUCKY FOR SOME

Each of the white squares in the diagram contains a different one of the numbers 1 to 13. From the clues given below, can you place the correct number in each of the squares?

Clues

1 There are no two-digit numbers in rows A or D, or in columns 1 or 4.

2 The 9 does not occupy a corner square.

3 The 6 is in direct line below the 2.

4 The number in E5 is one below the one in A3.

5 The 1 is diagonally below and to the left of the 12, and diagonally above and to the right of the 10.

6 The number in square B4 is two higher than the one in square D2.

7 The 8 is in direct line above the number 13.

Numbers: 1, 2, 3, 4, 5, 6, 7, 8, 9, 10, 11, 12, 13

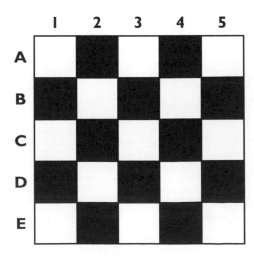

Starting tip: Start by placing the 1 in its correct position.

PIN MONEY

Along the High Street this evening five bank customers are inserting their cards into cash machines to get some cash for the night's entertainment. From the following information, can you work out which bank each is using, their individual PIN numbers, and the amount of cash each is withdrawing?

Clues

1 Mr Mclean has tapped in 4630 to withdraw half the amount being taken from the Westshire Bank cash machine by a customer whose number is not 4061.

2 Miss Hanson is withdrawing more than the customer whose number is 3989.

3 Mr Doyle is not the Lancashire Bank customer with the number 3162.

4 Mrs Bradley is a customer of the Bank of East Anglia.

5 The largest amount is being withdrawn from the Mercia Bank machine, but the smallest amount is not being withdrawn from the Midminster.

6 One customer has keyed in 6757 to take out £20.

	Mrs Bradley	Mr Doyle	Miss Hanson	Mrs Kerr	Mr Mclean	3162	3989	4061	4630	6757	£10	£20	£40	£80	£160
East Anglia															
Lancashire															
Mercia															
Midminster															
Westshire															
£10											
£20											
£40											
£80											
£160											
3162						
3989						
4061						
4630						
6757						

Bank	Customer	PIN number	Amount

QUICK ON THE DRAW

Quick on the Draw is a daytime TV programme in which five amateur artists compete for a prize by producing a finished drawing of a subject within a specified time. Today's contestants have been taken to a country park, where there are five Shetland ponies. Can you identify the artists, say how many ponies each has to draw, and work out how long ago each took up drawing? Also, can you work out who won the prize that day?

Clues

1 David has been drawing a year longer than the artist named Toobee, who is not Jane, and whose picture included one more pony than the former's.

2 The most recent arrival on the drawing scene managed to draw four ponies in the time allotted.

3 Mary concentrated all her efforts in depicting one single Shetland pony.

4 Sharpe is the name of the contestant who took up drawing four years ago.

5 The person who won the prize for the day's best effort drew one more pony than George, who has been drawing for longer than the contestant named Graffite.

6 It is just two years since Sally took up her artist's pencil for the first time.

7 Lead's completed picture included all five ponies; this contestant is less experienced artistically than Shading.

	Graffite	Lead	Shading	Sharpe	Toobee	1 pony	2 ponies	3 ponies	4 ponies	5 ponies	1 year	2 years	3 years	4 years	5 years
David															
George																
Jane																
Mary																
Sally																
1 year																
2 years																
3 years																
4 years																
5 years																
1 pony																
2 ponies																
3 ponies																
4 ponies																
5 ponies																

Artist	Surname	No of ponies	No of years

BONANZAH!

In the oil-rich sheikhdom of Bonanzah between 1998 and 2002, the ruling sheikh paid out gratuities to five junior sheikhs who each impressed him in some way. (Sadly none impressed him in either 2003 or 2004!) From the clues given below, can you name the sheikh honoured in each year, work out the amount of the award he was granted, and say for what achievement he was given it?

Clues

1 Sheikh Hays-el-rod, who used his water-divining talent to find water-holes in the Bonanzah desert, was rewarded with a grant of 2,500 gushas more than the most recent recipient of the sheikh's bounty.

2 The largest gratuity was paid out to the sheikh who bravely defended a desert oasis against a band of marauding nomads.

3 The 12,500 gushas reward was paid to Sheikh Ratl-en-rol, not the trainer of the successful string of racehorses.

4 The 1998 reward was exactly 10,000 gushas.

5 The sheikh who won the prestigious Bonanzah camel Derby in the year 2000, who was not Sheikh Yahand, was rewarded by a gratuity consisting of an exact number of thousands of gushas.

6 Sheikh Adu-bel-sichs gained favour in 2001.

	Sheikh Adu-bel-sichs	Sheikh Hays-el-rod	Sheikh Mahfist	Sheikh Ratl-en-rol	Sheikh Yahand	5,000 gushas	7,500 gushas	10,000 gushas	12,500 gushas	15,000 gushas	Defending oasis	Finding water	Sinking oil well	Training horses	Winning camel Derby
1998															
1999															
2000															
2001															
2002															
Defending oasis											
Finding water											
Sinking oil well											
Training horses											
Winning Derby											
5,000 gushas						
7,500 gushas						
10,000 gushas						
12,500 gushas						
15,000 gushas						

Year	Sheikh	Prize money	Achievement

SOOPERGROOP

Soopergroop is a rock band — the kind of musical unit that used to be known as a popular beat combo — comprising five members, whose pop careers began with five different groups back in the sixties. From the clues given below, can you say who plays which instrument, name the group with which each used to play, and work out how many chart hits each original group had?

Clues

1 The Bleatles had fewer hits than the group Mick used to play with, but more than the group to which the lead guitarist belonged.

2 Dick, whose original group was The Why, had more hits with them than Rick had with his sixties group.

3 The provider of Soopergroop's rhythm guitar had one fewer chart success than the player with the Bluesy Moods.

4 Chick's sixties group had four chart hits during his time with them.

5 The keyboard player first enjoyed success with The Froggs.

6 The Strolling Drones made it into the charts on three occasions back in the sixties.

7 The drummer achieved chart status twice with his former group.

Name	Instrument	Former group	No of hits

AN AMERICAN RAFFLES

The criminal proclivities of the Raffles family weren't confined to the British branch of the family: an American cousin, Annabelle Jemima Raffles specialised in conning wealthy ranchers into entrusting her with cash, then vanishing into the sunset. In 1895, she conned five and got away with $1,000,000! Can you work out which Wild West town she visited in each of the listed months, what she pretended to be and who she robbed?

Clues

1 Annabelle wasn't posing as an actress or a singer when she robbed Rusty Cooper (whose ranch was in a community with a two-word name) in an even-numbered month of the year.

2 Annabelle pretended to be a singer for the crime she undertook immediately before robbing Buck Wayne in Santa Fe, New Mexico.

3 Annabelle posed as an actress in Cheyenne, visited neither in June nor in the month when she robbed Mason Hart.

4 Her theft of more than $300,000 from Gus Stewart was the month after that in which she posed as a private detective from the Pinkerton Agency.

5 Her robbery of Sam Autry while pretending to be an army officer's widow didn't take place in March nor in the month she visited Tombstone.

6 It wasn't in August that Annabelle committed a crime in Dodge City, Kansas.

	Cheyenne	Dodge City	El Paso	Santa Fe	Tombstone	Actress	Detective	Heiress	Singer	Widow	Buck Wayne	Gus Stewart	Mason Hart	Rusty Cooper	Sam Autry
March															
May															
June															
August															
September															
Buck Wayne															
Gus Stewart															
Mason Hart															
Rusty Cooper															
Sam Autry															
Actress															
Detective															
Heiress															
Singer															
Widow															

Month	Town	Rôle	Victim

CAMP FIRE

The picture below shows the overnight camp of a group of travellers in America's Rocky Mountains in the 1870s — which is why one member of the party is awake and keeping watch for predators, animal or human. From the clues below, can you fill in the full name and age of each man?

Clues

1 Henry Volker's position is numbered one lower than the 19-year-old's.

2 Jim (figure 1) was in the same decade of his life as figure 4.

3 Dan, who was next anticlockwise to Mr Sutter, is indicated by a lower number than that of Orrin, who was next clockwise of Mr Redlaw.

4 O'Carroll, the prospector, wasn't 38 years old.

5 Bert was two places clockwise of 24-year-old Levi.

6 Figure 2 is the drifter surnamed Rizzo.

7 Mr Murray (aged 44) is indicated by an even number.

Forenames:
Bert; Dan; Henry; Jim; Levi; Orrin

Surnames:
Murray; O'Carroll; Redlaw; Rizzo; Sutter; Volker

Ages:
17; 19; 24; 31; 38; 44

	1	2	3	4	5	6
Forename						
Surname						
Age						

Starting tip: First position Murray and then find his first name.

THE WILD GEESE

In the bad old days, the Wild Geese were Irishmen driven abroad to seek employment, many as soldiers; the five children of Liam and Kathleen Casey from Ballydrum have also gone overseas to seek their fortunes, but this St Patrick's Day, they'll be at home with their parents, who are celebrating their Ruby Wedding. Can you work out what job each does, where they live and what they've brought for their parents' anniversary?

Clues

1 It isn't the young Casey who lives and works in Britain who has bought Liam and Kathleen a new tea set for their anniversary.

2 The painting of a sailing ship is a gift from their son who lives in the USA.

3 Neither the young Casey who has his own building business in Brazil nor Niall is giving his parents an anniversary gift of wine.

4 Sheilah Brady, nee Casey, now lives in Australia.

5 The Caseys' oldest son, who's a soldier, isn't giving them the painting.

6 Father Declan Casey, a parish priest in his adopted home-town, isn't giving his parents wine.

7 The police officer who's giving an anniversary gift of jewellery – cuff links for Liam and a bracelet for Kathleen – isn't Bridget Casey, who doesn't live in Britain.

	Builder	Folk-singer	Police officer	Priest	Soldier	Australia	Brazil	Britain	Spain	USA	Candlesticks	Jewellery	Painting	Tea set	Wine
Bridget															
Declan															
Kevin															
Niall															
Sheilah															
Candlesticks															
Jewellery															
Painting															
Tea set															
Wine															
Australia															
Brazil															
Britain															
Spain															
USA															

Forename	Occupation	Country	Gift

REGIMENTAL HISTORY

Having been commissioned to write the official history of the Barsetshire Fusiliers, military author Henry Martini has a problem; he's discovered that the well-known stories of certain ex-BFs' heroism at some of the great battles of the last 200 years are – well, not quite true. Can you identify each gentleman concerned, his final military rank, the battle in which he is supposed to have distinguished himself, and what really happened?

Clues

1 Oscar Ponto wasn't the Major-General who had been drunk in his tent.

2 The officer who missed the battle in which he was to have fought because he was visiting a friend at Divisional HQ wasn't the man who was supposed to have been a hero of El Alamein in 1942, whose name was not Joseph Knox.

3 Albert Bolt (who should have fought at Inkerman) achieved a final rank just below that of Joseph Knox.

4 Lieutenant-General Sidney Trow never claimed to have fought at Bloemfontein and wasn't on leave at the time of battle.

5 Enoch Fitch, whose final army rank was not Colonel, was laid up with gout when he should have been in battle.

6 The man laid up with fever during the battle of Waterloo did not become a Lieutenant-General.

	Lieutenant-Colonel	Colonel	Brigadier	Major-General	Lieutenant-General	Bloemfontein	Cambrai	El Alamein	Inkerman	Waterloo	Drunk	Had fever	Had gout	On leave	Visiting HQ
Albert Bolt															
Enoch Fitch															
Joseph Knox															
Oscar Ponto															
Sidney Trow															
Drunk															
Had fever															
Had gout															
On leave															
Visiting HQ															
Bloemfontein															
Cambrai															
El Alamein															
Inkerman															
Waterloo															

Name	Rank	Battle	Reason

A KORNE ANTIQUES

Adrian Korne, proprietor of A Korne Antiques had a good week last week: as well as a number of high-priced individual sales, he managed five 'doubles' where a married couple purchased two expensive items, one chosen by the husband and one by the wife. From the clues below, can you work out which two items he sold on each of the listed days, and the surnames of the couples (all tourists) who bought them?

Clues

1 The Georgian silver-mounted carriage lamp was chosen by the woman (not Mrs Yurkowitz from Philadelphia) who came in with her husband on Monday. On Tuesday, the 'double' customers were the Fujitas from Tokyo.

2 The 18th Century mirror was sold two days before Mr and Mrs Berg made their purchases. The music box was purchased the day after the silver loving-cup, which Adrian suspected might be a reproduction — something he forgot to tell the gentleman who admired it so much.

3 Mr McAndrew chose an 18th Century 'Brown Bess' musket.

4 The old naval telescope was sold on Thursday.

5 Mrs Hofmann bought a tallboy 'after the style of Sheraton' — a long way after.

6 One man bought a Stringer and Woolward walnut case grandmother clock for himself and a bust for his wife — no, a marble one, depicting a young peasant girl, artist unknown.

	Clock	Loving-cup	Musket	Tantalus	Telescope	Bust	Lamp	Mirror	Music box	Tallboy	Berg	Fujita	Hofmann	McAndrew	Yurkowitz
Monday															
Tuesday															
Thursday															
Friday															
Saturday															
Berg															
Fujita															
Hofmann															
McAndrew															
Yurkowitz															
Bust															
Lamp															
Mirror															
Music box															
Tallboy															

Day	Husband's buy	Wife's buy	Surname

BACK TO BACK

Two blocks of houses (one of which is a block of back-to-back houses) have been modernised and refurbished for single-person occupation. By coincidence, each is occupied by someone whose age is a different number of years between 18 and 29. From the clues given below, can you name and establish the age of the occupant of each of houses 1 to 12?

Clues

1 Liam's house is due south of the one occupied by the oldest resident, and due north of the one leased by the man five years older than him.

2 Katie's house is between Beverley's to the west, and a man's to the south; one of these three is 20 years old.

3 The person aged 22 lives in the next house east to the 19-year-old's (whose northern neighbour is Harry).

4 Gina's house, with a single-digit even number, is the eastern neighbour of that rented by Douglas, aged 28.

5 The woman aged 25 lives in the southernmost row.

6 The resident of No 4 is 23.

7 No 5 is rented by Eve, who is a year younger than the person in No 3.

8 The resident of house 1 is three years younger than the one who rents house 10, while the person in house 11 is one of the five youngest.

9 Claire lives in the same east-west row as the 24-year-old, who also lives in the same north-south line as John.

10 Frank is three years younger than the resident of No 9.

Names:
Angus; Beverley; Claire; Douglas; Eve; Frank; Gina; Harry; Iris; John; Katie; Liam

Ages:
18; 19; 20; 21; 22; 23; 24; 25; 26; 27; 28; 29

Name: _____ _____

Age: _____ _____   _____ _____

1	2	3	4
5	6	7	8

Name: _____ _____

Age: _____ _____   _____ _____

9	10	11	12

Name: _____ _____

Age: _____ _____   _____ _____

Starting tip: Begin by working out which house Liam lives in.

EXPECTANT DRONES

One particular week each of our old friends from the Drones Club was dragged off to an event which was not his particular cup of tea in order to accompany an elderly aunt, from whom he had expectations. From the clues given below, can you work out on which day which Drone escorted which Aunt to what event?

Clues

1 The flower show took place later in the week than the event to which Gerald Huntington escorted his Aunt Euphemia.

2 Aunt Victoria went out the day after the unwilling escort was Rupert de Grey.

3 Edward Tanqueray attended the art exhibition with his elderly relative.

4 Archie Fotheringhay (not Aunt Millicent's escort) did not go out on Monday.

5 Aunt Priscilla insisted on being escorted around the tapestry exhibition, but not on Friday.

6 Montague Ffolliott performed his spell of duty on Thursday.

7 The opera was attended on Wednesday evening.

8 Aunt Constance had her nephew dancing attendance on Tuesday.

	Archie Fotheringhay	Edward Tanqueray	Gerald Huntington	Montague Ffolliott	Rupert de Grey	Aunt Constance	Aunt Euphemia	Aunt Millicent	Aunt Priscilla	Aunt Victoria	Art exhibition	Ballet	Flower show	Opera	Tapestry exhibition
Monday															
Tuesday															
Wednesday															
Thursday															
Friday															
Art exhibition															
Ballet															
Flower show															
Opera															
Tapestry exhib															
Aunt Constance															
Aunt Euphemia															
Aunt Millicent															
Aunt Priscilla															
Aunt Victoria															

Day	Drone	Aunt	Outing

FRESHERS' WEEK

Five new students arrived at Goatsferry University last October and spent some time visiting the freshers' week club and society stands, where each joined a different group which attracted their interest. From the clues given below, can you name each student's home-town, say which subject each was about to start reading at Goatsferry, and work out which group each joined?

Clues

1 The girl from Croydon joined the university debating society.

2 The student (not Craig) interested by the photography club's stall is reading sociology.

3 The person reading French and the one from Bolton are of the same sex.

4 Luke (a student of the university's school of architecture) did not sign up with the music group.

5 Jane's subject was not physics, and Colin is not from Frome.

6 Debbie was soon signed up by the flourishing dramatic society.

7 The classics student is from Ipswich.

	Bolton	Croydon	Frome	Ipswich	Perth	Architecture	Classics	French	Physics	Sociology	Debating	Drama	Music	Orienteering	Photography
Colin															
Craig															
Debbie															
Jane															
Luke															
Debating															
Drama															
Music															
Orienteering															
Photography															
Architecture															
Classics															
French															
Physics															
Sociology															

Student	Home-town	Subject	Society

PRIDE OF SCOTLAND

Film star, Sholto Chisholm is proud of being a Scot – even his mansion in Spain is decorated in traditional tartans – and he plays every rôle with his trademark Edinburgh accent, regardless of the character's nationality. He has starred in one award-winning picture in each of the last five years; from the clues below, can you work out the title of the film released in each year, and the occupation and nationality of Chisholm's character?

Clues

1 Scorpion, in which Chisholm was cast as a secret agent whose Scots accent was explained by a remark that he had once studied at St Andrew's University, came out after the film in which he played an American.

2 His rôle as a physician who learned English from a Scottish ship's engineer was in the film that came out the year after the one in which he played a Russian.

3 Conspiracy was released in 2002.

4 In the 2001 release (not The Price), Chisholm played the part of a Saudi Arabian.

5 In 2000, he played a naval officer who had had a Scots nannie when young.

6 In the sci-fi film Nova, Chisholm's character came from Krysania.

7 The film in which he played a Swedish detective whose Scots accent (even when speaking Swedish!) was blamed on having a Glaswegian girlfriend came out the year before Firecracker.

	Conspiracy	Firecracker	Nova	Scorpion	The Price	Businessman	Detective	Naval officer	Physician	Secret agent	American	Krysanian	Russian	Saudi Arabian	Swedish
1999															
2000															
2001															
2002															
2003															
American															
Krysanian															
Russian															
Saudi Arabian															
Swedish															
Businessman															
Detective															
Naval officer															
Physician															
Secret agent															

Year	Title	Rôle	Nationality

GHOSTHUNTERS

The Goatsferry Ghosthunters Club has been investigating the supernatural for more than 100 years and is still going strong. Many of the students have an abiding interest in spirits (and also beer). The picture below shows six student Ghosthunters off to a vigil in their minibus. From the clues given, can you determine the name of each student, which college at Goatsferry he or she attends and their particular ghosthunting speciality?

Clues

1 Student number 5 is at St Magnus' College.
2 The Ghosthunters' site surveyor (from Pentecost College) is seated immediately in front of Ben Coston.
3 Joanne Kaye, who does all the research on houses where the Ghosthunters carry out investigations, is in the same row as the student from Gladstone College.
4 The Ghosthunters' interviewer, who talks to people who claim to have seen ghosts, has a lower-numbered seat than the student from Lyonesse College.
5 Len Miller is sitting next to the minibus' driver.
6 Peter Quist from Fairfax College is in the same row of seats as the team's sound recordist (not number 4).
7 Student 3 is the Ghosthunters' photography expert.
8 Sue Teague and the team leader are on opposite sides and opposite ends of the bus.

Students:
Ben Coston; Joanne Kaye; Len Miller; Mike Newman; Peter Quist; Sue Teague

Colleges:
Carnegie; Fairfax; Gladstone; Lyonesse; Pentecost; St Magnus'

Rôles: interviews; photography; research; site surveys; sound recording; team leader

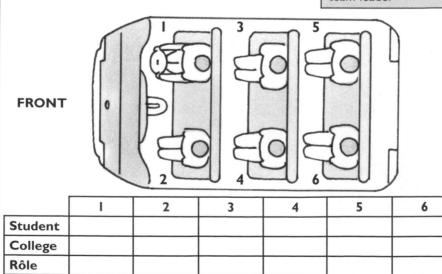

FRONT

	1	2	3	4	5	6
Student						
College						
Rôle						

Starting tip: Work out the rôle of student 6.

KNITTING NEEDLES

An elderly spinster, Jemima Kneedles, is a compulsive knitter with an unfortunate habit, due to her failing eyesight, of producing items in totally unsuitable colours, which she then presents to members of her family. In five successive months last year, she knitted one present per month. From the clues given below, can you name the work she knitted in each month, work out its colour, and say for whom it was intended?

Clues

1 The lime green bootees were knitted the month after the gift intended for Jemima's niece.

2 Jemima's great-nephew was not enamoured of the puce-coloured wool used to knit his present.

3 The work (not gloves) knitted in October was for Jemima's cousin.

4 Jemima's nephew was presented with the knitted tie.

5 The jersey (not mauve) was knitted in September.

6 The bright orange wool was used in July.

7 The shocking pink wool (not used in June) was knitted into something for a male relative.

	Bootees	Gloves	Jersey	Socks	Tie	Lime green	Mauve	Orange	Puce	Shocking pink	Cousin	Great-nephew	Great-niece	Nephew	Niece
June															
July															
August															
September															
October															
Cousin															
Great-nephew															
Great-niece															
Nephew															
Niece															
Lime green															
Mauve															
Orange															
Puce															
Shocking pink															

Month	Gift	Colour	Recipient

TWINS

Last Saturday, newspapers across the country reported an unusual wedding at the Church of St Thomas in Matchington, when five men who each have a twin sister each married the twin of one of the other men, but without any of the men's sisters marrying the brother of the woman her brother had married. From the clues below, can you work out the full name of each groom and the forename and maiden surname of his bride?

Clues

1 David's new wife, whose name isn't Julie, was formerly Miss McAlpine; her brother was married to Sarah on Saturday.

2 Nigel married Carol.

3 The former Tessa Haines didn't marry Peter Cammack.

4 Keith's new wife's maiden surname is the same as Karen's married surname.

5 The Mr Purchan who married the former Miss Cammack isn't Simon.

	Cammack	Haines	McAlpine	Purchan	Tweedale	Carol	Julie	Karen	Sarah	Tessa	Cammack	Haines	McAlpine	Purchan	Tweedale
David															
Keith															
Nigel															
Peter															
Simon															
Cammack															
Haines															
McAlpine															
Purchan															
Tweedale															
Carol															
Julie															
Karen															
Sarah															
Tessa															

Groom	His surname	Bride	Her surname

ON THE RACK

Visiting a friend serving in the United States Air Force in Suffolk, I noticed a rack on the wall of the mess-room holding a number of local newspapers from the USA, and thought what a good logic problem it would make – so here it is. From the clues below, can you fill in on the picture the name of the community in which each paper is published, the state in which that community stands and the name of the newspaper itself?

Clues

1 The paper from Pine Lake was immediately below the Journal and immediately right of the Florida tabloid.

2 The Ohio paper was in an even-numbered position.

3 The Riverside paper had a higher-numbered position than the one from Maine, which was one row below and one row right of the Fairview weekly.

4 The Star-Herald was in position 5, the paper from Arizona in 2 and the one published in Five Points in 7.

5 The Telegram, published in Indiana, was next left to the paper from Pleasant Hill. The Globe was immediately above the one published in Midway, Texas.

6 The Mount Lincoln paper was in the same horizontal row as that from Pennsylvania but further left. The Messenger was in the same vertical row as the Pennsylvanian paper.

7 The paper published in Illinois (not from Centerville) was on the same horizontal row as (and further right than) the Kentucky tabloid, which wasn't at the bottom.

8 The Enquirer was in the same vertical row as the Chronicle, but lower down.

9 One paper was the Oak Grove Recorder.

Communities:
Centerville; Fairview; Five Points; Midway; Mount Lincoln; Oak Grove; Pine Lake; Pleasant Hill; Riverside

States:
Arizona; Florida; Illinois; Indiana; Kentucky; Maine; Ohio; Pennsylvania; Texas

Newspaper titles:
Chronicle; Dispatch; Enquirer; Globe; Journal; Messenger; Recorder; Star-Herald; Telegram

	1	2	3
Community: State: Paper:			

	4	5	6
Community: State: Paper:			

	7	8	9
Community: State: Paper:			

RUNNERS AND RIDERS

Three jockeys who rode for the same trainer each had a mount at a different course on a different day last week. From the clues given below, can you say which horse each man rode on which day at which course?

Clues

1 Four-leafed Clover ran later in the week than Josh's mount at Newcaster.

2 Reggie's ride was not at Oldmarket.

3 Declan's race was on Wednesday.

4 Black Cat was the horse entered for the race at Mascott.

	Monday	Wednesday	Friday	Mascott	Newcaster	Oldmarket	Black Cat	Four-leafed Clover	Silver Horseshoe
Declan									
Josh									
Reggie									
Mascott									
Newcaster									
Oldmarket									
Black Cat									
Four-leafed Clover									
Silver Horseshoe									

Jockey	Day	Horse	Course

BROAD BASED

Three hired motor cruisers are tied up to the bank of Easton Broad, Norfolk, on a summer evening. Can you work out the colour of each boat's hull, the name of the family who are its current hirers and the period for which they have hired it?

Clues

1 The blue-hulled boat has been hired for one week longer than the Widgeon, which has been rented by the Fishers.

2 The family who have hired a boat for three weeks aren't the Nelsons, who have the vessel with a plain white hull.

3 The Daffodil hasn't been rented by the Drake family.

	Blue	Green	White	Drake	Fisher	Nelson	1 week	2 weeks	3 weeks
Daffodil									
Jewel									
Widgeon									
1 week									
2 weeks									
3 weeks									
Drake									
Fisher									
Nelson									

Boat	Colour	Family	Hire period

FOUR GUYS NAMED MOE

It's quite unusual to find men nicknamed Moe these days, I've been told, and yet in the village of Faraway, near where I live, there are four of them, all local men much involved in the day-to-day life of the community. From the clues given below, can you work out what Moe is an abbreviation for in each case, and the man's normal job and spare time pursuit?

Clues

1 Moe Shunless isn't the local scoutmaster, whose real first name is Morris.

2 Moe Quette, who represents Faraway on the local district council, has eight letters in the first name he was given by his parents.

3 The man christened Mortimer is Faraway's builder. Funnily enough, it isn't Moses who is the publican at The Bulrushes, Faraway's local hostelry.

4 The farmhand who works at Clockhouse Farm is also the lay reader who runs some of the Sunday services at St George's Church now that they can't afford a full-time minister.

5 Moe Torway, whose full name is Montague Oliver Torway, isn't the postman, nor is the postman Moe Shunless.

	Montague	Morris	Mortimer	Moses	Builder	Farmhand	Postman	Publican	Councillor	Lay reader	Scoutmaster	Special constable
Moe Hare												
Moe Quette												
Moe Shunless												
Moe Torway												
Councillor												
Lay reader												
Scoutmaster												
Spec constable												
Builder												
Farmhand												
Postman												
Publican												

Name	Full forename	Full-time job	Part-time job

SUNDAY SERMONS

The Reverend Milton Keynes is a member of a team ministry covering a number of parishes in Midlandshire. In May he is due to deliver Sunday sermons at four different churches, at the rate of one per week. From the clues given below, can you work out at which church he is due to speak on each Sunday, which village it is in, and on which rather obscure scripture he'll be basing that Sunday's sermon?

Clues

1 On Sunday, May 25, the Reverend Milton Keynes will be speaking in the parish church of St Rhea.

2 On May 18 the Reverend Keynes' text is taken from the Book of Jubilees, Chapter 12; this is not the day on which he will be preaching in Heaviwater.

3 The Reverend Keynes will be preaching at St Freya's Church in Cherrypit the Sunday after he delivers his sermon based on the Third Epistle to the Corinthians, Chapter 3, verses 7 to 14.

4 It's not on the second Sunday in May that the Reverend Keynes will be speaking on a text from the Book of Reuben at the parish church in Kerbstone.

5 The church in Ricefield where the Reverend Keynes will be giving the sermon on May 4 is not St Typhon's.

	St Freya's	St Nudd's	St Rhea's	St Typhon's	Cherrypit	Heaviwater	Kerbstone	Ricefield	3 Corinthians	Jubilees	Nicodemus	Reuben
May 4												
May 11												
May 18												
May 25												
3 Corinthians												
Jubilees												
Nicodemus												
Reuben												
Cherrypit												
Heaviwater												
Kerbstone												
Ricefield												

Sunday	Church	Village	Text

FOR A GOOD CAUSE

Employees of some local companies in Storbury have been running sponsored events to raise funds for the town's Willowtree Hospital. Last night at the Town Hall the money they had made was handed over to the hospital's treasurer. Can you work out the full name of each of the four people who presented the treasurer with cheques, which company they work for, what sponsored event they ran, and how much it made?

Clues

1 The employees of PennyCorp, the multinational Penny Corporation's Storbury operation, raised £800 by their sponsored efforts.

2 Pamela Rice works for Finch's Packaging.

3 The sponsored mountain climb, which raised £500, actually made use of a climbing wall at the sports centre, as there are no real mountains in Storbury; the company representative who handed over the £500 was of the same gender as the person who presented the profits from the sponsored quiz (they kept going for thirty-six hours!) run by employees of Grey and Hick.

4 Andrew Bell handed the treasurer a cheque for £600.

5 It was Fiona Green who presented the profits from the sponsored swim.

	Finch's	Grey and Hick	JJL	PennyCorp	Mountain climb	Quiz	Swim	Walk	£500	£600	£700	£800
Andrew Bell												
Fiona Green												
Keith Lloyd												
Pamela Rice												
£500												
£600												
£700												
£800												
Mountain climb												
Quiz												
Swim												
Walk												

Representative	Company	Event	Amount

WIZARD PLOT!

The popularity of a certain well-known junior wizard has led to a huge increase in the number of academies offering magical courses to would-be sorcerers. Below are details of five lucky candidates who have won places; from the information given, can you work out at which establishment each is a pupil, their main areas of study, and the Professor looking after each?

Clues

1 Larry Lester is at Porkwens Academy, but not to study invisibility; Prof Deerkey instructs in wandwork, but not at Porkwens or Hamboils.

2 Lottie Baxter is not at Boarpocks, and isn't being taught by Prof McTavish, who is not a specialist in flying.

3 Barry Carter is a pupil of Prof Tumbledown.

4 Carrie Foster is studying potions.

5 One of the five is attending Sowrash Academy to study fortune-telling.

6 Prof Squirrel is a fellow of Gruntpimples Academy.

	Boarpocks	Gruntpimples	Hamboils	Porkwens	Sowrash	Flying	Fortune-telling	Invisibility	Potions	Wandwork	Deerkey	McTavish	Snoop	Squirrel	Tumbledown
Lottie Baxter															
Barry Carter															
Gary Dexter															
Carrie Foster															
Larry Lester															
Deerkey															
McTavish															
Snoop															
Squirrel															
Tumbledown															
Flying															
Fortune-telling															
Invisibility															
Potions															
Wandwork															

Wizard	Academy	Area of study	Professor

MS FITT

Wanda B Fitt takes her physical condition very seriously, and every weekday she attends a different fitness class somewhere in her home town (then spends Saturday and Sunday trying to recover and summon up enough energy to start again on Monday). From the clues below, can you work out which instructor's class she visits on each day, where it's held, and what outfit she wore there last week?

Clues

1 Both Holly's aerobics class, for which Wanda wore a jogging suit last week, and Beth's step session are held in hired halls, but the group she goes to on Monday meets in a properly-equipped gymnasium.

2 Wanda wore a grey jogging-suit (not at Starr's Gymnasium) earlier in the week than the pink leotard (not worn at the community centre).

3 Kate's yoga class (for which Wanda wears a leotard) is not held in the church hall.

4 Last Wednesday, Wanda wore a green leotard.

5 The class held at Starr's gymnasium is not on Tuesdays.

6 Lisa's circuit class, for which Wanda appeared in black takes place the day before the one held at the community centre and the day after the one at the church hall.

	Beth	Heather	Holly	Kate	Lisa	Church hall	Community centre	School hall	Starr's gym	YWCA gym	Black leotard	Blue joggers	Green leotard	Grey joggers	Pink leotard
Monday															
Tuesday															
Wednesday															
Thursday															
Friday															
Black leotard															
Blue joggers															
Green leotard															
Grey joggers															
Pink leotard															
Church hall															
Comm centre															
School hall															
Starr's gym															
YWCA gym															

Day	Instructor	Location	Outfit

BATTLESHIPS

This puzzle is based on the old game of battleships. Your task is to find the vessels in the diagram. Some parts of boats or sea squares have already been filled in, and a number next to a row or column refers to the number of occupied squares in that row or column. The boats may be positioned horizontally or vertically, but no two boats or parts of boats are in adjacent squares – horizontally, vertically or diagonally.

Aircraft Carrier:

Battleships:

Cruisers:

Destroyers:

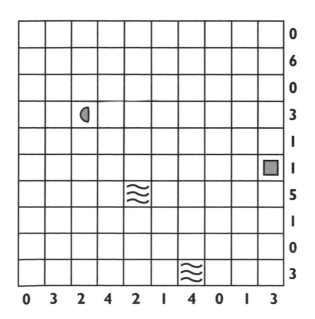

LOGI-5

Every row across and column down should contain five letters: A, B, C, D and E, appearing once each. Also every shape (shown by the thick lines) must contain each of the letters A, B, C, D and E, appearing once each. Can you fill the grid?

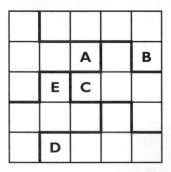

ABC

Every row across and column down is to have each of the letters A, B and C and two empty squares. The letter outside the grid shows the first or second letter in the direction of the arrow. Can you fill the grid?

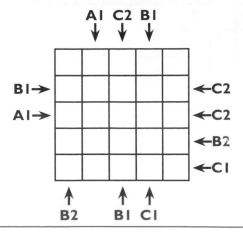

BUT IS IT ART?

Art collector Sir Archie Stahls specialises in modern art, the sort that leaves many people puzzled or just plain angry. Below are details of five recent acquisitions; from the information given, can you work out from which trendy gallery each was purchased, the name of the artist, what the 'work of art' consists of, and how much Stahls paid for each?

Clues

1 The Ivan Rippov piece, a stainless steel pyramid, was not bought from the Huddwinker Gallery, but cost twice as much as the piece from the Schamm Gallery.

2 The work by Monty Banks from the Foni Gallery cost £5,000 less than the piece on display at the Schamm.

3 The dustbin full of cans cost more than the broken glass in a frame.

4 The pile of old car tyres cost Sir Archie £10,000; it was not the work of Artie Fishall, who was also not responsible for the dustbin of cans.

5 The broken glass in the frame was on display at Fake Modern.

6 Sir Archie had to pay more for the Con Swindell work than for that by Esau Hoakes.

	Monty Banks	Artie Fishall	Esau Hoakes	Ivan Rippov	Con Swindell	Broken glass	Dustbin	Pile of tyres	Steel pyramid	Yellow kettle	£5,000	£10,000	£15,000	£20,000	£25,000
Fake Modern															
Foni															
Huddwinker															
Pinchbeck															
Schamm															
£5,000															
£10,000															
£15,000															
£20,000															
£25,000															
Broken glass															
Dustbin															
Pile of tyres															
Steel pyramid															
Yellow kettle															

Gallery	Artist	Work	Price

THE TEE-VEES

The latest arrivals on children's television are the Tee-Vees, five cuddly creatures living in a magical house on a faraway planet. From the following information, can you discover their names, their individual colours, the distinctive item of clothing each wears, and the job each performs around the house?

Clues

1 Luni is yellow, but Dipi is neither pink nor green.

2 The green Tee-Vee neither wears an apron, which is the cook's accessory, nor is responsible for the gardening.

3 The Tee-Vee who wears the top hat is not pink, and neither drives the others around nor does their laundry.

4 It's the purple Tee-Vee who does the laundry, but doesn't wear wellies while doing it.

5 Dafi cleans the house, but doesn't sport the top hat.

6 Bati always wears the sou'-wester, while the red Tee-Vee wears the waistcoat.

	Green	Pink	Purple	Red	Yellow	Apron	Sou'wester	Top hat	Waistcoat	Wellies	Cleaning	Cooking	Driving	Gardening	Laundry
Bati															
Dafi															
Dipi															
Gaga															
Luni															
Cleaning											
Cooking											
Driving											
Gardening											
Laundry											
Apron						
Sou'-wester						
Top hat						
Waistcoat						
Wellies						

Name	Colour	Clothing	Job

PLACE THE POOCHES

The families living at numbers 2 to 8 each have a dog. From the clues given below, can you name the family at each house and their dog, and identify the latter's breed?

Clues

1 The Kennels live at the house immediately to the right of the one which is home to Ricky, the Dalmatian.

2 The Barkers' house has a lower number than the one where the bulldog lives.

3 Butch lives at number 4.

4 The family at number 6 own the Labrador.

5 The spaniel, who is not called Simba, belongs to the Doggetts.

Families:
Barker; Doggett; Kennell; Yapp

Dogs:
Butch; Jack; Ricky; Simba

Breeds:
Bulldog; Dalmatian; Labrador; spaniel

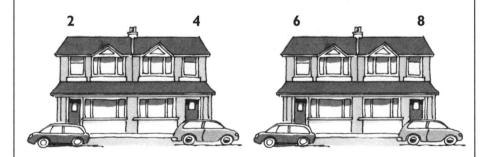

House number	Family	Dog	Breed

Starting tip: Start by working out where Ricky lives.

THE PASSAGE OF TIME

Four public clocks are on view on different buildings in a small town on the Isle of Chronos. From the clues given below, can you identify buildings 1 to 4, work out in which year the clock on each was installed, and name the street in which it stands?

Clues

1 Jubilee Road was re-named in 1897 in honour of Queen Victoria's Diamond Jubilee at the same time as the clock there was installed.

2 The timepiece celebrating the Coronation of 1953 is not on the school.

3 The oldest of the four clocks is the one on the parish church, which dates from 1735.

4 The clock on the library in Gregory Street is older than the one on building number 1.

5 The clock installed to celebrate the end of the Great War in 1918 is on building number 2.

6 The bank is not in Spicer Street, which is next anticlockwise from Long Lane.

Buildings:
Bank; church; library; school

Years:
1735; 1897; 1918; 1953

Streets:
Gregory Street; Jubilee Road; Long Lane; Spicer Street

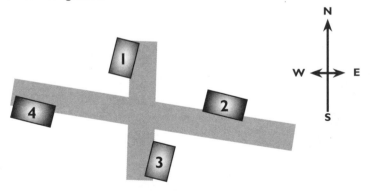

Number	Building	Year	Street

Starting tip: Start by working out the date of the library clock.

DRONES WILL BE DRONES

On their respective birthdays one year, each of the Drones about town celebrated only too well with his fellow members of the Drones Club, and later in the evening made a fool of himself in a different manner in various locations about the capital. From the clues given below, can you work out in which month each was born, and how and where he celebrated?

Clues

1 One Drone was debagged and then abandoned by his club colleagues in celebration of the birthday next after the one when another decided to take a swim in the Serpentine.

2 Rupert de Grey made a fool of himself in Piccadilly.

3 Montague Ffolliott purloined a policeman's helmet, but not in June.

4 It was in August that one Drone made a long, rambling speech, much to the amusement of the passing populace.

5 Edward Tanqueray celebrated his birthday in February; he did not disgrace himself in the Strand.

6 The June incident, which did not involve Gerald Huntington, took place on the Embankment, when the celebrant was not the man who took it into his head to burst into song.

	February	April	June	August	October	Debagged	Made speech	Sang	Stole helmet	Swam	Embankment	Piccadilly	Serpentine	Strand	Trafalgar Square
Archie Fotheringhay															
Edward Tanqueray															
Gerald Huntington															
Montague Ffolliott															
Rupert de Grey															
Embankment															
Piccadilly															
Serpentine															
Strand															
Trafalgar Square															
Debagged															
Made speech															
Sang															
Stole helmet															
Swam															

Drone	Month	Deed	Location

EVENING JOBS

Five young mums got talking at the playgroup, and discovered that, after spending the day at home with the children, each had an evening job. From the clues given below, can you work out how many children each woman has, say which evening job she does, and name her husband who looks after the children on the nights when she works?

Clues

1 Juliet has more children than John and his wife, who works three nights a week as a barmaid.

2 Louise is out working on nights when she can organise one of her parties to sell a specific company's products; she has more children than Sally.

3 Delia, who does not work as a cleaner, and her husband Neville, have one more child than Nick and his wife.

4 Tom has only one child to look after when his wife is out at work.

5 Andrea does not have two children.

6 The fitness instructor and her husband have a family of three children.

7 Ewan's family is not as large as the night-class teacher's.

	1	2	3	4	5	Barmaid	Cleaner	Fitness instructor	Night teacher	Party seller	Ewan	John	Neville	Nick	Tom
Andrea															
Delia															
Juliet															
Louise															
Sally															
Ewan															
John															
Neville															
Nick															
Tom															
Barmaid																
Cleaner																
Fitness instr																
Night teacher																
Party seller																

Name	Children	Job	Husband

GOOD NEWS, BAD NEWS

One day last week five neighbours each received two items in the post, one welcome and one not so welcome. From the clues given below, can you name the resident at each address, and describe the two items he or she received?

Clues

1 The person whose letter from a sister in Australia was matched by a summons to jury service lives at the number next higher than that of Jack Brown's house.

2 Naomi Potts was delighted to receive a wedding invitation.

3 The reminder about an overdue library book was sent to Annie Price, whose house does not have a single-digit number.

4 Tom Watson, who lives at number 12, did not receive the birthday card.

5 The gardening catalogue was the acceptable item delivered at number 4 (which is not the home of Debbie Blythe) and it was not accompanied by the begging letter from a student son, away from home.

6 The income tax demand went to number 11.

	Annie Price	Debbie Blythe	Jack Brown	Naomi Potts	Tom Watson	Birthday card	Gardening cat	Premium bond	Sister in Australia	Wedding invitation	Begging letter	Gas bill	Jury summons	Library reminder	Tax demand
Number 4															
Number 5															
Number 11															
Number 12															
Number 14															
Begging letter															
Gas bill															
Jury summons															
Library reminder															
Tax demand															
Birthday card															
Gardening cat															
Premium bond															
Sister in Australia															
Wedding invitation															

House No	Resident	Welcome	Unwelcome

ON THE RIGS

The diagram shows five men walking across the tarmac to a helicopter which is about to take them all to an offshore oil rig on which four of them work. From the clues given below, can you fully identify each of the men numbered 1 to 5, work out what he does, and say how old he is?

Clues

1 As they walk across the tarmac, the helicopter pilot has Mr Barrell immediately to his left and the man aged 44 immediately to his right.

2 Mr Field (aged 36) is somewhere to the right of Nathan as they head for the helicopter.

3 Number 5 in the diagram is not as old as Jack, who is not next but one to Mervyn in the line.

4 The 28-year-old (James) is immediately to the right of the foreman, and immediately to the left of Mr Hoyle.

5 Number 4 is Don.

6 Mr Sinker is the rig worker.

7 The chemist is numbered 2 in the line.

Forenames:
Don; Jack; James; Mervyn; Nathan

Surnames:
Barrell; Field; Hoyle; Sinker; Wells

Jobs:
Chemist; engineer; foreman; pilot; rig worker

Ages:
28; 33; 36; 41; 44

No	Forename	Surname	Job	Age

Starting tip: Start by placing the foreman.

TOO MANY COOKS

Somebody at Albion-TV has come up with a brilliant idea for yet another cookery programme, and five qualified chefs are competing to become the presenter. Can you work out each man's name, the particularly distinctive aspect of his appearance, the style of cookery in which he specialises, and in what part of London he runs a small but incredibly popular restaurant?

Clues

1 The man with the goatee beard cooks cuisine nouveau. Neither Tim Sweet-Bredd nor the fish specialist who runs Heart and Sole insists on wearing green.

2 The man with the shaven head has a restaurant in Lambeth, has no hyphen in his surname, and is neither Dirk D'Essert nor the specialist in British traditional fare.

3 Angus Bannock is an expert in Oriental cookery. Perry Rasher is recognised by his unusual facial hair.

4 The man whose restaurant is in Balham is a vegetarian in his private life as well as at his work.

5 Jay Hammond-Eggz, who wears his hair in a tightly-braided pigtail, does not have a restaurant in Hornsey.

6 Perry Rasher, who runs Chez Longue in Chelsea, is not an expert in fish cookery.

7 Tim Sweet-Bredd does not cook traditional British food.

	Dresses in green	Goatee beard	Pigtail	Shaven head	Walrus moustache	British traditional	Cuisine nouveau	Fish	Oriental	Vegetarian	Balham	Chelsea	Hornsey	Islington	Lambeth
Angus Bannock															
Dirk D'Essert															
Jay Hammond-Eggz															
Perry Rasher															
Tim Sweet-Bredd															
Balham															
Chelsea															
Hornsey															
Islington															
Lambeth															
British traditional															
Cuisine nouveau															
Fish															
Oriental															
Vegetarian															

Chef	Appearance	Speciality	Location

ME, ME, ME, ME, ME!

Five celebrity autobiographies are currently on sale in bookshops. From the following information can you discover the egotistical title of each book, the name of the author, his or her profession, and the cover price of each volume?

Clues

1 Guy Fuller's autobiography is The Fuller Story, while Caleb Ritty is a footballer.

2 Speaking Personally is on sale at £16.99, but its author is not the pop singer whose book is priced lower than Quite a Life.

3 The radio presenter's book, Talking of Me, has a lower cover price than Hugh Jeago's.

4 The MP's autobiography is only £15.99, but its author is not Ed Biggar.

5 I Say! isn't the £17.99 volume.

6 Emma Starr's autobiography is for sale at £18.99.

	Ed Biggar	Guy Fuller	Hugh Jeago	Caleb Ritty	Emma Starr	£15.99	£16.99	£17.99	£18.99	£19.99	Footballer	MP	Opera singer	Pop singer	Radio presenter
I Say!															
Quite a Life															
Speaking Pers'ly															
Talking of Me															
The Fuller Story															
Footballer															
MP															
Opera singer															
Pop singer															
Radio presenter															
£15.99															
£16.99															
£17.99															
£18.99															
£19.99															

Title	Author	Price	Profession

DETECTIVES' DETECTIVES

A friend who's a literary agent in the city of New York told me recently about five new clients he's picked up, each one a real-life detective of some sort who is working on a book about a fictional detective. From the clues below, can you work out the name and employer of each of the real-life detectives, and the name and occupation of the fictional investigator he or she has created?

Clues

1 The detective whose book features Sergeant Lucy Regan of the Internal Affairs Division (IAD) of an unnamed metropolitan police department, whose job is investigating fellow-cops, isn't employed by a police department.

2 Dave Carey's book, which isn't about Patsy-Ann Bowen, features a federal agent belonging to a special task force working against organised crime.

3 Wendy Vance created Maisie Hovik.

4 John Kengo is senior investigator for the Stern Agency. The Vice Squad detective from the Miami Police didn't create a private eye character.

5 The New York police officer (whose investigator is not Andy Gomez) and the detective writing about a small-town police chief are both male.

6 The investigator for Diamond Insurance, whose book is about a Military Police detective, isn't Marion Penn, whose detective is female.

	Boston police	Diamond Insurance	Miami police	New York police	Stern Agency	Andy Gomez	Carl Van Damm	Lucy Regan	Maisie Hovik	Patsy-Ann Bowen	Federal agent	IAD officer	Mil'y Police officer	Police chief	Private eye
Dave Carey															
John Kengo															
Marion Penn															
Saul Rossi															
Wendy Vance															
Federal agent																
IAD officer																
Mil'y Police officer																
Police chief																
Private eye																
Andy Gomez																
Carl Van Damm																
Lucy Regan																
Maisie Hovik																
Patsy-Ann Bowen																

Real detective	Employer	Fictional det've	Occupation

SUSIE'S QUILT

Granny Smith makes a quilt for each of her grandchildren when they are born. In the diagram we see baby Susie's quilt. Each alternate (shaded) square is made of pink checked material, but in the thirteen other squares Granny has embroidered a different motif on a different coloured background. Can you work out all the details, writing in the motifs and colours directly onto the patchwork squares?

Clues

1 The rabbit has the pale green square to its left and the pale red square to its right; they are in the row above the boat.

2 The grey square is somewhere directly above the one depicting the bird.

3 The elephant is diagonally immediately below and to the left of the yellow square. The lilac square is somewhere right of the elephant in the same row.

4 The motif in square C5 is not of a living creature.

5 The butterfly is diagonally immediately below and to the right of the apricot square, which is in the same horizontal row as the dark blue one.

6 The quilt's central square, C3, depicts the sun on a crimson background.

Motifs:
Ball; bird; boat; butterfly; doll; elephant; fish; flower; house; rabbit; sun; toadstool; tree

Colours:
Apricot; beige; brown; cream; crimson; dark blue; dark green; grey; lilac; pale blue; pale green; pale red; yellow

7 Square D4 is brown.

8 The fish is in square E5.

9 The toadstool is somewhere directly below the beige square in a column containing three non-pink squares.

10 The ball (which is in the same row as the tree) has the flower diagonally immediately below it to its right.

11 The pale blue square is in the column next to and right of that including the doll, and next to and left of that in which the cream square appears.

	1	2	3	4	5
A					
B					
C					
D					
E					

Starting tip:

Begin by placing the rabbit.

BEAUX AFLOAT

When the Napoleonic wars were safely concluded, Beaux Spritt made a summer cruise each year in his yacht, on which a different one of our Beaux was invited in each of the years 1816 to 1820, along with a young lady whose acquaintance he was eager to pursue. From the clues below, can you say which Beau was invited aboard in each year, and name the girl he was interested in, and her father's rank or occupation?

Clues

1 Matilda, whose father was an ambassador at the court of St James, was a guest on a cruise in a later year than the one on which Beau Nydel was invited.

2 Beau Legges and the admiral's daughter, who was not Augusta, were both Beau Spritt's guests in the year before Caroline went cruising.

3 Beau Belles was an earlier guest of Beau Spritt's than Beau Tighe.

4 Charlotte, whose father was not the rich merchant, was the young lady who appealed to Beau Streate; their cruise was not the first or last of the five.

5 1817 was the year in which Sophia was invited to travel on Beau Spritt's yacht.

6 The earl's daughter was the prize catch aboard Beau Spritt's yacht in 1818; she was not being pursued by Beau Belles.

	Beau Belles	Beau Legges	Beau Nydel	Beau Streate	Beau Tighe	Augusta	Caroline	Charlotte	Matilda	Sophia	Admiral	Ambassador	Baronet	Earl	Rich merchant
1816															
1817															
1818															
1819															
1820															
Admiral															
Ambassador															
Baronet															
Earl															
Rich merchant															
Augusta															
Caroline															
Charlotte															
Matilda															
Sophia															

Year	Beau	Lady	Father

A GOOD REPORT

When Sophie took her report home at the end of term her parents were, on the whole, quite pleased with it, though the grades she received varied between A and C+. From the clues given below, can you work out which grade she was given by which teacher in each of the five listed subjects, and say which summarising comment each teacher appended?

Clues

1 The A grade was naturally the one matched by the comment 'excellent', while the A- was not accompanied by the comment 'works hard'.

2 The grade given by Mr Dingle was not as good as the science grade, but higher than the one which drew the comment 'intelligent'.

3 'A steady worker' was Mrs Carter's assessment of Sophie.

4 Sophie received a B+ from her French teacher.

5 In history, Sophie was given a grade immediately higher than the one she received for maths, which she is not taught by Miss Roberts.

6 The B grade was awarded by Mrs Jefferson.

7 The English teacher, Mr Fletcher, awarded Sophie the grade immediately higher than the one which preceded the comment 'solid progress'.

	A	A-	B+	B	C+	Mrs Carter	Mr Dingle	Mr Fletcher	Mrs Jefferson	Miss Roberts	Excellent	Intelligent	Solid progress	Steady worker	Works hard
English															
French															
History															
Maths															
Science															
Excellent															
Intelligent															
Solid progress															
Steady worker															
Works hard															
Mrs Carter															
Mr Dingle															
Mr Fletcher															
Mrs Jefferson															
Miss Roberts															

Subject	Grade	Teacher	Comment

SCOTS WHA HAE ...

Five men have dominated their respective events over recent years at a small Highland Games meeting in northern Scotland. From the clues given below, can you fully identify each athlete, name his event, and say for how many successive years he has won the prize in his event?

Clues

1 The champion at tossing the caber has won that event for one more successive year than Gordon McAlpine has carried off his prize.

2 The miler has won for more years than the high jumper, but fewer than Iain.

3 Hamish has been successful at the last four games.

4 Gregor (whose event is throwing the hammer) has a record of success extending a year further back than Campbell's.

5 Bruce has won the cup in his event for five years in a row.

6 For the last six years the shot putt has been won by the same man.

7 Alistair has a longer-standing record of success than Stewart.

	Bruce	Campbell	Kennedy	McAlpine	Stewart	Caber	Hammer	Mile	High jump	Shot putt	3 years	4 years	5 years	6 years	7 years
Alistair															
Gordon															
Gregor															
Hamish															
Iain															
3 years															
4 years															
5 years															
6 years															
7 years															
Caber															
Hammer															
High jump															
Mile															
Shot putt															

Forename	Surname	Event	No of years

WANTED!

'Wanted' posters for notorious outlaws have gone up in five Wild West towns. From the information given below, can you discover where each poster has been nailed up, the crime for which each outlaw is wanted, and the reward being offered?

Clues

1 The townspeople at Harris Falls have put together a reward for the capture of Scotty McRae of $300 more than that being offered for the cattle rustler.

2 The $400 reward is being offered in Little Pine, but not for the capture of Hank Gilmore.

3 The reward being offered for the murderer is $100 more than the sum on the posters in White River, where an even number of hundreds of dollars is being offered.

4 Zack Monroe is a train robber.

5 The reward for Link O'Reilly's capture is $600.

6 The reward of $500 is not for the bank robber, who is wanted in Gibbsville.

	Baxter Gould	Hank Gilmore	Scotty McRae	Zack Monroe	Link O'Reilly	Bank robbery	Cattle rustling	Horse stealing	Murder	Train robbery	$400	$500	$600	$700	$1,000
Gibbsville															
Harris Falls															
Little Pine															
White River															
Yellow Creek															
$400															
$500															
$600															
$700															
$1,000															
Bank robbery															
Cattle rustling															
Horse stealing															
Murder															
Train robbery															

Town	Outlaw	Crime	Reward

SAILOR SAM

Sam had an urge to emulate his hero the pioneering single-handed, round-the-world yachtsman Joshua Slocum, but after five attempts in successive years, was persuaded by his family to give up his maritime ambitions. Can you say where he set out from in each year, where he was heading for and where, since he was almost totally lacking in the skills of both seamanship and navigation, he eventually ended up on each occasion?

Clues

1 Sam managed to get as far south as Bordeaux on a later voyage than the one when he attempted to sail to Gibraltar, and the year before he started his journey from Brighton.

2 One of Sam's voyages saw him end up in Dunkirk after setting sail for Algiers.

3 The trip from Dover was undertaken the year after the one when Sam came ashore in Calais.

4 Plymouth was not where Sam made his landfall after setting out from Worthing, which was not his departure point in 1899.

5 1901 was the year Sam's sense of direction led him to Torquay.

6 Tangier was Sam's intended destination on an earlier voyage than the one to Tunis, but a later one than the one to Madeira.

7 Portsmouth was Sam's chosen starting point for the last of his five epic voyages.

	Brighton	Dover	Portsmouth	Southend	Worthing	Algiers	Gibraltar	Madeira	Tangier	Tunis	Bordeaux	Calais	Dunkirk	Plymouth	Torquay
1899															
1900															
1901															
1902															
1903															
Bordeaux															
Calais															
Dunkirk															
Plymouth															
Torquay															
Algiers															
Gibraltar															
Madeira															
Tangier															
Tunis															

Year	From	To	Ended up in

BIRTHDAY BOOK

Alma keeps a book in which she has recorded the birthdays of her family and friends. The accompanying table contains a digest of twelve such dates in different months of the year, each being the birthday of a relative, or, in one case, a godchild. From the clues given below, can you fill in the relevant date, name and connection for each of the twelve months?

Clues

1 Alma's son has his birthday in April.
2 One of the men was born on March 1st.
3 The great-uncle's birthday is three months after the aunt's.
4 Alma's father, Henry, was born in a 30-day month.
5 The connections born in January and July are of the same sex, while the birthday on the 31st of the month is the month after the one on the 11th.
6 Melanie's birthday is on the 30th of the month after grandad's, which is also on an even date.
7 Alma's god-daughter has a birthday two months after Joyce's, and Rodney's is two months after Valerie's, which is on the 10th.
8 Helen (not Alma's mother) was born in June.
9 One cousin was born on the 8th of a month which is seven months before or after the other's birthday.
10 Alma's uncle's birthday is in the first half of the year on a date later than the 20th of the month following her grandma's, but on an earlier date in the month than Richard's.
11 A man was born in December.
12 The birthday on the 16th is the month before Alma's daughter's and three months before Derek's. Derek's is later in the year than the one on the 22nd, but earlier than the one on the 14th.
13 Stanley's birthday is two months later than Patricia's. Henry's is the month before that on the 27th.

Dates:
1st; 6th; 8th; 10th; 11th; 14th; 16th; 22nd; 23rd; 27th; 30th; 31st

Names:
Anne; Derek; George; Helen; Henry; Joyce; Melanie; Patricia; Richard; Rodney; Stanley; Valerie

Connections:
Aunt; cousin (male); cousin (female); daughter; father; god-daughter; grandad; grandma; great-uncle; mother; son; uncle

Month	Date	Name	Connection
January			
February			
March			
April			
May			
June			
July			
August			
September			
October			
November			
December			

YESTERDAY'S VILLAINS

While Joe and his wife were staying in the Cornish fishing village of Rathole last summer, they were introduced to a number of local men who were quite proud of being descended from villains of the 18th and 19th Centuries, when the county was a lot less law-abiding than it is these days! Can you work out the name and occupation of each of these men, and the first name and criminal profession of his infamous ancestor?

Clues

1 Alan Borlase's villainous ancestor had a shorter first name than Owen Pender's, who wasn't the notorious wrecker who used false navigation lights to lure merchant ships onto the rocks around Rathole Bay.

2 The publican from the Fisherman's Rest isn't the man descended from Sampson.

3 Yestin's modern-day descendant is a perfectly respectable solicitor; he is not Sam Trevian's ancestor, who was a murderer who would today be classified as a serial killer rather than a sort of folk hero.

4 Jack Kegwin drives a bus between Rathole and Mencarrow and back twice every weekday and three times on Saturdays.

5 Dewi, the smuggler, was killed in a running battle with excise men in 1819. Ivo, who died in 1773, wasn't the murderer.

6 Chris Davey, whose notorious 18th Century ancestor was Wynn Davey, isn't the Rathole ferryman who is descended from one of Cornwall's most famous highwaymen.

	Bus driver	Ferryman	Hotelier	Publican	Solicitor	Dewi	Ivo	Sampson	Wynn	Yestin	Forger	Highwayman	Murderer	Smuggler	Wrecker
Alan Borlase															
Chris Davey															
Jack Kegwin															
Owen Pender															
Sam Trevian															
Forger															
Highwayman															
Murderer															
Smuggler															
Wrecker															
Dewi															
Ivo															
Sampson															
Wynn															
Yestin															

Name	Occupation	Ancestor	Crime

PROBLEM PROBLEMS

Among the many wonderful suggestions for logic problems recently submitted by our expert compilers were some that were – well, frankly, totally unusable! Below are details of some of these which used well-known Logic Problems characters. Can you identify the name and home-town of the compiler who submitted each idea, the character or characters they used, and the unacceptable aspect of their suggestion?

Clues

1 One suggestion involved secret agent James Link and rather too much sex!

2 The compiler from Walsall who put forward an unacceptable suggestion for a Drones problem wasn't Mr Lupin.

3 Ms Glump's puzzle concerned the Knock-kneed Knights of the Round Table.

4 The suggestion from the resident of Norwich concerned cannibalism. This wasn't the problem which featured Miss Raffles, nor did she appear in the cricket puzzle.

5 The suggestion submitted by Mr Tufto from Malvern didn't involve sport.

6 Neither Miss Rugge's problem (rejected because it involved cruelty to animals) nor Mr Lupin's concerned the Regency Beaus.

7 Mrs Bleyes didn't submit the problem rejected because it required an expert knowledge of cricket.

8 The puzzle about pankration, an Ancient Greek martial sport, whose details are lost in the mists of time, was not submitted from Runcorn.

	Bristol	Malvern	Norwich	Runcorn	Walsall	Beaus	Drones	James Link	Knights	Miss Raffles	Animal cruelty	Cannibalism	Cricket	Pankration	Sex
Mrs Bleyes															
Ms Glump															
Mr Lupin															
Miss Rugge															
Mr Tufto															
Animal cruelty															
Cannibalism															
Cricket															
Pankration															
Sex															
Beaus															
Drones															
James Link															
Knights															
Miss Raffles															

Compiler	Home-town	Character/s	Theme

B&B AND EVENING MEAL

Last year, while my wife and I were visiting Cornwall, we took the opportunity to visit a number of villages, each the site of something she wanted to see; I was more concerned that each was also the site of an establishment where we could get a decent bed and breakfast and that could also provide an evening meal. Can you work out what we saw in each village, the name of the B&B there, and the evening meal provided?

Clues

1 Our evening meal at Haven House included chips, and very nice they were, too.

2 The B&B we stayed at in the village where we saw the standing stone called the May Maiden gave us a very fine and flavourful lamb curry for an evening meal.

3 On the night we stayed at Redgate in the village where we saw an ancient British hill fort (which wasn't Mencarrow) we didn't have pizza for our evening meal.

4 The Willows, where we had delicious fish and chips for our evening meal, wasn't the B&B in Rospentyr where our bedroom window actually gave us a fine view of the medieval Holy Well of St Buda which we had gone there to see.

5 Neither Polkear, where our B&B provided burgers and chips for our evening meal nor Henmelin, where we stayed at Camelot (though it wasn't the original!), boasted either a stone circle or a hill fort.

	Castle	Hill fort	Holy well	Standing stone	Stone circle	Camelot	Haven House	Redgate	St Piran's	The Willows	Burger and chips	Curry	Fish and chips	Pasty and chips	Pizza
Bosleven															
Henmelin															
Mencarrow															
Polkear															
Rospentyr															
Burger and chips															
Curry															
Fish and chips															
Pasty and chips															
Pizza															
Camelot															
Haven House															
Redgate															
St Piran's															
The Willows															

Village	Feature	B&B	Evening meal

AT A STANDSTILL

When an accident occurred on the northbound carriageway of a motorway, vehicles came to a halt in all three lanes. The first twelve drivers affected are the ones we ask you to identify, using the diagram and the clues below. Can you fill in the correct name in each vehicle?

Clues

1 Sue is immediately behind Bill, and has Ruth at a standstill in the lane outside her.

2 Laura's car in the slow lane has Don's immediately diagonally behind her and to her right.

3 Mike is somewhere, but not immediately, behind Leon in the same lane of the motorway.

4 Tina's odd-numbered vehicle is in the row behind Jack's car.

5 Vehicle 7 has Jill at the wheel, while the one behind her has a male driver.

6 Cars 9 and 11 have drivers of the same sex, the latter's name having the same initial letter as that of the person in car 1.

Drivers:
Bill; Dick; Don; Jack; Jill; Laura; Leon; Mary; Mike; Ruth; Sue; Tina

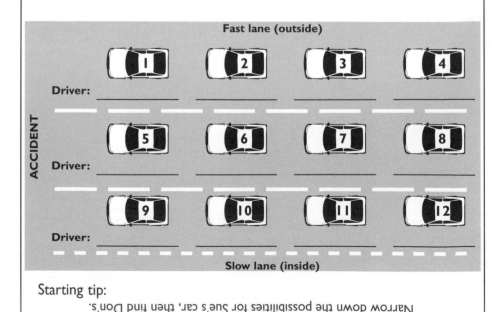

Fast lane (outside)

1 2 3 4

Driver: _____ _____ _____ _____

ACCIDENT

5 6 7 8

Driver: _____ _____ _____ _____

9 10 11 12

Driver: _____ _____ _____ _____

Slow lane (inside)

Starting tip:

Narrow down the possibilities for Sue's car, then find Don's.

BATTLESHIPS

This puzzle is based on the old game of battleships. Your task is to find the vessels in the diagram. Some parts of boats or sea squares have already been filled in, and a number next to a row or column refers to the number of occupied squares in that row or column. The boats may be positioned horizontally or vertically, but no two boats or parts of boats are in adjacent squares – horizontally, vertically or diagonally.

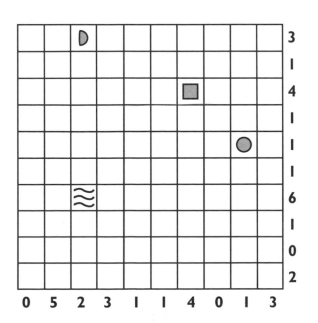

LOGI-5

Every row across and column down should contain five letters: A, B, C, D and E, appearing once each. Also every shape (shown by the thick lines) must contain each of the letters A, B, C, D and E, appearing once each. Can you fill the grid?

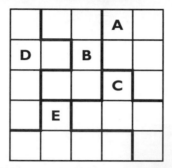

ABC

Every row across and column down is to have each of the letters A, B and C and two empty squares. The letter outside the grid shows the first or second letter in the direction of the arrow. Can you fill the grid?

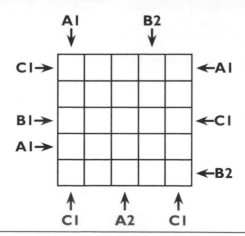

SOMETHING SPECIAL

Kay Terring is Northchester's leading organiser of wedding receptions, and has been booked to run the wedding celebrations for five rather out-of-the-ordinary marriages. Can you work out the name of the bride and groom concerned in each of them, where the actual ceremony will take place and what Kay is charging for doing the reception?

Clues

1 Kay's bill for the reception at the Northchester City football ground after Jon Ireton and his bride, both dressed in City colours, have been united (sorry) in matrimony will be lower than the one for the former Liz Monk's do.

2 Rachel Shaw's reception is going to cost her parents exactly £2000.

3 Mark Lewis' reception is going to cost £2400; he isn't the gentleman who will be getting married in the basket of a hot-air balloon!

4 Clare Dane and her husband-to-be have arranged for their wedding to be on the shore of a beautiful woodland lake.

5 Kay's bill for the reception after the wedding at the stately home called Northchester Towers will be £1600.

6 The cost of the reception after Alison Bell's marriage to Simon Ryder will be £400 more than the bill which will be sent to Nick Murphy's in-laws-to-be.

	Daniel Clark	Jon Ireton	Mark Lewis	Nick Murphy	Simon Ryder	Football ground	Hot-air balloon	Lake shore	Stately home	Tudor chapel	£1400	£1600	£1800	£2000	£2400
Alison Bell															
Clare Dane															
Emma Finch															
Liz Monk															
Rachel Shaw															
£1400															
£1600															
£1800															
£2000															
£2400															
Football ground															
Hot-air balloon															
Lake shore															
Stately home															
Tudor chapel															

Bride	Groom	Location	Cost

MUSIC AND ...

Five lovers of classical music were all travelling on a train, each in one of five successive coaches, which we will call A to E, starting from the front of the train. During the journey each was reading a different type of material while listening on headphones to the work of a different composer. From the clues given below, can you work out the full details?

Clues

1 Julia was reading the financial report in the carriage behind the one occupied by the Mozart aficionado.

2 Martin (whose musical preference is for the symphonies of Haydn) was not in the carriage immediately in front of the one in which the novel reader was travelling.

3 Bella's carriage was further back in the train than the one in which the magazine reader was listening to Beethoven.

4 John, who was travelling in coach C, was not reading the newspaper.

5 The studious passenger reading the textbook was in coach B of the train.

6 Bach was the favourite composer of the coach D passenger.

	Coach A	Coach B	Coach C	Coach D	Coach E	Financial report	Magazine	Newspaper	Novel	Textbook	Bach	Beethoven	Handel	Haydn	Mozart
Bella															
Carole															
John															
Julia															
Martin															
Bach															
Beethoven															
Handel															
Haydn															
Mozart															
Financial report															
Magazine															
Newspaper															
Novel															
Textbook															

Name	Coach	Reading	Composer

... MEALS ON WHEELS

The passengers in the previous problem all decided to visit the buffet car at about the same time, and were in five successive positions in the queue waiting to be served. From the clues given below, together with the information obtained by solving the previous problem, can you name the person in each position in the queue, and work out his or her sandwich and drink preference?

Clues

1 The only passenger whose order in the queue matched that of the position of his or her coach in the train chose both a ham salad sandwich and orange juice.

2 Lager was the drink ordered by the person standing immediately behind Carole in the queue for the buffet car. The lager-drinker didn't have a chicken salad sandwich.

3 Coffee was chosen by the passenger from the coach immediately in front of Martin's.

4 The second passenger in the queue was the one who had been reading the novel.

5 The person who drank shandy was queueing immediately in front of one of the male passengers, who was somewhere nearer the front of the queue than the consumer of the cheese salad sandwich.

6 The newspaper reader ordered the ham and tomato sandwich.

	First	Second	Third	Fourth	Fifth	Cheese/tomato	Cheese salad	Chicken salad	Ham/tomato	Ham salad	Coffee	Lager	Orange juice	Shandy	Tea
Bella															
Carole															
John															
Julia															
Martin															
Coffee															
Lager															
Orange juice															
Shandy															
Tea															
Cheese/tomato															
Cheese salad															
Chicken salad															
Ham/tomato															
Ham salad															

Passenger	Queue order	Sandwich	Drink

LITERARY ASSOCIATIONS

Among the many interesting buildings in the ancient University city of Goatsferry are some historic pubs that have associations with famous writers. From the clues below, can you work out in which street of old Goatsferry each of the listed establishments stands, the year in which the building was completed, and the name of the writer who has an association – no matter how tenuous – with it?

Clues

1 Dorothy L Sayers stayed at the Royal Dragoon several times, and liked it so much that she had Lord Peter Wimsey drop in there for a drink.

2 The Hawk and Hound stands in Dog Lane. The Devil and Boot is an older hostelry than the pub where Charles Dickens once spent a couple of nights.

3 Ian Fleming, creator of James Bond, often stayed overnight at the pub dating from 1776 while – it's said – romancing one of the lady dons from the University.

4 E M Forster often visited Goatsferry, and it is claimed that on every visit he dined at the pub in the Market Place, which was not built in 1689 or 1740.

5 The oldest pub is in Leman Street and has no known connection with J R R Tolkien.

6 The Old Ship was completed in 1824.

7 The Jack O'Lantern isn't in Queen's Road. The pub built in 1740 doesn't stand in Rose Street.

	Dog Lane	Leman Street	Market Place	Queen's Road	Rose Street	1612	1689	1740	1776	1824	Charles Dickens	Ian Fleming	E M Forster	Dorothy L Sayers	J R R Tolkien
Devil and Boot															
Hawk and Hound															
Jack O'Lantern															
Old Ship															
Royal Dragoon															
Charles Dickens											
Ian Fleming											
E M Forster											
D L Sayers											
J R R Tolkien											
1612					
1689					
1740					
1776					
1824					

Pub	Address	Year	Writer

APRIL FOOLERY

On April 1st three lads played April Fool jokes on different teachers at their school. From the clues given below, can you fully identify each lad, and say which teacher of which lesson he managed to con?

Clues

1 Jimmy managed to catch the female biology teacher off her guard.

2 Young Diddler succeeded in fooling Mrs Baker.

3 The maths teacher fell for Catcher's wiles.

4 Tommy's victim was not Mr Green, and Danny did not trick the English teacher, who is not Miss Jones.

	Catcher	Diddler	Kidham	Mrs Baker	Mr Green	Miss Jones	Biology	English	Maths
Danny									
Jimmy									
Tommy									
Biology									
English									
Maths									
Mrs Baker									
Mr Green									
Miss Jones									

Forename	Surname	Teacher	Subject

LOGI-5

Every row across and column down should contain five letters: A, B, C, D and E, appearing once each. Also every shape (shown by the thick lines) must contain each of the letters A, B, C, D and E, appearing once each. Can you fill the grid?

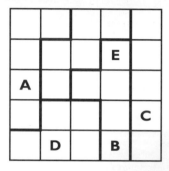

ABC

Every row across and column down is to have each of the letters A, B and C and two empty squares. The letter outside the grid shows the first or second letter in the direction of the arrow. Can you fill the grid?

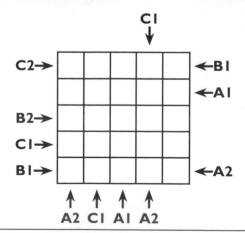

PILE UP

These piles of bricks aren't the random results of a child's play but clues to a final, at present blank, pile on the right. Like the rest, that one has six bricks each with a different one of the six letters.

The numbers below the heaps tell you two things:

(a) The number of adjacent pairs of bricks in that column which also appear adjacent in the final pile.

(b) The number of adjacent pairs of bricks that make a correct pair but the wrong way up.

So: would score one in the 'Correct' row if the final heap had an A directly above a C and a one in the 'Reversed' row if the final heap had a C on top of an A. From all this, can you create the final pile before it topples?

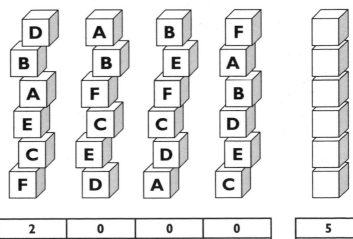

Correct	2	0	0	0	5
Reversed	0	0	0	1	0

BACK TO SCHOOL

Three teachers have just been employed by Storbury Upper School, the very place where they were educated and where each captained a sports team in the distant past. From the clues given below, can you work out what subject each man now teaches, what sport he once captained the school's team in, and the year that he did so?

Clues

1 Bruce Otway captained a school sports team later than the man who now teaches geography.

2 Alan Newton headed his team earlier than the captain of cricket.

3 The English teacher who was captain of the swimming team isn't Clive Price.

4 The biology teacher isn't the man who was captain of the rugby team in 1975.

	Biology	English	Geography	Cricket	Rugby	Swimming	1970	1975	1980
Alan Newton									
Bruce Otway									
Clive Price									
1970									
1975									
1980									
Cricket									
Rugby									
Swimming									

Teacher	Subject	Sport	Year

ALL THE As

In the 18th Century, the Duchy of Aylettria was ruled successively by four Duke Antons – and, by the sort of pure coincidence so handy for writers of logic puzzles, each had a nickname beginning with an A (the T in 'The' doesn't count!), a wife whose name began with A and even a cause of death that began with A – provided you used the right word to describe it. Can you identify each Anton's nickname, wife and cause of death?

Clues

1 It wasn't Duke Anton IV who was known as 'the Asinine'.

2 Anton the Abominable, who was married to the Duchess Anastasie, wasn't the Duke who died from the effects of a cerebrovascular accident – or, as they used to call it in the 18th Century, apoplexy.

3 Anton II was the husband of Duchess Agathe.

4 Anton the Amiable, who wasn't married to the Duchess Adamante, owed his amiability to the quantity of brandy he consumed daily, which – with the remainder of the wines and spirits he drank – meant he eventually died from alcohol abuse.

5 Duchess Astrud's husband, who died when his ducal hunting party was ambushed by revolting peasants in the valley of the River Ay, ruled after the Duke known as Anton the Arrogant.

	The Abominable	The Amiable	The Arrogant	The Asinine	Adamante	Agathe	Anastasie	Astrud	Alcoholism	Ambush	Apoplexy	Arsenic poisoning
Anton I												
Anton II												
Anton III												
Anton IV												
Alcoholism												
Ambush												
Apoplexy												
Arsenic												
Adamante												
Agathe												
Anastasie												
Astrud												

Duke	Nickname	Duchess	Cause of death

BATSWOMEN

The latest edition of The Monthly Journal of Women's Cricket carries news stories about the leading batswomen from four different county teams playing in the Albion-TV British Ladies Cricket League. From the clues given below, can you work out each woman's full name, which county team she plays for in the ATVBLCL, and the nature of the story?

Clues

1 Ms Ball is Sarah, although she's usually referred to as 'Thunda' Ball by tabloid journalists, because – well, that's the sort of thing tabloid journalists are expected to say; Ms Wicket is the top scorer for Cheshire this season.

2 According to the report in the MJoWC (which isn't a tabloid), Carol, who plays for a county which isn't a 'shire', was arrested for assaulting a TV celebrity during a recording of the popular sports quiz Somebody Said It Was Finished; she denies the charge and says that it was pure accident that her bat came into contact with his … er, body.

3 It's the top player from the Essex team who has announced that she's pregnant and will be taking the rest of the season off.

4 Ms Field, who has just announced her engagement to a fellow-player (well, of course he's a fellow), isn't Lucy.

	Ball	De Clare	Field	Wicket	Cheshire	Durham	Essex	Hampshire	Arrest	Engagement	Pregnancy	Retirement
Carol												
Ellen												
Lucy												
Sarah												
Arrest												
Engagement												
Pregnancy												
Retirement												
Cheshire												
Durham												
Essex												
Hampshire												

Batswoman	Surname	County	Story

SYNCHRONISE YOUR ...

... watches! They've gone over the plan dozens of times. The crack force of five specially trained agents – each with a 'bird' codename – will approach the enemy compound at 23.00 hours, each with his own job to do, timed to the second. From the following information, can you discover at what time each agent is to make his move, what his mission is, and in which building, each being designated Shed A to E?

Clues

1 At precisely 23.00 hours 'Raven' will move off, but not heading for Shed A, followed at 23.01 by the agent heading for Shed B; 2 minutes later the generator will be knocked out.

2 'Condor' will make his move 1 minute after another agent has set off to plant explosives.

3 Two minutes before one of the agents will begin running towards Shed C, 'Hawk' will set off.

4 The objective for 'Eagle' is Shed D.

5 The diversion will be created by 'Falcon'.

6 The vehicles in Shed E must be disabled.

	"Condor"	"Eagle"	"Falcon"	"Hawk"	"Raven"	Create diversion	Destroy radio	Disable vehicles	KO generator	Plant explosives	Shed A	Shed B	Shed C	Shed D	Shed E
23.00															
23.01															
23.03															
23.04															
23.05															
Shed A										
Shed B										
Shed C										
Shed D										
Shed E										
Create diversion					
Destroy radio					
Disable vehicles					
KO generator					
Plant explosives					

Time	Agent	Job	Location

CELEBRITY PETS

This morning, four top showbiz celebrities phoned famous veterinary surgeon and animal psychologist Noah Zarke (a celebrity in his own right) and asked him to treat their pets. From the clues below, can you work out what sort of animal each celebrity owns, what it's called, and what they alleged was wrong with it?

Clues

1 Fido is a rabbit – a house-rabbit, not your ordinary stuck-in-a-hutch-in-the-garden variety but one who's allowed to roam his owner's luxury home at will; and he's never tried to run away, which is why he's called Fido, meaning faithful.

2 The budgie's owner claims that it is obviously suffering from headaches, although the bird hasn't confirmed this verbally.

3 Singer Phil Rubio's pet isn't the one that's supposed to be suffering from depression, which isn't called Tigger.

4 Actress Anna Bell calls her pet Prince; apparently she's always called her pets Prince, regardless of their species, because it saves time.

5 The guinea pig belonging to TV presenter Jay Jaye isn't called Rover.

6 Supermodel Vikki White's pet has a sore foot.

	Budgie	Guineau pig	Rabbit	Tree frog	Fido	Prince	Rover	Tigger	Depression	Headache	Indigestion	Sore foot
Anna Bell												
Jay Jaye												
Phil Rubio												
Vikki White												
Depression												
Headache												
Indigestion												
Sore foot												
Fido												
Prince												
Rover												
Tigger												

Celebrity	Pet	Name	Problem

DINNER LADIES

In the school dining hall five dinner ladies are lined up to serve lunches to the pupils. Details of the first five children to pass along the serving counter are given below. Can you discover the name and year of each, and work out which dinner lady is serving what item to which child and that child's year at school?

Clues

1 Annie is serving the beans, but Kay is on neither the potatoes nor the pie.

2 Neither Shelley, who is in year 8, nor the child in year 9 is having potatoes.

3 Nicky is not in year 10 or 11 and isn't being served pie; he is also not the year 7 pupil being served by Mavis.

4 The year 10 child, who is not Rosie, is having a generous helping of peas.

5 Lee is having fish fingers for lunch.

6 Wendy is serving Matthew.

	Beans	Fish fingers	Peas	Pie	Potatoes	Lee	Matthew	Nicky	Rosie	Shelley	Year 7	Year 8	Year 9	Year 10	Year 11
Annie															
Hazel															
Kay															
Mavis															
Wendy															
Year 7															
Year 8															
Year 9															
Year 10															
Year 11															
Lee															
Matthew															
Nicky															
Rosie															
Shelley															

Dinner lady	Food	Pupil	Year

BATTLESHIPS

This puzzle is based on the old game of battleships. Your task is to find the vessels in the diagram. Some parts of boats or sea squares have already been filled in, and a number next to a row or column refers to the number of occupied squares in that row or column. The boats may be positioned horizontally or vertically, but no two boats or parts of boats are in adjacent squares – horizontally, vertically or diagonally.

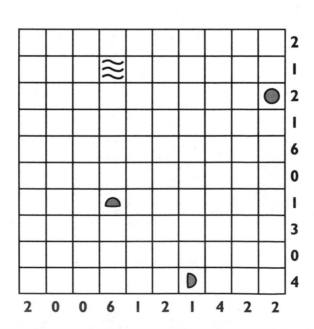

Aircraft Carrier:

Battleships:

Cruisers:

Destroyers:

LOGI-5

Every row across and column down should contain five letters: A, B, C, D and E, appearing once each. Also every shape (shown by the thick lines) must contain each of the letters A, B, C, D and E, appearing once each. Can you fill the grid?

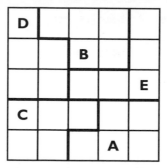

ABC

Every row across and column down is to have each of the letters A, B and C and two empty squares. The letter outside the grid shows the first or second letter in the direction of the arrow. Can you fill the grid?

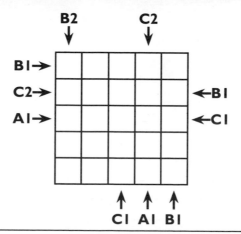

WHAT THE BUTLER SAW

Back in the days when domestic service was a commonplace, five gentlemen's gentlemen, accompanying their employers at a country house party, were chatting below stairs about incidents they had witnessed earlier in their careers involving illicit canoodling by their then employer with various females in different locations. Can you name the two parties who featured in each tale and the location where they were seen?

Clues

1 Lord Portington was often overheard in later years telling his friends "Howe-Green was my valet", unaware that he had been seen in a compromising situation by the latter, in a location inside the house.

2 The governess discovered in the garden summerhouse was not seen by Walcott.

3 Groombridge did not see Sir Jeremy Catkin's amatory encounter.

4 The woman stumbled upon in flagrante in a cupboard on the landing was not a titled Lady.

5 The Hon Augustus Rimmington was caught with Lady Violet, but not by Bickerstaffe, who saw the goings-on in the library.

6 The chambermaid's indiscretions came to the notice of Masters; she was not in the 20-acre arboretum.

7 Viscount Drummond was seen canoodling in the billiard room.

	Viscount Drummond	Sir J Catkin	Lord Portington	Hon F Wythenshawe	Hon A Rimmington	Lady Antonia	Lady Violet	Chambermaid	Governess	Kitchen-maid	Arboretum	Billiard room	Landing cupb'd	Library	Summerhouse
Bickerstaffe															
Groombridge															
Howe-Green															
Masters															
Walcott															
Arboretum															
Billiard room															
Landing cupb'd															
Library															
Summerhouse															
Lady Antonia															
Lady Violet															
Chambermaid															
Governess															
Kitchen-maid															

Manservant	Male offender	Female offender	Location

FRIENDS AT COURT

After a session at the juvenile court last week, five of the offenders, having been found guilty, were assigned to the care of probation officers as part of their sentence. From the clues given below, can you say which offence each of the five, whose names have been changed, committed, and fully identify the probation officer to whom each was referred?

Clues

1 Jonathan was found guilty of taking a vehicle without the owner's consent.

2 Rachel Atkins did not follow up the public disorder offence.

3 Marlon was not the shoplifter, the surname of whose probation officer was Martin; the latter's first name is not Nathan.

4 The man into whose charge Christian was assigned and the man looking after the youth found guilty of assault have first names of equal length.

5 The mugging offence was the crime of which the client of James, who is not Holloway, was convicted.

6 Farouk's probation officer was the one named Lowther; the former had not been charged with a public disorder offence.

	Assault	Mugging	Public disorder	Shoplifting	Taking without consent	Barry	James	Nathan	Pamela	Rachel	Atkins	Berryman	Holloway	Lowther	Martin
Christian															
Craig															
Farouk															
Jonathan															
Marlon															
Atkins															
Berryman															
Holloway															
Lowther															
Martin															
Barry															
James															
Nathan															
Pamela															
Rachel															

Client	Offence	Forename	Surname

CUTE QUADS

Four little boys who are quadruplets had a photo taken on their fourth birthday. Although identical, each was dressed in a different coloured shirt to allow them to be distinguished. From the clues given below, can you name quads 1 to 4 in the photo, say what coloured shirt each was wearing, and say in which order they were actually born?

Clues

1 The third of the quads to be born is pictured immediately to the right of his brother Kevin as you look at the photo.

2 The last of the four boys to put in an appearance is wearing a blue shirt; he is depicted somewhere to the right of Stuart.

3 The boy in red is somewhere to the left of the eldest quad.

4 Andrew, in position 3, arrived in the maternity ward immediately before his sibling wearing the yellow shirt.

Brothers:
Andrew; Kevin; Mervin; Stuart

Shirt colours:
Blue, green, red, yellow

Order born:
First, second, third, fourth

Number	Brother	Shirt	Order born

Starting tip:
Start by working out the position in the photo of the quad born third.

ON CALL

A country vet was called out on successive days of the week to each of the farms numbered 1 to 4 on the map. From the clues given below, can you name the farmer who summoned him to each location, say which particular animal needed his ministrations, and work out on which day of the week he paid each visit?

Clues

1 The vet was summoned by Plowman the day after attending to the sick cow on the farm next west from his.

2 The Wednesday visit was paid to the farm numbered 1 on the map.

3 The chickens were not ailing on farm 2, and farm 3 was visited the day before Field's.

4 The sheepdog, which did not belong to Hayes, was the Monday patient, but not on farm 4.

Farmers:
Hayes; Herd; Field; Plowman

Sick animals:
Chickens; cow; pigs; sheepdog

Days:
Monday; Tuesday; Wednesday; Thursday

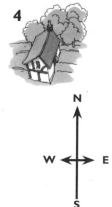

Farm No	Farmer	Sick animal	Day

Starting tip:
Start by working out on which day the vet visited Plowman's farm.

A DRIVING AMBITION

In the years just before the Second World War, five Londoners each achieved a childhood ambition to become drivers of public service vehicles of various kinds. From the clues given below, can you fully identify each man, say which type of transport he drove, and work out the year in which he achieved his ambition?

Clues

1 Perhaps it was his surname which inspired the young Wheeler's ambition to be a London bus-driver; he was not Eric, and he did not start work in the Silver Jubilee year of King George V, 1935.

2 Pascoe had a shorter first name than the tram driver.

3 Wilfred was taken on by the Great Western Railway as a train driver some time after Rogers started work.

4 The underground train driver fulfilled his ambition the year after George.

5 Arthur Niven's realised ambition was not to be a London taxi-driver.

6 Oakman's public service career got under way in 1932.

7 1934 saw the start of Eric's career, but Herbert did not commence his duties in the previous year.

	Niven	Oakman	Pascoe	Rogers	Wheeler	Bus	Taxi	Train	Tram	Underground	1931	1932	1933	1934	1935
Arthur															
Eric															
George															
Herbert															
Wilfred															
1931															
1932															
1933															
1934															
1935															
Bus															
Taxi															
Train															
Tram															
Underground															

Forename	Surname	Transport	Year

CRIME IN THE STREETS

Recently, Newtwick has become notorious for the number of car thefts there; yesterday five vehicles were reported stolen, although all were recovered — or, at least, found — by the end of the day. Can you work out in which street each theft took place, what car was stolen, whose it was and its condition on recovery?

Clues

1 The Ford (not Mr Mason's) was stolen from the car park in Spice Street.

2 Mr Kennedy's Toyota was taken from outside his home.

3 The car taken from Herring Street was found late in the evening, burned out on wasteland behind the old steelworks.

4 The car which crashed on the Great South Road in the early evening is neither the property of Mrs Robins nor the Renault (not stolen in Myrtle Street) which belongs to her friend.

5 Mr Green's car, taken from Barracks Street, isn't the one which was crashed.

6 The BMW was recovered, but only after it had been dismantled for spare parts.

7 Mr Mason's car (which had been repainted) was taken from a street with a name one letter longer than that of the street from which the car found abandoned but undamaged was taken.

	BMW	Ford	Renault	Toyota	Volvo	Mr Green	Mr Kennedy	Mr Mason	Mrs Robins	Ms Wells	Abandoned	Burned out	Crashed	Dismantled	Repainted
Barracks Street															
Herring Street															
Myrtle Street															
Spice Street															
York Street															
Abandoned															
Burned out															
Crashed															
Dismantled															
Repainted															
Mr Green															
Mr Kennedy															
Mr Mason															
Mrs Robins															
Ms Wells															

Street	Car	Owner	Recovered

DAILY DOZEN

Here's a gentle mental exercise. Each of the twelve squares contains a different one of the numbers 1 to 12. From the clues given below, can you place them correctly?

Clues

1 The 12 is in square B2. The numbers immediately to its left and diagonally below it to the left both divide into 12, one being the 3.

2 The 6 is adjacent to the 10 in the same row, and is to be found in the same vertical column as the 8.

3 The numbers in squares A1 and C3, added together, give the one in square C4.

4 The 7 is immediately below the 4, and immediately to the right of the 5.

5 Neither the 2 nor the 1 is in column 1, though the 2 is in a column further left than the column containing the 11.

Numbers:
1; 2; 3; 4; 5; 6; 7; 8; 9; 10; 11; 12

	1	2	3	4
A				
B				
C				

Starting tip: First place the numbers referred to in clue 1.

THE MOLTONS OF MOLTON

Sir Giles Molton, head of the family of Molton House, Suffolk, had five sons, all of whom took orders in the church and were appointed to parishes of which their father held the advowson (right to name the minister); this meant they didn't have to work too hard, and each also gained fame as a writer. Can you say when each man was born, the name of his parish and the kind of writing with which he made his reputation?

Clues

1 The Reverend Anthony Molton, rector of Molton St John, made his name as a writer of fiction.

2 The oldest of Sir Giles' sons, who went on to become rector of Great Molton and eventually to succeed his father in the baronetcy, was not Dominic.

3 The Molton who was rector of Castle Molton, and had been born two years before Greville, wasn't the brother who wrote the famous novels Bertram Ryder and Marcus Clydesdale.

4 The hymn-writing brother was born in 1813.

5 The Reverend Quentin Molton achieved fame for his scriptural commentaries.

6 The rector of Molton St Mary, who only achieved literary fame late in life with the publication of his diary as Journal of A Country Clergyman, wasn't Matthew, who was born in 1809.

	1805	1807	1809	1811	1813	Castle Molton	Great Molton	Little Molton	Molton St John	Molton St Mary	Commentaries	Diary	Ghost stories	Hymns	Novels
Anthony															
Dominic															
Greville															
Matthew															
Quentin															
Commentaries															
Diary															
Ghost stories															
Hymns															
Novels															
Castle Molton															
Great Molton															
Little Molton															
Molton St John															
Molton St Mary															

Name	Date of birth	Parish	Wrote

JUST RAMBLING

After a bracing six-mile hike, five stalwarts of the Stepwell Ladies' Walking Group have stopped to eat their packed lunch at a favourite viewpoint. From the clues given below, can you work out which colour fleece each woman is wearing, say what she is having for lunch, and work out exactly where she is sitting as she eats?

Clues

1 Neither the woman in the green fleece sitting by the gate nor Donna Dale has brought sandwiches for lunch.

2 The woman eating the tuna sandwich is not wearing the blue fleece.

3 Una P Hill is sitting up against the dry-stone wall.

4 The woman with a ham roll and wearing an amber coloured fleece isn't by the large rock.

5 The chicken sandwich is being enjoyed by the woman by the stream (not Flo Wingbrook, whose fleece is not red).

6 Barbie Wyre (dining on hard-boiled eggs), is not sitting by the gate.

7 Hy Styles has a brown fleece.

	Amber	Blue	Brown	Green	Red	Chicken sandwich	Eggs	Ham roll	Soup	Tuna sandwich	By gate	By rock	By stream	By tree	By wall
Barbie Wyre															
Donna Dale															
Flo Wingbrook															
Hy Styles															
Una P Hill															
By gate															
By rock															
By stream															
By tree															
By wall															
Chicken sandwich															
Eggs															
Ham roll															
Soup															
Tuna sandwich															

Rambler	Fleece	Lunch	Location

THE NOMINATIONS ARE ...

We are lucky to be able to reveal advance information about some of the nominees for the forthcoming Netherlipp Film Festival Awards, the Lippies. From the following information, can you discover for which award each person has been nominated, the title of the film concerned, and the month it was released during the year?

Clues

1 Rachel Morris has been nominated for an award for the November film, which has a two-word title, while Miranda Kemp is up for the Best Actress Lippie.

2 A woman has been nominated for the Best Director award for her film The Marked Man.

3 Hugh Talbot has not been nominated for his work in special effects; the film being rewarded for its effects, released in May, is not One Rainy Day.

4 The nominated costume designer worked on a film released four months after the one for which Imogen Penn has been nominated.

5 Desert Ice is not one of the films up for the Lippie for Best Score.

6 Queen of Manhattan was released in July.

	Desert Ice	Funny Business	One Rainy Day	Queen of Manhattan	The Marked Man	Costume design	Director	Leading actress	Score	Special effects	Miranda Kemp	Duncan McKee	Rachel Morris	Imogen Penn	Hugh Talbot
May															
July															
September															
November															
January															
Miranda Kemp															
Duncan McKee															
Rachel Morris															
Imogen Penn															
Hugh Talbot															
Costume design															
Director															
Leading actress															
Score															
Special effects															

Month	Film	Award	Nominee

A DAY AT THE SEASIDE

On a bright summer Saturday, five young couples from the South-East of England drove to the popular seaside resort of Brightbourne for the day – a day which proved to be memorable for all of them, in one way or another. From the clues, can you work out the names of each young couple, where they are from and what was memorable about their day at the seaside?

Clues

1 Lynne Lee and her boyfriend (not Alan Blake) had a good time in Brightbourne.

2 Eve Flynn is from Croydon. Pam Scott and her boyfriend, who aren't from South London, were already engaged when they left for Brightbourne that day.

3 Dan Gibbon and his girlfriend (not Jane Joad) had a terrible row over lunch on the Central Pier and by the end of the day had irrevocably broken up; Dan even had to travel home by train, as they had travelled in her car.

4 John Maple did not fall into the sea with his girlfriend (whose forename and surname begin with different letters).

5 The Maidstone couple were arrested after trying to pay a bill with someone else's credit card.

6 Peter Rowe and the girl he took out live in Guildford.

7 Toby Wells and his girlfriend Gail Hope are not Londoners.

	Eve Flynn	Gail Hope	Jane Joad	Lynne Lee	Pam Scott	Croydon	Guildford	Maidstone	South London	West London	Arrested	Broke up	Fell in sea	Got engaged	Had good time
Alan Blake															
Dan Gibbon															
John Maple															
Peter Rowe															
Toby Wells															
Arrested															
Broke up															
Fell in sea															
Got engaged															
Had good time															
Croydon															
Guildford															
Maidstone															
South London															
West London															

Boyfriend	Girlfriend	Home-town	Event

WORKING TITLES

Movie actress Donna Prima has been offered starring rôles in five films soon to go into production; all pay well, but there are certain other pros and cons that she has to consider. From the clues below, can you work out the working title of each script Donna's been sent, what type of film it is, and what factors there are in favour and against her accepting the rôle?

Clues

1 Deep Water (not a horror film) has a director who's really hot at the moment (his last four films have been nominated for Academy Awards) and there are none of Donna's ex-boyfriends to complicate things.

2 The thriller is based on a bestselling book. Road Hog isn't the film which offers Donna the chance to appear with a really hot co-star.

3 The film with a great script but which, sadly, is a remake isn't the science fiction film, Blue Devil.

4 The producer of the war movie (shot entirely in the studio!) which hasn't the best of scripts, is unfortunately one of Donna's numerous ex-boyfriends.

5 Night Watch involves many nude scenes, and Donna has reached an age when she really prefers to avoid that sort of thing!

	Comedy	Horror	Science fiction	Thriller	War	Based on b'seller	Great locations	Great script	Hot co-star	Hot director	Ex-boyfriend directs	Ex-boyfriend produces	Low budget	Nude scenes	Remake
Blue Devil															
Deep Water															
Night Watch															
Road Hog															
Wild Wings															
Ex- directs															
Ex- produces															
Low budget															
Nude scenes															
Remake															
Based on b'seller															
Great locations															
Great script															
Hot co-star															
Hot director															

Working title	Type of film	For	Against

SAFE HARBOUR

The picture below shows the harbour at Santa Marta Island, in the West Indies, one day in 1805; the Napoleonic Wars are raging in Europe, but Santa Marta is a safe harbour because Napoleon and his allies have few troops or warships in the Caribbean. From the clues below, can you work out the name of each of the ships tied at anchor, what kind of vessel it is, and the name of its captain?

Clues

1 Captain Bower's privateer is next to the Jane Cary.

2 Ship C is commanded by Captain Nathaniel Lee.

3 The Post Office packet boat is anchored next to and east of the Royal Navy brig, whose captain is not named Hatch.

4 The Sceptre is anchored next west of Captain Moor's vessel; the merchantman is anchored next west of the Merlin.

5 Ship D is a Royal Navy frigate, resupplying with gunpowder and provisions after a raid on a French merchant convoy.

6 Captain Fay's Rainbow is anchored two places west of the island trader.

7 Ship B is the Pole Star.

8 Captain Wake's vessel has a one-word name and is next to the Dolphin.

Ships:
Dolphin; Jane Cary; Merlin; Pole Star; Rainbow; Sceptre

Types:
Brig; frigate; island trader; merchantman; packet boat; privateer

Captains:
Bower; Fay; Hatch; Lee; Moor; Wake

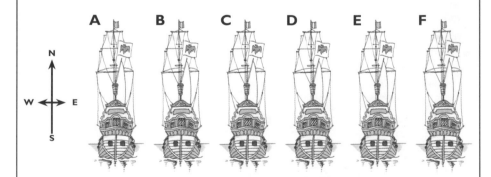

A B C D E F

N
W ← → E
S

Ship						
Type						
Captain						

Starting tip: Decide which type of ship is at A.

NIGHT COURT

'Night Court' is a US legal institution, in which a junior judge presides over cases involving minor charges outside normal working hours. In the city of New Manchester, five detectives have had to go down to the Night Court to give evidence. Can you work out which of the city's police precincts each detective is from, the name of the person he is giving evidence against, and the crime that person is charged with?

Clues

1 The detective from the 4th Precinct is giving evidence in the case of Zeke Weiss, who is not the prisoner charged with vandalising a subway train.

2 Sergeant Noah Penny isn't involved in the drunk-driving case nor is he the detective from the 9th Precinct who arrested the man charged with stealing.

3 Detective Joe Keegan will be testifying against the shoplifter, who he arrested trying to make off with several bottles of cheap wine from a liquor store.

4 Gus Herero is going to give evidence against Benny Capone.

5 Mary O'Brian has been charged with assaulting a police officer.

6 Detective Ross Trani from the 16th Precinct has no involvement in the case against Ed Dillinger, who was arrested by a cop from a higher-numbered precinct than was Vic Torrio.

7 Neither Sergeant Bill Adler nor the cop from the 7th Precinct is giving evidence in the drunk-driving case.

	4th	7th	9th	12th	16th	Benny Capone	Ed Dillinger	Mary O'Brian	Vic Torrio	Zeke Weiss	Assault	Drunk-driving	Shoplifting	Stealing	Vandalism
Bill Adler															
Gus Herero															
Joe Keegan															
Noah Penny															
Ross Trani															
Assault															
Drunk-driving															
Shoplifting															
Stealing															
Vandalism															
Benny Capone															
Ed Dillinger															
Mary O'Brian															
Vic Torrio															
Zeke Weiss															

Detective	Precinct	Prisoner	Charge

KNIGHTLY AILMENTS

King Arthur grew so concerned about the persistent pusillanimity of our friends the knock-kneed knights of the Round Table that he sent them to see his court physician on successive days of the week. Each was diagnosed as suffering from a different complaint, and was prescribed a different form of treatment. From the clues given below, can you work out all the details?

Clues

1 The knight given pills after being diagnosed with pavidus rigidus was seen the day after Sir Spyneless de Feete.

2 Sir Sorely à Frayde was suffering from extreme dracophobia.

3 The potion was prescribed for the court physician's Tuesday patient.

4 Gallinacardia was the verdict on the knight treated the day after the one given lozenges.

5 The liniment was given to Sir Poltroon à Ghaste.

6 Sir Timid was seen on Thursday.

7 A bout of flavostriatus was diagnosed on Wednesday.

	Monday	Tuesday	Wednesday	Thursday	Friday	Alba penna syndrome	Dracophobia	Flavostriatus	Gallinacardia	Pavidus rigidus	Liniment	Lozenges	Ointment	Pills	Potion
Sir Coward de Custarde															
Sir Poltroon à Ghaste															
Sir Sorely à Frayde															
Sir Spyneless de Feete															
Sir Timid de Shayke															
Liniment															
Lozenges															
Ointment															
Pills															
Potion															
Alba penna syndrome															
Dracophobia															
Flavostriatus															
Gallinacardia															
Pavidus rigidus															

This list may help you to identify some diagnoses:
alba = white, draco = dragon, flavus = yellow, gallina = hen, pavidus = terrified

Knight	Day	Diagnosis	Treatment

MOUNTAIN RESCUE

As the winter snows deepen five mountain rescue centres in the Scottish Highlands are kept busy with climbers getting into difficulties. Below are details of five recent rescues; from the information given, can you discover the name of the team leader at each centre, the number of climbers in the party needing assistance, and their location?

Clues

1 Ben Peake isn't the leader of the rescue team from the Glenmoine centre, which was searching for a smaller party than the one lost on Craigmore and being sought by the Achnadubh team.

2 Two climbers were in difficulties in Glen Tarvie, but they weren't being helped by Miles Trudge's or Ben Peake's rescue teams; Miles Trudge's team was also not looking for the party of three or the climbers on Culmor Crags.

3 Alan Slyde was searching for two more people than were stuck at Meall Lodge.

4 The Gordonburn rescue team were going to the assistance of four climbers.

5 Will Findham leads the Kilcarn team.

6 Cliff Ledge and his team went to the assistance of the largest group of climbers.

	Will Findham	Cliff Ledge	Ben Peake	Alan Slyde	Miles Trudge	2 climbers	3 climbers	4 climbers	5 climbers	6 climbers	Crask Forest	Craigmore	Culmor Crags	Glen Tarvie	Meall Lodge
Achnadubh															
Glenmoine															
Gordonburn															
Kilcarn															
Strathness															
Crask Forest															
Craigmore															
Culmor Crags															
Glen Tarvie															
Meall Lodge															
2 climbers															
3 climbers															
4 climbers															
5 climbers															
6 climbers															

Rescue centre	Team leader	No in party	Location

PILE UP

These piles of bricks aren't the random results of a child's play but clues to a final, at present blank, pile on the right. Like the rest, that one has six bricks each with a different one of the six letters.

The numbers below the heaps tell you two things:

(a) The number of adjacent pairs of bricks in that column which also appear adjacent in the final pile.

(b) The number of adjacent pairs of bricks that make a correct pair but the wrong way up.

So:

would score one in the 'Correct' row if the final heap had an A directly above a C and a one in the 'Reversed' row if the final heap had a C on top of an A. From all this, can you create the final pile before it topples?

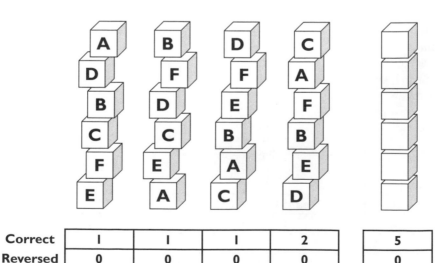

| Correct | 1 | 1 | 1 | 2 | | 5 |
| Reversed | 0 | 0 | 0 | 0 | | 0 |

BATTLESHIPS

This puzzle is based on the old game of battleships. Your task is to find the vessels in the diagram. Some parts of boats or sea squares have already been filled in, and a number next to a row or column refers to the number of occupied squares in that row or column. The boats may be positioned horizontally or vertically, but no two boats or parts of boats are in adjacent squares — horizontally, vertically or diagonally.

Aircraft Carrier:

Battleships:

Cruisers:

Destroyers:

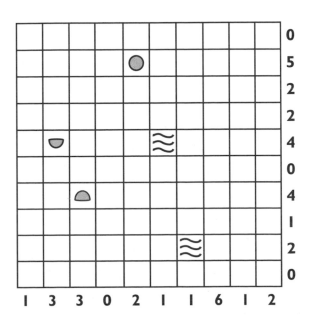

UP, UP AND AWAY

Recently five people were treated to trips in hot-air balloons to mark different milestones in their lives. Although all had expressed a wish to make such a trip, their reactions to it varied greatly. Towards the end of each trip adverse weather conditions blew up, and all landed safely, but in rather unorthodox places. From the clues given below, can you work out all the details?

Clues

1 One man felt airsick during his flight, which terminated amidst herd of cows.

2 The person (not retired) whose balloon ended up in someone's back garden is of the same sex as the one who remained calm and serene throughout the flight.

3 David was just terrified all the time he was aloft.

4 John's trip was not to mark his retirement. Mary's was paid for by her parents as a reward for passing her A-levels.

5 Ronald's flight, during which he did not express excitable enjoyment, ended when his balloon came down in the middle of a busy roundabout.

6 The person who couldn't bear to look down was celebrating a big job promotion.

7 The birthday tripper (not Pauline) got a bit wet when the balloon came down at the edge of a pond.

	Birthday	Job promotion	Passing A-levels	Retirement	Ruby wedding	Airsick	Calm and serene	Couldn't look	Enjoyed excitedly	Terrified	Beach	Garden	Herd of cows	Pond	Roundabout
David															
John															
Mary															
Pauline															
Ronald															
Beach															
Garden															
Herd of cows															
Pond															
Roundabout															
Airsick															
Calm and serene															
Couldn't look															
Enjoyed excitedly															
Terrified															

Name	Reason	Reaction	Landed

GOOD NIGHTS – AND BAD

My wife and I weren't the only people who visited Cornwall this year; Mr and Mrs Cuthbert also spent five days there, staying each night at a different bed-and-breakfast establishment. From the clues given below, can you work out the name of the B&B they used each night, which town or village it was in, and what the Cuthberts thought of it?

Clues

1 The Cuthberts visited the B&B they described as 'poor' the night after they stayed in Looe and the night before they spent the night in the Eagle's Nest.

2 The Seven Pillars in the village of Menmellick provided the Cuthberts' B&B the night after they stayed at the establishment they described as 'great!'.

3 The 'disappointing' B&B visited on Monday night wasn't in Tredew.

4 The B&B in Pendowgan, which the Cuthberts decided was 'acceptable', had a two-word name.

5 On Wednesday, the Cuthberts stayed at Grasmere.

6 Acapulco Lodge was, in the opinion of Mr and Mrs Cuthbert, 'pretty bad' – but what would you expect with a name like that?

	Acapulco Lodge	Eagle's Nest	Grasmere	Seven Pillars	Versailles	Looe	Menmellick	Pendowgan	St Orgo	Tredew	Acceptable	Disappointing	Great!	Poor	Pretty bad
Monday															
Tuesday															
Wednesday															
Thursday															
Friday															
Acceptable															
Disappointing															
Great!															
Poor															
Pretty bad															
Looe															
Menmellick															
Pendowgan															
St Orgo															
Tredew															

Day	B&B	Location	Opinion

MUSICAL BOXES

A mail-order music club once produced a series of boxed CDs featuring music from five different decades, each set being tastefully packaged in a coloured case with either gold or silver lettering, and containing an accompanying booklet. From the clues given below, can you name the set issued in each year, describe the colours of its box, and say of how many pages its booklet consists?

Clues

1 The set named The Sizzling 70s was produced some time before one of the sets in a silver-lettered box, which did not have 26 pages in its booklet.

2 The silver and green box had a booklet with four more pages than the one in the set issued the previous year.

3 The red box with the gold lettering had a 24-page booklet inside it.

4 The very first of the boxed sets in the series had a red-coloured cover.

5 The gold-lettered box containing the 22-page booklet was produced the year before The Fighting 40s.

6 The Thrilling 30s was issued in the year 2000; its booklet had more pages than the one which appeared the following year.

7 The Fabulous 50s (with a 28-page booklet) was produced some time later than The Swinging 60s (not in the box with a silver and red cover, which had a booklet with fewer pages than the one with the 1999 set).

	The Fabulous 50s	The Fighting 40s	The Sizzling 70s	The Swinging 60s	The Thrilling 30s	Gold and blue	Gold and red	Silver and blue	Silver and green	Silver and red	22 pages	24 pages	26 pages	28 pages	30 pages
1998															
1999															
2000															
2001															
2002															
22 pages															
24 pages															
26 pages															
28 pages															
30 pages															
Gold and blue															
Gold and red															
Silver and blue															
Silver and green															
Silver and red															

Year	Set	Colours	Pages

ON THE CLOCK

The four cars lined up outside the second-hand car dealer's showrooms each had different 'guaranteed mileages' on the clock. From the clues given below, can you work out the exact mileage shown on each car's mileometer, and identify its make and colour?

Clues

1 Each of the digits 0 to 9 appears twice in all, while no car's mileage contains a repeated digit, and no two digits appear in the same position on two different clocks.

2 Car 2 has done less than 30,000 miles. None of the four cars has yet reached a total of 50,000.

3 The first number on the clock of car 3 is two lower than the one in the same position on car 1, whose clock also displays an 8.

4 The blue car, which is next to the Fiat in the line, has the largest total on its mileometer, while the red car's second digit on the clock is a 9.

5 The third digit displayed on car 2 is the same as the last digit on car 4.

6 One zero is the third figure on one clock, and the other 0 is in the last position, but not on an adjacent vehicle.

7 The fourth number on the display of car number 1 is a 4.

8 The last three figures on the mileometer of the black Volvo are 735.

9 There is no 7 showing on the Audi's clock, the last digit of which is a 1.

10 The digits 65 appear in that order, consecutively, on one clock. The digits 98 appear in that order, consecutively, and in the same relative position on another clock.

Cars:
Audi; Fiat; Ford; Volvo

Colours:
Black; blue; green; red

Digits:
0; 0; 1; 1; 2; 2; 3; 3; 4; 4; 5; 5; 6; 6; 7; 7; 8; 8; 9; 9

	1	2	3	4

Clock:

Car:

Colour:

Starting tip:

First work out the first digit on each car's mileometer display.

BATTLESHIPS

This puzzle is based on the old game of battleships. Your task is to find the vessels in the diagram. Some parts of boats or sea squares have already been filled in, and a number next to a row or column refers to the number of occupied squares in that row or column. The boats may be positioned horizontally or vertically, but no two boats or parts of boats are in adjacent squares – horizontally, vertically or diagonally.

Aircraft Carrier:

Battleships:

Cruisers:

Destroyers:

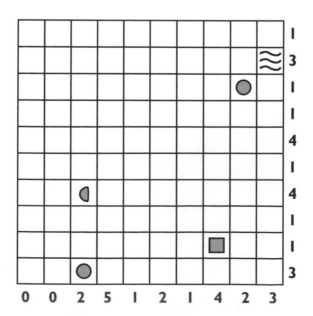

LOGI-5

Every row across and column down should contain five letters: A, B, C, D and E, appearing once each. Also every shape (shown by the thick lines) must contain each of the letters A, B, C, D and E, appearing once each. Can you fill the grid?

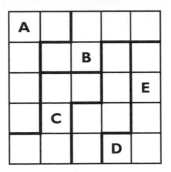

ABC

Every row across and column down is to have each of the letters A, B and C and two empty squares. The letter outside the grid shows the first or second letter in the direction of the arrow. Can you fill the grid?

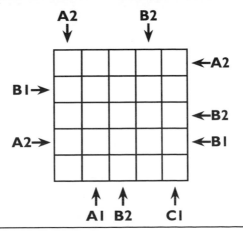

ROMEOS AND JULIETS

Iris Sadleigh-Penham is a writer of romantic fiction with a difference — the hero and heroine are invariably star-crossed lovers whose romance ends in tears. From the clues given below, can you work out the titles of Iris Sadleigh-Penham's five most recent works, and name the hero and heroine who are the unhappy pair featured in each tale?

Clues

1 The heart-rending tale of Raymond and Jeanette was published the year after Amour No More.

2 Julia was the heroine of the novel which immediately preceded A Heavy Heart.

3 The Last Goodbye was the title which first appeared in 1998.

4 Roland was the hero of the next novel after the one featuring Roger.

5 The book published in the year 2000 recounted Rupert's ruined romance, which was not with Jayne.

6 The Loneliest Nights was the novel immediately preceding the one describing Rory's unhappy affair.

7 Josephine was jilted at the altar in the most recent novel by Iris Sadleigh-Penham.

	A Fond Farewell	Heavy Heart	Amour No More	The Last Goodbye	The Loneliest Nights	Raymond	Roger	Roland	Rory	Rupert	Jacqueline	Jayne	Jeanette	Josephine	Julia
1998															
1999															
2000															
2001															
2002															
Jacqueline															
Jayne															
Jeanette															
Josephine															
Julia															
Raymond															
Roger															
Roland															
Rory															
Rupert															

Year	Novel	Hero	Heroine

ON THE LEVEL

Before it was replaced by automatic barriers, the level-crossing at Creekey Gates was in regular use. Below are details of one weekday morning, when the signalman had to shut the gates five times in half an hour. Can you work out at what times the gates were closed across the road, the train that passed on each occasion, the number of minutes the gates remained closed, and the total number of vehicles held up on each occasion?

Clues

1 The gates remained closed for the longest time when the lumbering up goods passed, while the largest number of vehicles were held up when the gates were closed for 5 minutes.

2 The gates were closed for 4 minutes at 10.23, which was later than when eight vehicles waited for the passing of the express passenger train.

3 Both the 10 o'clock closure and the 3-minute closure were for goods trains, and on both occasions fewer vehicles were held up than when the gates were closed for the local passenger train.

4 The next train after the local passenger was a coal train.

5 More vehicles waited while the gates were closed for 2 minutes than when the down goods passed.

6 Only five vehicles had to wait at the level crossing at 10.15.

	Coal	Down goods	Express passenger	Local passenger	Up goods	2 minutes	3 minutes	4 minutes	5 minutes	6 minutes	5 cars	8 cars	11 cars	12 cars	14 cars
10.00															
10.10															
10.15															
10.23															
10.31															
5 cars											
8 cars											
11 cars											
12 cars											
14 cars											
2 minutes						
3 minutes						
4 minutes						
5 minutes						
6 minutes						

Time	Train	Minutes closed	Vehicles

HOLIDAY READING

Janet likes to read romantic novels when she's on holiday, and for this year's trip to the West Indies took along five from her favourite publishing company. From the clues below, can you work out the title and author of each, and say in what business or organisation the lovers are employed and in which city it was set?

Clues

1 Kingwood was set in a major hospital somewhere in Britain; Ruth Pound's book, which is set outside Britain, is not the one about the manageress of a top restaurant and its new owner.

2 One of the books was about the romance between a researcher and a producer in a Manchester TV studio; Emma Donne's novel wasn't the one set in Edinburgh.

3 Gail Frost's book was called Castaway.

4 Lucy Keats had written about the love between an antiques expert and an administrator in a famous auction house, in a book with a title one letter longer than that of Zena Wilde's romance.

5 Sunbeam, the novel set in Los Angeles, was not about members of a car racing team.

6 Glow Worm was not the book set in Sydney, Australia.

	Emma Donne	Gail Frost	Lucy Keats	Ruth Pound	Zena Wilde	Auction house	Car racing team	Hospital	Restaurant	TV studio	Bristol	Edinburgh	Los Angeles	Manchester	Sydney
Castaways															
Glow Worm															
Kingwood															
Sunbeam															
Whirlwind															
Bristol															
Edinburgh															
Los Angeles															
Manchester															
Sydney															
Auction house															
Car racing team															
Hospital															
Restaurant															
TV studio															

Title	Writer	Business	City

PILE UP

These piles of bricks aren't the random results of a child's play but clues to a final, at present blank, pile on the right. Like the rest, that one has six bricks each with a different one of the six letters.

The numbers below the heaps tell you two things:

(a) The number of adjacent pairs of bricks in that column which also appear adjacent in the final pile.

(b) The number of adjacent pairs of bricks that make a correct pair but the wrong way up.

So:

would score one in the 'Correct' row if the final heap had an A directly above a C and a one in the 'Reversed' row if the final heap had a C on top of an A. From all this, can you create the final pile before it topples?

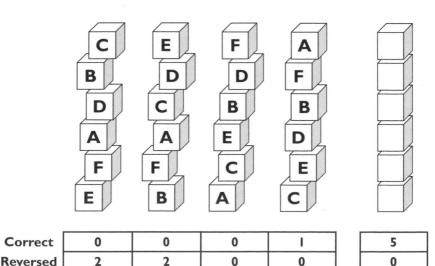

Correct	0	0	0	1		5
Reversed	2	2	0	0		0

LOGI-5

Every row across and column down should contain five letters:
A, B, C, D and E, appearing once each. Also every shape (shown by the
thick lines) must contain each of the letters A, B, C, D and E, appearing
once each. Can you fill the grid?

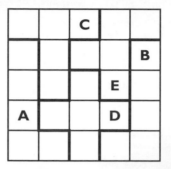

ABC

Every row across and column down is to have each of the letters A, B and
C and two empty squares. The letter outside the grid shows the first or
second letter in the direction of the arrow. Can you fill the grid?

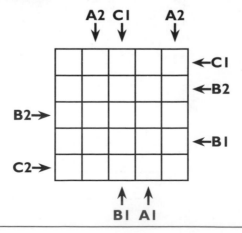

CUCKOO

This year, as every year, a number of readers of the local paper wrote in to claim to have been the first to hear a cuckoo. From the clues given below, can you fully identify and describe each claimant, and work out the date on which the great event took place in each case?

Clues

1 Bird claimed an earlier date than James, the vicar.

2 Millicent heard her first cuckoo some time before the nurse, whose surname is not Clutch.

3 Norah did not claim the 17th April as the crucial date.

	Bird	Clutch	Nest	Librarian	Nurse	Vicar	16th April	17th April	18th April
James									
Millicent									
Norah									
16th April									
17th April									
18th April									
Librarian									
Nurse									
Vicar									

Forename	Surname	Occupation	Date

MEET THE FAMILY

The McAdam family are all returning home to Edinburgh for a reunion, and Mickey McAdam – who still lives in the city – is picking up three of the returnees tomorrow morning. From the clues below, can you work out his relationship to each of the trio, and when and where he's supposed to be meeting them?

Clues

1 Mickey's collecting his nephew from the city bus station.

2 Mickey will be meeting Andy before he picks up his cousin, who isn't coming in by aircraft.

3 Ernie is Mickey's older brother.

4 At 10.00am, Mickey will be meeting one of the other McAdams at the railway station.

	Brother	Cousin	Nephew	Andy	Ernie	Jack	Airport	Bus station	Rail station
Andy									
Ernie									
Jack									
Airport									
Bus station									
Rail station									
9.00am									
10.00am									
11.00am									

Name	Relationship	Time	Location

A MOVING STORY

On the first day of her visit to Russia, British chess prodigy Queenie King, aged 14, played and defeated the adult champions from four different cities. From the clues below, can you work out the full name of her opponent in each game and the city from which he came?

Clues

1 Boris was from the famous city of Gorki, while the other champions came from cities not so well known.

2 Rookov, Queenie's second opponent, was not the man from the city of Yorki, centre of the Russian chocolate industry.

3 Piotr, who was the first Russian to play – and be beaten by – Queenie wasn't Pawnchev.

4 Bishopnik played Queenie immediately after Ivan and immediately before the man from Corki.

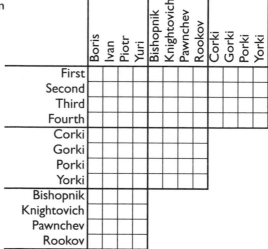

Order	Forename	Surname	Home city

VIP(ICTURES)

Famous portrait photographer Phil Frame has been commissioned by a major publisher to produce pictures of four people who are the writers or subjects of books they will be bringing out in the next few months. From the clues below, can you work out which four appointments in his busy schedule (day and time) Phil has allotted to this work, and the name and occupation of the person to whom each appointment has been allocated?

Clues

1 Amanda Barker will be making her way to Phil's studio in Beaton Street on Tuesday.

2 The single-handed round-the-world sailor whose picture is needed for the cover of Voyage Of The Witch has an appointment with Phil at noon on the day after he photographs Rebecca Say, who won't be visiting his studio at 4.00pm.

3 Martina Nash's appointment is two hours earlier than the one Phil has allocated to the Member of the European Parliament (MEP) for West Eastshire, whose book about Britain's economic future is about to be published – though, of course, the two appointments are not on the same day!

4 Jean Keeler is having her picture taken before midday, but not on Thursday; she isn't the barrister who has edited a new collection of humorous – and scandalous – true stories about lawyers and the law.

Day	Appointment	Name	Occupation

DOING THEIR BITS

Four doctors from surgeries in different parts of Northchester have undertaken various sponsored activities to raise funds for various establishments in less affluent countries. From the clues given, can you work out which surgery each doctor works at, what event he or she is taking part in and what they're raising money for?

Clues

1 Dr Shana Naruda's efforts are raising funds to purchase operating theatre equipment for a community hospital in Southeast Asia.

2 The doctor who is based at the Milton House surgery is neither the one who is undertaking a sponsored six-hundred-mile bicycle ride nor the one whose surname immediately precedes the cyclist's in the alphabetical list and is the longer of the two.

3 The name of the doctor who is raising funds for an orphanage in Eastern Europe appears in the alphabetical list between those of the GP who's doing a sponsored parachute jump and the one from the Saxon Road Medical Centre who is raising funds for a nursing school in East Africa.

4 The doctor who works at The Beeches has a longer surname than the one who is doing a sponsored canoe trip from Northchester to London.

	Milton House	The Piper Centre	Saxon Road	The Beeches	Canoe trip	Cycle ride	Marathon	Parachute jump	Community hospital	Maternity clinic	Nursing school	Orphanage
Dr Adams												
Dr Harwood												
Dr Naruda												
Dr Wood												
Comm hospital												
Maternity clinic												
Nursing school												
Orphanage												
Canoe trip												
Cycle ride												
Marathon												
Parachute jump												

Doctor	Surgery	Event	Good cause

IDOL THOUGHTS

Archaeologists are excavating the ruined city of a lost South American people, and are discovering the identities of their five principal gods. From the following information, can you discover what each deity was god of, the animal form each took, and the main period when each was worshipped?

Clues

1 Pangul was the god of mountains, while Knualei took the form of a lizard.

2 Luaho was worshipped in the spring, but Jagradi was not the winter god; the winter god did not take the form of a dragon.

3 Bahamatotl (not worshipped in the autumn) was not represented by a monkey.

4 The eagle god was worshipped in the summer months, and had a name one letter shorter than that of the god of forests.

5 The river god took the form of a fish and had a name of six or seven letters.

6 The sun god was worshipped on midsummer day.

	Dance	Forests	Mountains	River	Sun	Dragon	Eagle	Fish	Lizard	Monkey	Spring	Summer	Midsummer day	Autumn	Winter
Bahamatotl															
Jagradi															
Knualei															
Luaho															
Pangul															
Spring															
Summer															
Midsummer day															
Autumn															
Winter															
Dragon															
Eagle															
Fish															
Lizard															
Monkey															

God's name	God of	Form taken	Season

GENTLEMEN OF THE ROAD

Near the village of Gibbet Hill lived five brothers who all worked at a normal trade by day, but became highwaymen by night. Each brother had a trusty horse and a favourite area of road near the village where he plied his evil trade. Can you work out all the details?

Clues

1 Neither Handsome Hal nor his brother, the daytime flour-miller, who held up his victims by Devil's Dyke, had a horse with a two-word name.

2 The tailor was not the owner of Black Shadow.

3 Happy Tom lurked at Crow's Corner to prey upon unsuspecting travellers.

4 Hairy Jem carried out his nefarious secondary trade on the back of Midnight.

5 Flyer's owner plied his daytime trade as a blacksmith. Neither he nor the owner of Fleetfoot chose the summit of Gibbet Hill.

6 Hardhearted Jack was an ostler at the Gallows Inn in Gibbet Hill, which allowed him to pick up much useful information about travellers who were potential victims.

7 Grey Mist's rider (not Hateful Dan) had a predilection for Witch Wood as a hunting-ground for ill-gotten gains. Hateful Dan was not the cobbler.

	Blacksmith	Cobbler	Flour miller	Ostler	Tailor	Black Shadow	Fleetfoot	Flyer	Grey Mist	Midnight	Crow's Corner	Dead Oak Dell	Devil's Dyke	Gibbet Hill	Witch Wood
Hateful Dan															
Handsome Hal															
Hardhearted Jack															
Hairy Jem															
Happy Tom															
Crow's Corner															
Dead Oak Dell															
Devil's Dyke															
Gibbet Hill															
Witch Wood															
Black Shadow															
Fleetfoot															
Flyer															
Grey Mist															
Midnight															

Brother	Trade	Horse	Location

A MATTER OF TASTE

At a recent wine-tasting, experts were asked to give a percentage rating to five new wines. From the following information, can you work out the name, type and country of origin of the five wines, and the rating each was given, in particular the one meriting the full 100%?

Clues

1 The Farrell Brothers wine, which wasn't the rosé, received the lowest rating.

2 The sparkling wine was given the 60% rating.

3 The German wine merited a 10% higher rating than the Drake River, which wasn't given 50% or 70%.

4 Chateau de Lisle is a French wine; it wasn't given the 50% rating.

5 Black Knight was the dessert wine, and was given a rating 30% higher than the Californian offering.

6 The white wine was from South Africa.

	Dessert	Red	Rosé	Sparkling	White	Australia	California	France	Germany	South Africa	40%	50%	60%	70%	100%
Black Knight															
Chateau de Lisle															
Clay Hill															
Drake River															
Farrell Brothers															
40%															
50%															
60%															
70%															
100%															
Australia															
California															
France															
Germany															
South Africa															

Name	Type	Origin	Rating

KNIGHTS OF THE THEATRE

In an attempt to impart courage and self-confidence to the five knights of the Round Table, King Arthur's chief psychologist had them join the CADS (Camelot Amateur Dramatic Society), where, in successive productions, they were each given the part of a classical hero to play, but the strategy was doomed to failure, as all failed to measure up in different ways to the challenge. From the clues given below, can you work out all the details?

Clues

1 The knight who played Theseus (who tripped over the dead Minotaur) appeared directly after Sir Timid de Shayke.

2 The knight who completely dried up was earlier than Sir Spyneless de Feete in facing an audience.

3 Sir Coward de Custarde (not the second CADS debutant) was wildly miscast as Apollo.

4 The knight who developed a stammer appeared some time before the one cast as Ajax.

5 The fourth knight to make his stage debut was Sir Sorely à Frayde.

6 The knight who shivered and shook was in the third CADS production.

7 Sir Poltroon à Ghaste's performance came to an undignified conclusion when he fainted.

8 Hercules was played by the first of our Round Table debutants.

	Sir Coward de Custarde	Sir Poltroon à Ghaste	Sir Sorely à Frayde	Sir Spyneless de Feete	Sir Timid de Shayke	Ajax	Apollo	Hector	Hercules	Theseus	Developed stammer	Dried up	Fainted	Shivered	Tripped
First															
Second															
Third															
Fourth															
Fifth															
Dev'd stammer															
Dried up															
Fainted															
Shivered															
Tripped															
Ajax															
Apollo															
Hector															
Hercules															
Theseus															

Order	Knight	Character	Result

ON THE ROPES

The diagram shows four soldiers on an assault course, crossing a stream by means of a rope. From the clues given below, can you fully identify the men numbered 1 to 4 in the direction in which they are heading, and say whereabouts each is from?

Clues

1 Brett, from Dorset, is somewhere behind Squaddey as they cross the stream.

2 Sandy is not leading the line as they make their crossing.

3 Bullett is immediately behind the soldier from Suffolk.

4 Soldier 3 hails from Berkshire.

5 Gunn's home county is Cheshire; he is right behind Pete on the rope.

Forenames:
Brett; Dave; Pete; Sandy

Surnames:
Bullett; Gunn; March; Squaddey

Counties:
Berkshire; Cheshire; Dorset; Suffolk

Forename: _____ _____ _____ _____

Surname: _____ _____ _____ _____

County: _____ _____ _____ _____

Starting tip: Start by working out the home county of soldier 1.

MAKING THEIR MARK

Four young people are pictured awaiting the attentions of a tattooist. Each chose a different design and a different site for his tattoo. From the clues given below, can you name the person on each of chairs 1 to 4 each disguising their nerves by reading the paper, describe the tattoo each requested, and work out its location?

Clues

1 Warren, whose tattoo was on his chest, is pictured immediately to the right of the person who was adorned by a dragon.

2 James is sitting next to the person who had the butterfly tattoo, neither choosing to have a shoulder decorated.

3 The eagle design was tattooed on the customer in chair 1, who was not Andrew.

4 The occupant of chair 3 is Charlie, whose left-hand neighbour did not opt for a tattooed back.

Names:
Andrew; Charlie; James; Warren

Tattoos:
Butterfly; dragon; eagle; heart

Locations:
Back; chest; forearm; shoulder

Name: _____ _____ _____ _____

Tattoo: _____ _____ _____ _____

Location: _____ _____ _____ _____

Starting tip: First place Warren.

CHAMBER OF HORRORS

Master torturer Will Makeham-Tork has a full morning ahead in the torture chamber. Five miscreants are chained in the waiting room booked in for a variety of excruciating ordeals – from the information given below, can you discover the time of each victim's appointment, his crime, and the piece of diabolical equipment that Will has reserved for him?

Clues

1 Edward Brake is booked into the chamber after 10 o'clock; he's not the traitor.

2 Angus Hyghe's appointment is later than the thief's, but he's not the miscreant due on the rack at 9 o'clock.

3 Will Yeald is not the thief.

4 Alleged sorcerer Watt Payne is to be tortured more than seventy minutes later than the mutineer, who's due for the thumbscrews.

5 The blasphemer is not to be lashed.

6 Marcus Brand is to suffer the hot irons.

	Edward Brake	Marcus Brand	Angus Hyghe	Watt Payne	Will Yeald	Blasphemy	Mutiny	Sorcery	Theft	Treason	Hot irons	'Iron maiden'	Lashing	Rack	Thumbscrews
8.00															
9.00															
9.20															
10.30															
10.50															
Hot irons										
'Iron maiden'										
Lashing										
Rack										
Thumbscrews										
Blasphemy						
Mutiny						
Sorcery						
Theft						
Treason						

Time	Victim	Crime	Torture

RED FACES AT THE FETE

Westmead's Summer Fête is organised by the parish council with help from the head of the local school, the local publican and the village's police officer. However, it was embarrassing this year when the winning raffle tickets all proved to have been sold to members of the organising committee! Can you discover each ticket's number, the prize it won and the name and position of the lucky, if red-faced, ticket-holder?

Clues

1 The publican from Westmead's solitary pub, the Man in the Moon, had a lower-numbered winning ticket than the Parish Clerk.

2 The Head Teacher, who won with ticket number 245, is neither Harry Gadway nor the person (not Harry) who won the dozen bottles of Champagne.

3 Carol Brooke, whose family have lived in Westmead for five hundred years, is officially Chair of the parish council.

4 Sam Ratcliffe's winning ticket was number 482.

5 The police constable, who won the luxury food hamper, bought just the one ticket, which was numbered less than two hundred lower than Judy Iverson's, which won her a DVD player.

6 The short-break holiday in Brightbourne went to the holder of ticket 110.

	Champagne	DVD player	Hamper	Holiday	Portable TV	Carol Brooke	Harry Gadway	Judy Iverson	Nigel Moore	Sam Ratcliff	Chair of PC	Head Teacher	Parish Clerk	Police officer	Publican
110															
245															
367															
482															
599															
Chair of PC															
Head Teacher															
Parish Clerk															
Police officer															
Publican															
Carol Brooke															
Harry Gadway															
Judy Iverson															
Nigel Moore															
Sam Ratcliff															

Ticket	Prize	Winner	Rôle

BATTLESHIPS

This puzzle is based on the old game of battleships. Your task is to find the vessels in the diagram. Some parts of boats or sea squares have already been filled in, and a number next to a row or column refers to the number of occupied squares in that row or column. The boats may be positioned horizontally or vertically, but no two boats or parts of boats are in adjacent squares – horizontally, vertically or diagonally.

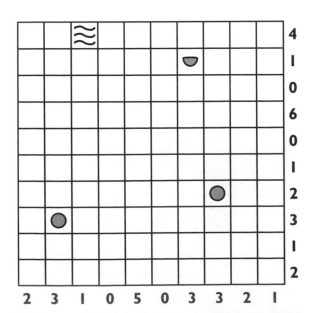

Aircraft Carrier:

Battleships:

Cruisers:

Destroyers:

LOGI-5

Every row across and column down should contain five letters:
A, B, C, D and E, appearing once each. Also every shape (shown by the
thick lines) must contain each of the letters A, B, C, D and E, appearing
once each. Can you fill the grid?

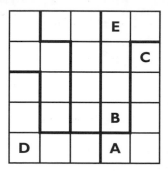

ABC

Every row across and column down is to have each of the letters A, B and
C and two empty squares. The letter outside the grid shows the first or
second letter in the direction of the arrow. Can you fill the grid?

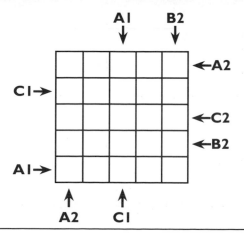

THE MERRY MONTH

Each of the twelve squares contains one of the twelve listed words, each of which may follow the word May in a well-known phrase. From the clues given below, can you place the correct word in each of the squares?

Clues

1 APPLE is immediately to the right of BUG, and immediately above BLOSSOM.

2 FLY is somewhere right of FLOWER in one row, and POLE is somewhere above DAY in one column.

3 LILY is the word in square B4.

4 The words in squares A2 and C2 begin with the same letter of the alphabet.

5 TIME is in the same horizontal row as QUEEN, separated by one other word.

6 Square A4 contains a word with five letters.

7 TREE is in the same horizontal row as FAIR, but further to the left.

Words to be inserted:
APPLE; BLOSSOM; BUG; DAY; FAIR; FLOWER; FLY; LILY; POLE; QUEEN; TIME; TREE

	1	2	3	4
A				
B				
C				

Starting tip:

Begin by naming the word in square A4.

STUDENTS AT WAR

Distinguished military historian, Vincent Fox is preparing a book on five Goatsferry students who, in 1939, broke off their studies to go into various forms of Government service and ended up spending most of the next six years somewhere very different from their tranquil academic community. Can you work out where each student was from, what he or she was studying, and where they spent their wartime years?

Clues

1 The chemistry student from London wasn't Colin Finch, who was studying law.

2 The student from Sheffield, who had a four-letter surname, was in Washington 1940 to 1945, working as secretary to the head of British intelligence there.

3 Ann Dale joined the Special Operations Executive and was based in Paris.

4 The engineering student, who worked on bomb disposal for the Royal Navy in Liverpool from the end of 1939 to mid-1946, wasn't Eric Hay, whose home wasn't in North London.

5 The woman born in Oxford chose to go to Goatsferry to read history.

6 The student (not born in Dover) was sent into Berlin as a 'sleeper' agent of British Intelligence.

7 The art student (not Paul Shaw) had a four-letter surname.

	Dover	North London	Oxford	Sheffield	West London	Art	Chemistry	Engineering	History	Law	Berlin	Bletchley Park	Liverpool	Paris	Washington
Ann Dale															
Colin Finch															
Eric Hay															
Julia Moor															
Paul Shaw															
Berlin															
Bletchley Park															
Liverpool															
Paris															
Washington															
Art															
Chemistry															
Engineering															
History															
Law															

Student	Home-town	Subject	Location

MINE'S A CORNET

Five musicians visited a music shop on different days last week to try out various examples of their particular instrument with a view to replacing their existing one. From the clues given below, can you work out who visited the shop on which day to seek which instrument, and say how long he or she spent in the shop before deciding which model to buy?

Clues

1 The Wednesday customer, who was not looking for a new guitar, spent longer in the music shop than Greg.

2 Karen made the quickest decision, taking less than half an hour to select her new instrument; this was not on Thursday.

3 The Friday visitor spent just 30 minutes making a selection; the longest visit was some time before the double-bass was purchased.

4 The electric guitar was bought the day before Rose visited the shop.

5 It took one customer 45 minutes to pick the right model of acoustic guitar.

6 Steve dropped in to the music store on Tuesday.

7 The cornet was bought the day after Nick's instrument.

	Acoustic guitar	Cornet	Double-bass	Electric guitar	Saxophone	Monday	Tuesday	Wednesday	Thursday	Friday	25 minutes	30 minutes	40 minutes	45 minutes	50 minutes
Greg															
Karen															
Nick															
Rose															
Steve															
25 minutes															
30 minutes															
40 minutes															
45 minutes															
50 minutes															
Monday															
Tuesday															
Wednesday															
Thursday															
Friday															

Name	Instrument	Day	Time taken

FIELD TRIPS

George enjoys visiting the sites of famous battles, and below are details of five that he explored last year. From the information given, can you discover the date of each battle, the name of the victorious commander, and how the battlefield is marked today?

Clues

1 The site of the 1294 battle, which isn't Gorfield, is marked by a chapel.

2 Lord Duncraig's forces won the Battle of Forton in the century after the battle that is marked by a tower.

3 The museum deals with a battle fought the century after Rowtingham, but the century before Prince Cuthbert's victory.

4 The Duke of Radnor's victory was commemorated by the planting of a wood.

5 An obelisk marks the location of the Battle of Pressholme, which was not won by an Earl.

6 The Earl of Ashby saw victory in 1435.

	Forton	Gorfield	Killin	Pressholme	Rowtingham	Duke of Radnor	Earl of Ashby	Earl of Kenilworth	Lord Duncraig	Prince Cuthbert	Chapel	Museum	Obelisk	Tower	Wood
1294															
1372															
1435															
1509															
1640															
Chapel											
Museum											
Obelisk											
Tower											
Wood											
Duke of Radnor						
Earl of Ashby						
Earl of K'worth						
Lord Duncraig						
Prince Cuthbert						

Year	Battle	Victor	Marked by

DEADWINTER DEATHS

One of the characteristics of the popular TV police drama series Deadwinter Deaths is the high body-count in the murders in the villages around Deadwinter being investigated by Chief Inspector Rudge. Below are details of last night's story – from the information given, can you work out the jobs of the five victims, the order in which they were dispatched by the murderer, and the murder weapon used in each case?

Clues

1 The first victim, who wasn't the publican, was shot, followed by Di Carnidge, who wasn't attacked with a cudgel.

2 Celia Fayte wasn't the third victim, while the doctor was fourth.

3 The murderer had already used and disposed of the cudgel before he felt it necessary to dispatch Guy Slade.

4 Hugh Dunnett was stabbed before the farmer met his end.

5 The gardener was poisoned with weedkiller.

6 Donna Waywith was an actress.

	Actress	Doctor	Farmer	Gardener	Publican	First	Second	Third	Fourth	Fifth	Cudgel	Explosives	Gun	Knife	Poison
Di Carnidge															
Hugh Dunnett															
Celia Fayte															
Guy Slade															
Donna Waywith															
Cudgel															
Explosives															
Gun															
Knife															
Poison															
First															
Second															
Third															
Fourth															
Fitfth															

Victim	Job	Order	Weapon

TO MEET THE QUEEN

The diagram shows the producer and cast of six in a West End play lined up to meet the Queen after she had attended a performance of their show. From the clues given below, can you fully identify the producer and the six thespians numbered 1 to 6 in the line-up?

Clues

1 The person named Mathers is somewhere further to the right in the line-up than Watson.

2 Angus is standing immediately between the two people named Brand and Goodman; the latter is not Clifford.

3 Rick is separated from Meade by two others in the line.

4 Simmons is the same distance down the line from the producer as Samantha is from Simmons.

5 Clifford is not standing next to the woman named Arnold.

6 As you look at the waiting line Melinda is immediately to the left of Bradley.

Forenames:
Angus; Bradley; Clifford; Julia; Melinda; Rick; Samantha

Surnames:
Arnold; Brand; Goodman; Mathers; Meade; Simmons; Watson

	Producer	1	2
Forename			
Surname			

	3	4	5	6
Forename				
Surname				

Starting tip:

Begin by working out the positions occupied by Samantha and Simmons.

SOUGHT AND BOLD

Samantha, who is somewhat of a tomboy, has been much in demand, having been engaged for a short period of time in successive years to various active chaps who have eventually rebelled against her headstrong nature. From the clues given below, can you name and describe the man to whom she was betrothed in each of the years in question, and work out his age at the time?

Clues

1 Sam broke up with Bruce the year before she became engaged to the rally driver, who was a year younger at the time than her 1998 fiancé.

2 Gerard, the jockey, was two years older when he bought Sam a ring than was his successor in her affections.

3 The man aged 25 entered into an engagement with Samantha in 2001.

4 The fiancé aged 26 was not the footballer.

5 The test pilot proposed to Sam, and was accepted, in the year 2000.

6 Dennis was 27 when he popped the question, and was accepted by Sam.

7 Garth and Samantha announced their engagement in 1999; he was not the commando.

	Bruce	Darren	Dennis	Garth	Gerard	Commando	Footballer	Jockey	Rally driver	Test pilot	24	25	26	27	28
1998															
1999															
2000															
2001															
2002															
24															
25															
26															
27															
28															
Commando															
Footballer															
Jockey															
Rally driver															
Test pilot															

Year	Name	Description	Age

TRUCKERS ...

Five HGV drivers working for the same company each headed off to a different place the other morning with their loads. From the clues given below, can you fully identify each man, say to which destination he drove, and work out the total length of his journey?

Clues

1 Slingsby, who took his load to Kidborough, had further to travel than Andy.

2 The longest of the five journeys was the one to Treadwell.

3 Lewis Patterson's drive was shorter than the one to Worlington.

4 Stonemarket is not 193 miles from the depot.

5 Fletcher was given the assignment involving the 20-mile journey.

6 Warren's trip was longer than Clyde's.

7 Vinnie's route covered 186 miles.

	Burley	Fletcher	Patterson	Slingsby	Warren	Ashfield	Kidborough	Stonemarket	Treadwell	Worlington	158 miles	186 miles	193 miles	207 miles	220 miles
Andy															
Clyde															
Lewis															
Mel															
Vinnie															
158 miles															
186 miles															
193 miles															
207 miles															
220 miles															
Ashfield															
Kidborough															
Stonemarket															
Treadwell															
Worlington															

Forename	Surname	Destination	Mileage

... TUCK IN

On their way to their various destinations, each of the five drivers featured in the preceding problem stopped off for a meal at a greasy spoon café on the route. From the clues given below, plus the facts established by solving the previous problem, can you say at what time each man stopped, name the establishment at which he ate, and work out which item he chose from the menu on offer?

Clues

1 The man who was on his way to Worlington ate quarter of an hour before the driver who ordered the beef pie, and quarter of an hour after the one who patronised Luigi's.

2 The man whose journey covered 193 miles ate his lunch at Meals-R-Us.

3 It was the driver named Burley who stopped to eat at half-past twelve.

4 Mr Fletcher did not visit Dan's Diner, famous for its mixed grill.

5 Irish stew was the choice of the last of the five drivers to stop for food, who was not on his way to Ashfield.

6 The man travelling to Treadwell stopped to eat quarter of an hour before the one who had fish and chips for lunch.

7 The Cosy Café was not visited by a man travelling over 200 miles.

	12.15	12.30	12.45	1.00	1.15	Cosy Café	Dan's Diner	Eataway	Luigi's	Meals-R-Us	Beef pie	Curry	Fish and chips	Irish stew	Mixed grill
Andy															
Clyde															
Lewis															
Mel															
Vinnie															
Beef pie															
Curry															
Fish and chips															
Irish stew															
Mixed grill															
Cosy Café															
Dan's Diner															
Eataway															
Luigi's															
Meals-R-Us															

Driver	Time	Café	Meal

PILE UP

These piles of bricks aren't the random results of a child's play but clues to a final, at present blank, pile on the right. Like the rest, that one has six bricks each with a different one of the six letters.

The numbers below the heaps tell you two things:

(a) The number of adjacent pairs of bricks in that column which also appear adjacent in the final pile.

(b) The number of adjacent pairs of bricks that make a correct pair but the wrong way up.

So:

would score one in the 'Correct' row if the final heap had an A directly above a C and a one in the 'Reversed' row if the final heap had a C on top of an A. From all this, can you create the final pile before it topples?

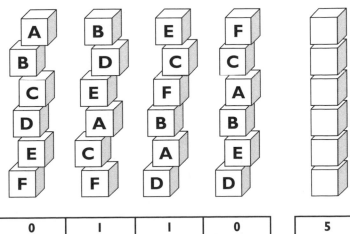

Correct	0	1	1	0		5
Reversed	0	1	2	0		0

BATTLESHIPS

This puzzle is based on the old game of battleships. Your task is to find the vessels in the diagram. Some parts of boats or sea squares have already been filled in, and a number next to a row or column refers to the number of occupied squares in that row or column. The boats may be positioned horizontally or vertically, but no two boats or parts of boats are in adjacent squares – horizontally, vertically or diagonally.

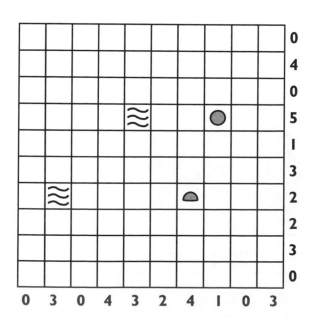

Aircraft Carrier: ◖■■■◗

Battleships: ◖■◗   ◖■◗

Cruisers: ◖◗   ◖◗   ◖◗

Destroyers: ●   ●   ●   ●

										0
										4
										0
				≈			●			5
										1
										3
		≈				◠				2
										2
										3
										0

0	3	0	4	3	2	4	1	0	3

BECAUSE IT'S THERE

Intrepid mountaineer Will E Climate has visited five different areas over the last five years, taking a different climbing companion with him on each occasion. From the clues given below, can you say where Will went climbing in each of the listed years, and fully identify his fellow mountaineer on each expedition?

Clues

1 Armand Piton was Will's companion the year before he made his visit to the Scottish Highlands.

2 The ambitious climb in the Himalayas took place the year after Will chose to climb with Scales.

3 Victor was with Will on his expedition of 2001.

4 Clarence accompanied Will two years either before or after Cleft.

5 The 1999 climb took place in the Alps.

6 Julian went climbing with Will in the Rockies some time before Boulder's climb.

7 Peake accompanied Will on his climb in 2000.

	Alps	Andes	Himalayas	Rockies	Scots Highlands	Armand	Clarence	Julian	Timothy	Victor	Boulder	Cleft	Peake	Piton	Scales
1998															
1999															
2000															
2001															
2002															
Boulder															
Cleft															
Peake															
Piton															
Scales															
Armand															
Clarence															
Julian															
Timothy															
Victor															

Year	Mountains	Forename	Surname

NIGHTMARES

Occasionally, I find myself troubled by bad dreams; I put it down to my imagination, although my wife blames my habit of having cheese for supper. Anyway, last week I had a full-blown nightmare every night, finding myself being pursued through an inhospitable environment by evil creatures led by an even more evil creature. Can you work out where I dreamed I was each night, what was chasing me, and who their leader was?

Clues

1 My nightmare about being pursued by zombies came two nights after my dream pursuers had been led by the Star Wars arch-villain Darth Vader.

2 The Mummy had his evil horde (not orcs) hunting me through a deserted city.

3 The nightmare in which I was running from monsters led by Ann Robinson in full Weakest Link mode came earlier in the week than the one where I was trapped in a cave complex (which wasn't on Thursday).

4 In one nightmare, giant rats pursued me through sewers.

5 It wasn't on Thursday that I found myself the quarry of Count Dracula and his army of vampires.

6 The monsters in Tuesday's nightmare were under the control of Medusa the Gorgon, but not chasing me through a trackless forest.

7 In Wednesday's nightmare I was chased around a Gothic castle.

	Cave	Deserted city	Forest	Gothic castle	Sewers	Giant rats	Giant spiders	Orcs	Vampires	Zombies	Anne Robinson	Count Dracula	Darth Vader	Medusa	The Mummy
Monday															
Tuesday															
Wednesday															
Thursday															
Friday															
Anne Robinson															
Count Dracula															
Darth Vader															
Medusa															
The Mummy															
Giant rats															
Giant spiders															
Orcs															
Vampires															
Zombies															

Day	Location	Monster	Leader

SPOILT FOR CHOICE

Drinkers in Pubsville are spoilt for choice, as the town boasts nine excellent public houses with popular licensees. Can you name each of the inns numbered 1 to 9, and its host or hostess?

Clues

1 The Galloping Major is due west of the Wallingfen Arms, and due north of Marion's establishment.

2 Alan's pub is immediately north-west of the Cheshire Cheese, which has a lower number than Terence's inn.

3 Wilf's hostelry is north-east of the White Horse.

4 Public house number 5 is the Red Lion.

5 Sandra's pub is south-west of the Three Tuns.

6 Lorna is the landlady of pub number 6.

7 Malcolm owns the Cat and Fiddle, which is somewhere to the east of the Green Dragon in the same street (which does not include Graham's pub, which has an even number and is not in alignment either north-south or east-west with Trixie's).

Pubs:
Blue Boar; Cat and Fiddle; Cheshire Cheese; Galloping Major; Green Dragon; Red Lion; Three Tuns; Wallingfen Arms; White Horse

Licensees:
Alan; Graham; Lorna; Malcolm; Marion; Sandra; Terence; Trixie; Wilf

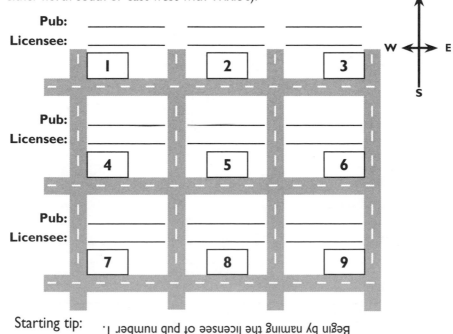

Pub: _____ _____ _____
Licensee: _____ _____ _____

N
W ← → E
S

1   2   3

Pub: _____ _____ _____
Licensee: _____ _____ _____

4   5   6

Pub: _____ _____ _____
Licensee: _____ _____ _____

7   8   9

Starting tip: Begin by naming the licensee of pub number 1.

BRIGHTBOURNE WEEKEND

Brightbourne, the seaside resort, used to have a racy reputation, so when our friends from the Drones Club received invitations from girlfriends to spend a weekend there, they wondered why. However, they needn't have worried because in each case they were merely joining parties at the town's hotels. Can you identify each Drone's girlfriend, the hotel where they spent the weekend, and the girl's father who hosted the party?

Clues

1 Neither Archie Fotheringhay's girlfriend Angela nor the young lady who invited one Drone to the Esplanade Hotel was the daughter of a Lord.

2 Edward Tanqueray spent his weekend at the Marine Hotel, where he found himself attending a convention of existentialist astrologers.

3 The name of the girl (not Melanie) who invited her Drone to the Grand Hotel appears in the list immediately after that of Lord Hartopp's daughter.

4 Sir Guy Graeme hosted the party at the Links Hotel.

5 Daphne was the daughter of Major-General Drew, Gerald Huntington's girlfriend was not the daughter of Lord St Simon. Phyllis did not invite Rupert de Grey.

6 Hannah was at the Normandie.

7 Montague Ffolliott's girlfriend is the daughter of Admiral Humphrey Tagg.

	Angela	Daphne	Hannah	Melanie	Phyllis	Esplanade	Grand	Links	Marine	Normandie	Admiral Tagg	General Drew	Lord Hartopp	Lord St Simon	Sir Guy Graeme
Archie Fotheringhay															
Edward Tanqueray															
Gerald Huntington															
Montague Ffolliott															
Rupert de Grey															
Admiral Tagg															
General Drew															
Lord Hartopp															
Lord St Simon															
Sir Guy Graeme															
Esplanade															
Grand															
Links															
Marine															
Normandie															

Drone	Girlfriend	Hotel	Father

ALL-DAY BREAKFAST

The All-Day Café on the A762 serves one basic meal, its famous All-Day Breakfast: chips, baked beans, fried tomato, fried egg, fried bacon, a (fried) sausage and buttered toast – but customers can request variations. For instance, the five-man crew of a Pickwick Removals pantechnicon came in the other day and ... well, can you work out what drink each man ordered, and what he had taken from and added to his All-Day Breakfast?

Clues

1 Brian doesn't like mushrooms and never drinks black coffee.

2 Nelson, who never thinks a meal is complete without a couple of rounds of toast, had white coffee, but neither a burger nor a poached egg.

3 Jonathan couldn't face the fried tomatoes.

4 The man who drank orange juice asked for his baked beans to be replaced. One man asked for scrambled egg rather than sausage.

5 Ray was neither the man who had the fried egg taken off his breakfast nor the one who had a poached egg added; both egg-swapping men had shorter names than their mate (who had a burger added to his breakfast, but didn't drink black coffee).

6 The tea-drinker (who dunked his toast in it!) had mushrooms added to his breakfast.

	Black coffee	Cola	Orange juice	Tea	White coffee	Beans	Fried egg	Sausage	Toast	Tomato	Black pudding	Burger	Mushrooms	Poached egg	Scrambled egg
Brian															
Gary															
Jonathan															
Nelson															
Ray															
Black pudding															
Burger															
Mushrooms															
Poached egg															
Scrambled egg															
Beans															
Fried egg															
Sausage															
Toast															
Tomato															

Name	Drink	Item omitted	Item added

HANOVER CAPTAINS

On a visit to the USA, when I dropped in to see an old friend in the city of Hanover, New Jersey, who happens to be a cop, I met five newly-appointed precinct captains. Can you work out each one's full name, the number of their precinct and the name of the city district it covers?

Clues

1 Captain Wesley Seaborg's precinct is numbered three lower than that covering the area called Jamestown.

2 Captain Callaghan isn't in charge at the 14th Precinct.

3 The Lancaster district is covered by a precinct numbered three lower than Abraham's, but more than three higher than Captain Negretti's, which is in an area with a one-word name, unlike either Callaghan's or the 14th.

4 Both Rosina and the man in charge of policing the Oak Glen area (neither of whom is De Torres) command lower-numbered precincts than Captain Kreisky (not Martin), whose precinct is numbered six higher than that covering Oak Glen.

5 Captain de Torres' precinct is numbered three lower than the one in South Ridge.

	Callaghan	De Torres	Kreisky	Negretti	Seaborg	2nd	5th	8th	11th	14th	Jamestown	Lancaster	Middlewood	Oak Glen	South Ridge
Abraham															
Colleen															
Martin															
Rosina															
Wesley															
Jamestown															
Lancaster															
Middlewood															
Oak Glen															
South Ridge															
2nd															
5th															
8th															
11th															
14th															

Forename	Surname	Precinct	Area

TEAM DE RONDA

De Ronda Motors, the famous manufacturers of sports cars, entered five vehicles in the recent Circum-Britain Rally, but unfortunately all came to grief at the high-speed stage on Salisbury Plain. From the clues below, can you work out the name of each of the Team De Ronda drivers, his or her co-driver, the model of De Ronda they were driving, and what happened to that car on the Plain?

Clues

1 Jim Salt's co-driver was Esther Lyon; their car wasn't either of the Zarca models.

2 The car driven by Dinah Morris skidded out of control on a tight forest bend and crashed into a tree, while the one which had Stephen Guest as co-driver lost a wheel and overturned.

3 Mary Garth was co-driver of the De Ronda Romola; this wasn't the vehicle driven by William Dane, which wasn't the one which dropped out of the rally with a jammed gearbox.

4 It was the engine of the De Ronda Bardo which blew up.

5 The De Ronda Zarca GT, which didn't crash into anything, had a crew which was at least partly female.

6 Martin Poyser drove the De Ronda Melema; his co-driver wasn't Don Silva.

	Celia Brooke	Don Silva	Esther Lyon	Mary Garth	Stephen Guest	Bardo	Melema	Romola	Zarca GT	Zarca GTi	Blew up engine	Gearbox jammed	Hit tree	Hit wall	Lost wheel
Dinah Morris															
Godfrey Cass															
Jim Salt															
Martin Poyser															
William Dane															
Blew up engine															
Gearbox jammed															
Hit tree															
Hit wall															
Lost wheel															
Bardo															
Melema															
Romola															
Zarca GT															
Zarca GTi															

Driver	Co-driver	Car model	Reason

ONE TO GO

Five friends are playing a game of seven-card rummy, and each is waiting for just one card to go out, having four of one set, two of another, and an unwanted card to discard. From the clues given below, can you work out the hand each player holds?

Clues

1 John's unwanted card is required to allow the hand with four Jacks to declare.

2 The player with a pair of 4s has an unwanted 7 in his hand.

3 Mike has no picture cards or Aces in his hand; his unwanted card is a higher one than Bob's, which bears an even number of pips.

4 Frank needs an 8 to be able to turn his pair into a three and claim victory.

5 The card Kevin is hoping to acquire is not a 4.

6 The full set of four Kings is in Bob's hand, while the hand with all four 5s does not have an unwanted Queen.

7 The hand with all four 3s also holds an unwanted 2.

8 The four 9s and two 6s are not in the same player's hand.

	3s	5s	9s	Jacks	Kings	Aces	4s	6s	8s	Queens	2	4	7	10	Queen
Bob															
Frank															
John															
Kevin															
Mike															
2															
4															
7															
10															
Queen															
Aces															
4s															
6s															
8s															
Queens															

Player	Set	Pair	Unwanted

TWO'S COMPANY

Five Stone Age acquaintances each went into business partnership with a friend. From the clues given below, can you say in which order each began trading, name his partner, and describe the nature of the business they set up?

Clues

1 No one entered into a business partnership with a man whose name rhymed with his own.

2 Jigg pooled his talents with a friend immediately before one pair, who included Clogg, started out as wheelwrights to capitalise on a recent new invention.

3 Agg was one of the fourth pair to set up in partnership.

4 The shoemakers started business next before Igg.

5 The bakers' business was founded next after the one involving Egg, who did not go into partnership with Flagg.

6 The third couple to go into partnership were fishmongers.

7 Ugg and Kegg set up next after the pair who were in the fur trade.

	Agg	Egg	Igg	Ogg	Ugg	Clogg	Flagg	Jigg	Kegg	Lugg	Bakers	Fishmongers	Furriers	Shoemakers	Wheelwrights
First															
Second															
Third															
Fourth															
Fifth															
Bakers															
Fishmongers															
Furriers															
Shoemakers															
Wheelwrights															
Clogg															
Flagg															
Jigg															
Kegg															
Lugg															

Order	Name	Partner	Business

SMALL CRAFT

The East Coast port of Luckstowe is usually associated with big container ships, but on a recent visit there I got talking to some men who operate small craft from the old harbour for a variety of purposes. From the clues below, can you work out the name of each boat, what it's used for and the the name of its 'captain' and his one-man crew?

Clues

1 The Seagull was a fishing boat: not a trawler or drifter, as you'd once have seen off the East Coast, but one that's for hire to parties of sea anglers. Its crewman wasn't the man known just as Jack (no crewman was known by his surname).

2 John Briggs' boat was called the Dolphin.

3 Tom Platt's crewman answered to the name of 'Spud'.

4 Terry was the crewman on the boat that takes parties of sightseers around the harbour.

5 Dave Lewis' boat, which bore a girl's name, wasn't that used to take divers out to shipwrecks.

6 The crewmen of both the Melanie and the crabbing boat were known only by their nicknames.

7 The crewman who worked with Sam Watson operating the foot ferry between Luckstowe and Harestone Quay wasn't 'Ginger', who didn't work on the Prudence.

	Crabbing	Diving	Fishing	Foot ferry	Sightseeing	Dave Lewis	John Briggs	Nick Bady	Sam Watson	Tom Platt	Ginger	Jack	Mike	Spud	Terry
Dolphin															
Hercules															
Melanie															
Prudence															
Seagull															
Ginger											
Jack											
Mike											
Spud											
Terry											
Dave Lewis											
John Briggs											
Nick Bady											
Sam Watson											
Tom Platt											

Boat	Use	Captain	Crewman

PILE UP

These piles of bricks aren't the random results of a child's play but clues to a final, at present blank, pile on the right. Like the rest, that one has six bricks each with a different one of the six letters.

The numbers below the heaps tell you two things:

(a) The number of adjacent pairs of bricks in that column which also appear adjacent in the final pile.

(b) The number of adjacent pairs of bricks that make a correct pair but the wrong way up.

So: would score one in the 'Correct' row if the final heap had an A directly above a C and a one in the 'Reversed' row if the final heap had a C on top of an A. From all this, can you create the final pile before it topples?

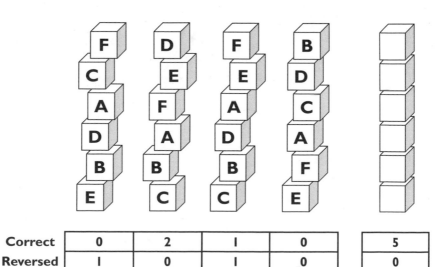

Correct	0	2	1	0	5
Reversed	1	0	1	0	0

LOGI-5

Every row across and column down should contain five letters:
A, B, C, D and E, appearing once each. Also every shape (shown by the
thick lines) must contain each of the letters A, B, C, D and E, appearing
once each. Can you fill the grid?

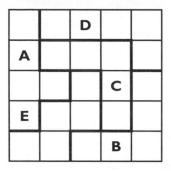

ABC

Every row across and column down is to have each of the letters A, B and
C and two empty squares. The letter outside the grid shows the first or
second letter in the direction of the arrow. Can you fill the grid?

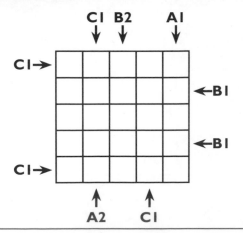

WEEKEND WALKS

Three couples recently spent the entire weekend walking in different areas of the countryside. From the clues given below, can you match the pairs, say where they walked, and work out which type of weather they encountered at the weekend?

Clues

1 Edward and his partner enjoyed sunny weather on their weekend walk.

2 Charles did not go walking on Exmoor, and his companion was not Naomi.

3 Esther had to put up with drizzle on her outing, which was not to the beautiful Peak District.

4 The couple in the Yorkshire Dales found the sky overcast.

	Esther	Joyce	Naomi	Exmoor	Peak District	Yorkshire Dales	Drizzle	Overcast	Sunny
Charles									
Edward									
Stuart									
Drizzle									
Overcast									
Sunny									
Exmoor									
Peak District									
Yorkshire Dales									

Man	Woman	Location	Weather

SURVIVORS

Over a period of 120 years, three sailors were shipwrecked alone on the island of Santa Maria in the Caribbean. From the clues below, can you work out the name of each man, his position in his ship's crew, the name of the ship and the year he was shipwrecked?

Clues

1 It wasn't in 1810 that the bosun of the Sturgeon found himself alone on Santa Maria.

2 The man who was third mate of one vessel was shipwrecked before Ben Cable, who wasn't on the Pole Star.

3 Hugh Keel wasn't the survivor from the Rose.

4 Sam Thole, who wasn't the bosun, was marooned on Santa Maria when his ship sank in a storm in 1750.

	Bosun	Cook	Third mate	Pole Star	Rose	Sturgeon	1690	1750	1810
Ben Cable									
Hugh Keel									
Sam Thole									
1690									
1750									
1810									
Pole Star									
Rose									
Sturgeon									

Name	Position	Ship	Date

IS THAT A FOLK SONG?

The traditional answer to the above question, when applied to something that may or may not be a folk song, is "Well, I never heard a cow sing it". None of the singers in this problem are cows, and all they sing is folk songs. Can you identify each male singer and his female partner, the name they perform under and the type of folk songs they sing?

Clues

1 Although he was born in Munich, Hans Gruber and his partner sing only traditional English folksongs.

2 Nancy O'Hara is the Rose half of Rose and Thorn.

3 One of the men whose surname begins with a vowel sings with Carol Dodds, while the other performs traditional American material with partner Jane Kenny.

4 Peter Owen and his partner – who resemble each other not at all – perform as the Starr Twins; Ben Ashby isn't one of the Merlyns.

5 The male half of the duo who perform folk-type songs of their own composition has a first name one letter longer than that of Sue Rogers' partner.

	Carol Dodds	Jane Kenny	Nancy O'Hara	Sue Rogers	Dirk and Daisy	Merlyns	Rose and Thorn	Starr Twins	American	English	Irish	Own compositions
Ben Ashby												
Hans Gruber												
Peter Owen												
Steven Thorp												
American												
English												
Irish												
Own compositions												
Dirk and Daisy												
Merlyns												
Rose and Thorn												
Starr Twins												

Male singer	Female singer	Duo name	Folk songs

SPORTS WRITERS

Four celebrated sportspersons have each just written a book and found a publisher – not difficult if you're famous enough, even if the book's rubbish. From the clues below, can you work out what sport each of them has become famous for, the title of her book and what type of book it is?

Clues

1 The writer of Lifetime Ambition has a longer first name than the tennis star.

2 The golfer, whose book is a potted history of the sport, has a first name the same length as that of the author of Championship, whose surname is the same length as the racing driver's.

3 Amanda Bourn, whose book is a biting satire on the top names in her particular sport, is not a fencer – the only foil she's used to handling is the stuff they wrap chocolate bars in.

4 Emma Ford's book, which she has entitled Winning And Losing, is not a whodunnit; Emma does not play tennis.

	Fencing	Golf	Motor racing	Tennis	Championship	Lifetime Ambition	Top of the World	Winning and Losing	Autobiography	History	Satire	Whodunnit
Amanda Bourn												
Emma Ford												
Katie Lloyd												
Sally Tate												
Autobiography												
History												
Satire												
Whodunnit												
Championship												
Lifetime Ambition												
Top of the World												
Winning and Losing												

Name	Sport	Title	Genre

HAUNTED HOUSTEAD

Not far from where I live is the town of Houstead, where – according to local legend – four of the oldest dwellings in the town are haunted by the ghosts of people who lived and died in them. From the clues below, can you work out the name of each house, the period of construction of its oldest part and the name and description of its (allegedly) resident ghost?

Clues

1 The building which dates partly from the Early Tudor period, which is said to be visited regularly by the ghost of someone murdered in the reign of King James the First, has a name two letters shorter than that of the domicile said to be haunted by the phantom known as 'Little Tam'.

2 The house which has foundations and cellars dating from Norman times is haunted by 'Old John', who is not the phantom mongrel dog.

3 No part of the house called Ashepound dates from Saxon times; Okehurst isn't the building where 'Grey Susan' manifests herself in the older part of the ground floor.

4 'Wicked Peter' is the ghost of an alchemist who died – when, it's claimed, the Devil came to collect the soul he'd sold in exchange for worldly success – during the period when Oliver Cromwell ruled England as Lord Protector.

5 Helm Grange isn't the house said to be haunted by a former resident who committed suicide in the days of King George the Third.

	Norman	Early Tudor	Late Tudor	Saxon	'Grey Susan'	'Little Tam'	'Old John'	'Wicked Peter'	Alchemist	Dog	Murder victim	Suicide
Ashepound												
Helm Grange												
Martyn's												
Okehurst												
Alchemist													
Dog										
Murder victim										
Suicide										
'Grey Susan'													
'Little Tam'													
'Old John'													
'Wicked Peter'													

House name	Building period	Ghost's name	Description

SECTS AND THE CITY

In the 19th Century, in the melting-pot of the Industrial Revolution, many strange religious and spiritualist sects sprang up in Britain's cities. Below are details of five. From the information given, can you discover in which city each sect was established, the year, and the name of its founder?

Clues

1 The Pakorians first met in Manchester at least seven years after Saul Bunkham founded his sect.

2 Amos Strangefellow founded his sect in 1860, but it wasn't the Sennonists and wasn't based in London. Nor was the group known as the Sennonists based in London.

3 The followers of Evan Waites were known as Waitists; Waitism wasn't founded in 1865.

4 The Grisinians sect was founded in 1875.

5 Ellen Brimstone gathered her followers in Birmingham.

6 One sect was established in Cardiff in 1871.

	Birmingham	Cardiff	Glasgow	London	Manchester	1860	1865	1871	1875	1884	Ellen Brimstone	Saul Bunkham	Amos Strangefellow	Connor Swindell	Evan Waites
Grisinians															
Marsillians																
Pakorians																
Sennonists																
Waitists																
Ellen Brimstone											
Saul Bunkham											
Amos Strangefellow											
Connor Swindell											
Evan Waites											
1860					
1865					
1871					
1875					
1884					

Sect	City	Year founded	Founder

JACKS OF ALL TRADES

Below are details of five tradesmen, all by strange coincidence called Jack. Can you discover which trade each is in, the name of the current client of each, and the address where each is working?

Clues

1 Jack Naylor is neither a builder nor a decorator, while the builder is neither working for Mr and Mrs Plummer in Brick Road nor working in Tyler Street.

2 The Joyners do not live in either Millers Way or Cobblers Drive, and are not employing the decorator.

3 The carpet-layer is working in Cobblers Drive, but not for Mr and Mrs Butcher.

4 Jack Gardner is working in Locksmith Lane, but not for the Joyners.

5 The sweep is clearing the Bakers' chimney.

6 Jack Glaser is an electrician, and Jack Painter is working for the Pipers.

	Builder	Carpet-layer	Decorator	Electrician	Sweep	Baker	Butcher	Joyner	Piper	Plummer	Brick Road	Cobblers Drive	Locksmith Lane	Millers Way	Tyler Street
Jack Carpenter															
Jack Gardner															
Jack Glaser															
Jack Naylor															
Jack Painter															
Brick Road															
Cobblers Drive															
Locksmith Lane															
Millers Way															
Tyler Street															
Baker															
Butcher															
Joyner															
Piper															
Plummer															

Tradesman	Trade	Customer	Address

BATTLESHIPS

This puzzle is based on the old game of battleships. Your task is to find the vessels in the diagram. Some parts of boats or sea squares have already been filled in, and a number next to a row or column refers to the number of occupied squares in that row or column. The boats may be positioned horizontally or vertically, but no two boats or parts of boats are in adjacent squares – horizontally, vertically or diagonally.

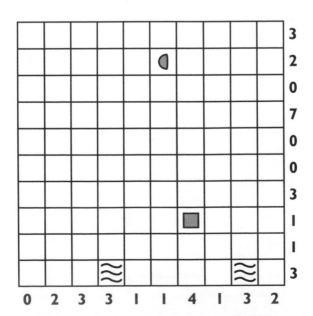

Aircraft Carrier:

Battleships:

Cruisers:

Destroyers:

Columns: 0 2 3 3 1 1 4 1 3 2

Rows: 3 2 0 7 0 0 3 1 1 3

LOGI-5

Every row across and column down should contain five letters:
A, B, C, D and E, appearing once each. Also every shape (shown by the
thick lines) must contain each of the letters A, B, C, D and E, appearing
once each. Can you fill the grid?

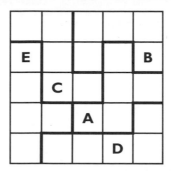

ABC

Every row across and column down is to have each of the letters A, B and
C and two empty squares. The letter outside the grid shows the first or
second letter in the direction of the arrow. Can you fill the grid?

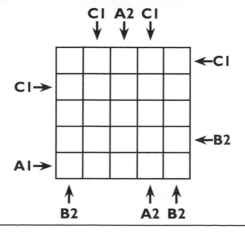

LORD PRESERVE US

The WI's summer fair is fast approaching, and Mrs Marjoribanks, who is in charge of the preserves stall, has been checking up to see which of her regular suppliers has produced what for her stall. From the clues given below, can you work out the full name of five of her contributors featured here, and say what amount of which item each has made this year?

Clues

1 Mildred has produced one pound more of her preserve than Mrs Jamieson, who always makes lemon curd for the summer fair.

2 Mrs Potterton has provided 8 lbs of her normal product.

3 The weightiest contribution to the fair has been made by Jane.

4 7 lbs of plum jam is one WI member's offering for Mrs Marjoribanks' stall.

5 Betty Storton has made more preserve than Mrs Banks.

6 Phyllis' speciality is raspberry jam.

7 Less strawberry jam has been forthcoming than jars of Mrs Fraser's preserve.

	Banks	Fraser	Jamieson	Potterton	Storton	6 lbs	7 lbs	8 lbs	9 lbs	10 lbs	Bramble jelly	Lemon curd	Plum jam	Raspberry jam	Strawberry jam
Betty															
Fenella															
Jane															
Mildred															
Phyllis															
Bramble jelly															
Lemon curd															
Plum jam															
Raspberry jam															
Strawberry jam															
6 lbs															
7 lbs															
8 lbs															
9 lbs															
10 lbs															

Forename	Surname	Amount	Preserve

THE SIXTH PASSENGER

On an evening in 1899, six passengers boarded a carriage of the LSWR express to Holcaster; when it arrived, five were asleep and the other had disappeared, along with a bag of diamonds. The police were sure that the sixth passenger had been Miss Raffles, but none of the descriptions given by them sounded like her. Can you work out the name and occupation of each passenger and his description (appearance and dress) of the sixth?

Clues

1 Norton Oates, who was sure that the sixth passenger was 'a foreign man – possibly Italian or Spanish', was not the jeweller's specially-employed bodyguard, who swore that the missing traveller had been wrapped in a brown cloak.

2 Joseph Kilne described the sixth passenger as wearing a lightish grey duster coat.

3 One of the passengers was sure that his disappearing fellow-traveller had been 'a young woman dressed in a black waterproof'.

4 Ernest Finch, the jeweller whose diamonds had been stolen, was adamant that the passenger had been male.

5 Albert Busby (not the factory owner) did not say the sixth passenger was 'a motherly woman'; it wasn't the factory owner who thought the traveller had been in 'a sort of bluey-grey Inverness'.

6 The Member of Parliament was certain that the sixth passenger was 'a tall man'.

	Bank manager	Bodyguard	Factory owner	Jeweller	MP	Foreign man	Motherly woman	Tall man	Young man	Young woman	Black waterproof	Blue coat	Brown cloak	Grey duster	Inverness
Albert Busby															
Ernest Finch															
Joseph Kilne															
Norton Oates															
Percy Ruskin															
Black waterproof											
Blue coat											
Brown cloak											
Grey duster											
Inverness											
Foreign man						
Motherly woman						
Tall man						
Young man						
Young woman						

Name	Occupation	Description	Dress

THE GREAT ESCAPE

The diagram shows four prisoners of war using an escape tunnel they have excavated in order to leave the infamous Chilpitz Castle, where recidivist escaping officers were incarcerated. From the clues given below, can you work out the nickname and surname of each of tunnellers 1 to 4, and say in which branch of the armed forces he served?

Clues

1 'Biggles' who, of course, is the RAF member, is somewhere behind Mr Marshall in the tunnel.

2 'Kipper', named for his ability to sleep in the most uncomfortable situations, is currently wide awake as he crawls down the tunnel immediately ahead of the navy man, Mr Valliant.

3 Mr Goodhart is number 2.

4 'Puffer', who usually smokes a foul pipe, is crawling immediately behind Mr Bottle.

5 'Jingo' is further along the tunnel than the artillery officer.

Nicknames:
'Biggles'; 'Jingo';
'Kipper'; 'Puffer'

Surnames:
Bottle; Goodhart;
Marshall; Valliant

Services:
Artillery; RAF;
Royal Marines;
Royal Navy

Number	Nickname	Surname	Service

Starting tip: First work out the surname of escaper number 4.

IN ORBIT

The planet Ragnarok is earthlike, but has no inhabitants, so the Interplanetary Commission has permitted a Terra/Lamorak Consortium to exploit it. They have four satellites in orbit, each crewed by an administrator and a technician; two satellites have a Terran administrator and a Lamorakian technician, and the other two have a Lamorakian administrator and a Terran technician. Can you discover the facts?

Clues

1 Administrator B'Kap and Administrator Smith are not assigned to consecutively-numbered satellites.

2 Technician Maz'k is assigned to satellite 4, which is not the Custodian.

3 Satellite 2, the Sentinel, has a Terran administrator.

4 Administrator D'Poj is assigned to the satellite Watchman; this is not satellite 1, which is not the one to which Technician Thomas has been assigned.

Satellites:
Custodian;
Guardian; Sentinel;
Watchman

Administrators:
B'Kap (Lamorakian);
D'Poj (Lamorakian);
Jones (Terran);
Smith (Terran)

Technicians:
Brown (Terran);
Lo'Bu (Lamorakian);
Maz'k (Lamorakian);
Thomas (Terran)

1

4   2

3

Number	Satellite	Administrator	Technician

Starting tip: Work out the name of the technician on satellite 2.

LOGI-PATH

Use your deductive reasoning to form a pathway from the box marked 'START' to the box marked 'FINISH', moving either horizontally or vertically (but not diagonally) from square to adjacent square. The number at the beginning of every row or column indicates exactly how many boxes in that row or column your pathway must pass through. The small diagram at the bottom of the page is given as an example of how it works.

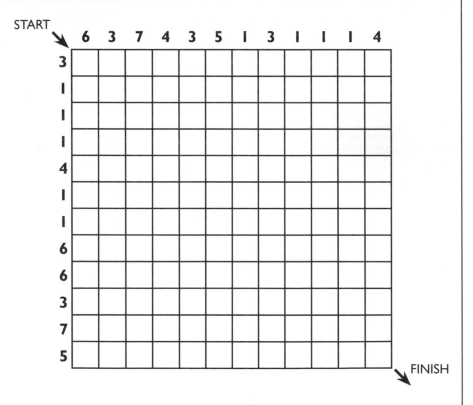

START

6 3 7 4 3 5 1 3 1 1 1 4

3
1
1
1
4
1
1
6
6
3
7
5

FINISH

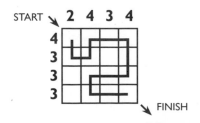

START 2 4 3 4

4
3
3
3

FINISH

DOMINO SEARCH

A standard set of dominoes has been laid out, using numbers instead of dots for clarity. With the aid of a sharp pencil and a keen brain, can you draw in the lines to show where each domino has been placed? You may find the check grid useful – crossing off each domino as you find it.

2	4	1	3	1	6	5	4
5	0	6	3	0	5	5	3
6	6	3	4	4	0	2	5
0	1	0	4	4	1	2	6
2	5	3	1	2	6	6	5
4	1	1	4	3	2	3	3
2	5	0	6	2	0	0	1

0							
1							
2							
3							
4							
5							
6							
	0	1	2	3	4	5	6

STOR DETECTIVES

The Stor Valley Metal Detecting Club (the Stor Detectives!) had a meeting in Storbury last night, at which some of the members showed off the most unusual finds they had made (always, of course, on land they had permission to search – the Stor Detectives would never go on to anyone's property without their permission). Can you work out who found what, and the name of the actual location and village where it was found?

Clues

1 Turkey Bridge spans the Stor in the village of Boxstone.

2 The whaling harpoon, one of the hand-thrown variety used in the early 19th Century, which wasn't discovered by Mick O'Leary, was found thirty miles inland, at Chapel Farm, which is not in Lavenstead.

3 No-one has ever explained how an Inca helmet found its way from Peru to the Suffolk village of Waldleigh where it was found, though not at Hazel Farm.

4 While searching farmland, Bob Dean discovered the World War II Russian medal; the Japanese samurai sword was not the item discovered in the grounds of one village's Rectory.

5 Jack Lowe made his find on Bluegate Farm, which belongs to his Uncle Walter.

6 Eddie Green's discovery was made in his home village of Glemsfield, but not on a farm.

	Arab dagger	Inca helmet	Japanese sword	Russian medal	Whaling harpoon	Bluegate Farm	Chapel Farm	Hazel Farm	The Rectory	Turkey Bridge	Boxstone	Glemsfield	Lavenstead	Mellingford	Waldleigh
Bob Dean															
Eddie Green															
Jack Lowe															
Mick O'Leary															
Paul Ray															
Boxstone															
Glemsfield															
Lavenstead															
Mellingford															
Waldleigh															
Bluegate Farm															
Chapel Farm															
Hazel Farm															
The Rectory															
Turkey Bridge															

Name	Find	Location	Village

DISHONOURABLE MEMBERS

Sadly, more stories of political sleaze have hit the headlines recently, involving backbenchers from five different parties. Luckily these have all been fabricated for the benefit of this puzzle. From the information given below, can you work out which MP belongs to which party, the name of his constituency, and the nature of his misdemeanour?

Clues

1 Phil Pocket is a LibDem MP, but he's not been accused of not declaring some of his earnings, while the Conservative's affair has been exposed; neither the Conservative nor the Labour MP is the member for Tainton.

2 The MP with the underworld connections, Ben de Rooles, the MP for Giltley and the Labour politician are four different people; Will Fiddle is also not the member for Giltley.

3 Lou Smorrells is not a Labour MP, but is member for a constituency beginning with the letter C.

4 The member for Chiselham is accused of accepting cash for questions.

5 The Scottish National Party MP is member for Crooklow.

6 Sir Ivor Vyce is MP for Blotton.

	Conservative	Independent	Labour	LibDem	Scottish National	Blotton	Chiselham	Crooklow	Giltley	Tainton	Affair	Cash for questions	Insider dealing	Undeclared earnings	Underworld connections
Will Fiddle															
Phil Pocket															
Ben de Rooles															
Lou Smorrells															
Sir Ivor Vyce															
Affair															
Cash for questions															
Insider dealing															
Undeclared earnings															
U'world connections															
Blotton															
Chiselham															
Crooklow															
Giltley															
Tainton															

Name	Party	Constituency	Misdemeanour

PASSING THE TEST

Spectators were entering the ground for the first day of a cricket test match through the turnstiles lettered A and B in the diagram. From the clues given below, can you work out the names of the first six people in the line at each turnstile at the moment our snapshot was taken?

Clues

1 Edward was two places behind Salim in one of the lines, both being in odd-numbered positions.

2 The man at the head of the queue for turnstile A has a six-letter name.

3 Ravi is somewhere in line behind Denzil; they are not in the same queue as Farouk, who is not in the same relative position as either of them.

4 Chester is the third in line at turnstile B.

5 Johnny is two places behind Owen in one of the lines.

6 Number 4 at turnstile A has a longer name than his opposite number at turnstile B.

7 One of the number 5s is Faisal; he is in the same queue as, but not adjacent to, Keith, whose opposite number is Michael.

Names:
Chester; Denzil; Edward; Faisal; Farouk; Gareth; Johnny; Keith; Michael; Owen; Ravi; Salim

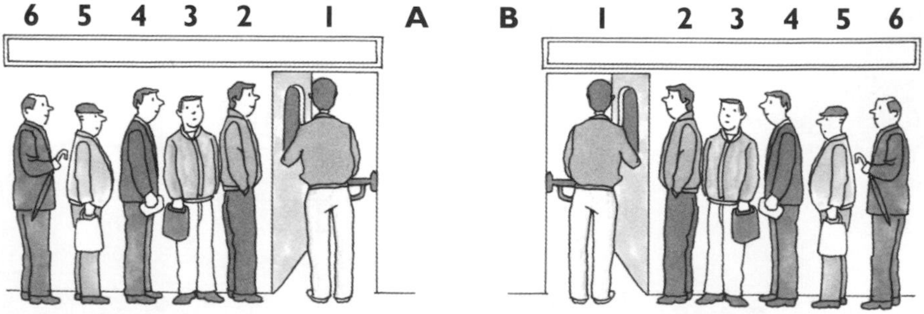

6	5	4	3	2	I	A	B	I	2	3	4	5	6

Gate A	6	5	4	3	2	I
Name						

Gate B	6	5	4	3	2	I
Name						

Starting tip:

First place Edward and Salim.

END OF THE YEAR

Towards the end of the academic year five Goatsferry University students each met with their personal tutors on the same day to discuss their progress. From the clues given below, can you match each student with his or her tutor, say at what time they met, and work out how each tutor summarised his or her charge's progress?

Clues

1 The 'favourable' assessment was made later in the day than Amanda's interview with Dr Nurse.

2 The 'adequate' comment was made some time after the one concerning Tara.

3 Damien's end of term interview was arranged for 3pm.

4 Mrs Cram was not charged with monitoring James' progress.

5 The last of the five meetings produced a 'competent' assessment.

6 Prof Groom arranged to see the student he was tutoring at 11am.

7 Mr Moldham described his student's efforts as 'promising'.

8 Caroline was highly delighted to hear her year's work summarised as 'excellent'.

	Mrs Cram	Miss Foster	Prof Groom	Mr Moldham	Dr Nurse	10.00am	11.00am	2.00pm	3.00pm	4.00pm	'Adequate'	'Competent'	'Excellent'	'Favourable'	'Promising'
Amanda															
Caroline															
Damien															
James															
Tara															
'Adequate'										
'Competent'										
'Excellent'										
'Favourable'										
'Promising'										
10.00am					
11.00am					
2.00pm					
3.00pm					
4.00pm					

Student	Tutor	Time	Comment

LAMBS TO THE SLAUTA

When Dave and Carol Lamb took their three kids to the island of Slauta, they spent their mornings on the beach belonging to their hotel and their afternoons getting into trouble with Slauta's somewhat draconian police (though all the charges were dismissed at once by the magistrate, who was head of the tourist authority). Where did they go each afternoon, which of the family was arrested there and with what were they charged?

Clues

1 Gemma was arrested at the vineyard, but not on Monday or Tuesday.

2 During the visit to the temple ruins, one of the Lamb family was charged with spying after taking a photograph just as one of the Carnajian Air Force's 'top secret' MiG-21 fighters flew overhead.

3 On Thursday, when they visited a local fishing port, the Lamb arrested was not Dave, and the charge was not theft.

4 On Tuesday one of the Lambs was charged with being indecently dressed. The Roman villa trip wasn't on Monday or Tuesday.

5 Jake Lamb was arrested for picking a flower, but not on Wednesday or Thursday.

6 Andrew was not arrested during the family's visit to the weekly market, nor was he the one charged with 'insulting the flag of the republic of Carnajia'.

	Fishing port	Temple ruins	Villa ruins	Village market	Vineyard	Andrew	Carol	Dave	Gemma	Jake	Indecently dressed	Insulting the flag	Picking a flower	Spying	Theft
Monday															
Tuesday															
Wednesday															
Thursday															
Friday															
Indecently dressed															
Insulting flag															
Picking flower															
Spying															
Theft															
Andrew															
Carol															
Dave															
Gemma															
Jake															

Day	Place	Family member	Charge

OFF COURSE ON COURSE

When our five old friends the Drones about town decided to play golf one afternoon, each had his round interrupted at a different hole by an untoward occurrence, and each ended up with rather a large total of strokes taken at the end of the round. From the clues given below, can you work out all the details?

Clues

1 One Drone spent a long time trying to dig his way out of a bunker at the unlucky thirteenth; his final total for the round was an odd number of strokes.

2 The monocle was mislaid as its owner searched for his ball in the deep rough further along the course than the location of the incident involving Edward Tanqueray, who completed his round with a score of 108.

3 The 'best' score of 96 was achieved by whoever had to take a penalty when he lost his original ball in a hollow tree.

4 Archie Fotheringhay suffered the next mishap after his friend's ball was taken by a squirrel.

5 The Drone who scored 101 had a bad experience at the eighth.

6 Montague Ffolliott (who tore a hole in the seat of his plus-fours whilst in the rough) took fewer strokes overall than Rupert de Grey.

7 The tenth was the hole where Gerald Huntington got into difficulties.

	Tore plus-fours	Squirrel	Lost monocle	Hollow tree	Bunker	Third	Eighth	Tenth	Thirteenth	Seventeenth	96	99	101	108	115
Archie Fotheringhay															
Edward Tanqueray															
Gerald Huntington															
Montague Ffolliott															
Rupert de Grey															
96															
99															
101															
108															
115															
Third															
Eighth															
Tenth															
Thirteenth															
Seventeenth															

Drone	Mishap	Hole	Strokes taken

KNIGHTS ON THE CARDS

As an advertising venture, the Camelot Mead Co issued a series of cards, one given with each purchase of a bottle; showing an artist's portrait on the front and a picture of Round Table knights on the back. Our five craven acquaintances appeared in the series. Can you work out the series number of the card bearing each knight's portrait and what (according to the picture) was the pet hate and favourite food item of each?

Clues

1 Custard was the favourite food quoted by Sir Coward de Custarde, whose card had a higher number in the series than that showing the knight who hated jousting.

2 Jelly was mentioned on a lower-numbered card than the one depicting Sir Timid de Shayke.

3 Card 48 was the one devoted to Sir Spyneless de Feete, whose pet hate was not ugly ogres.

4 Trifle and polishing armour did not feature on the same card.

5 It was Sir Poltroon à Ghaste who stated that his pet hate was mice.

6 The pet hate quoted on card number 40 in the series was dragons.

7 The pen portrait on card 50 gave junket as its subject's favourite food.

	Sir Coward de Custarde	Sir Poltroon à Ghaste	Sir Sorely à Frayde	Sir Spyneless de Feete	Sir Timid de Shayke	Dragons	Jousting	Mice	Polishing armour	Ugly ogres	Blancmange	Custard	Jelly	Junket	Trifle
Card 40															
Card 42															
Card 45															
Card 48															
Card 50															
Blancmange															
Custard															
Jelly															
Junket															
Trifle															
Dragons															
Jousting															
Mice															
Polishing armour															
Ugly ogres															

Card No	Knight	Pet hate	Favourite food

IN THE ROUND

Each of the circles numbered 1 to 8 forming the two rings lettered A and B contains a different digit between 1 and 8. From the clues given below, can you place all eight digits in their correct position in each of the two rings?

Clues

1 No digit appears in a circle indicated by the same number as itself, and no digit appears in the same numbered space in both rings.

2 Circle 5 of ring B contains a 2.

3 The number in circle 1 of ring A has a value twice that of the number in the corresponding circle of ring B.

4 The 4 in ring B is in a higher-numbered circle than the one in ring A, which is diametrically opposite to the 8.

5 An 8 is to be inserted in the circle next clockwise from the 3 in ring B.

6 The 3 in ring A is two positions anticlockwise from the 6, and two places clockwise from the 1.

7 The same digit appears in circle 7 of ring B as in circle 5 of ring A.

8 The 7 in ring B is in a circle numbered one lower than the 7 in ring A.

9 The 5 in ring A is in a lower-numbered circle than the 2, but the reverse is the case in ring B, where they are not in adjacent circles.

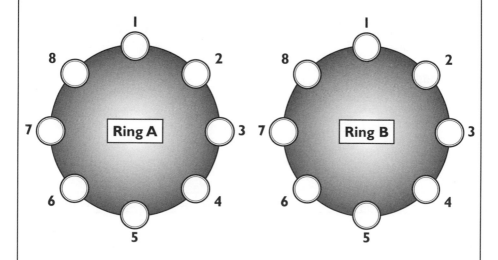

Starting tip: First work out the number in circle 1 of ring B.

GHOST STORIES

Soon after they bought the Old Vicarage at Borleigh, Dick and Jane Keane discovered it was haunted; each night a phantom woman walked through their bedroom wall, wailing mournfully. When they asked some of the neighbours to help identify the ghost they found that everyone had a different story. Can you work out the five names and descriptions ascribed to the ghost, and the details of the people to whom they spoke?

Clues

1 Mr Price's version of the ghost story identified the phantom as a bride who died on her wedding day.

2 Miss Duke is the Borleigh postmistress.

3 According to Mr Wayne (who is neither the librarian nor the publican) the ghost is named Lily but is not the woman who was cursed as a bride.

4 The librarian told of a governess (not known as Harriet) who committed suicide after being seduced and abandoned.

5 The member of the parish council named the ghost as Valerie. The local historian didn't say that the ghost was that of a pining housekeeper.

6 One man told them that the ghost was of Abigail, a maid murdered by her married lover.

	Cursed bride	Jilted bride	Murdered maid	Pining Housekeeper	Seduced governess	Miss Duke	Mr Jarvis	Mr Price	Mrs Selby	Mr Wayne	Librarian	Local historian	Parish councillor	Postmistress	Publican
Abigail															
Harriet															
Lily															
Phyllis															
Valerie															
Librarian															
Local historian															
Parish councillor															
Postmistress															
Publican															
Miss Duke															
Mr Jarvis															
Mr Price															
Mrs Selby															
Mr Wayne															

Ghost	Description	Informant	Position

SPUN OFF

Albion-TV's popular sitcom Red Gables, about five students at Goatsferry University who share a house on the outskirts of the town, has come to the end of its run, but the producers have decided to 'spin off' each of the main characters into a series of his or her own. From the clues below, can you work out the name of each character, what they've been studying at Goatsferry, the title of their spin-off series and its basic premise?

Clues

1 In City Lights, one former student will move to London and have to find a home, a job and new friends.

2 The new comedy series about the George Todd character will have him accidentally killed in the first episode, then follow his comic adventures as a ghost.

3 The male theology student will move on to a series (not Number 7) in which he gets a job in the Religious Affairs Department of a TV company and is shocked by the attitudes of his fellow workers.

4 Room 102 will feature the former engineering student.

5 Pinkies is the spin-off series for the Brenda Owen character.

6 In Red Gables, Kenny Young studied archaeology.

7 The series in which one former student inherits a title includes a number in its title.

8 The ex-drama student (not George Todd) isn't the one who marries an ambitious politician and won't feature in Number 7.

	Archaeology	Drama	Engineering	Medicine	Theology	City Lights	Hard Times	Number 7	Pinkies	Room 102	Becomes ghost	Gets job in TV	Inherits title	Marries politician	Moves to London
Brenda Owen															
Esther Reid															
George Todd															
Ian Vickers															
Kenny Young															
Becomes ghost															
Gets job in TV															
Inherits title															
Marries politician															
Moves to London															
City Lights															
Hard Times															
Number 7															
Pinkies															
Room 102															

Character	Subject	Series title	Series idea

ASK AN ACQUAINTANCE

The popular TV game show Who Wants to Win a Wad? offers the contestants the opportunity to seek help from the studio audience or by 'Asking an Acquaintance'. Five recent contestants did the latter; from the following information can you discover who phoned whom, the contestant's relationship to the acquaintance, and the answer that the latter suggested was the correct one?

Clues

1 Graham spoke with Charlie on the phone, who is not a college friend.

2 Charlie wasn't the acquaintance who suggested to his neighbour that 'Liverpool' was the correct answer, nor was that Gary.

3 Dave didn't seek help from Terry, and wasn't recommended the answer 'Pink'; 'Pink' was also not the answer suggested by the cousin.

4 Sharon is the sister of one of the contestants.

5 Annie thought the correct answer was 'Atlas'.

6 Linda went with her acquaintance's suggestion and plumped for 'Elizabeth I', while Scott sought help from a workmate.

	Annie	Charlie	Gary	Sharon	Terry	College friend	Cousin	Neighbour	Sister	Workmate	'Atlas'	'Elizabeth I'	'Liverpool'	'Pink'	'Rhododendron'
Dave															
Graham															
Kirsty															
Linda															
Scott															
'Atlas'															
'Elizabeth I'															
'Liverpool'															
'Pink'															
'Rhododendron'															
College friend															
Cousin															
Neighbour															
Sister															
Workmate															

Contestant	Acquaintance	Relationship	Answer

PILE UP

These piles of bricks aren't the random results of a child's play but clues to a final, at present blank, pile on the right. Like the rest, that one has six bricks each with a different one of the six letters.

The numbers below the heaps tell you two things:

(a) The number of adjacent pairs of bricks in that column which also appear adjacent in the final pile.

(b) The number of adjacent pairs of bricks that make a correct pair but the wrong way up.

So:

would score one in the 'Correct' row if the final heap had an A directly above a C and a one in the 'Reversed' row if the final heap had a C on top of an A. From all this, can you create the final pile before it topples?

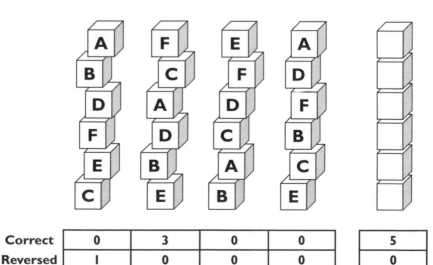

Correct	0	3	0	0		5
Reversed	1	0	0	0		0

BATTLESHIPS

This puzzle is based on the old game of battleships. Your task is to find the vessels in the diagram. Some parts of boats or sea squares have already been filled in, and a number next to a row or column refers to the number of occupied squares in that row or column. The boats may be positioned horizontally or vertically, but no two boats or parts of boats are in adjacent squares – horizontally, vertically or diagonally.

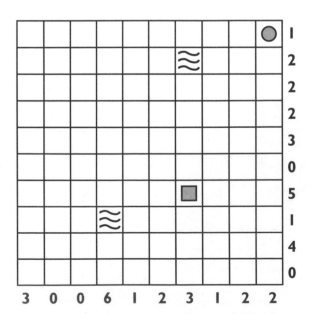

Aircraft Carrier: ◖■■■◗

Battleships: ◖■◗   ◖■■◗

Cruisers: ◖◗   ◖◗   ◖◗

Destroyers: ●   ●   ●   ●

Grid row numbers (top to bottom): 1, 2, 2, 2, 3, 0, 5, 1, 4, 0

Grid column numbers (left to right): 3, 0, 0, 6, 1, 2, 3, 1, 2, 2

A CARD FROM SANDRA

Sandra is on holiday at Bracing Bay, and has sent a postcard to each of her five work colleagues back at the office. From the clues given below, can you fully identify each recipient, describe the card he or she received, and work out the message inscribed on each?

Clues

1 It was one of Sandra's female friends who was told she was 'Getting quite brown', but not on the card featuring the floral clock on the promenade, while the picture of the abbey ruins went to one of the men.

2 The 'Weather good' message was on the back of the Bracing Bay lighthouse card.

3 Parker, who is of the same sex as the person surnamed Green, received the card with a view of Bracing Bay pier; Parker has a first name longer than that of Jones.

4 Adam was not told that Sandra was 'Having a great time'.

5 The 'Wish you were here' message went to Mr/Ms Evans.

6 Mary's card had a picture of the smugglers' cave.

7 Julie, whose surname is not Green, was told 'Hotel excellent'.

8 Cathy is Ms Smith.

	Evans	Green	Jones	Parker	Smith	Abbey ruins	Floral clock	Lighthouse	Pier	Smugglers' cave	'Getting quite brown'	'Having a great time'	'Hotel excellent'	'Weather good'	'Wish you were here'
Adam															
Cathy															
Harry															
Julie															
Mary															
'Getting quite brown'															
'Having a great time'															
'Hotel excellent'															
'Weather good'															
'Wish you were here'															
Abbey ruins															
Floral clock															
Lighthouse															
Pier															
Smugglers' cave															

Forename	Surname	Picture	Message

HAPPY COUPLES

Five couples got married in successive months last year. From the clues given below, can you name the bride and groom in each month's ceremony, and say which location each pair had chosen for their honeymoon?

Clues

1 Sheila did not marry Peter; her wedding took place the month after the one which led to the Paris honeymoon.

2 Patrick and Sarah were married on the 31st of the month.

3 Paul's Florida honeymoon was over some time before Sally got married.

4 Perry was married some time after the pair who travelled to Barbados.

5 The honeymoon in Rome was embarked upon by the pair married in May.

6 Susan spent her honeymoon in New York.

	Patrick	Paul	Perry	Peter	Philip	Sally	Samantha	Sarah	Sheila	Susan	Barbados	Florida	New York	Paris	Rome
April															
May															
June															
July															
August															
Barbados															
Florida															
New York															
Paris															
Rome															
Sally															
Samantha															
Sarah															
Sheila															
Susan															

Month	Groom	Bride	Honeymoon

PHOTO-FINISH

The picture below shows the finish of this year's Citrus Fizz Trophy race at Sundown Park. It isn't a 'real' photo-finish (because you can see quite clearly who came where, though the horses were close together), but we have to get a title from somewhere! Can you work out the race-number of each of the horses shown, its name and the name of its jockey?

Clues

1 Horse number 6, Colin Archer's mount, did not win this year's Citrus Fizz Trophy.

2 Phil Richards rode a good race, but his horse could only secure third place.

3 Horse number 3 finished two places behind Geoff Watts' mount, which wasn't number 7.

4 Ed Scott's mount bore a number two lower than that of Proud Dancer, which finished second.

5 Jack Carson (on Dandy Hill) was two places behind (and had a lower race number than) Bold Venture.

6 Mr Golden carried the number 5 in the race.

7 Red Rag's race number was two higher than Thunder Away's, but lower than that of Mark Buckle's mount.

Race numbers:
3; 4; 5; 6; 7; 8

Horses:
Bold Venture; Dandy Hill; Mr Golden; Proud Dancer; Red Rag; Thunder Away

Jockeys:
Colin Archer; Ed Scott; Geoff Watts; Jack Carson; Mark Buckle; Phil Richards

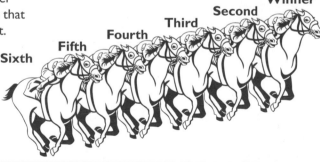

Winner
Second
Third
Fourth
Fifth
Sixth

Position	Race No	Horse	Jockey

Starting tip: Work out the race number of Red Rag.

LIGHTHOUSE FAMILY

Below are details about five fictional lighthouses around the coast of Britain. From the following information can you discover on which coast each is located, its age, and the name of the Senior Keeper?

Clues

1 Flint Head lighthouse is not as old as St Mary's Point, and doesn't look out across the English Channel; the Senior Keeper at St Mary's is Don C Fowkes.

2 Eddie Stone looks after the 70-year-old lighthouse, which does not guard either the Atlantic or English Channel coasts. The Atlantic lighthouse is neither 80 years old nor kept by Harry Mote.

3 The lighthouse on the North Sea is 20 years older than the one kept by Des O'Lett.

4 West Nab lighthouse is 90 years old.

5 The oldest lighthouse is beside the Irish Sea.

6 Mull of Dounsay lighthouse is in the Orkneys.

	Atlantic	English Channel	Irish Sea	North Sea	Orkneys	70 years old	80 years old	90 years old	100 years old	110 years old	Ray Beames	Don C Fowkes	Harry Mote	Des O'Lett	Eddie Stone
Flint Head															
Highburgh															
Mull of Dounsay															
St Mary's Point															
West Nab															
Ray Beames															
Don C Fowkes															
Harry Mote															
Des O'Lett															
Eddie Stone															
70 years old															
80 years old															
90 years old															
100 years old															
110 years old															

Lighthouse	Location	Age	Senior Keeper

HOLIDAY READING

My friend Fran loves historical novels, and when she went on holiday this year she took with her five, recommended by various friends and acquaintances; when she returned, she told me – in fairly blunt terms – that she hadn't thought much of any of them, and the reasons why. From the clues given below, can you work out which book was recommended by each of Fran's friends, who it was by, and what her opinion of it was?

Clues

1 Rupert's Woman (which Fran found 'boring') wasn't the Kate Lovel book recommended by Audrey. The novel recommended by Patsy was 'pornographic'.

2 The name of the woman who recommended Empress appears next alphabetically after that of whoever recommended the Lucy Mowiss novel; neither was the one Fran said was 'infantile', which was recommended by a woman whose name is one letter shorter than that of the woman who recommended Constantinople.

3 Both Passion Fruit and the book Jane suggested are the work of writers with the same initial for forename and surname. Jane's suggestion had more than one word in its title, unlike both Patsy's and the Greta Hallaby opus.

4 The writer of Lord of Eagles has a shorter surname than the author of the book recommended by Zoe (not that described as 'mildly amusing').

5 The book recommended by Dawn wasn't by Coral Carey.

	Constantinople	Empress	Lord of Eagles	Passion Fruit	Rupert's Woman	Coral Carey	Greta Hallaby	Kate Lovel	Lucy Mowiss	Saul Snape	Badly researched	Boring	Infantile	Mildly amusing	Pornographic
Audrey															
Dawn															
Jane															
Patsy															
Zoe															
Badly researched																
Boring																
Infantile																
Mildly amusing																
Pornographic																
Coral Carey												
Greta Hallaby												
Kate Lovel												
Lucy Mowiss												
Saul Snape												

Friend	Title	Writer	Opinion

ELEGANT VICTIMS

Those who think that street crime and mugging are of recent origin may be surprised to hear that each of our five friends the Regency Beaux was robbed in the same year in a different London street. From the clues given below, can you work out when and where each man was attacked, and say which particular item was taken from him?

Clues

1 Beau Tighe was attacked close by Temple Bar earlier in the year than his friend's gold watch was stolen, but later than the incident in which the silver-topped cane was grabbed.

2 The attack in Aldgate came earlier in the year than the one which took place in the Strand, which was not where Beau Streate was walking.

3 The top hat was snatched on Ludgate Hill in the attack which immediately preceded the one on Beau Nydel.

4 The March crime was carried out in Cheapside.

5 The purse full of guineas was taken from one of our friends in July.

6 Beau Belles fell victim to a street thief in May; he did not have his gloves stolen.

Beau	Month	Location	Item stolen

POOLED RESOURCES

In the middle of the sixties a manufacturing company employed a typing pool of nine women as shown in the diagram. From the clues given below, can you fully identify the woman in each position? NB – 'Left' and 'right' refer throughout to the viewpoint of the woman concerned as she sits at her work.

Clues

1 As they sit at their desks Alicia is immediately behind Ms Myers, and immediately left of Ms Jordan.

2 Beverley works at the same table as Ines, who is not seated directly in front of or behind Eve; the two former are separated by Ms Quigley.

3 Diane is in the row behind Ms Ryan, but not immediately behind her.

4 Cassandra Orton, who is not in the back row, is directly in line to the right of Ms Lawson.

5 Ms Prentice uses the central typewriter in the middle row.

6 Ms Kettley's position has a higher number than Ms Nolan's.

7 Position 6 in the diagram is occupied by Harriet, whose surname contains an even number of letters.

8 Frances works diagonally behind and to the right of Gill.

Forenames:
Alicia; Beverley; Cassandra; Diane; Eve; Frances; Gill; Harriet; Ines

Surnames:
Jordan; Kettley; Lawson; Myers; Nolan; Orton; Prentice; Quigley; Ryan

No	Forename	Surname

Starting tip:

Begin by placing Myers.

BATTLESHIPS

This puzzle is based on the old game of battleships. Your task is to find the vessels in the diagram. Some parts of boats or sea squares have already been filled in, and a number next to a row or column refers to the number of occupied squares in that row or column. The boats may be positioned horizontally or vertically, but no two boats or parts of boats are in adjacent squares – horizontally, vertically or diagonally.

Aircraft Carrier:

Battleships:

Cruisers:

Destroyers:

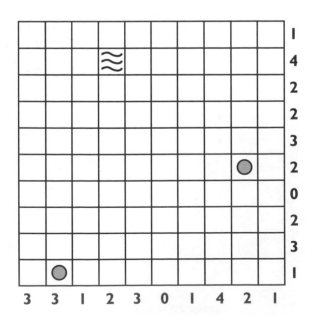

LOGI-5

Every row across and column down should contain five letters:
A, B, C, D and E, appearing once each. Also every shape (shown by the
thick lines) must contain each of the letters A, B, C, D and E, appearing
once each. Can you fill the grid?

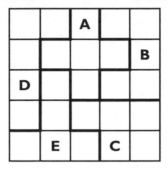

ABC

Every row across and column down is to have each of the letters A, B and
C and two empty squares. The letter outside the grid shows the first or
second letter in the direction of the arrow. Can you fill the grid?

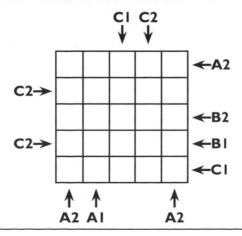

CROP SWAP

Five long-established farmers have, over the last few years, changed the main emphasis of their holdings in line with modern thinking. From the clues given below, can you say which former crop each man produced and to what he has now turned, and work out how many years ago each of the changes took place?

Clues

1 It is now seven years since Rampleigh changed the main product on his farm.

2 One farmer changed from potatoes to growing rapeseed two years after Linton switched things around.

3 The man who turned to raising pigs did so longer ago than the time when another stopped growing beans.

4 The most recent change involved the decision to stop growing oats.

5 Vereker is the man who used to grow wheat; he made his changeover some time before the man who started to produce linseed.

6 Corbyn's change of emphasis was the one which immediately preceded the one made by the man who is now a chicken farmer.

	Alfalfa	Beans	Oats	Potatoes	Wheat	Chickens	Linseed	Pigs	Rapeseed	Turkeys	3 years	5 years	7 years	10 years	12 years
Corbyn															
Grant															
Linton															
Rampleigh															
Vereker															
3 years															
5 years															
7 years															
10 years															
12 years															
Chickens															
Linseed															
Pigs															
Rapeseed															
Turkeys															

Farmer	Formerly	Now	Time span

CELEBRITY HOUSEHOLD

One of those fashionable interactive TV programmes was screened recently, in which five celebrities with different claims to distinction were assembled together, and voted out one at a time following telephone calls by the viewers. From the clues given below, can you fully identify and describe the five, and work out in which order they were expelled from the household, or, in one case, survived and won?

Clues

1 The TV personality was next to be expelled from the household after Clyde Crowe.

2 The former MP (not Headstrong) was given a much larger majority in being voted off first than had ever been seen in the constituency at past elections.

3 The male radio presenter's surname is not Boast.

4 Pushey (not Linda) stayed longer than the former international athlete, but was not the eventual winner.

5 Loudleigh was still a member of the household after the departure of the gossip columnist, who was not voted off third.

6 Max was expelled at the end of the second session of voting.

7 Headstrong did not survive as long as Adrienne, who isn't the gossip columnist.

	Boast	Crowe	Headstrong	Loudleigh	Pushey	Former MP	Gossip columnist	Radio presenter	Retired athlete	TV personality	First	Second	Third	Fourth	Winner
Adrienne															
Clyde															
Linda															
Max															
Steve															
First															
Second															
Third															
Fourth															
Winner															
Former MP															
Gossip columnist															
Radio presenter															
Retired athlete															
TV personality															

Forename	Surname	Claim to fame	Order

SUMMER SEASONS

Andrew Brown sings, dances, plays the piano, tells jokes and juggles (none of them well) and it was people like him who helped kill the variety theatres. His main work is in summer seasons at seaside theatres. Can you work out which resort he worked at in each of the listed years (he spent the summer of 1999 'resting' after a disagreement with his agent), and the name of the theatre and the show in which he worked there?

Clues

1 Andrew appeared as song-and-dance man and stand-up comedian in Fun in the Sun! in Brightbourne the year before he was one of the Summer Stars! at the decrepit fleapit known as the Galleon Theatre.

2 Andrew was at the Neptune Theatre in Swanmouth the year before he performed at the Marine Pier Theatre.

3 Neither the theatre at which he performed in 2000 nor the one in Havensands mentions a pier in its name.

4 Dingle-on-Sea (not where Andrew spent the summer of 1998) wasn't where Andrew performed in Seaside Sensation!

5 Hooray for Holidays! was the 2002 show.

	Brightbourne	Dingle-on-Sea	Havensands	Marlcliff	Swanmouth	Anchorage	Galleon	Marine Pier	Neptune	Pierhead	Fun in the Sun!	Hooray For Holidays!	Seaside Sensation!	Song of Summer!	Summer Stars!
1998															
2000															
2001															
2002															
2003															
Fun in the Sun!															
Hooray For Holidays!															
Seaside Sensation!															
Song of Summer!															
Summer Stars!															
Anchorage															
Galleon															
Marine Pier															
Neptune															
Pierhead															

Year	Resort	Theatre	Show

FOR THE LOVE OF MELANIE

In 1936, Melanie Gourlay-Smythe was considered to be the most eligible debutante in London and five bachelors, each exceedingly eligible in his own right, conducted a campaign to try to make her his wife. Of course, only one succeeded; but can you work out the name and occupation of each of Melanie's suitors, where he lived, and the outcome of his attempts to win her hand?

Clues

1 After she chose someone else as her husband, Melanie's stockbroker suitor (not Peregrine Quex) salved his broken heart by marrying a wealthy American widow and taking her to live in his country home.

2 Ambrose Boulby was a well-known racing driver.

3 The man whose home was a country manor in rural Surrey was very upset when Melanie refused his offer of marriage and volunteered for the Royal Navy.

4 Having decided that if he couldn't marry Melanie he would never marry, Lambert Moodie became a monk.

5 The hotelier's home occupied a wing of one of his seaside hotels.

6 The solicitor (whose home wasn't the penthouse flat in Mayfair) wasn't Meredith Nyman, whose home was a Georgian townhouse.

7 The 'man-about-town' didn't emigrate.

	Hotelier	Man-about-town	Racing driver	Solicitor	Stockbroker	Country cottage	Country manor	Penthouse flat	Seaside hotel	Town house	Became monk	Emigrated	Joined navy	Married Melanie	Married widow
A Boulby															
B Coggesby															
L Moodie															
M Nyman															
P Quex															
Became monk															
Emigrated															
Joined navy															
Married Melanie															
Married widow															
Country cottage															
Country manor															
Penthouse flat															
Seaside hotel															
Town house															

Name	Occupation	Home	Result

PILE UP

These piles of bricks aren't the random results of a child's play but clues to a final, at present blank, pile on the right. Like the rest, that one has six bricks each with a different one of the six letters.

The numbers below the heaps tell you two things:

(a) The number of adjacent pairs of bricks in that column which also appear adjacent in the final pile.

(b) The number of adjacent pairs of bricks that make a correct pair but the wrong way up.

So:

would score one in the 'Correct' row if the final heap had an A directly above a C and a one in the 'Reversed' row if the final heap had a C on top of an A. From all this, can you create the final pile before it topples?

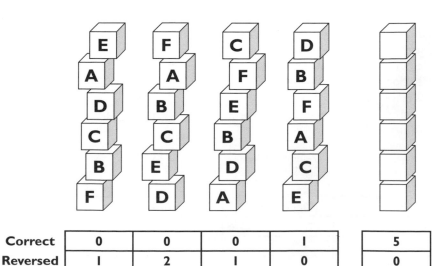

Correct	0	0	0	I		5
Reversed	I	2	I	0		0

LOGI-5

Every row across and column down should contain five letters:
A, B, C, D and E, appearing once each. Also every shape (shown by the
thick lines) must contain each of the letters A, B, C, D and E, appearing
once each. Can you fill the grid?

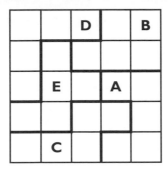

ABC

Every row across and column down is to have each of the letters A, B and
C and two empty squares. The letter outside the grid shows the first or
second letter in the direction of the arrow. Can you fill the grid?

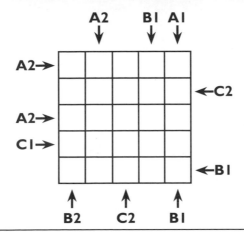

TAKING FLIGHT

Three holidaymakers left the airport at different times the same morning, on their way to distant destinations. From the clues given below, can you work out the full names of the three passengers, say where they were bound and discover their time of take-off?

Clues

1 The flight to Melbourne had the next take-off time after Alicia's plane.

2 Glenda was not aboard the 9.40 flight.

3 The passenger surnamed Faraday took the plane which left at 9.20.

4 The ticket for Seattle was held by the passenger surnamed Newton, who is not Cicely.

	Faraday	Fleming	Newton	Bangkok	Melbourne	Seattle	9.20	9.30	9.40
Alicia									
Cicely									
Glenda									
9.20									
9.30									
9.40									
Bangkok									
Melbourne									
Seattle									

Forename	Surname	Destination	Time

STAR SPORTS STARS

Star Sports, retailers of sports clothes and equipment, have hired three sports stars to reopen three of their newly-refurbished stores in the south-east of England next week. From the clues given, can you identify each sports star, his or her sport, the day on which he or she is opening a shop and the location of that shop?

Clues

I The Monday opening will be performed by a man. Dawn Pearce will be appearing at a Star Sports shop two days before their St Albans store has a celebrity visitor.

2 The judo champion will be reopening the Guildford shop.

3 Barry Noble will be performing an opening later in the week than the golfer has been booked to appear at one of the shops.

4 The Maidstone shop will not be reopened on Wednesday of next week.

	Golf	Judo	Tennis	Monday	Wednesday	Friday	Guildford	Maidstone	St Albans
Barry Noble									
Dawn Pearce									
Fergus Ross									
Guildford									
Maidstone									
St Albans									
Monday									
Wednesday									
Friday									

Star	Sport	Opening day	Location

DIG THIS!

Professor Rosetta Stone, the eminent British archaeologist, is considering offers to participate in four different 'digs' next year. Can you work out the name of the fellow-archaeologist making each offer, which university he is from, what is to be excavated and its location?

Clues

1 Professor Azimovic wants Rosetta to join him for an expedition into the wild highlands of Peru.

2 The University of New York expedition is being mounted to excavate the site of a two thousand-year-old temple.

3 Professor Katsouris isn't organising the expedition that is going to excavate an ancient fort.

4 The site in the Takla Makan desert of China to be investigated by the University of Arizona expedition is not that of a villa.

5 Professor Voelkner of the University of Berlin has no connection to the projected expedition to excavate a newly-discovered pyramid in Egypt's Nile delta.

	Arizona	Berlin	Miami	New York	Fort	Pyramid	Temple	Villa	China	Egypt	Peru	Scotland
Prof Azimovic												
Prof Katsouris												
Prof Partington												
Prof Voelkner												
China												
Egypt												
Peru												
Scotland												
Fort												
Pyramid												
Temple												
Villa												

Professor	University	Excavation	Location

MONSIEUR LE DUC

In the 1930s, the Duc de Baucherie was a charter member of High Society in Europe and frequently featured in the gossip columns and scandal magazines of the era. Amongst other things, he married four wealthy American heiresses, then (having spent each one's fortune) divorced them. From the clues given below, can you work out from where each heiress's family money came and the city and year in which she married the Duc?

Clues

1 Neither the banking heiress who married the Duc de Baucherie in 1938 nor Horatia Hampton, whose father was an oil millionaire, was at the Athens wedding – even as a guest.

2 One of the Duc's weddings took place in Berlin in 1936, during the Olympic Games.

3 The Monte Carlo wedding was earlier than the Duc's marriage to Mabelle Oakland.

4 The family of Regina Stamford, the Duc's 1934 bride, had no major involvement in the automobile industry.

5 Drusilla Camden met and married the Duc in Paris, all within a week.

	Automobiles	Banking	Mining	Oil	Athens	Berlin	Monte Carlo	Paris	1932	1934	1936	1938
Drusilla Camden												
Horatia Hampton												
Mabelle Oakland												
Regina Stamford												
1932												
1934												
1936												
1938												
Athens												
Berlin												
Monte Carlo												
Paris												

Bride	Business	City	Year

TEACHERS' LITTLE SECRETS

Young Damien Hacker, a brilliant though unruly pupil at Storbury Upper School, has managed to gain illicit access to the staff employment records in the school's computer, and discovered that four teachers have previously unpublicised achievements in their pasts. From the clues below, can you work out the nickname of each of the teachers involved, the subject he or she teaches and the nature of each one's little secret?

Clues

1 Damien has discovered that Miss Ashby was (in her younger days) seen as being the player who would restore the glory days of British women's lawn tennis; alas, like so many others, she failed to do so.

2 Mr Green is quite a personable sort of man, and was allocated the nickname Slime solely on the basis of his surname; nobody seems quite sure why the history teacher is known as Thumper, however.

3 The teacher nicknamed Blondie was a member of the late-1970s one-hit wonder pop group, The Peaches.

4 The maths teacher is an ex-astronaut – sort of; she was selected for astronaut training whilst serving in the armed forces, but was dropped at the end of the second stage of training.

5 The former naval officer, who served on a frigate off the Falklands (twelve years after the war there, in a crew which included male and female officers and ratings) doesn't teach physics.

	Blondie	Slime	The Dragon	Thumper	English	History	Maths	Physics	Ex-astronaut	Ex-naval officer	Ex-pop singer	Ex-tennis star
Miss Ashby												
Mr Green												
Mr King												
Mrs Polton												
Ex-astronaut												
Ex-naval officer												
Ex-pop singer												
Ex-tennis star												
English												
History												
Maths												
Physics												

Teacher	Nickname	Subject	Secret

MOVIE MAYHEM

Five film stars of the thirties and forties were noted within the industry for their erratic behaviour while making films. From the clues given below, can you say which star was involved in shooting which type of movie in which year, and describe each star's disruptive behaviour?

Clues

1 Betty Garble giggled constantly during the shooting of a film made the year after the screwball comedy.

2 Rita Worthless was cast in the movie set at the time of the French Revolution.

3 Clark Bagel was the star signed up for the picture produced in 1939.

4 The failure to show up on set occurred during the shooting of an earlier movie than the one in which Cary Grunt starred, but a later movie than the Western, in which the main character showed no real grasp of the scripted lines.

5 The gangster movie was shot in 1941.

6 The outbreak of brawling with a co-star happened on the set of the picture made in 1940.

	Betty Garble	Cary Grunt	Clark Bagel	Greta Garbage	Rita Worthless	French Revolution	Gangster movie	Murder mystery	Screwball comedy	Western	Brawled with co-star	Giggled constantly	Failed to show up	Hadn't learned lines	Threw tantrums
1938															
1939															
1940															
1941															
1942															
Brawled with co-star															
Giggled constantly															
Failed to show up															
Hadn't learned lines															
Threw tantrums															
French Revolution															
Gangster movie															
Murder mystery															
Screwball comedy															
Western															

Year	Star	Movie	Behaviour

BEEN RUNNERS

A recent reunion brought together some of the greatest track athletes of recent decades. From the following information, can you discover which athlete broke records in which event, and the venue and year in which each had their greatest triumph?

Clues

1 One of the women took the 1500m record in 1962, while Vic Torrius is remembered for his win in 1956.

2 The athlete who took the gold at Edinburgh in 1953 was not Aled Field, and the race concerned was not the 400m hurdles.

3 Miles Farster won in London, but not a hurdles race.

4 The Berlin event was six years after the 200m triumph.

5 Wanda Gold didn't win her event in Milan.

6 One of the athletes is remembered for the 800m win in Paris.

	Aled Field	Enya Marks	Miles Farster	Wanda Gold	Vic Torrius	Berlin	Edinburgh	London	Milan	Paris	100m hurdles	200m	400m hurdles	800m	1500m
1953															
1956															
1959															
1962															
1965															
100m hurdles															
200m															
400m hurdles															
800m															
1500m															
Berlin															
Edinburgh															
London															
Milan															
Paris															

Year	Athlete	Venue	Event

THE ARMY NAME

Many of the Regiments of the British Army have, or used to have, unusual nicknames, arising from their appearance or incidents in their history. Here are five real examples; from the information given, can you discover the number and type of each regiment, its nickname, and the decade when it was first applied?

Clues

1 Bingham's Dandies bear the number 17, but the Cherry-Pickers are not the 1st or 4th.

2 The '1st' regiment isn't one of Foot, and its nickname does not date from the 1830s, while the nickname of the regiment of Lancers (who are not the 4th Lancers) wasn't applied in the 1760s or 1810s.

3 One of the regiments, not of Lancers, was nicknamed the Cheesemongers in the 1780s, while the '2nd' regiment isn't one of Life Guards, but was nicknamed from the 1760s.

4 The regiment of Foot gained its nickname in the 1730s.

5 One of the regiments is the 11th Hussars.

6 The Queen's Bays is a regiment of Dragoon Guards.

	1st	2nd	4th	11th	17th	Dragoon Guards	Foot	Hussars	Lancers	Life Guards	1730s	1760s	1780s	1810s	1830s
Barrell's Blues															
Bingham's Dandies															
Cheesemongers															
Cherry-Pickers															
Queen's Bays															
1730s															
1760s															
1780s															
1810s															
1830s															
Dragoon Guards															
Foot															
Hussars															
Lancers															
Life Guards															

Nickname	Number	Type	Year applied

AWAY FROM IT ALL

Five married couples took holidays abroad in different months last year. From the clues given below, can you match the couples, and say in which month they holidayed in which location?

Clues

1 Sally's holiday took place some time after John's.

2 David and Mary were the next couple to go away after the pair who went off to Jamaica.

3 Alan went away earlier in the year than the couple who enjoyed a holiday in Spain.

4 John and his wife took a later holiday than Deborah and her husband.

5 Malta wasn't the location chosen by Julia and her husband for their holiday, and no one visited Australia in July.

6 As this is a Logic Problem, we have seen to it that none of the initial letters in any of the four categories match each other.

	Alan	David	John	Martin	Simon	Angela	Deborah	Julia	Mary	Sally	Australia	Denmark	Jamaica	Malta	Spain
April															
May															
July															
September															
December															
Australia															
Denmark															
Jamaica															
Malta															
Spain															
Angela															
Deborah															
Julia															
Mary															
Sally															

Month	Husband	Wife	Country

HOLE IN THE WALL

Four men are queueing up to draw money from a hole-in-the-wall cash machine. From the clues given below, can you identify and describe each of the men numbered 1 to 4, and work out how much money he is withdrawing?

Clues

1 Both Graham and the student are somewhere in front of the person drawing out £50.

2 Reg is immediately ahead of the soldier, who isn't drawing out £80.

3 Liam is the person who has come to take out £100.

4 Tom's position in the queue is immediately ahead of the plumber.

5 The taxi-driver is further back in the line than the person making the smallest withdrawal of £30, who isn't number 2 in the diagram.

Names:
Graham; Liam; Reg; Tom

Descriptions:
Plumber; soldier; student; taxi-driver

Amounts:
£30; £50; £80; £100

Name: _____ _____ _____ _____

Description: _____ _____ _____ _____

Amount: _____ _____ _____ _____

Starting tip: Start by naming the man fourth in line.

A TROUBLED COACH

It wasn't long after the departure of the coach taking a senior citizens group on an outing before some of those aboard began to complain. From the clues given below, can you name the passenger who started complaining at each of the listed times, match them with the number of their seats on the coach, and work out the nature of their complaints? NB – Lower numbers are nearer the front of the coach.

Clues

1 The first complaint made to the accompanying carer was from the woman who claimed that she had not been allocated her usual window seat.

2 Mrs Clooney, who complained of being too far back on the coach, wasn't nearest the front; the previous complaint to hers had been made by Mrs Rogers.

3 The woman who requested a toilet stop complained earlier than Mrs Harper, but later than the woman in seat 20.

4 Mrs Simpkins in seat 13 complained earlier on in the journey than the woman who felt travel sick.

5 The complaint made at 9.07 was uttered by the woman in seat 7, who wasn't Mrs Bowyer. The one in seat 34 didn't complain at 9.12.

6 The occupant of seat 25 was the next to complain after the one who discovered she had left her handbag behind.

	Mrs Bowyer	Mrs Clooney	Mrs Harper	Mrs Rogers	Mrs Simpkins	Seat 7	Seat 13	Seat 20	Seat 25	Seat 34	Felt travel sick	Left handbag	Toilet stop	Too far back	Window seat
9.03															
9.05															
9.07															
9.10															
9.12															
Felt travel sick															
Left handbag															
Toilet stop															
Too far back															
Window seat															
Seat 7															
Seat 13															
Seat 20															
Seat 25															
Seat 34															

Time	Passenger	Seat	Complaint

OFF THE PEG

Twelve primary school children were allocated pegs in the cloakroom in three rows of four, as shown in the diagram. They were allocated in strict alphabetical order of surname, but this will not help you, as this problem concerns only their first names. From the clues given below, can you correctly allocate names to pegs, writing the names below the coats?

Clues

1 As you look at the pegs, Barry's is somewhere directly behind Annette's.

2 Rows A and C each serve either one girl and three boys or one boy and three girls (both of these arrangements being present), the odd one of each sex having the same numbered peg.

3 Dean's peg isn't in row A; its number is two lower than that of another child with a four-letter first name.

4 Owen's peg is two places to the right of Candice's in the same row.

5 Tom's peg is immediately to the left of Robert's; Neil's is in the row behind, and Lucy's in the row in front, none of the four having pegs bearing the same number.

6 Kylie and Josie have pegs in the same row, the latter's having the higher number.

7 Shelley hangs her coat on peg C1.

Names:
Annette; Barry;
Candice; Dean;
Josie; Kylie;
Lucy; Neil;
Owen; Robert;
Shelley; Tom

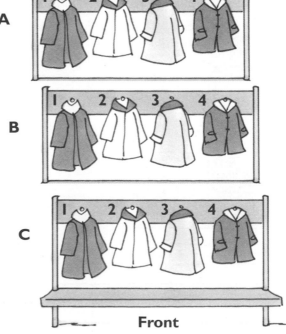

Front

Starting tip:

Begin by locating Dean's peg.

FERRY TALES

Many small foot and car ferries ply between the remoter Western Isles of Scotland. Below are details of five such routes; from the details given, can you discover which ferry works between which two islands, and how often the journey is made each week?

Clues

1 The Corray to Ballinch ferry operates half as often as the Western Countess, which doesn't sail to Glenholm.

2 Maid of Mull sails from one of the islands to Dunsay; Braemar sails from Kilgarry.

3 The ferry from Sheillin is more frequent than that to Scalnish.

4 Lady Moira makes her journey more than once a week.

5 Kinloch Castle makes the most journeys each week.

6 The ferry to Ardray operates twice a week.

	Corray	Dunsay	Kilgarry	Orinsay	Sheillin	Ardray	Ballinch	Dunsay	Glenholm	Scalnish	1	2	4	8	16
Braemar															
Kinloch Castle															
Lady Moira															
Maid of Mull															
Western Countess															
1															
2															
4															
8															
16															
Ardray										
Ballinch										
Dunsay										
Glenholm										
Scalnish										

Ferry	From island	To island	Times per week

MUSH!

The day after it snowed, four dads were persuaded into taking their offspring sledging on the common. From the clues given below, can you name the father pulling each of the sledges numbered 1 to 4, identify his child, and work out the latter's age?

Clues

1 Jasmine is on a sledge further back in the line than the one pulled by Brendan, whose child is a year older than the one on sledge 3.

2 The five-year-old is on a sledge somewhere in front of the one bearing Noel's boy, Adam.

3 The four-year-old is on a sledge further to the rear than the one Tony is pulling.

4 Henry is on a sledge somewhere behind the one bearing the three-year-old child.

5 The sledge pulled by Kevin and the one carrying Katie are adjacent to each other in the line.

Dads:
Brendan; Kevin; Noel; Tony

Children:
Adam; Henry; Jasmine; Katie

Ages:
3; 4; 5; 6

Sledge No	Dad	Child	Age

Starting tip: Start by naming the man fourth in line.

DUTIFUL DRONES

Each of our old friends the Drones was requested by a female relative on a different day of the same week to carry out a delicate task on her behalf. From the clues given below, can you name each Drone's relative, and say which task he dutifully undertook for her on which day of the week?

Clues

1 Archie Fotheringhay was asked to deliver a love-letter.

2 Aunt Sophia asked her nephew to collect a secret package from the jeweller without his uncle's knowledge; this was the day after Montague Ffolliott carried out a commission for his cousin Ariadne.

3 Whoever told someone that his feelings weren't reciprocated did so later in the week than Rupert de Grey's task.

4 Cousin Griselda's errand was on Tuesday.

5 The bet on a horse wasn't placed two days before sister Hermione's request.

6 On Wednesday one Drone bought a risqué novel for a relative who didn't wish to be recognised by the bookseller.

7 Edward Tanqueray carried out his family obligation (not imposed upon him by his sister) on Monday.

	Aunt Ermintrude	Aunt Sophia	Cousin Ariadne	Cousin Griselda	Sister Hermione	Buy risqué novel	Collect package	Deliver letter	Put money on horse	Tell of feelings	Monday	Tuesday	Wednesday	Thursday	Friday
Archie Fotheringhay															
Edward Tanqueray																
Gerald Huntington																
Montague Ffolliott																
Rupert de Grey																
Monday																
Tuesday																
Wednesday																
Thursday																
Friday																
Buy risqué novel																
Collect package																
Deliver letter																
Put money on horse																
Tell of feelings																

Drone	Relative	Task	Day

NUMBER ONE

It so happened that when five well-known people were asked to name their favourite classic film for a magazine feature, each chose a film with a number in its title. From the clues given below, can you identify the five, establish their status, and say which film each chose?

Clues

1 The title of Stella's chosen film had a larger number in it than the one selected by the television gardener, but a lower number than that in the one named by Henson.

2 It was the interviewee named Agnew who put forward the film 1984 as her all-time favourite.

3 The first name of the trade union leader is Tony.

4 The title of the ballet-dancer's favourite film contained a lower number than that selected by the novelist.

5 Adam chose a film with a higher number in its title than Jefferson's.

6 The Thirty-Nine Steps was the unhesitating choice of the tennis-player, whose surname isn't Wignall.

7 Marcia's film choice was 101 Dalmatians.

	Agnew	Briggs	Henson	Jefferson	Wignall	Ballet-dancer	Novelist	TV gardener	Tennis-player	Union leader	Magnificent Seven	Catch-22	Thirty-Nine Steps	101 Dalmatians	1984
Adam															
Charlotte															
Marcia															
Stella															
Tony															
Magnificent Seven															
Catch-22															
Thirty-Nine Steps															
101 Dalmatians															
1984															
Ballet-dancer															
Novelist															
TV gardener															
Tennis-player															
Union leader															

Forename	Surname	Status	Film choice

LUNCH IN ACAPULCO

It's lunchtime in a hotel in Acapulco, Mexico, and six US visitors are taking meals – but one is a thief who stole cash, jewellery and other items from a safety deposit in the city of Columbus, Ohio, who is about to get a nasty shock. Can you discover the full name of each of the people lunching, say which one's the thief – and who each of the other five (working together to recover the loot and take the thief back for trial) is working for?

Clues

1 Russ, who's a Detective Lieutenant with the Ohio State Police, is seated at the same table as Miss Van Buren.

2 Figure 2 is a tall, rugged guy in a stylish linen suit.

3 Figure 5 is Candy, a pretty blonde who looks too young to be – whatever she is.

4 The gorgeous but "hard-as-nails" lady who is an investigator for Eagle Insurance isn't surnamed Lincoln.

5 The person called (or, at least, using the name) Adams is lunching at the left-hand table.

6 The thief isn't Kent Tyler, the Val Kilmer lookalike, whose position is indicated by a number two above that which marks the beautiful red-haired Natasha's.

7 Figure 3, whose surname is Grant, is seated at the same table as the investigator from the Bank of Ohio, but in a moment the investigator is going to give a signal, and then all hell will break loose …

8 One of the even-numbered figures is the private eye surnamed Munroe, an employee of the Hammett Detective Agency looking after the interests of some of the people whose property was taken from the bank.

First names:
Candy; Kent; Lauren; Natasha; Nick; Russ

Surnames:
Adams; Grant; Lincoln; Munroe; Tyler; Van Buren

Employer/rôle:
Bank of Ohio; Eagle Insurance; FBI; Hammett Agency; Ohio State Police; thief

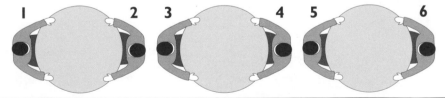

1	2	3	4	5	6

Number	Forename	Surname	Rôle

COUNTY LINE

Not much has changed in Black Rock County, Texas, since the days of the old Wild West except that modern transport has replaced stagecoaches, etc. However there are still only seven roads leading in and out of the county, and the Sheriff's Office has a plan to seal them all off, if it's ever necessary. Can you fill in on the map the name of the point where each will be blocked and the call sign of the police car assigned to it?

Clues

1 The Gold River Bridge roadblock has a lower number than the one at Buffalo Canyon; the numbers of these two, added together, equal the number of the one assigned to car Zebra-1.

2 The car assigned to set up a roadblock by the ruins of Fort Clark has a call sign numbered one higher than that of the vehicle (not Zebra-5) assigned to roadblock 1, but one lower than that covering the Cactus River Bridge.

3 Car Zebra-6 isn't the vehicle detailed to set up roadblock 2.

4 Car Zebra-3 (which will block the road at Eagle Creek Bridge) has a lower call number than the car assigned to set up roadblock 6 outside Murphy's Diner.

5 The car detailed to set up the Comanche Butte roadblock has a call sign numbered one lower than that of the roadblock 5 vehicle.

6 There is no bridge at roadblock 3, to which car Zebra-4 is assigned.

Roadblocks:
Buffalo Canyon; Cactus River Bridge; Comanche Butte; Eagle Creek Bridge; Fort Clark; Gold River Bridge; Murphy's Diner

Car call signs:
Zebra-1; Zebra-2; Zebra-3; Zebra-4; Zebra-5; Zebra-6; Zebra-7

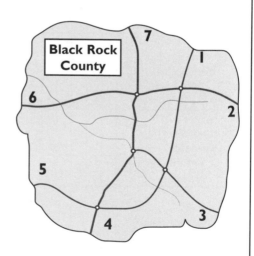

Number			
Roadblock			
Call sign			

Number			
Roadblock			
Call sign			

JAM SALES

At a recent Women's Institute Market, the county's five best jam makers had home-made preserves for sale. From the information given below, can you work out to which WI each lady belongs, the flavour of jam and number of jars each was selling?

Clues

1 Mrs Jarritt had ten jars, but it was not blackberry and apple jam, fewer jars of which were for sale than of the jam made by Mrs Boyle.

2 The stall carried fewer jars of Miss Setwell's gooseberry jam than were brought by the Bramblewood WI member.

3 The eight jars of blackcurrant jam were not from Canefield, while the raspberry jam had been made by a Hedgeley member.

4 The Pickwell WI member made 17 jars of jam.

5 The 15 jars of jam were not the work of Mrs Potts.

6 Miss Pecktin is a member of Great Punnett WI.

	Bramblewood	Canefield	Great Punnett	Hedgeley	Pickwell	8	10	15	17	18	Blackberry/apple	Blackcurrant	Gooseberry	Raspberry	Strawberry
Mrs Boyle															
Mrs Jarritt															
Miss Pecktin															
Mrs Potts															
Miss Setwell															
Blackberry/apple											
Blackcurrant											
Gooseberry											
Raspberry											
Strawberry											
8						
10						
15						
17						
18						

Member	WI	No of jars	Jam

INSPECTORS ALL

Five residents of Checkett Road have something in common –
they are all inspectors. Can you fully identify the man who lives at each
listed number in the street, and say what kind of inspector he is?
NB – Odd numbers are on one side of the road,
and even numbers on the other.

Clues

1 Lindsay Naylor's house is on the opposite side of the road from that of the police inspector, whose surname is not Thompson.

2 Charlie is a ticket inspector with the local bus company; his house bears a higher street number than Edward's.

3 The tax inspector's surname is Priestley; his house has a lower number than Thompson's.

4 The Dobbs family lives at 22 Checkett Road; Mr Dobbs is not the building inspector.

5 Mr Carson's house in Checkett Road does not bear the highest or lowest number of the five.

6 Harry's house is number 103.

7 The school inspector lives at number 68; his first name is not Robin.

	Charlie	Edward	Harry	Lindsay	Robin	Carson	Dobbs	Naylor	Priestley	Thompson	Building inspector	Police inspector	School inspector	Tax inspector	Ticket inspector
7															
22															
51															
68															
103															
Building inspector															
Police inspector															
School inspector															
Tax inspector															
Ticket inspector															
Carson															
Dobbs															
Naylor															
Priestley															
Thompson															

House No	Forename	Surname	Type

HEALTH WORKERS

Four friends, all employed in non-medical jobs at Feelwell General Hospital, have each made two New Year's resolutions – one to cut out something that is damaging their health and one to take up a pursuit that should improve it. From the clues given below, can you work out each person's job at the hospital, and what they have resolved to give up and to take up?

Clues

1 Eddie Ford, who's a senior porter at the General, isn't taking up aerobics because his wife already does those and he doesn't want to get into competition with her – experience has taught him that's asking for trouble!

2 The clerk from the Records Department has a surname beginning with a consonant, while the person who has resolved to give up smoking has a vowel for a surname initial.

3 The Health Service worker who has resolved to give up getting drunk every Saturday night and take up jogging has a surname initial in the same half of the alphabet as that of the security officer, who is the same gender as the person who has given up – or, at least, expressed the intent to give up – eating chocolate.

4 Ann Barratt, who has resolved to swim at least five lengths every morning before work, is not the person who has given up takeaway meals after becoming convinced that eating vindaloo and chips twice a day isn't good for you.

	Cleaner	Clerk	Porter	Security officer	Chocolate	Getting drunk	Smoking	Takeaway meals	Aerobics	Cycling	Jogging	Swimming
Ann Barratt												
Eddie Ford												
Nina O'Toole												
Tom Usher												
Aerobics								
Cycling								
Jogging								
Swimming								
Chocolate				
Getting drunk				
Smoking				
Takeaway meals				

Name	Job	Giving up	Taking up

WINNINGTON WINNERS

Last month, four residents of the London district of Winnington actually became big winners in different competitions. From the clues given below, can you work out each winner's full name and occupation, and say what prize they won?

Clues

1 Donald, the taxi-driver, has a surname the same length as that of the person who has won a newly-built house in the 'stockbroker belt' in a building society's competition.

2 Julie has won a world cruise for herself and her partner in a travel company's Internet competition.

3 Pyke has won the latest Japanese sports car in a scratchcard game run by a petrol company.

4 It wasn't Angela Strong who won £2.4 million on the National Lottery.

5 The waitress' surname isn't Cobb.

	Benton	Cobb	Pyke	Strong	Policeman	Saleswoman	Taxi-driver	Waitress	Car	House	£2.4 million	World cruise
Angela												
Donald												
Julie												
Martin												
Car												
House												
£2.4 million												
World cruise												
Policeman												
Saleswoman												
Taxi-driver												
Waitress												

Forename	Surname	Occupation	Prize

MISSING IN ACTION

At the end of a major exercise, four soldiers from a Territorial Army infantry unit had to report that they had lost certain quite important items of their equipment. From the clues given below, can you work out the rank and full name of each unfortunate warrior, and say what it was he had lost?

Clues

1 Steve's rank is immediately between that of David and that of the man who lost his sleeping bag.

2 The Private was unfortunate to lose his boots while he was asleep during the last night of the exercise; he suspected that they had been 'borrowed' by one of his comrades whose own footwear had become wet through.

3 The Sergeant is neither Mike Gordon nor Buller, who had managed to mislay his mess kit; the ranks of these two are separated only by that of the man who committed one of the worst sins a soldier can: he lost his rifle!

4 Moore's first name isn't David.

	David	Geoff	Mike	Steve	Buller	Gordon	Moore	Wolfe	Boots	Mess kit	Rifle	Sleeping bag
Private												
Lance-Corporal												
Corporal												
Sergeant												
Boots												
Mess kit												
Rifle												
Sleeping bag												
Buller												
Gordon												
Moore												
Wolfe												

Rank	Forename	Surname	Item lost

NOT SO STATELY

Bellendale is just part of Grancaster these days but until it was engulfed in the 19th-Century expansion of that city it was a rural area in which stood five stately homes, none of which still survives. (In fact, the earliest two were already ruins, courtesy of Cromwell's Roundheads, when the last was built). From the clues given below, can you work out who built each house, in which year it was finished and what now occupies its site?

Clues

1 Lord Casby built Pincot House (not personally, you understand) in the same century that saw the construction of another great house whose name is now only remembered as that of the housing estate which now occupies its former site.

2 Part of one wall of Bevil House still stands, incorporated into the comprehensive school built on its site in the 1960s; Hugby House was built after Bevil House.

3 The public park occupies the former site of an 18th-Century building and its gardens, and is named for its builder.

4 It was not Lord Quale's house that was completed in 1723.

5 The Earl of Pyke's home, finished in 1685, is not the building whose site is today occupied by an industrial estate.

6 Tatham Manor was the last of the buildings to be completed.

7 Fermin Place was constructed in the century after Lord Gowan's house.

8 The zoo is on the site of Sir Hugh Fern's home.

	Earl of Pyke	Lord Casby	Lord Gowan	Lord Quale	Sir Hugh Fern	1579	1634	1685	1723	1767	Housing estate	Industrial estate	Public park	School	Zoo
Bevil House															
Fermin Place															
Hugby House															
Pincot House															
Tatham Manor															
Housing estate											
Industrial estate											
Public park											
School											
Zoo											
1579					
1634					
1685					
1723					
1767					

House	Builder	Year finished	Current use

HEAD OF THE QUEUE

As usual, there's a queue for the January sale at Wigglesworth & Golightly, Colncaster's biggest department store, and (as usual) the local Evening Mail has published a front-page picture of the ladies at the head of the queue, who have already been there for 48 hours with another 24 still to go. Can you fill in the names of the four bargain-hunters shown, which of the special offer bargains she's after, and its price?

Clues

1 The lady who wants to buy a wide-screen, flat-screen, stereo-sound, all-singing, all-dancing, nuclear-powered, state-of-the-art TV set with built-in DVD player for £40 is immediately ahead of Karen Brass.

2 Donna Nubbles is queuing to buy herself a new coat.

3 The bargain washing machine isn't priced at £30.

4 Becky Quilp is in second place in the queue.

5 The lady in fourth place isn't planning to spend as much as Sharon Jarley.

6 The bargain-hunter in third position has her eye on a bargain priced at just £10.

Shoppers:
Becky Quilp; Donna Nubbles; Karen Brass; Sharon Jarley

Bargains:
Coat; tea set; TV; washing machine

Prices:
£10; £20; £30; £40

	First	Second	Third	Fourth
Shopper:	_____	_____	_____	_____
Bargain:	_____	_____	_____	_____
Price:	_____	_____	_____	_____

Starting tip:

Work out the position in the queue of the shopper after the TV set.

FIRST BIRTHDAYS

Penny Corporation's Storbury operation is about to honour five employees who were born on January 1st – exactly 60, 50, 40, 30 and 20 years ago (laws prevent PennyCorp from employing 10-year-olds) by presenting them with a brooch or pair of cufflinks, according to gender. Can you work out the details of those qualifying for this giveaway by being born in each listed year: forename, surname and their department?

Clues

1 The load planner from the Transport Department is ten years younger than Thorne but ten years older than Pamela.

2 The section leader from Accounts is ten years older than Maxine Cooper.

3 The Customer Service manager, who was born on January 1st, 1943, is not Kent.

4 Ms Forbes works on the computers in Administration.

5 Donald was born on January 1st, 1963.

6 Esther is an account executive in Sales.

	Donald	Esther	Maxine	Pamela	Rodney	Cooper	Forbes	Green	Kent	Thorne	Accounts	Administration	Customer Service	Sales	Transport
1943															
1953															
1963															
1973															
1983															
Accounts															
Administration															
Customer Service															
Sales															
Transport															
Cooper															
Forbes															
Green															
Kent															
Thorne															

Year of birth	Forename	Surname	Department

WITH A VIEW TO PURCHASE

Two salespersons who work for a firm of estate agents, Claire and Jason, each escorted four couples round properties for sale the other day. From the clues given below, can you name the couple and the location involved in each viewing session listed on the chart?

Clues

1 The Olivers were shown round by Claire at exactly the same time as Jason was carrying out his duties in Chestnut Close.

2 The McCoys, whose guide's previous appointment that day had been with the Littles, were shown round at the same time as the couple in Sycamore Crescent.

3 Claire showed the Moodys round immediately before rushing off to her appointment in Birch Street an hour later.

4 The Clarkes were the couple who viewed the house in Lime Avenue.

5 The salesperson who was in Hawthorn Road during the morning session did not visit Oak Lane in the afternoon.

6 Jason was in Maple Drive at 3.30 that afternoon.

7 Claire's 2.30 appointment was with the couple named Baker.

8 Jason's second task that day was to show the Smythes round a property.

Couples:
Baker; Clarke; Little; McCoy; Moody; Oliver; Smythe; Taylor

Properties:
Birch Street; Chestnut Close; Hawthorn Road; Lime Avenue; Maple Drive; Oak Lane; Poplar View; Sycamore Crescent

	Claire		Jason	
	Couple	**Address**	**Couple**	**Address**
10.30				
11.30				
2.30				
3.30				

Starting tip:

First establish the time at which Claire was in Birch Street.

FIRST PAST THE POST

Below are details of the five winners at yesterday afternoon's meeting at Epwell Park. From the information given, can you work out which horse won each race, the name of the jockey, and the odds?

Clues

1 Impetus didn't win the 2.45 or the 3.45, and its jockey wasn't Phil Sadler; Micko's odds weren't 5-1.

2 Miles Littler's mount won at 3-1, but not in the 2.15.

3 Harve Pynte, on Red Tape, won the race before that in which Guy Smallhouse came in first.

4 The name of the winning horse in the 3.45, which came home at 7-2, is longer than that of the horse that won at 5-4.

5 Sparkler won at 10-1 in the race before Phil Sadler came in first.

6 Les Waite won the 3.15.

	Guy Smallhouse	Harve Pynte	Les Waite	Miles Littler	Phil Sadler	Gaelic Boy	Impetus	Micko	Red Tape	Sparkler	3-1	5-1	5-4	7-2	10-1
2.15															
2.45															
3.15															
3.45															
4.15															
3-1															
5-1															
5-4															
7-2															
10-1															
Gaelic Boy															
Impetus															
Micko															
Red Tape															
Sparkler															

Race	Jockey	Horse	Odds

DEAR SIR ...

I Dudgeon is well-known to local newspaper editors as a prolific writer of complaining letters. Last week he had a letter published in each of our five local papers. From the following information, can you discover which paper featured each day's letter, the subject of Mr Dudgeon's rant, and the number of words in each letter?

Clues

1 One of his letters appeared in Tuesday's Daily Courier, while his complaint about vandalism in the park was published two days later than the 115-word letter.

2 'Dear Sir, The state of the pavements in the town is deplorable...' began Monday's tirade; it wasn't published in the Daily Reporter, and didn't run to 80 words.

3 The longest letter appeared in an evening paper on Thursday.

4 'Dear Sir, The amount of litter in the town centre is dreadful...' began the Morning Clarion letter, which was of more than 100 words.

5 'Dear Sir, Could the local bus service get any worse?' was not the letter published in the Evening Bugle.

6 The shortcomings of the proposed one-way system were outlined in a 120-word letter.

	Daily Courier	Daily Reporter	Evening Bugle	Evening Herald	Morning Clarion	Bus service	Litter	One-way system	Pavements	Vandalism	80 words	90 words	115 words	120 words	130 words
Monday															
Tuesday															
Wednesday															
Thursday															
Friday															
80															
90															
115															
120															
130															
Bus service															
Litter															
One-way system															
Pavements															
Vandalism															

Day	Newspaper	Subject	No of words

IN THE NICK

Coldridge is a small town in Cumbria, and its exposed, high-altitude position means that it often gets cut off in snowy weather. That's why, late one January night with a blizzard blowing, the police station has all five cells occupied, one by an offender and four by stranded innocents. Can you work out the full name of each person 'overnighting' in the cells, their cell number and occupation?

Clues

1 Joanne is sleeping soundly in cell 4.

2 The off-duty Detective-Sergeant in cell 3, who decided to stay over after the local radio reported that the road to Kirkosbert was impassable, isn't Vince.

3 Susan, a housewife who has become stranded on the way home from a visit to her mother, is in the cell numbered immediately below that occupied by Maybrick.

4 Palmer, in cell 1, isn't the police surgeon who was called to Coldridge nick to check out a drunk driver and then couldn't get home again.

5 Armstrong, who isn't in cell 4 or 5, isn't Brian.

6 Mike Crippen's cell is numbered immediately above that of the nick's one real prisoner, a sailor on leave from the Royal Navy who has been charged with drunk-driving and assaulting a police officer.

	Armstrong	Crippen	Maybrick	Palmer	Seddon	Cell 1	Cell 2	Cell 3	Cell 4	Cell 5	Detective-Sgt	Housewife	Police surgeon	Sailor	Van driver
Brian															
Joanne															
Mike															
Susan															
Vince															
Detective-Sgt															
Housewife															
Police surgeon															
Sailor															
Van driver															
Cell 1															
Cell 2															
Cell 3															
Cell 4															
Cell 5															

Forename	Surname	Cell	Occupation

OUTLOOK FAIR

Five young people are attending an education and employment fair to gain information which will help them decide on their next step in life. From the clues given below, can you match each with his or her age, say which stand at the fair each is currently visiting, and work out how long each has spent so far discussing matters with that organisation's representative?

Clues

1 Stella's 10-minute discussion has not been with the representative of an educational establishment.

2 Rob is two years older than the young person involved in discussion at the stand run by an internationally famous department store.

3 The 12-minute discussion has occupied the person aged 20.

4 Jane (who isn't 18) has ambitions to work in a bank, and is discussing the possibilities of this.

5 The longest discussion has not involved the young person considering a course at the FE college, who is 19; the latter is not Lisa.

6 Nick, who is 21 years old, has no ambitions to take a university degree.

7 The shortest discussion so far is the one at the stand run by the computer company.

	17	18	19	20	21	Bank	Computer co	Department store	FE college	University	5 minutes	10 minutes	12 minutes	15 minutes	18 minutes
Jane															
Lisa															
Nick															
Rob															
Stella															
5 minutes															
10 minutes															
12 minutes															
15 minutes															
18 minutes															
Bank															
Computer Co															
Dept store															
FE college															
University															

Name	Age	Stand	Length of time

OH YES THEY DID!

Five children were each taken to the pantomime at the theatre in their home-town. Can you say where each lives, name the theatre there, and work out which pantomime it is staging this year?

Clues

1 Ann-Marie was taken to see Robinson Crusoe.

2 Cinderella was on for a season at the Empire.

3 The girl who saw Dick Whittington is not the child who visited the Civic theatre, which is not in Northwold.

4 Desmond lives in Waterburn.

5 The theatre where Damien enjoyed a visit to the pantomime was the Grand; the show there was not Babes in the Wood.

6 The New Theatre in Kingsford was not the one to which Janine was taken.

7 This year's pantomime in Petershill is Aladdin; the youngster who saw it is the same sex as the one taken to the Palace.

	Greenwell	Kingsford	Northwold	Petershill	Waterburn	Civic	Empire	Grand	New	Palace	Aladdin	Babes in the Wood	Cinderella	Dick Whittington	Robinson Crusoe
Ann-Marie															
Damien															
Desmond															
Janine															
Laura															
Aladdin															
Babes in the Wood															
Cinderella															
Dick Whittington															
Robinson Crusoe															
Civic															
Empire															
Grand															
New															
Palace															

Name	Town	Theatre	Pantomime

ARMS AND THE MEN

Below are details of the coats of arms of five eminent families, each of which bears a particular animal and some other prominent device, as well as the family motto in Latin. From the information given, can you work out which animal and device belongs on which arms, and the English translation of the motto beneath it?

Clues

1 The arms of Lord Knowes bear some kind of living plant, but not a dragon; neither the arms of Earl Stones nor the ones featuring the cross-keys or the dragon bears the motto 'Fear none'.

2 The cross-keys are not part of the arms of Viscount Vickers; the castle is found on the crest of the Dukes of Ellington.

3 A boar surmounts the motto 'Unity in faith'; the sword is found on neither the crest with the boar nor the one with the dragon.

4 The eagle is the emblem of Lord Meyer, but 'Strong of arm' is not the Meyer family motto.

5 A rose surmounts the motto 'Truth and honour'.

6 The lion and the oak tree share a crest.

	Boar	Dragon	Eagle	Lion	Stag	Castle	Cross-keys	Oak tree	Rose	Sword	'Always loyal'	'Fear none'	'Strong of arm'	'Truth and honour'	'Unity in faith'
Dukes of Ellington															
Earl Stones															
Lord Knowes															
Lord Meyer															
Viscount Vickers															
'Always loyal'															
'Fear none'															
'Strong of arm'															
'Truth and honour'															
'Unity in faith'															
Castle															
Cross-keys															
Oak tree															
Rose															
Sword															

Family	Animal	Other device	Motto

FOOTBALLERS' WIVES

The front pages of this morning's newspapers are full of stories about the wives of various Premiership footballers who have all begun new careers despite lacking any talent whatsoever (not just for the aforesaid careers – for anything). Can you work out to whom each of the women is married, what club he plays for and what she's going to be doing with her life from here on?

Clues

1 Billi-Jo's husband doesn't play for Newdale or Oxham Town; the Newdale player, whose wife hasn't just signed a contract to become a pop singer, isn't Danny Tyler, whose gorgeous but air-headed blonde spouse has been cast as the heroine of a big-budget movie.

2 Jay Duffy's wife isn't going to be a pop singer or a TV presenter; Jay doesn't play for Newdale or Oxham Town.

3 The woman who will present Albion-TV's revamped MegaMorning Show is married to the Hillby United footballer, who isn't Heinz Lammer.

4 Vangi, who's just starting out as a couturier, isn't Mrs Jay Duffy.

5 Rick Broom is Langwood's famous sweeper.

6 Daffodil is married to Nico Solti; Maribelle's husband plays for Riverton.

	Rick Broom	Jay Duffy	Heinz Lammer	Nico Solti	Danny Tyler	Hillby United	Langwood	Newdale	Oxham Town	Riverton	Couturier	Film actress	Model	Pop singer	TV presenter
Billi-Jo															
Daffodil															
Maribelle															
Shannon															
Vangi															
Couturier															
Film actress															
Model															
Pop singer															
TV presenter															
Hillby United															
Langwood															
Newdale															
Oxham Town															
Riverton															

Wife	Husband	Team	Career

STORBURY BOOKS

The owner of Storbury Books has just placed in the window a display of four books 'of local interest' (which means that, interesting or not, they've been written by people who live in the town, whose friends and acquaintances might be interested in purchasing – and maybe even reading – a copy). Can you decide the titles of the volumes shown, the names of their writers, and what kind of book (apart from 'of local interest') each is?

Clues

1 The travel book, which is not called The Trumpeter, is at the far right of the display.

2 You probably won't be surprised to learn that Georgian Storbury is a book about local history.

3 Over the Water is displayed immediately right of the book by local bank manager Simon Talbot and immediately left of the autobiography.

4 The whodunnit is the work of Carol Dillon, who taught at Storbury Upper School before her retirement.

5 Going West is not the book penned by John Keene in the time he could spare from his work as a partner in a local law practice.

Titles:
Georgian Storbury; Going West; Over the Water; The Trumpeter

Writers:
Carol Dillon; John Keene; Martin North; Simon Talbot

Types of book:
Autobiography; local history; travel; whodunnit

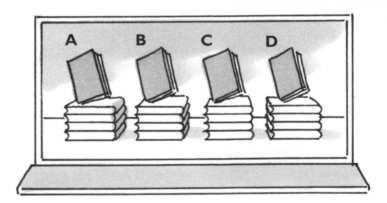

Title:	____	____	____	____
Writer:	____	____	____	____
Book type:	____	____	____	____

Starting tip: Work out which book is the autobiography.

AS I WAS GOING TO ...

... St Ives, I couldn't believe my eyes when I met a man with seven wives, who insisted on introducing them to me. He seemed a bit simple, so I hadn't the heart to tell him he was a serial bigamist. However, when he explained his marital arrangements to me, telling me each wife's different rôle, I began to wonder if he was as simple as he at first appeared. Can you name the numbered wives in the line, and outline each one's duties?

Clues

1 I couldn't help noticing that each wife had seven cats, but the man explained to me that two of the seven wives spent all their time attending to them, the one who groomed them being three places behind the one who fed them; and Kate was further back than both.

2 Sarah, who looks after the man's garden, was two places behind Jill.

3 Wife number 2 washes all the clothes for the household.

4 Valerie immediately precedes in the line the wife who cooks for them all.

5 Lucy is wife number 3 on the road from St Ives.

6 Annie is two places behind the wife who does all the sewing and mending.

7 Marjorie is not the wife responsible for keeping the house clean.

Wives:
Annie; Jill; Kate; Lucy; Marjorie; Sarah; Valerie

Duties:
Cleans house; cooks; does garden; feeds cats; grooms cats; sews; washes clothes

Number			
Name			
Duty			

Number			
Name			
Duty			

Starting tip: Begin by naming wife number 1 in the line.

HEADS AND TAILS

The children at a birthday party were playing the age-old game 'Pin the Tail on the Donkey'. As they were, of course, blindfolded, their efforts were all fairly widely off the mark. From the clues given below, can you name the children in the order in which they made their attempts, describe each one's status at the party, and say to which portion of the donkey's anatomy each tried to pin the tail?

Clues

1 Kevin, the birthday girl's brother, made his attempt some time before the person who pinned the tail to the donkey's front leg.

2 The shoulder was picked out by the player who immediately followed the birthday girl herself, who did not make the first attempt.

3 The birthday girl's sister had her go some time before the invited friend.

4 The donkey's head was adorned by the tail pinned by the third person to compete, who was not Madeleine.

5 The fourth child to be blindfolded and given the donkey's tail was Helen.

6 It was Samantha who pinned the tail to the donkey's back leg; she went immediately after the birthday girl's cousin, who was a later participant in the game than Agnes.

	Agnes	Helen	Kevin	Madeleine	Samantha	Birthday girl	Brother	Cousin	Friend	Sister	Back	Back leg	Front leg	Head	Shoulder
First															
Second															
Third															
Fourth															
Fifth															
Back															
Back leg															
Front leg															
Head															
Shoulder															
Birthday girl															
Brother															
Cousin															
Friend															
Sister															

Order	Name	Status	Donkey part

EVERYDAY STORY OF ...

Country Folk is a daily radio serial which typically ends each day's episode with a mini crisis or surprise revelation involving one or other of the regular characters. From the clues given below, can you work out the name and description of the character who provided this denouement on each day last week, and match them with their storylines?

Clues

1 The climax of Wednesday's programme put the spotlight on Brian.

2 The person who works behind the bar in the local pub was the one involved in the ending of Thursday's episode.

3 The visit of a long-lost brother wasn't featured in Friday's programme.

4 The proposal of marriage was made in the episode following that involving Sheila, and accepted at the start of the following day's programme (which itself terminated with a storyline involving the vet).

5 Brenda, the village shopkeeper, was at the centre of events at the end of the programme next after the one in which it was announced that a baby was on the way.

6 The doctor's decision to retire was taken the day before Stan's storyline was broadcast.

	Brenda	Brian	Laura	Sheila	Stan	Bar attendant	Doctor	Farmer	Shopkeeper	Vet	Baby expected	Marriage proposal	Retirement	Visit of brother	Win on lottery
Monday															
Tuesday															
Wednesday															
Thursday															
Friday															
Baby expected															
Marriage proposal															
Retirement															
Visit of brother															
Win on lottery															
Bar attendant															
Doctor															
Farmer															
Shopkeeper															
Vet															

Day	Name	Rôle	Event

TRICK OR TREAT

Last Hallowe'en five young friends went 'trick or treating' in Elm Street. From the information given, can you work out which scary costume each child wore, the number of the house at which each called, and the type of sweets distributed by the householders to avoid a trick?

Clues

1 Belinda was given fruit jellies at a house with a number lower than the one that Holly was calling at; Holly was not the child dressed as Dracula who was given chocolate buttons.

2 Tim, dressed as a ghost, visited a house numbered two less than that where the skeleton knocked on the door.

3 Zoe was at No 13, but unluckily was not given a chocolate bar.

4 James was not calling at No 8.

5 The witch was at No 5.

6 The householder at No 11 gave the children toffees.

	Belinda	Holly	James	Tim	Zoe	Dracula	Frankenstein	Ghost	Skeleton	Witch	Chews	Chocolate bar	Chocolate buttons	Fruit jellies	Toffees
3															
5															
8															
11															
13															
Chews															
Chocolate bar															
Choc buttons															
Fruit jellies															
Toffees															
Dracula															
Frankenstein															
Ghost															
Skeleton															
Witch															

House	Child	Costume	Treat

SANTA'S LITTLE ELVES

Six students have been forced, by lack of cash to take jobs as elves in Santa's Grotto at a local store. They'd have preferred jobs which didn't require them to dress in tights and coloured tunics and be friendly to ghastly kids (their job description, not the shop's) and have adopted names based on those of Snow White's dwarfs. Can you decide each student's name, the colour he or she is wearing, and his or her nickname?

Clues

1 The elf in the lilac tunic and matching tights is immediately left of Jo and immediately right of the person who has chosen to be known as 'Fusty' (when the management aren't around).

2 Penny, whose elf costume is orange, is next to 'Grotty'.

3 The pink-clad elf is next but one to the right of 'Droopy'.

4 Elf D has chosen to be called 'Nasty'. The student who has chosen the nickname 'Spotty' isn't in position F.

5 Elf E is dressed all in yellow. Elf A isn't in pale green.

6 'Grimy', dressed in a pale blue outfit which is, if truth be told, not absolutely pristine, is next but one to Steve.

7 Elf C is Dilly – no, that's her real name, or, at least the one she's normally known by. Elf B is not Nicci.

Students:
Dilly; Frank; Jo; Nicci; Penny; Steve

Outfit colours:
Lilac; orange; pale blue; pale green; pink; yellow

Nicknames:
'Droopy'; 'Fusty'; 'Grimy'; 'Grotty'; 'Nasty'; 'Spotty'

Identity	Student	Colour	Nickname

Starting tip: Work out the nickname of elf F.

SCHOOLREUNION.COM

Five friends have subscribed to the popular reunion website schoolreunion.com, and already have been contacted by old school-friends that they haven't seen for many years. From the information given, can you work out which person from the past has contacted each, the class that the two of them were in together when they were friends, and the year they last met?

Clues

1 Ruth was contacted by someone she hadn't seen since 1974, but it wasn't John Gibson.

2 Vanessa got in touch with her old best friend from 2A, but they hadn't last been in touch in 1975.

3 Steve Dale sent a message to Mark; they had last met three years more recently than the subscriber and his or her friend in 5B.

4 Paul hadn't seen his old school-friend since an even-numbered year, while the contact from the days of class 3A hadn't been in touch since one year after that.

5 One of the subscribers hadn't spoken to Neil Murphy since 1976.

6 Tracey Evans used to be in class 4B.

	Pamela Clifford	Steve Dale	Tracey Evans	John Gibson	Neil Murphy	2A	3A	3C	4B	5B	1974	1975	1976	1977	1980
Mark															
Paul															
Robert															
Ruth															
Vanessa															
1974															
1975															
1976															
1977															
1980															
2A															
3A															
3C															
4B															
5B															

Subscriber	Contact	Class	Year

ON THE FIDDLE

The visiting Women's Chamber ensemble is a quintet of classical musicians from former Iron Curtain countries. From the clues given below, can you determine which country each artiste is from, work out her age, and say which instrument she plays in the ensemble?

Clues

1 Elena, from Bulgaria, does not play the viola.

2 The Russian musician is not 27.

3 Maria is 28; she plays the same instrument as the woman from the Czech Republic.

4 Anna, who plays the cello, is not yet in her thirties; she is not from the Ukraine.

5 The woman aged 30 does not play an instrument preceded by the word 'second' in the ensemble.

6 The first violin is played by the instrumentalist from Poland, who is the immediate senior in age in the ensemble of Katarina.

	Bulgaria	Czech Republic	Poland	Russia	Ukraine	25	27	28	30	31	Cello	First viola	First violin	Second viola	Second violin
Anna															
Basia															
Elena															
Katarina															
Maria															
Cello															
First viola															
First violin															
Second viola															
Second violin															
25															
27															
28															
30															
31															

Name	Country	Age	Instrument

LEGIONARIES

Five regulars were having a natter at the Royal British Legion club, reminiscing over their wartime experiences. From the clues given below, can you fully identify the five ex-servicemen, work out their respective ages, and name the branch of the armed forces in which each had fought during the war?

Clues

1 Thomas is two years older than the man who served in the Fleet Air Arm.

2 James Coates is younger than his friend who was in the RAF.

3 The Eighth Army veteran is older than the ex-serviceman named Graham.

4 Donald recently celebrated his 82nd birthday.

5 The ex-Royal Navy man, who is not William, is now 81.

6 Johnstone's branch of the services was the Royal Marines; he is a year younger than Abbott.

	Abbott	Coates	Graham	Johnstone	Markham	80	81	82	83	84	Eighth Army	Fleet Air Arm	RAF	Royal Marines	Royal Navy
Donald															
James															
Thomas															
Walter															
William															
Eighth Army															
Fleet Air Arm															
RAF															
Royal Marines															
Royal Navy															
80															
81															
82															
83															
84															

Forename	Surname	Age	Service

ZEROING IN

Twenty of the twenty-five squares in the diagram each contain a different one of the numbers 1 to 20, while each of the other five squares contains a zero. From the clues given below, can you place the correct number in each square? NB – Where the phrase 'number' or 'single-digit number' occurs in a clue, this does not include zeros.

Clues

1 No row, column or diagonal (long or short) contains more than one zero.

2 The 19 in square B3 is the only two-digit number in that row, while the 7 is the only single-digit number in row 2.

3 The 9 is immediately below the 16, and immediately left of the 12.

4 The numbers in column E total 45, and those in row 2 total 51.

5 The number in A4 is five higher than the one in E5, which is itself one higher than the one in C2.

6 The 11 is immediately to the right of the 5 in row 4, while the 2 is to be found in a higher row than the 4.

7 The 17 appears in column D, somewhere below a zero, and somewhere above the 8.

8 The four numbers in column C are all even numbers, but do not include the 18.

9 The number 1 can be found in row 5, and the 6 in row 1.

10 The 10 is in the same column as the 3, but higher up.

	A	B	C	D	E
1					
2					
3					
4					
5					

Starting tip:

Begin by placing the 9.

COPYCATS

Five employees of a large organisation arrived within moments of each other at the firm's only functioning photocopier, the others being all temporarily out of order, and awaiting the attentions of the engineer. From the clues given below, can you work out in what order the five arrived, and say in which department each works, and how many copies each urgently needed to make?

Clues

1 Jayne used the photocopier next after the person from accounts, who needed fewer copies than Jayne.

2 The planning department employee, who required 12 copies, used the machine immediately before James.

3 The person from the personnel department used the machine earlier than whoever needed 24 copies (who doesn't work in customer services).

4 Claire didn't want a number of copies divisible by 6.

5 Sarah had to wait patiently till the other four had finished before she got to use the photocopier; she needed more copies than Nick, who wasn't first in the queue.

6 The person from the firm's records department was fourth in the queue.

7 15 copies were made by the second person to use the photocopier.

	Claire	James	Jayne	Nick	Sarah	Accounts	C services	Personnel	Planning	Records	10	12	15	20	24
First															
Second															
Third															
Fourth															
Fifth															
10															
12															
15															
20															
24															
Accounts															
Customer services															
Personnel															
Planning															
Records															

Order	Name	Department	Copies

BOX NUMBERS

Postman Roy L Mayle is making his evening collection from postboxes around the town. From the following information, can you discover the location and emptying time of each box, the kind of box it is, and the number of items in each on this particular evening?

Clues

1 Neither the 5.00 collection nor that from the brick-built pillar-box were made in a Street, and both contained fewer items than the box in Mill Street.

2 The Mill Street collection is made immediately before that from Highgate, while the 5.30 collection from the box in the shop wall is made later than that in Rose Street which this evening yielded 43 items.

3 There was more post in the box attached to the telegraph pole than in that in Victoria Road.

4 The box emptied at 5.20 contained just 30 items.

5 The box with most items was that inside the supermarket.

6 The metal pillar-box is in Market Close.

	Highgate	Market Close	Mill Street	Rose Street	Victoria Road	Brick pillar-box	In shop wall	Inside supermarket	Metal pillar-box	On telegraph pole	30	43	51	62	68
5.00															
5.10															
5.20															
5.30															
5.40															
30															
43															
51															
62															
68															
Brick pillar-box															
In shop wall															
Inside supermarket															
Metal pillar-box															
On telegraph pole															

Collection	Location	Type of box	No of items

AHOY!

One fine day last summer four visitors from different Yorkshire towns were using money-in-the-slot telescopes along the seafront of a popular east coast resort. From the clues given below, can you name the person using each telescope, identify his home-town, and say on what precise object each was focusing at the time?

Clues

1 The person focusing on the ship which takes holidaymakers for a cruise round the bay is somewhere to the left of Richard, from Sheffield.

2 The visitor from Hull, who is not Simon, is next to the person watching a surfer perform.

3 Telescope number 2, which is being used by Marcus or Simon, is trained on a group of seabirds.

4 John, who was watching the manoeuvrings of a motorboat, is somewhere to the left of the person from Rotherham along the seafront.

Names:
John; Marcus; Richard; Simon

Towns:
Halifax; Hull; Rotherham; Sheffield

Watching:
Cruise ship; motorboat; seabirds; surfer

| | 1 | 2 | 3 | 4 |

Name:	___	___	___	___
Town:	___	___	___	___
Watching:	___	___	___	___

Starting tip:
First work out what the person using telescope 4 is watching.

READING MATTERS

I belong to a book group, and every month we read a different book, then meet to discuss it. From the following information, can you discover which books by which authors we read this summer, and my comment on each?

Clues

1 April's book, which was not Dark Guest, I found 'gripping'.

2 We read Dusty Death by Maeve McCarthy the month after the book I thought was 'trashy'.

3 The 'unputdownable' novel came the month after we read Daybreak and the month before we tried something by Anne Gavin.

4 In June we read a work by Leo Tanner.

5 The 'hilarious' Rosie Jones was written by a woman.

6 I found Jenny Royle's book 'too long'.

	Dark Guest	Daybreak	Dusty Death	King's Park	Rosie Jones	Anne Gavin	Brian Maxwell	Maeve McCarthy	Jenny Royle	Leo Tanner	'Gripping'	'Hilarious'	'Too long'	'Trashy'	'Unputdownable'
April															
May															
June															
July															
August															
'Gripping'															
'Hilarious'															
'Too long'															
'Trashy'															
'Unputdownable'															
Anne Gavin															
Brian Maxwell															
Maeve McCarthy															
Jenny Royle															
Leo Tanner															

Month	Book	Author	Comment

COUPLING

We're planning a series of supper parties, and are trying to decide which pairs of couples to invite, as not all our friends get on with others. From the following comments, can you discover which foursomes we eventually decided on for each date, and the main course we're intending to serve on each occasion?

Clues

1 'Let's invite Annie and Tom on the 24th, and Jane and Paul on the 3rd, although Paul doesn't like fish.'

2 'Heather and Alan can only make the weekend after Pat and Ray, and Sheila and Peter would get on really well with Jane and Richard.'

3 'Sue and Tony have already had my paella, but that's OK because I'm planning that for the party a fortnight later.'

4 'I'll do my famous boeuf bourguignon on the 10th.'

5 'I'll do roast lamb for Margaret and Jim.'

6 'I'll have a go at pheasant when Jan and Andy come.'

	Heather and Alan	Jane and Paul	Margaret and Jim	Sheila and Peter	Sue and Tony	Annie and Tom	Elaine and Robert	Jan and Andy	Jane and Richard	Pat and Ray	Boeuf bourguignon	Paella	Pheasant	Poached salmon	Roast lamb
3rd															
10th															
24th															
31st															
7th															
Boeuf bourg'n															
Paella															
Pheasant															
Poached salmon															
Roast lamb															
Annie and Tom															
Elaine and Robert															
Jan and Andy															
Jane and Richard															
Pat and Ray															

Date	First couple	Second couple	Main course

ON THE PISTE

Five families have arranged short winter break skiing holidays this year. Can you name the country each family will visit, say on which date their holiday starts, and work out how long it lasts?

Clues

1 The Terry family, whose holiday starts next after that of the family going to Austria, will spend one less day on the piste.

2 The Italian holiday starts immediately before the one due to last eight days.

3 The Bentleys will set off two days before the family heading for Norway.

4 The holiday which lasts just seven days will begin on 16th January.

5 The Robinsons are going away for a nine-day break.

6 The Nevilles will go skiing in the French Alps; they will not set off immediately before the Lonsdales, who will be the last of the five families to put on their skis and will be away longer than the family going to Norway.

	Austria	France	Italy	Norway	Switzerland	10th January	12th January	14th January	16th January	18th January	6 days	7 days	8 days	9 days	10 days
Bentley															
Lonsdale															
Neville															
Robinson															
Terry															
6 days															
7 days															
8 days															
9 days															
10 days															
10th January															
12th January															
14th January															
16th January															
18th January															

Family	Country	Date	Length of stay

HAT PARADE

The front pews on either side of the aisle in church at the carol concert were occupied by elderly ladies, each wearing a hat of a different colour. From the clues given below, can you name the lady in each of positions 1 to 8, and work out the respective colours of their hats?

Clues

1 Madge is sitting next to both the lady in the pink hat and the one wearing brown, the latter being in a position numbered either three higher or three lower than the position taken by the wearer of the white hat.

2 Polly is in the pew to the left of the aisle, and is sitting next to and left of the lady in the yellow hat.

3 Dorothy's position in the diagram has a lower number than Joyce's, the latter not being in a position corresponding with that of Polly in the other pew.

4 Lucy is in position 6; one of her immediate neighbours has a blue hat, while the green hat is worn by a lady in the pew on the other side of the aisle, who is seated next to Ellen.

5 Sarah, whose hat is beige, has an odd-numbered seat in her pew, in which she sits next to Winifred.

6 The black hat is on the head of the lady in seat 8.

Ladies:
Dorothy; Ellen; Joyce; Lucy; Madge; Polly; Sarah; Winifred

Hats:
Beige; black; blue; brown; green; pink; white; yellow

	Name	Hat			Name	Hat
1				5		
2				6		
3				7		
4				8		

Starting tip:

BATTLESHIPS

This puzzle is based on the old game of battleships. Your task is to find the vessels in the diagram. Some parts of boats or sea squares have already been filled in, and a number next to a row or column refers to the number of occupied squares in that row or column. The boats may be positioned horizontally or vertically, but no two boats or parts of boats are in adjacent squares – horizontally, vertically or diagonally.

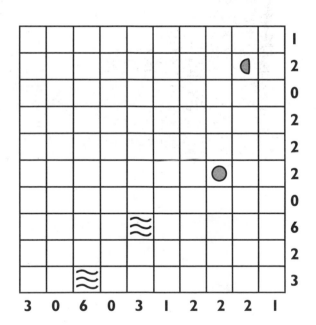

Aircraft Carrier:

Battleships:

Cruisers:

Destroyers:

LOGI-5

Every row across and column down should contain five letters: A, B, C, D and E, appearing once each. Also every shape (shown by the thick lines) must contain each of the letters A, B, C, D and E, appearing once each. Can you fill the grid?

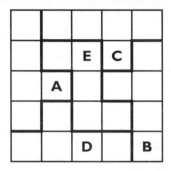

ABC

Every row across and column down is to have each of the letters A, B and C and two empty squares. The letter outside the grid shows the first or second letter in the direction of the arrow. Can you fill the grid?

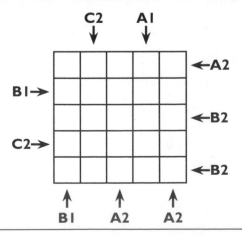

JOINT OPERATIONS

The nature of intelligence organisations being what it is, it's not unusual for an agent to be working with representatives of other friendly agencies. Britain's newest group MCIS-7 is currently running five operations jointly with Russia's CVRS, trying to recover former Soviet military hardware. Can you work out which MCIS-7 agent is involved in each operation, the name of his CVRS partner, and the city in which the operation is based?

Clues

1 Jeff Bruce has been assigned to Operation BARD.

2 Justin Bell is involved in the operation based in Budapest, Hungary.

3 One MCIS-7 agent is with Major Vera Luvina in Manila, capital of the Phillipines.

4 John Blake, who has been assigned to an operation with a five-letter codename, hasn't teamed up with CVRS agent Boris Monokov.

5 Both Operation NOMAD and that in which Olga Kozlova is involved are based in European cities.

6 Jack Booth and Yuri Sidrov are working together, but aren't the agents based in Oslo, Norway, who aren't involved in Operation SALVO.

7 Ivan Bykov is part of Operation TOGA, which isn't based in Havana, Cuba.

	Jack Booth	Jeff Bruce	Jeremy Bray	John Blake	Justin Bell	Boris Monokov	Ivan Bykov	Olga Kozlova	Vera Luvina	Yuri Sidrov	Budapest	Havana	Manila	Oslo	Tokyo
BARD															
ICON															
NOMAD															
SALVO															
TOGA															
Budapest															
Havana															
Manila															
Oslo															
Tokyo															
Boris Monokov															
Ivan Bykov															
Olga Kozlova															
Vera Luvina															
Yuri Sidrov															

Operation	MCIS-7 agent	CVRS agent	City

STATELY GARDENS

Five owners of stately homes open to the public have added new attractions to their grounds over the last few years. From the clues given below, can you match each pile with its owner and its new garden attraction, and say in which year the new feature was installed?

Clues

1 Lord Underdale's new attraction was viewed for the first time by the public two years after the one at Wilton Towers.

2 The knot garden was the brainchild of Lord Gleneaton.

3 The orangery was opened at a later date than the feature provided at Tinkerton Hall by the Marquess of Dunroamin.

4 The waterlily lake proved a success in attracting new visitors to Sunbury Castle, which isn't Sir Jeremy Wilson's seat.

5 Viscount Fetlocke provided his new feature the year before the cascades came on stream.

6 The Japanese garden was completed in 2001, but not for an owner whose title was simply 'Lord'.

7 The grounds at Fullwell House were embellished in the year 2000.

	Lord Gleneaton	Lord Underdale	Marq of Dunroamin	Sir Jeremy Wilson	Viscount Fetlocke	Cascades	Japanese garden	Knot garden	Orangery	Waterlily lake	1998	1999	2000	2001	2002
Fullwell House															
Moatbridge Manor															
Sunbury Castle															
Tinkerton Hall															
Wilton Towers															
1998															
1999															
2000															
2001															
2002															
Cascades															
Japanese garden															
Knot garden															
Orangery															
Waterlily lake															

House	Owner	Feature	Year

LUCKY WINNERS

At the grand Agricultural Show last summer, raffle tickets from books of several different colours were on sale, and by chance, the five main prizes were all won by different coloured tickets. From the clues given below, can you name the winner of each prize in the draw, say what colour each winner's ticket was, and work out which number it bore?

Clues

1 Mr Vernon's number was called out earlier than that on the yellow ticket, which was a lower one.

2 'On the green ticket, number 293', announced the master of ceremonies when one of the tickets had just been drawn.

3 Mr Marchant's ticket bore the number 615.

4 The third number to be drawn was 508, which wasn't on a pink ticket.

5 Mrs Evans had bought a strip of white tickets, one of which won her a prize.

6 The winner of the fifth prize in the raffle wasn't Miss Ryder.

7 A blue ticket won its purchaser the fourth prize. Its number was lower than the one which carried off the first prize.

	Mrs Evans	Mrs Harkness	Mr Marchant	Miss Ryder	Mr Vernon	Blue	Green	Pink	White	Yellow	293	337	472	508	615
First															
Second															
Third															
Fourth															
Fifth															
293															
337															
472															
508															
615															
Blue															
Green															
Pink															
White															
Yellow															

Prize	Winner	Colour	Number

JACK THE LAD

Jack Ladd has a busy social diary, having reached a position where he's simultaneously dating five girls, each of whom is unaware of the existence of the other four. On different days last week he was out walking with one of the five when he spotted one of the others approaching, and took the required evasive action, taking his baffled companion with him. From the clues given below, can you work out the full details?

Clues

1 Jack had no contact whatever with Wendy on Monday last week.

2 Annabel was suddenly swept into a pub by Jack as he tried to avoid another girl seeing him; this was the day before he caught sight of Stella in a crowded street.

3 Jack was with Caroline only the day before he was horrified to see her approaching in the distance.

4 It wasn't while he was walking with Stella that Jack made the swift about turn.

5 Jack's sudden decision to cross the road in front of a stream of oncoming traffic was made to avoid Wendy seeing him escorting another girl (not Stella).

6 Paula was with Jack when he had to take evasive action to prevent her being sighted by Annabel.

7 Jack darted into a shop on Thursday, making a rather feeble excuse to his companion.

	Annabel	Caroline	Paula	Stella	Wendy	Annabel	Caroline	Paula	Stella	Wendy	Crossed road	Darted in shop	Dashed in pub	Leapt on to bus	Swift about turn
Monday															
Tuesday															
Thursday															
Friday															
Saturday															
Crossed road															
Darted in shop															
Dashed in pub															
Leapt on to bus															
Swift about turn															
Annabel															
Caroline															
Paula															
Stella															
Wendy															

Day	With	Saw	Action

NOVEMBER NIGHT OUT

Five boys from the same class at St Guido's School in the suburb of Fawkeston each went to a firework display on the evening of November 5th – a different display, at a different location and starting at a different time. From the clues given below, can you work out whose display each boy attended, the location's street address and its starting time?

Clues

1 Alan Bush stayed at home and attended the display put on by his family.

2 The display which took place in Tresham Walk began at 8.00pm.

3 The Community Centre in Fawkeston is a long way from Catesby Road.

4 The display in Bates Lane started thirty minutes before the one attended by Joey Keene and thirty minutes after the one at the stadium of the local football club.

5 Wayne York went to the display in Winter Hill, which started thirty minutes before the one at the King's Head to which one of the boys was taken by his mum and dad.

6 The Cubs of the Fawkeston 3rd Scout Group put on the first display to start.

7 Chris Day didn't go to the display which started at 7.30pm.

	Community Centre	Cubs	Football club	Home	King's Head	Bates Lane	Catesby Road	Percy Drive	Tresham Walk	Winter Hill	7.00pm	7.30pm	8.00pm	8.30pm	9.00pm
Alan Bush															
Chris Day															
Joey Keene															
Ricky Salt															
Wayne York															
7.00pm															
7.30pm															
8.00pm															
8.30pm															
9.00pm															
Bates Lane															
Catesby Road															
Percy Drive															
Tresham Walk															
Winter Hill															

Name	Location	Address	Starting time

ON SCREEN

In each of their bedrooms in the family home, four siblings are using their TV screens for different activities. From the clues given below, can you say who has each of bedrooms 1 to 4, and work out their respective ages, and the purpose to which each screen is being devoted?

Clues

1 The door of Alicia's room is directly opposite that of her sibling who is watching sport on television.

2 Marcus is two years younger than his sibling who is avidly surfing the internet.

3 Jennifer, who is 13, has an even-numbered bedroom on the plan.

4 The youngest child of the family is watching a favourite video.

5 Someone is watching a film on television in bedroom 3; this person is younger than Tim.

6 The person in room 1 is older than the one in room 2.

Names:
Alicia; Jennifer; Marcus; Tim

Ages:
9; 11; 13; 15

Activities:
Internet; TV film; TV sport; video

1

Name: _____

Age: _____

Activity: _____

2

_____

_____

_____

4

Name: _____

Age: _____

Activity: _____

3

_____

_____

_____

Starting tip:

First work out the age of the child in room 3.

COVER GIRLS

Storbury Council publishes a quarterly booklet, distributed to all the houses in the town. Each issue has a picture of a local celebrity on the cover; and this year's happen all to have been female (although to call them 'cover girls' would be an insult to their maturity – although it does make quite a nice title, doesn't it?). Can you work out the full name and occupation of the woman featured on each issue of this year's booklets?

Clues

1 Louise and the traffic warden who works around the centre of Storbury (but who didn't appear on the front cover of the July booklet) both featured on covers in the same half of the year. The July cover didn't feature Ms Crabtree.

2 The January booklet featured a picture of Ms Sharp.

3 Caroline, whose picture appeared on the April booklet, has a surname one letter longer than that of the charity worker who was on the front of the October booklet.

4 The teacher appeared on an earlier issue of the booklet than the mayoress. The other woman whose photograph appeared on the booklet cover in the same half of the year as that of the mayoress isn't Julia.

	Caroline	Helen	Julia	Louise	Crabtree	Forman	Marsden	Sharp	Charity worker	Mayoress	Teacher	Traffic warden
January												
April												
July												
October												
Charity worker												
Mayoress												
Teacher												
Traffic warden												
Crabtree												
Forman												
Marsden												
Sharp												

Month	Forename	Surname	Occupation

LOOKS FAMILIAR

Five people work for a 'lookalike' agency and, on Saturday, each had an engagement at an opening ceremony. From the following information, can you discover which famous person each looks like, the time of their engagement and what each opened in the guise of their character?

Clues

1 Imogen Spitton opened the village fête, which was later in the day than Bess Mimwick's engagement.

2 Bess Mimwick doesn't look like Baroness Thatcher, and neither Baroness Thatcher nor Madonna was the lookalike celebrity who opened the charity football match at 12.30pm.

3 Madonna neither appeared at 1 o'clock nor was she the celebrity who opened the supermarket (not at 1 o'clock).

4 Marilyn Monroe's engagement was an hour later than the opening of the village hall.

5 Arthur Fishall looks like Prince Charles. Isla Fakenham assumed her lookalike identity for the 1.30pm opening.

6 Liza Minnelli's appearance was at 2.30pm.

	Baroness Thatcher	Liza Minnelli	Madonna	Marilyn Monroe	Prince Charles	12.30	1.00	1.30	2.00	2.30	Charity football	Sport shop	Supermarket	Village fête	Village hall
Arthur Fishall															
Bess Mimwick															
Carrie Cature															
Imogen Spitton															
Isla Fakenham															
Charity football											
Sports shop											
Supermarket											
Village fête											
Village hall											
12.30					
1.00					
1.30					
2.00					
2.30					

Name	Lookalike	Time	Opening

TRANSPORTS OF DELIGHT

This is the slow season for the Wheelwright's Farm Transport Museum and the owners are taking advantage of the fact to purchase, refurbish and install five new exhibits, all built in different parts of England. From the clues, can you work out the name of each new exhibit, what it is, and where and when it was built?

Clues

1 One exhibit (not the traction engine) was built in Hertford in 1881.

2 The narrowboat Unity was built seven years after one of the other exhibits was constructed in Doncaster.

3 Minerva was built in Ipswich.

4 The fishing boat, which will join the other vessels moored on the lake at Wheelwright's Farm, was built in Brixham.

5 The locomotive, which is not called Pegasus, dates from 1895.

6 Galahad was built in 1909.

	Fishing boat	Horse-bus	Locomotive	Narrowboat	Traction engine	Brixham	Doncaster	Hertford	Ipswich	Nantwich	1881	1888	1895	1902	1909
Amazon															
Galahad															
Minerva															
Pegasus															
Unity															
1881															
1888															
1895															
1902															
1909															
Brixham															
Doncaster															
Hertford															
Ipswich															
Nantwich															

Name	Exhibit	Place built	Date built

THEATRICAL DIGS

In the golden days of travelling theatre, five distinguished thespians have digs with Mrs Drarmer. From the following information, can you discover at which theatre each is appearing, the kind of production, and the number of weeks each will be staying?

Clues

1 Kirton Cawles is appearing in a comedy, and will be staying with Mrs Drarmer for fewer weeks than the actor who is on at the Queen's Theatre.

2 Bill Topper, who is not in the whodunnit, has a room for three weeks. The actor in the whodunnit will not be staying for as long as Treadwell Boards.

3 Will Hammett is not in the four-week run. Barnes Tormer is appearing at the Empire Theatre.

4 The J B Priestley play is having the shortest run, but not at the Palace.

5 The five-week run is at the Hippodrome.

6 The variety show is on at the Albion Theatre.

	Albion	Empire	Hippodrome	Palace	Queen's	2 weeks	3 weeks	4 weeks	5 weeks	6 weeks	Comedy	J B Priestley	Shakespeare	Variety	Whodunnit
Barnes Tormer															
Bill Topper															
Kirton Cawles															
Treadwell Boards															
Will Hammett															
Comedy											
J B Priestley											
Shakespeare											
Variety											
Whodunnit											
2 weeks						
3 weeks						
4 weeks						
5 weeks						
6 weeks						

Actor	Theatre	Weeks	Production

A CROP OF PIMPERNELS

Of course, pimpernels are wild flowers, so you don't actually get crops of them, but this problem refers to the League of the Scarlet Pimpernel, a body of noble Englishmen who saved so many French 'aristos' from the guillotine during the French Revolution. Can you work out in which city each aristocrat was rescued, the description the authorities had of the rescuer and the name of the League member hidden behind that guise?

Clues

1 Sir John Merton didn't carry out a rescue in Paris.

2 Lord Geraldin adopted the guise of a drunken, filthy tramp to free one prisoner.

3 Lord Bidmore effected the escape of an aristocrat (not a Comte) from Falaise.

4 The man who saved the Vicomtesse d'Elbes wasn't disguised as a labourer.

5 It wasn't in Rennes that the Comte de Passy was taken away for 'questioning about his treasonous activities' by an Englishman posing as an officer of the revolutionary army.

6 The Chevalier de Sauverne was saved from execution in Lille. The Marquis de St Menard was freed by the Hon Jack Hallam, but wasn't the aristocrat liberated from Amiens prison by an 'old lady' who was, of course, a League member in disguise.

	Amiens	Falaise	Lille	Paris	Rennes	Army officer	Chimney sweep	Drunken tramp	Labourer	Old lady	Hon Jack Hallam	Lord Bidmore	Lord Geraldin	Sir John Merton	Sir Simon Bolt
Chevalier de Sauverne															
Comte de la Roche															
Comte de Passy															
Marquis de St Menard															
Vicomtesse d'Elbes															
Hon Jack Hallam											
Lord Bidmore											
Lord Geraldin											
Sir John Merton											
Sir Simon Bolt											
Army officer									
Chimney sweep									
Drunken tramp									
Labourer									
Old lady									

Aristocrat	City	Description	Rescuer

FOLK CLUB

Five performers appeared at the folk club last night. From the following information can you discover the order in which each went on stage, the title of the tune he performed, and the instrument he played or with which he accompanied himself?

Clues

1 First up wasn't accordionist Danny Lane, and the second performer didn't give us Sweet Susannah.

2 Third on stage was Ralph Oakes, and he was followed by a pianist who sang a song containing a girl's name that was longer than the name in the title of the song sung by the guitarist.

3 Jake Field didn't sing Sweet Susannah.

4 The song entitled Lady Sarah wasn't performed on the tin whistle.

5 Toby Straw gave us Heloise the Milkmaid immediately before Willy Hedges sang.

6 Bridget Be Mine was performed on the Irish bagpipes immediately before Jake Field's song.

	Danny Lane	Jake Field	Ralph Oakes	Toby Straw	Willy Hedges	Bridget Be Mine	Heloise the Milkmaid	Lady Sarah	Queen Guinevere	Sweet Susannah	Accordion	Guitar	Irish bagpipes	Piano	Tin whistle
First															
Second															
Third															
Fourth															
Fifth															
Accordion															
Guitar															
Irish bagpipes															
Piano															
Tin whistle															
Bridget Be Mine															
Heloise the Milkmaid															
Lady Sarah															
Queen Guinevere															
Sweet Susannah															

Order	Singer	Title	Instrument

CALLING ALL CARS

During the early hours of the morning five police cars dealt with five different incidents. From the information given below, can you work out where each car was sent, the name of the PC driving it, the time, and the nature of the incident?

Clues

1 At half past midnight there was a traffic accident, but it wasn't in Parkway and PC Collarfield wasn't called to the scene; he also did not attend the Parkway incident.

2 The incident at 01.20 wasn't the assault that PC Custerdy dealt with.

3 An hour later, at 02.20, one of the cars went to Queen Square.

4 PC Cawtion answered the 3 o'clock call.

5 PC Cuffham went to Station Street more than 1hr 10min after the domestic incident.

6 The break-in was in Blackbird Lane.

	Blackbird Lane	London Road	Parkway	Queen Square	Station Street	00.30	01.20	02.20	03.00	04.30	Assault	Break-in	Disturbance	Domestic	Traffic accident
PC Cawtion															
PC Collarfield															
PC Coppall															
PC Cuffham															
PC Custerdy															
Assault											
Break-in											
Disturbance											
Domestic											
Traffic accident											
00.30						
01.20						
02.20						
03.00						
04.30						

Constable	Location	Time	Incident

LOGI-PATH

Use your deductive reasoning to form a pathway from the box marked 'START' to the box marked 'FINISH', moving either horizontally or vertically (but not diagonally) from square to adjacent square. The number at the beginning of every row or column indicates exactly how many boxes in that row or column your pathway must pass through. The small diagram at the bottom of the page is given as an example of how it works.

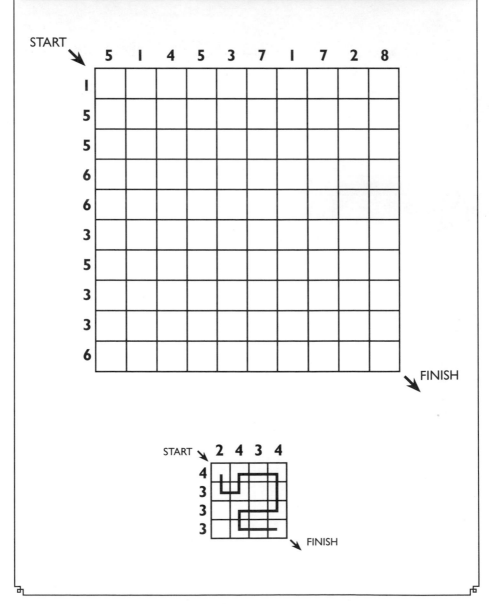

MAKING THE GRADES

My daughter and four of her friends are off to university this autumn, having each attained the necessary grades for their chosen courses. From the following information, can you discover which grades each student required, their chosen course, and the university each will be attending?

Clues

1 Liz didn't need to get ABB or CCC; the ABB requirement is neither for the Philosophy course at Lernham nor the Studiard University course.

2 Helen is going to Knolledge University; she is not the English student, who didn't need to get CCC and will not be attending Traynham or Reedmoor Universities.

3 The Reedmoor student required BCC, but her chosen course is not Physics.

4 Zoe got her required three Bs.

5 BBC grades have enabled one of the students to read Modern Languages.

6 Cathy will be studying Music.

	ABB	BBB	BBC	BCC	CCC	English	Modern languages	Music	Philosophy	Physics	Knolledge	Lernham	Reedmoor	Studiard	Traynham
Cathy															
Helen															
Liz															
Samantha															
Zoe															
Knolledge															
Lernham															
Reedmoor															
Studiard															
Traynham															
English															
Modern languages															
Music															
Philosophy															
Physics															

Student	A-level grades	Course	University

PILE UP

These piles of bricks aren't the random results of a child's play but clues to a final, at present blank, pile on the right. Like the rest, that one has six bricks each with a different one of the six letters.

The numbers below the heaps tell you two things:

(a) The number of adjacent pairs of bricks in that column which also appear adjacent in the final pile.

(b) The number of adjacent pairs of bricks that make a correct pair but the wrong way up.

So:

would score one in the 'Correct' row if the final heap had an A directly above a C and a one in the 'Reversed' row if the final heap had a C on top of an A. From all this, can you create the final pile before it topples?

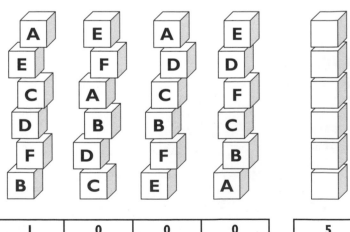

Correct	1	0	0	0		5
Reversed	0	0	2	2		0

FRIENDS & NEIGHBOURS

Four women who live in neighbouring streets have known each other for many years. From the clues given below, can you fully identify the woman who lives in each of the houses numbered 1 to 4 on the street plan, and work out the name of the street in which each friend lives?

Clues

1 Joan lives in the next house south of that occupied by her friend in Chestnut Road, which is not the address where house 3 is located.

2 Mrs Adams lives in Union Street, which is further north than the street where Mrs Green lives.

3 Mrs Skinner's street runs eastwards from the main road, but Marion's runs west; the latter is not Mrs Gilbert.

4 The house in Nelson Street is the one numbered 2 on the plan; neither Lily nor her best friend lives there, the latter living further south than the former.

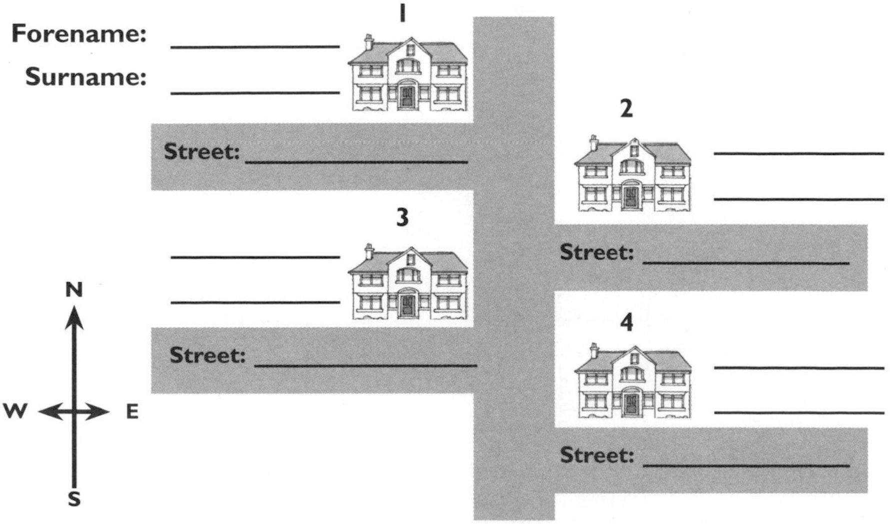

Forenames:
Chloë; Joan; Lily; Marion

Surnames:
Adams; Gilbert; Green; Skinner

Streets:
Chestnut Road; Melbourne Avenue; Nelson Street; Union Street

Forename: _____

Surname: _____

1

Street: _____

2

_____

Street: _____

3

_____

_____

Street: _____

4

_____

Street: _____

N

W ← → E

S

Starting tip:

Begin by naming the street where house 4 stands.

QED

The PLC-Mega Corporation has five main subsidiaries, located in different towns, each with its own specialist product and its own board of directors, a different number in each case. From the clues given below, can you work out the full details?

Clues

1 There are fewer directors on the board of the company based in Stockport than there are running HJK, but more than on the board of the textiles firm.

2 The makers of farm equipment operate from Cardiff.

3 VRC is not the firm located in Walsall; four directors sit on the board of the machine tools company.

4 The earthmovers are made by a firm with a smaller board of directors than the company based in Mansfield.

5 The six-man board meets in Derby.

6 The chemicals firm has fewer directors than QLH.

7 MDE is the company whose board of directors consists of eight members.

	Cardiff	Derby	Mansfield	Stockport	Walsall	Chemicals	Earthmovers	Farm equipment	Machine tools	Textiles	4	6	8	10	12
BGN															
HJK															
MDE															
QLH															
VRC															
4											
6											
8											
10											
12											
Chemicals						
Earthmovers						
Farm equipment						
Machine tools						
Textiles						

Firm	Location	Product	No on board

INVASION CANCELLED

An alien race, the Xbloing, decided to invade Earth and sent five scouts ahead to take over the bodies of natives for a few days and spy out the land. They landed in Britain and, after they reported back, the Xbloing decided not to bother and headed off elsewhere! Can you work out where each alien scout landed, and the name and occupation of the local earthperson it took over to do its scouting?

Clues

1 Xpj'ioz was dropped by flying saucer on the outskirts of Solihull and made its way into the town to find a victim; Diane Sims was taken over by the Xbloing scout who landed in Port Talbot.

2 Qdh'adv took over the body of Richard Frazier: his friend (who made the traffic warden its victim) is neither Bdr'aal, who didn't land in Wimbledon, nor Ghl'uik.

3 Knp'eoc took over the body of a male bus-driver.

4 Estate agent Seymour Griffiths was taken over by one of the alien scouts, but not Ghl'uik.

5 The aliens' victim in Wimbledon was neither Richard Frazier nor the fast food cook; the civil servant who was taken over by one of the Xbloing wasn't from Oldham.

	Gateshead	Oldham	Port Talbot	Solihull	Wimbledon	Diane Sims	Karen Wainwright	Paul Metcalfe	Richard Frazier	Seymour Griffiths	Bus-driver	Civil servant	Estate agent	Fast food cook	Traffic warden
Bdr'aal															
Ghl'uik															
Knp'eoc															
Qdh'adv															
Xpj'ioz															
Bus-driver															
Civil servant															
Estate agent															
Fast food cook															
Traffic warden															
Diane Sims															
Karen Wainwright															
Paul Metcalfe															
Richard Frazier															
Seymour Griffiths															

Alien	Town	Victim	Occupation

DAY-TRIPPERS

Back in the summer Mr and Mrs Borden took a cruise on the waterways of Holland. On Wednesday their vessel tied up at Groothaven, and on Thursday the Bordens passengers were given their choice of seven day-trips by coach to nearby places of interest. From the clues below, can you work out the details of each trip – the town or village to which it was going, and the particular feature that was to be visited there?

Clues

1 The trip to the giant craft market at Slechtfoort (where you could actually watch a clog-maker at work before buying his products) was indicated by an odd number on the list.

2 The windmill museum, which has probably the largest collection of windmills in the world, is not at Zachteveld.

3 The trip to the shopping centre (called, interestingly, a winkelwijk in Dutch) was numbered two higher than the one to Houdenwijk.

4 If you add together the number of the trip that went to the world-famous zoo and the (lower) number of the trip that visited Bochtingen, you'll end up with the number of the trip to Bushalteborg.

5 Trip number 1 went to Verkeerhoven, which is not the location of the botanical gardens where the Bordens saw, perhaps unsurprisingly, an awful lot of tulips.

6 Trip number 5, which didn't go anywhere near Rijdendoorn, visited a museum.

7 The barge museum, which has probably the world's largest collection of barges, was visited by trip number 7.

Places:
Bochtingen;
Bushalteborg;
Houdenwijk;
Rijdendoorn;
Slechtfoort;
Verkeerhoven;
Zachteveld

Features:
Barge museum;
botanical gardens;
cheese museum;
craft market;
shopping centre;
windmill museum;
zoo

	Place	Feature
1		
2		
3		
4		
5		
6		
7		

Starting tip:
Decide which excursion was to Slechtfoort.

SOLUTIONS

At the Races (No 1)

Ben is Farley (clue 3), so John, who isn't Richmond (clue 1), is Watson, who backed Horseshoe Falls (clue 2), and, by elimination, Richmond is Leo. Horseshoe Falls cannot have run at 4.30 (clue 1) and Lucky Jim was the winner of the 3.30 race (clue 4), so Horseshoe Falls won the 4 o'clock race and Four-leafed Clover won the 4.30. From clue 1, this was Leo Richmond's winner, so, by elimination, Ben Farley backed Lucky Jim in the 3.30.

In summary:

Ben Farley, 3.30, Lucky Jim.
John Watson, 4.00, Horseshoe Falls.
Leo Richmond, 4.30, Four-leafed Clover.

Nurses (No 2)

The nurse on Anderson qualified in 2000 (clue 4), so the one who qualified in 1998, who isn't on Blackwood (clue 3), is on Nightingale and is thus Ann Bowles (clue 1). By elimination, the nurse on Blackwood qualified in 1996, in London (clue 2). Pam Raynes didn't qualify in 1996 (clue 4), so in 2000. Pam Raynes didn't qualify in London (clue 2) so (clue 4) in Cardiff and Ann Bowles qualified in Glasgow. By elimination, Gail Hart trained in London.

In summary:

Ann Bowles, Glasgow, 1998, Nightingale.
Gail Hart, London, 1996, Blackwood.
Pam Raynes, Cardiff, 2000, Anderson.

Sons of Storbury (No 3)

Catchpole is buried in Dublin and the soldier on Cape Cod (clue 3), so Lambkin the cartographer, whose grave isn't in Alexandria (clue 1), is buried in St Malo and was thus Abel (clue 4). Thus the painter was Edmund and the ship's captain was Gilbert (clue 2), leaving Christopher as the soldier. We know he isn't Catchpole or Lambkin and clue 2 tells us he wasn't Saward, so he was Parfitt. Catchpole wasn't Edmund (clue 3), so he was Gilbert the ship's captain, and (by elimination) Saward was Edmund, the painter, who, by elimination, is buried in Alexandria.

In summary:

Abel Lambkin, cartographer, St Malo.
Christopher Parfitt, soldier, Cape Cod.
Edmund Saward, painter, Alexandria.
Gilbert Catchpole, ship's captain, Dublin.

Four Card Gamble (No 4)

Kay Jones worked in Kitchenware (clue 2), the girl in Shoes got the card with the roses (clue 2) and the girl in Sports got the card signed 'Your secret lover' (clue 3), so the Miss Brown who got the card with the champagne which was signed 'Mystery Man' (clue 4) worked in Lingerie. She wasn't Ann Brown, whose card was signed 'Mr X'

(clue 1), so she was Zoë Brown. We now know a name or department to go with three signatures, so Kay Jones from Kitchenware received the one signed 'Your secret admirer'. Thus it didn't show the hearts (clue 5). Her department tells us it didn't show roses and the signature tells us it didn't show champagne, so the picture was lovebirds. By elimination, the girl in Shoes received the card signed 'Mr X', so was Ann Brown; thus the girl from Sports was Sue Smith, whose card showed hearts.

In summary:

Ann Brown, Shoes, roses, 'Mr X'.
Kay Jones, Kitchenware, lovebirds, 'Your secret admirer'.
Sue Smith, Sports, hearts, 'Your secret lover'.
Zoë Brown, Lingerie, champagne, 'Mystery Man'.

Meeting the People (No 5)

Ava's 4.00pm speech in Farewell (clue 4) can't have been to the parish councillors (clue 3) and neither were they the audience at Touchwood Village Hall (clue 3). She spoke at Luce End to the farmers (clue 2), so Ava talked to the parish councillors in Runndown. By elimination, her 4.00pm talk in Farewell was in the Tithe Barn, to the parents (clue 1) and her talk in Touchwood Village Hall was to shop owners. We know the latter wasn't at 4.00pm, so the talk to the parish councillors in Runndown can't have been at 2.00pm (clue 3) or 12.00 noon (clue 4), so it was at 10.00am and thus (clue 3) Ava was at Touchwood at 12.00 noon. By elimination, the Luce End talk to the farmers was at 2.00pm, not in St Mark's School (clue 2), so in the Church Hall and St Mark's School was the venue in Runndown.

In summary:

10.00am, Runndown, St Mark's School, parish councillors.
12.00 noon, Touchwood, Village Hall, shop owners.
2.00pm, Luce End, Church Hall, farmers.
4.00pm, Farewell, Tithe Barn, parents.

Eyewitnesses (No 6)

The arson case is being dealt with at desk D (clue 6) and detective Tucci is at desk F (clue 2), so clue 4 rules out desks A, C, E and F for the bank robbery witness who is thus Alma LaFarge at desk B (clue 7). Now, from clue 4, the mugging witness is at desk A and Kravitz at desk C. We now know either the detective or the crime for five desks, so McManus, who's dealing with the car theft witness (clue 3), is at desk E. Thus, from clue 3, Sorvino and Elmer Smith, who we know aren't at desk B or C, is at desk A, talking about the mugging and, from the same clue, Sam Dominici, the assault witness, is with Kravitz

SOLUTIONS

at desk C. By elimination, the fraud witness is with Tucci at desk F, so, from clue 5, McManus' car theft witness at E is Jack Fernandez. The detective on the arson case isn't Eckler (clue 6), so is Grant, leaving Eckler talking to Alma LaFarge at desk B. Finally, Grant isn't talking to Jane Murphy (clue 1), so is taking Ned Ogorzov's statement, leaving Jane Murphy talking to Tucci about the fraud at desk F.

In summary:
A, Sorvino, Elmer Smith, mugging.
B, Eckler, Alma LaFarge, bank robbery.
C, Kravitz, Sam Dominici, assault.
D, Grant, Ned Ogorzov, arson.
E, McManus, Jack Fernandez, car theft.
F, Tucci, Jane Murphy, fraud.

Deep Phil (No 7)

The malted multi-grain sandwiches contain tomato, but neither ham nor chicken (clue 5), nor do they contain smoked salmon, which is in the soft rolls (clue 2), or tuna, which is accompanied by lettuce (clue 6), so they contain egg. The service station owner has ordered 10 ham snacks (clue 4), so the wholemeal bread sandwiches are not the six sandwiches containing avocado (clue 3) and the avocado are not on crusty white or malted multi-grain bread, so they are the baguettes. We know that these do not contain ham, egg, tuna or smoked salmon, so chicken. The soft rolls do not contain chutney (clue 2) or lettuce (clue 6), so cucumber, leaving the chutney as accompanying the ham sandwiches. There are 12 soft rolls (clue 2) and, from clue 1, 10 wholemeal and 14 egg. Thus the wholemeal sandwiches are ham and chutney and, by elimination, there are eight with tuna and lettuce on crusty white bread.

In summary:
6 baguettes, chicken and avocado.
8 crusty white, tuna and lettuce.
10 wholemeal, ham and chutney.
12 soft rolls, smoked salmon and cucumber.
14 malted multi-grain, egg and tomato.

On the Scent (No 8)

D Klein's perfume is 'Sapphire' (clue 5). Bacque D'Or's scent is neither 'Spirit', 'Impetuous' nor 'Dawn' (clue 3), so it's 'Time'. The perfume being promoted in Rackworths is 'Impetuous' (clue 4), but this isn't the scent from D Klein, Bacque D'Or, Fray Grant, which is being sampled at Mark Evans (clue 6), or Villa Roma (clue 4), so it's the Shamelle fragrance being demonstrated by Carla (clue 6). Maggie is working in Harridges (clue 1) and since Ingrid isn't in John Harvey or Lewishams, she is demonstrating the Fray Grant perfume in Mark Evans. This scent isn't

'Sapphire', 'Time', 'Impetuous' or 'Dawn', being demonstrated by Rachel (clue 3), so it's 'Spirit'. By elimination, Rachel is demonstrating the Villa Roma perfume. Since the one being promoted in John Harvey isn't 'Spirit' by Fray Grant or the D Klein scent (clue 2), it's Rachel's Villa Roma product. The Bacque D'Or scent isn't being promoted in Lewishams (clue 3), so it's Maggie's in Harridges, and, by elimination, Jan is the demonstrator in Lewishams, brandishing a bottle of 'Sapphire'.

In summary:
Carla, Rackworths, Shamelle, 'Impetuous'.
Ingrid, Mark Evans, Fray Grant, 'Spirit'.
Jan, Lewishams, D Klein, 'Sapphire'.
Maggie, Harridges, Bacque D'Or, 'Time'.
Rachel, John Harvey, Villa Roma, 'Dawn'.

I'm a Celebrity... (No 9)

Warren Asbean was a footballer (clue 1) and Miles Older is the prank show host-to-be (clue 4), so the former TV cook, who will be presenting a new chat show, who isn't Stella Eusterby or Willy Cwmbach (clue 2), is Hugh Wozzey. His new show isn't due to be screened from May (clue 3), April, which is when Willy Cwmbach will be seen again (clue 1), January, when the makeover show starts (clue 5), or February, the month when the former DJ gets his or her new show (clue 6), so it's March. Willy Cwmbach isn't the former magician (clue 1), so he must once have been a well-known newsreader. Thus his new opportunity isn't the chat show, the makeover show or the prank show, or the celebrity secrets show (clue 3), so Willy is hosting April's new game show. May's new show isn't about celebrity secrets (clue 3), so it's Miles Older's prank show. By elimination, the celebrity secrets show is earmarked for the former DJ in February. The DJ isn't footballer Warren Asbean, so by elimination is Stella Eusterby. Thus Warren Asbean is the host of January's makeover show and Miles Older is the once well-known magician.

In summary:
January, Warren Asbean, footballer, makeover show.
February, Stella Eusterby, DJ, celebrity secrets.
March, Hugh Wozzey, TV cook, chat show.
April, Willy Cwmbach, newsreader, game show.
May, Miles Older, magician, prank show.

Conservat-ive Estimates (No 10)

The 6x10 conservatory has been ordered by a woman (clue 4), but it isn't Mrs Clifton's 8ft-wide one (clue 3), so it's Mrs Knox's. The Florida conservatory will be 9x14 (clue 6) and Mr Deacon has ordered the 8x11 (clue 1), so Mr Eaton's Buckingham, which isn't 8x10 (clue 1), is

8x12 and thus will cost him £10,000 (clue 2). Mrs Clifton isn't buying the 9x14 conservatory (clue 3), so it's the 8x10 one, leaving Mr Griffin as the purchaser of the 9x14 Florida, for which he will pay £9,000 (clue 2). We know that the £8,000 Ashridge isn't the 6x10 or 8x10 conservatory (clue 3), so it's the 8x11 and was ordered by Mr Deacon. Mrs Clifton isn't paying £7,000 for her conservatory (clue 3), so it's £6,000, leaving £7,000 as Mrs Knox's bill for her 6x10 conservatory. Finally, Mrs Clifton isn't paying £6,000 for an Aurora conservatory (clue 5), so it's the Goldcrest and Mrs Knox bought the Aurora.

In summary:
Mrs Clifton, Goldcrest, 8x10, £6,000.
Mr Deacon, Ashridge, 8x11, £8,000.
Mr Eaton, Buckingham, 8x12, £10,000.
Mr Griffin, Florida, 9x14, £9,000.
Mrs Knox, Aurora, 6x10, £7,000.

Something About a Sailor ... (No 11)
Parcel D's from Archie (clue 2), so parcel E can't be Glen's with the bracelet or Jim's (clue 6). Nor is it the parcel from Ray on Sentinel (clue 7), so it's Tony's gift. Thus (clue 5) the chocolates from the man on Greyhound is parcel D. Parcel C holds perfume (clue 3). Parcel A can't contain lingerie or earrings (clue 1), so the bracelet. Thus (clue 6) parcel B is from Jim, who is serving on Adamant (clue 4). By elimination, the parcel from Ray is C. From clue 2, the man on Osprey is Tony, and, by elimination, Glen, who sent parcel A is on Pendragon. Finally, from clue 1, the lingerie is in parcel B and E contains earrings.

In summary:
A, Glen, Pendragon, bracelet.
B, Jim, Adamant, lingerie.
C, Ray, Sentinel, perfume.
D, Archie, Greyhound, chocolates.
E, Tony, Osprey, earrings.

The Likely Lairds (No 12)
The Duke of Carndale's estate covers 20,000 acres (clue 1). The 12,000-acre deer-farming estate isn't that of Lord Roskill, the Earl of Brora (clue 2) or Lord Calvie (clue 5), so it's the Earl of Kilbrae's, whose estate is Kilbrae (clue 1). The salmon-fishing estate is either 14,000 or 16,000 acres (clue 5), but as the Duke of Carndale owns 20,000 acres, Lord Calvie's estate is 18,000 acres and the salmon-fishing estate is 14,000. The latter's owner isn't Lord Roskill (clue 2), so it's the Earl of Brora. By elimination, the 16,000-acre Invercarn estate (clue 6) is owned by Lord Roskill. It's main income isn't from forestry (clue 3), or agriculture, which is Balnaloch (clue 4), so tourism. As Glenkinnon isn't the Earl of Brora's (clue 2), it isn't 14,000 acres. Invercarn is smaller

than Balnaloch (clue 4), so it's 18,000 acres of forestry. Thus Balnaloch is the 20,000-acre agricultural estate (clue 4). By elimination, the Earl of Brora's estate is Strathbeag.

In summary:
Balnaloch, Duke of Carndale, 20,000 acres, agriculture.
Glenkinnon, Lord Calvie, 18,000 acres, forestry.
Invercarn, Lord Roskill, 16,000 acres, tourism.
Kilbrae, Earl of Kilbrae, 12,000 acres, deer-farming.
Strathbeag, Earl of Brora, 14,000 acres, salmon-fishing.

Surprise! (No 13)
Someone's mother is organising the 40th birthday treat (clue 2), so the person for whom a brother is organising a surprise, who isn't 50, 70 or 100 (clue 4) is celebrating a 60th birthday and is thus Barry (clue 6). The person being taken to the West End show is celebrating a 70th birthday (clue 4). Margaret, who is 30 years older than the person being taken for the family meal (clue 1), cannot be 100, so her daughter is marking her mother's 70th birthday. Also from clue 1, the 40-year-old is having the family meal. Eileen is going on a balloon flight (clue 3) and the flight on Concorde is being organised by somebody's nephew (clue 5), so Barry's brother is setting up the steam loco driving treat. By elimination, Eileen's balloon flight is being arranged by her husband. The nephew isn't marking a 50th birthday (clue 5), so his 100th, leaving the 50th birthday as Eileen's. The 40th birthday treat being arranged by somebody's mother isn't for Charles (clue 2), so Mike, leaving Charles as the person being taken on Concorde.

In summary:
Brother, Barry, steam loco driving, 60.
Daughter, Margaret, West End show, 70.
Husband, Eileen, balloon flight, 50.
Mother, Mike, family meal, 40.
Nephew, Charles, flight on Concorde, 100.

Reassigned (No 14)
Room 103 was the Foreign Secretary's (clue 6), so, from clue 1, the Minister of Supply's room, now used by Mr Edkins, is Room 107 and Room 108 houses the person in charge of light bulbs. We know Room 108 wasn't meant for the Foreign Secretary or the Minister of Supply, nor can it have been the Prime Minister's (clue 3), or the Minister of Defence's, now used by the person in charge of first-aid kits (clue 4), so it was the Home Secretary's. We know the Minister of Defence wasn't assigned Room 103 or Room 107, so, from clue 4, his was Room 101. It's not now used by Mr Trott (clue 4), who we know doesn't use Room 107 either, so from

clue 4 he must use Room 103, once the Foreign Secretary's. We now know the present user or his or her responsibility for four rooms, so Mrs Bullamy, the tsarina of the washrooms (clue 2), must use Room 104, which was, by elimination, the Prime Minister's. Thus, from clue 3, Mr Rugg uses the Home Secretary's old Room 108, leaving the first-aid kit boss in the Minister of Defence's Room 101 as Miss Lobbs. Finally, from clue 5, Mr Edkins, now in Room 107, isn't in charge of drinks machines, so he is responsible for cleaning equipment, leaving the drinks machines as the responsibility of Mr Trott in the Foreign Secretary's former Room 103.

In summary:
Room 101, Minister of Defence, Miss Lobbs, first-aid kits.
Room 103, Foreign Secretary, Mr Trott, drinks machines.
Room 104, Prime Minister, Mrs Bullamy, washrooms.
Room 107, Minister of Supply, Mr Edkins, cleaning equipment.
Room 108, Home Secretary, Mr Rugg, light bulbs.

Valentine 2500 (No 15)

The science officer who got one card isn't Lt Brown from Terra (clue 1) and clue 3 tells us Ensign Lolo got more than one card. Ensign Ruppet's the astrogator (clue 4) and Lt Grigik got nine cards (clue 5), so the science officer is Lt Vanaya, who isn't from New Hope (clue 2). The Pilot is from Qaid (clue 3) and the woman from Andros got twelve cards (clue 6), so Lt Vanaya is from Beulah. We know the Pilot got at least five cards, so (clue 3) Ensign Lolo got at least seven. Ensign Ruppet didn't get five cards (clue 4), so Lt Brown got five. The Communications Officer got at least five cards, so clue 7 rules that out as the number received by the armaments officer, so Lt Brown is the communications officer. We now know that the Pilot got at least seven cards and that Lt Grigik got nine, so, from clue 3, Ensign Lolo got twelve and is thus from Andros. By elimination, Ensign Ruppet received seven cards. Ensign Lolo's not the pilot (clue 3), so is the armaments officer, leaving Lt Grigik as the Pilot. She's from Qaid (clue 3), so Ensign Ruppet's home world must be New Hope.

In summary:
Lt Brown, Terra, communications officer, 5 cards.
Lt Grigik, Qaid, Pilot, 9 cards.
Ensign Lolo, Andros, armaments officer, 12 cards.
Ensign Ruppet, New Hope, astrogator, 7 cards.
Lt Vanaya, Beulah, Science officer, 1 card.

Going Airside (No 16)

Patrick's surname is Collins (clue 4) and figure 4 is Wilson (clue 6), so Paul, figure 3, whose surname isn't Fisher (clue 1), Smith or Stevens (clue 3), is Hill. Figure 6 can't be Arnold (clue 1), Patrick Collins (clue 4), Dennis (no hand baggage, clue 2) or Joshua (clue 8), so figure 6 is Clive. Thus Patrick isn't figure 5 (clue 4) nor is he figure 2, so he is figure 1. Figure 5 is going to Pittsburgh (clue 7). Arnold, who is going to Boston and is standing immediately ahead of Mr Fisher (clue 1), can't be figure 2, thus he's figure 4 and figure 5 is Mr Fisher. Mr Fisher isn't Dennis (clue 1), so is Joshua. By elimination, figure 2 is Dennis. Clive is going to Memphis (clue 8), so Stevens who is going to Detroit (clue 5) is Dennis, and, by elimination, Clive's surname is Smith. The person going to Cleveland isn't Paul (clue 3), so is Patrick, leaving Paul Hill's destination as Syracuse.

In summary:
1, Patrick Collins, Cleveland.
2, Dennis Stevens, Detroit.
3, Paul Hill, Syracuse.
4, Arnold Wilson, Boston.
5, Joshua Fisher, Pittsburgh.
6, Clive Smith, Memphis.

Knights Off (No 17)

The holiday in Glastonbury began on 10th August (clue 5). The one starting on 17th August can't have been at The Lair in Mousehole (clue 1), Tintagel (clue 4), or in Brittany (clue 7), so was taken in Marazion by Sir Sorely (clue 6). Since someone stayed at the Chicken Run in August (clue 7), the 20th July (earliest) holiday wasn't in Brittany; nor was it in Tintagel (clue 4), so it was in Mousehole. Thus Sir Spyneless was away from 27th July (clue 1). Sir Coward was at Shivery Nook (clue 2) and Sir Timid was away from 3rd August (clue 3), so Sir Poltroon went to Mousehole. By elimination, the knight who stayed in Glastonbury from 10th August was Sir Coward. Sir Timid's holiday wasn't in Brittany (clue 7), so it was in Tintagel, leaving Sir Spyneless in Brittany. The Chicken Run was in Tintagel (clue 7). The Yellow was in Marazion (clue 4), so the White Feathers was in Brittany.

In summary:
20th July, Sir Poltroon à Ghaste, Mousehole, The Lair.
27th July, Sir Spyneless de Feete, Brittany, White Feathers.
3rd August, Sir Timid de Shayke, Tintagel, Chicken Run.
10th August, Sir Coward de Custarde, Glastonbury, Shivery Nook.
17th August, Sir Sorely à Frayde, Marazion, Yellow Cottage.

SOLUTIONS

In the Van (No 18)
Cyril headed north (clue 5). The green van, which went south, wasn't driven by Malcolm (clue 3) and Bryan's van was red (clue 1), so it was Dennis who went south to Heatherford (clue 4) and Cyril's van which went north was blue; and (clue 1) went to Broxton. By elimination, Malcolm drove the white van. Malcolm didn't go to Weirhead (clue 2), so to Fernlea. This isn't the village due east (clue 6), so it's to the west. Thus Brian went to Weirhead.

In summary:

North, Broxton, Cyril, blue.
East, Weirhead, Bryan, red.
South, Heatherford, Dennis, green.
West, Fernlea, Malcolm, white.

Bar Attenders (No 19)
Since the cider drinker isn't in seat 4, Steve cannot be the man in seat 1 (clue 3), nor can Ernie (clue 2). Since the man in seat 3 has salt and vinegar crisps (clue 1), clue 5 also rules out seat 1 for Lawrie, so it's occupied by Jack, who is the Guinness drinker (clue 4). The man who drinks mild with his plain crisps cannot be in seat 4 (clue 2) and we know he isn't in seat 1 or seat 3, so he is in seat 2. This person cannot be Steve, who is immediately clockwise of the cider drinker (clue 3) and we know that Steve does not drink Guinness, so his drink is a pint of bitter. Since number 2 drinks mild, Steve cannot be in seat 3 (clue 3), so in seat 4. Jack's crisps are smoky bacon flavoured (clue 3) and number 3 is the cider drinker. By elimination, Steve's crisps are cheese and onion, so (clue 5) Lawrie is in seat 2, leaving Ernie in seat 3.

In summary:

1, Jack, Guinness, smoky bacon.
2, Lawrie, mild, plain.
3, Ernie, cider, salt and vinegar.
4, Steve, bitter, cheese and onion.

Home From Home (No 20)
Archie's landlord from 2nd May was Mrs Bossey (clue 2). The following week he cannot have stayed with Mrs Knaggs and played the Alhambra (clue 1), or with Mrs Rule (clue 3) and clue 5 rules out that week for Mrs Draggon, so, by elimination, from 9th May he was staying with Mrs Tumbrill in Listerby (clue 6). He didn't stay with Mrs Rule from 11th April (clue 3) nor, since he was at the Palace on the week beginning 25th April (clue 4), was he with Mrs Rule from the 18th (clue 3). We know his two May landladies, so he was at Mrs Rule's from 25th April while playing the Palace. From Thus from 2nd May (clue 3), he was at the Locarno in Gladwell. The week of 11th April wasn't in Radbury (clue 1), or Steepleigh (clue 5), so in Twistleton, where his

landlady wasn't Mrs Draggon (clue 5), so it was Mrs Knaggs. This leaves 18th April as the date on which Archie's stay with Mrs Draggon began. The Tivoli isn't in Listerby (clue 6), so the Continental is, leaving the Tivoli as the theatre Archie played in the week of 18th April. This isn't in Steepleigh (clue 5), so in Radbury, leaving Steepleigh as the home of the Palace.

In summary:

11th April, Alhambra, Twistleton, Mrs Knaggs.
18th April, Tivoli, Radbury, Mrs Draggon.
25th April, Palace, Steepleigh, Mrs Rule.
2nd May, Locarno, Gladwell, Mrs Bossey.
9th May, Continental, Listerby, Mrs Tumbrill.

Digging In (No 21)
Ken Thomas was at Mrs Draggon's with Archie from 18th April (clue 1) and Billy Lawton stayed with Mrs Rule in Handley Lane (clue 5), so Alf Marshall, who wasn't at Mrs Bossey's or Mrs Tumbrill's (clue 2), stayed with him at Mrs Knaggs' establishment in Twistleton in (clue 1) Murdoch Road. Since the magician appeared with Archie at the Continental (clue 7), they shared digs at Mrs Tumbrill's, so Arthur Wright, the song and dance man (clue 6), stayed with Mrs Bossey in Gladwell. By elimination, the magician who stayed with Mrs Tumbrill was Dennis Green. Flanagan Terrace isn't in Gladwell (clue 8), so Mrs Bossey cannot have received Arthur Wright there and it was the ventriloquist who stayed in Askey Street (clue 4), so, by elimination, Mrs Bossey's house is in Miller Drive. Either the act or the address rules out four names for the man in Askey Street, so that was where Ken Thomas stayed with Mrs Draggon and, by elimination, Mrs Tumbrill lives in Flanagan Terrace. Billy Lawton wasn't the juggler (clue 3), so the ballad singer. Alf Marshall was the juggler.

In summary:

Mrs Bossey, Arthur Wright, song and dance man, Miller Drive.
Mrs Draggon, Ken Thomas, ventriloquist, Askey Street.
Mrs Knaggs, Alf Marshall, juggler, Murdoch Road.
Mrs Rule, Billy Lawton, ballad singer, Handley Lane.
Mrs Tumbrill, Dennis Green, magician, Flanagan Terrace.

Men About Town (No 22)
The BMW driver was to give evidence in a court case (clue 2) and the man who parked car 4 was in town to assess an insurance claim (clue 4). Roland, who came to purchase an engagement ring (clue 6), cannot be the driver of the Jaguar parked in position 2, nor had the latter come to town to make a will (clues 6 and 7), so he is the man applying for a bank loan. Marvin's

Citroën is car 3 (clue 1) and Hall parked car 4. His name, and the make or position of his car, rule out four reasons for Marvin's trip to town, so he came to make a will. From clue 5, Jeremy's car cannot be in any of positions 1, 2 or 5, so it's in position 4 and he is Hall. Car 5 is the Volvo (clue 5). Since we have matched four reasons for visits with either a position or make of vehicle, the Volvo belongs to Roland, who is purchasing the engagement ring. Now, by elimination, Jeremy's car is the Mercedes and the BMW is car 1. So, from clue 8, Roland's surname is Walker. We now know Anthony's car is 1 or 2, so, from clue 3, Godber's is 3 or 4. We know it isn't in position 4, so it's car 3 and Godber is Marvin, and, from clue 3, Anthony is the owner of the BMW parked in position 1. This leaves the Jaguar as Lloyd's car. He isn't Levitt (clue 8), so Frankish, leaving Levitt as Anthony.

In summary:
1, BMW, Anthony Levitt, witness in court.
2, Jaguar, Lloyd Frankish, apply for bank loan.
3, Citroën, Marvin Godber, make will.
4, Mercedes, Jeremy Hall, assess insurance claim.
5, Volvo, Roland Walker, purchase engagement ring.

What Was Their Line? (No 23)

From the job title used, the waitress working in Norwich (clue 1) is female. Melanie was working as a data inputter (clue 5) and Gemma lives in Rhyl (clue 7), so the waitress is Anna. The delivery van driver studying Geography isn't Philip (clue 4) and John's subject is Chemistry (clue 6). We know neither Melanie nor Anna did that job, so the van driver is Gemma. John, who wasn't the call centre clerk (clue 6), was the filing clerk, leaving the call centre clerk as Philip. So, from clue 2, the student from Grimsby is a girl and thus can only be Melanie. John's subject rules him out as the History student from Romford (clue 3), so his home town is Tavistock, leaving Philip as the resident of Romford studying History. Melanie's degree subject isn't German (clue 2), so it's Maths, leaving German as the subject Anna, from Norwich, is reading.

In summary:
Anna, Norwich, German, waitress.
Gemma, Rhyl, Geography, delivery van driver.
John, Tavistock, Chemistry, filing clerk.
Melanie, Grimsby, Maths, data inputter.
Philip, Romford, History, call centre clerk.

A-traction Engine (No 24)

The engine driving the circular saw was built in 1907 (clue 6), Victoria was demonstrating heavy haulage (clue 1) and the road-roller was built later than Samson (clue 1), so Goliath of 1906, which wasn't powering the roundabout (clue

2), was driving the threshing machine and was thus owned by Bernie Cole (clue 5). Leviathan's building date, which was the year after Hugh Jimney's engine (clue 2) wasn't 1907 or 1909. Guy Chuffin's engine dated from 1909 (clue 4), thus Leviathan wasn't built in 1910, so 1911. Hugh Jimney's dated from 1910 (clue 2). Lady Patricia was Bill Large's (clue 3), thus was built in 1907. The road-roller wasn't Samson (clue 1), so Leviathan and Samson dated from 1909 and was powering the roundabout. Thus Samson was Guy Chuffin's engine (clue 4), Hugh Jimney's was Victoria and Matt Black owned Leviathan.

In summary:
1906, Goliath, Bernie Cole, threshing machine.
1907, Lady Patricia, Bill Large, circular saw.
1909, Samson, Guy Chuffin, roundabout.
1910, Victoria, Hugh Jimney, heavy haulage.
1911, Leviathan, Matt Black, road-rolling.

Radio Romance (No 25)

Wendy's partner is Bill (clue 1) and Maggie's partner's forename begins with a vowel. Keith's partner isn't Helen or Aileen (clue 3), so Rachel from Kessworth (clue 6). Venice was nominated by Ian's partner (clue 2) and a South Sea island by the finalist from Mannbridge (clue 5). Rachel didn't nominate the Orient Express (clue 3) or Serengeti Park (clue 6), so Casablanca. Alan lives in Stowburgh (clue 2). Trevor isn't from Mannbridge or Thetbury (clue 4), so Wyndfield. As Ian's partner nominated Venice, they are from Thetbury (clue 5). Thus Wendy and Bill live in Mannbridge, nominating the South Seas and (clue 1) Maggie's partner is Alan. Helen doesn't live in Thetbury (clue 3), so she lives in Wyndfield. She didn't nominate the Orient Express (clue 3), so the Serengeti Park. By elimination, Aileen is from Thetbury and Maggie is the finalist who nominated the Orient Express.

In summary:
Aileen, Ian, Thetbury, Venice.
Helen, Trevor, Wyndfield, Serengeti Park.
Maggie, Alan, Stowburgh, Orient Express.
Rachel, Keith, Kessworth, Casablanca.
Wendy, Bill, Mannbridge, South Sea island.

Murder in Mind (No 26)

Henri came under suspicion in chapter 9 (clue 6). The main suspect in chapter 2 cannot have been Gaspard (clue 5), or Véronique, who was suspected in either chapter 5 or chapter 8 (clue 8) and clue 1 rules out Juliette, so he was Jean-Pierre, the junior partner (clue 3). The business rival cannot be Henri, suspected in chapter 9 (clue 1) and, since this person's motive was believed to be to corner the market (clue 1), this rules out chapter 8, where spite was thought to be the motive (clue 4). The mistress came under suspicion in chapter 6 (clue 7), so, by elimination, it was in chapter 5 that the business rival headed the list of suspects. Juliette is the mistress suspected in chapter 6 (clue 1). The business rival isn't Véronique (clue 8), so he is Gaspard; and Véronique is the suspect in chapter 8. Thus (clue 8) the chauffeur is Henri and Véronique is the secretary. Since we know her presumed motive was spite, from clue 2, it's Juliette whose motive was thought to be revenge. From clue 5, Jean-Pierre was suspected of being jealous, which leaves Henri's presumed motive as financial gain.

In summary:
Chapter 2, Jean-Pierre, junior partner, jealousy.
Chapter 5, Gaspard, business rival, desire to corner market.
Chapter 6, Juliette, mistress, revenge.
Chapter 8, Véronique, secretary, spite.
Chapter 9, Henri, chauffeur, financial gain.

On Parade (No 27)
Brian is No 2 in row C (clue 4). No 4 in that row isn't occupied by Charles, Edward or William (clue 1), Alan or Robin (clue 2), Miles, Norris or Shaun (clue 3), Donald (clue 6) or Paul (clue 5), so Ian is No 4 in C and Donald is No 3 (clue 6). Since Shaun isn't in row A (clue 5), from clue 3 he is in row B, Norris in row A and Miles in C, where the only position remaining unfilled is No 1. Shaun's position in B isn't No 1 or No 2 (clue 3), so (clue 5) it's 4 and Paul is No 1 in row A. Since we now know Charles isn't in row C, from clue 1, he is in row B and Edward and William are in A. Their positions are either 2 and 3, or 3 and 4 (clue 1), so Norris, cannot be No 3 in A. Clue 3 rules him out as No 1 or No 4, so he is No 2. William is No 3 (clue 1) and Edward No 4, with Charles as No 3 in row B. Robin is No 1 in row B (clue 2) and Alan is No 2.

In summary:
Row A: 1, Paul; 2, Norris; 3, William; 4, Edward.
Row B: 1, Robin; 2, Alan; 3, Charles; 4, Shaun.
Row C: 1, Miles; 2, Brian; 3, Donald; 4, Ian.

Café Regulars (No 28)
Wednesday's meal was at table 2 (clue 2). My Friday companion was the pharmacist (clue 7), so we weren't at table 6, favoured by the lawyer (clue 4), nor, since I lunched with Raymond Grey on Thursday (clue 6), can my Friday companion have been at table 12 (clue 5). Clue 3 rules out Friday for Jim Smart, who sits at table 15, so on Friday I sat at table 8. Dominic Taylor is the post office clerk (clue 5), so (by elimination) he was at table 2 and Thursday's meal was at table 12. Monday's wasn't at table 6 (clue 4), so, table 15 and the meal with lawyer was on Tuesday. The lawyer isn't Simon Benson (clue 4), so Terry

Jones, leaving Friday's companion as Simon Benson. Clue 1 now reveals Jim Smart as the bank clerk, so Raymond Grey is the shoe shop manager.

In summary:
Monday, Jim Smart, table 15, bank clerk.
Tuesday, Terry Jones, table 6, lawyer.
Wednesday, Dominic Taylor, table 2, post office clerk.
Thursday, Raymond Grey, table 12, shoe shop manager.
Friday, Simon Benson, table 8, pharmacist.

Come to Sunny Shinglethorpe (No 29)
The April event hasn't been staged for 10 (clue 3), 15 (clue 4), or 11 years (clue 5). The one-day carnival (clue 6) isn't the May event (clue 1), so clue 6 rules out April for the event of 12 years standing, so the event held in April has a history of 9 years. This isn't the balloon fiesta (clue 1), or carnival (clue 6), while clue 7 rules out the jazz festival. The May event hasn't a 15-year history (clue 1), so April isn't the month of the classic car rally (clue 4), thus the folk festival is in April. This does not last two days (clue 5) and we know it isn't the one-day event. The five-day event is staged in June (clue 2). Clue 5 now tells us the three-day event with an 11-year history is in May, so the folk festival lasts four days. The two-day event isn't in August (clue 3), so July and the one-day carnival takes place in August and has a 10-year history. Thus (clue 6) the two-day July event was staged for 12 years. By elimination, the five-day event in June has a 15-year history, so (clue 4) the classic car rally is in May, and (clue 1) the balloon fiesta is the two-day event in July, leaving the June event as the jazz festival.

In summary:
April, folk festival, 4 days, 9 years.
May, classic car rally, 3 days, 11 years.
June, jazz festival, 5 days, 15 years.
July, balloon fiesta, 2 days, 12 years.
August, carnival, 1 day, 10 years.

In the Swim (No 30)
Dorsell is 17 (clue 7) and Damon is 16 (clue 4). The backstroke swimmer is 14 (clue 6). Glyn Scales cannot be 13 or 15 (clue 1), so he's 14 and the butterfly swimmer is 13. Jacqueline does the crawl (clue 3). Damon doesn't do the breaststroke (clue 4), so (clue 5) he's the diver named Fish. Finn isn't 13 (clue 2), so 15 and Gill is the butterfly swimmer. Finn isn't Stephanie (clue 2) or Anna (clue 6), so Jacqueline is. Thus Dorsell is the breaststroke swimmer. Dorsell isn't Stephanie (clue 2), so is Anna, leaving Stephanie as the youngster named Gill.

SOLUTIONS

In summary:
Anna Dorsell, breaststroke, 17.
Damon Fish, diving, 16.
Glyn Scales, backstroke, 14.
Jacqueline Finn, crawl, 15.
Stephanie Gill, butterfly, 13.

Family Pets (No 31)

The Olivers live at number 5 (clue 4). The family at number 1 cannot be the Keiths (clue 1), or the Ansons (clue 3). Since the stick insects live at number 2 (clue 6), clue 5 rules out number 1 for the Colemans and clue 8 rules out the Evans family and their hamster. Since the Olivers' pet isn't a bird (clue 4), the Evans family cannot live at number 4 (clue 8), so, from clue 3, the Gardners cannot live at number 1. Clue 1 rules out the Keiths for number 4, so clue 3 rules out the Morgans for number 1. So, by elimination, the family who live there is the Iggledens. Now, from clue 7, the tortoise belongs to the Olivers at number 5, and, from clue 3, the Gardners must live at number 4. So the Ansons cannot own number 2 (clue 2), so they own number 6. The Ansons don't own the python (clue 2), the parrot (clue 5), the goldfish (clue 6) or the budgerigar (clue 8), so they own the tropical fish. So the Keiths live at number 8 (clue 1). Thus, from clue 4, the Morgans must live at number 2. Clues 5 and 8 rule out the parrot and the budgerigar as the pet of the Iggledens at number 1 and clue 2 rules out the python, so they own the goldfish. The python cannot live at number 7 (clue 2), so, from that clue, it must live at number 3. We have now allocated a family or a pet to seven houses, so the Evans and their hamster must live at number 7. So the budgie belongs to the Keiths at number 8 (clue 8), which leaves the parrot at number 4. The Colemans own the python.

In summary:
1, Iggleden, goldfish.
2, Morgan, stick insects.
3, Coleman, python.
4, Gardner, parrot.
5, Oliver, tortoise.
6, Anson, tropical fish.
7, Evans, hamster.
8, Keith, budgerigar.

On Escort Duty (No 32)

The WI dance took place on June 25th (clue 2). The lady who wore the blue dress on July 9th (clue 5) wasn't escorted to the Licensed Victuallers' function (clue 1), or the film premiere (clue 3) and clue 6 rules out July 9th for Corinne's outing to the mayor's reception, so, by elimination, the lady in blue attended the Hunt Ball. The lady in scarlet was Don's client on July 2nd (clue 4). The dress worn on June

11th cannot have been Marjorie's green one (clue 1), or the white one (clue 3), so it was pink. Since the blue dress was worn on July 9th, clue 1 rules out the July 2nd outing as the Licensed Victuallers' function and clue 3 rules out the film premiere, thus it was on July 2nd that Corinne went to the mayor's reception in the scarlet dress. Enid went to the Hunt Ball (clue 6) on July 9th. We now know the pink dress worn on June 11th didn't belong to Corinne, Enid or Marjorie, nor (clue 7) to Vanessa, so it was Yvonne's, and the white dress was worn by Vanessa. This wasn't on June 18th (clue 7), so Vanessa attended the WI dance and Marjorie's outing in the green dress was on June 18th. From clue 1, Yvonne was escorted to the Licensed Victuallers' function on June 11th, so the film première was on June 18th.

In summary:
June 11th, Licensed Victuallers, Yvonne, pink.
June 18th, film premiere, Marjorie, green.
June 25th, WI dance, Vanessa, white.
July 2nd, mayor's reception, Corinne, scarlet.
July 9th, Hunt Ball, Enid, blue.

The Good Doctor ... (No 33)

Lord Tilney challenged Captain Ferrars (clue 3) and Colonel Vernon and his offender both deloped (clue 6), so the man who challenged Sir Darcy Croft to a duel in which both were wounded, not Sir Henry Hurst or Sir Nick Price (clue 4), was the Hon Toby Ward. Sir Henry Hurst was Wednesday's challenger (clue 5), so Major Steele wasn't the offender on Monday, when the challenger was wounded (clue 2). Nor was Monday's offender the Hon Miles Martin (clue 1), so he was Lord Osborne. By elimination, Sir Nick Price was Monday's challenger and was wounded. Lord Tilney and Captain Ferrars weren't the pair who both missed (clue 3) so in their duel the offender was wounded, leaving the pair who both missed as Sir Henry Hurst and his opponent on Wednesday. From clue 2, the duel in which Lord Tilney wounded Captain Ferrars was on Thursday, with Major Steele being the Wednesday offender and the Hon Toby Ward and Sir Darcy Croft wounding each other on Friday. By elimination, Colonel Vernon's duel was with the Hon Miles Martin on Tuesday.

In summary:
Monday, Sir Nick Price, Lord Osborne, challenger wounded.
Tuesday, Colonel Vernon, Hon Miles Martin, both deloped.
Wednesday, Sir Henry Hurst, Major Steele, both missed.
Thursday, Lord Tilney, Captain Ferrars, offender wounded.
Friday, Hon Toby Ward, Sir Darcy Croft, both wounded.

SOLUTIONS

Miss Raffles' Revenge (No 34)

The pearls were stolen in April (clue 2) and the London theft was in June (clue 6), so the theft of the sapphires in Rome, which wasn't in January or November (clue 1), was in August. The prince robbed in June wasn't Siegfried (clue 6) nor Constantin (clue 5). Patrizius was robbed in Berlin, not London (clue 4) and Hugebert was robbed immediately before the theft of the emeralds (clue 7), which we know weren't stolen in August, so the June victim was Adelbert himself. So the jewels he lost weren't rubies (clue 3). The month of the theft rules out two other jewels and it was Constantin who lost his diamonds (clue 4), so Adelbert was robbed of emeralds. So, from clue 7, Hugebert was robbed in April, of the pearls. He wasn't robbed in Vienna (clue 7). We know he wasn't robbed in Berlin or London and the month of the crime rules out Rome, so he was robbed in Paris. As Patrizius was robbed in Berlin, he can't have been the August victim, so it was Siegfried who was robbed of his sapphires in Rome in that month. Now, by elimination, Constantin was robbed in Vienna and Patrizius lost the rubies. Thus, he wasn't robbed in January (clue 3), so lost his stones in November, leaving Constantin as the January victim.

In summary:
Prinz Adelbert, emeralds, June, London.
Prinz Constantin, diamonds, January, Vienna.
Prinz Hugebert, pearls, April, Paris.
Prinz Patrizius, rubies, November, Berlin.
Prinz Siegfried, sapphires, August, Rome.

Well-wishers (No 35)

Telegram 5 is from Larry (clue 6) so, from clue 3, the message from the player in Dead on Time can't be telegram 3; nor can telegram 3 be the 'All the best!' from the player in Outlaw which isn't in vertical or horizontal line with Wayne's message (clue 1). Telegram 6 is from the player in BMP (clue 5). Telegram 2 reads 'Break a leg!' (clue 4), so clue 7 tells us the player from Nurses didn't send telegram 3, while the telegram from Pat of Blue Eyes is even-numbered (clue 2), so, by elimination, telegram 3 is from the player in Green Valley. So, GG, who we know didn't send telegram 5, sent telegram 1. So Pat from Blue Eyes' message can't be telegram 2 (clue 2) and we know it's not telegram 6, so, from clue 2, it's telegram 4. The message from the player in Nurses can't be telegram 1 or 2 (clue 7) and we've already identified the film/show for telegrams 3, 4 and 6, so the player from Nurses sent telegram 5 and is thus Larry and 'I knew you'd make it!' is the message of telegram 4, sent by Pat from Blue Eyes (clue 7). We now know the message or film/show for five telegrams, so,

by elimination, the one wishing 'All the best!' from the player from Outlaw is message 1 and the sender of message 2 played in Dead on Time. The sender of telegram 3 wasn't Wayne (clue 1) or Joanne (clue 9), so Shari and thus says 'Good luck!' (clue 8). Telegram 2 wasn't from Wayne (clue 1) so Joanne and Wayne sent telegram 6. Larry's telegram doesn't read 'You're a star!' (clue 6), so 'Knock 'em dead!' and Wayne's reads 'You're a star!'.

In summary:
1. 'All the best!', GG, Outlaw.
2, 'Break a leg!', Joanne, Dead on Time.
3, 'Good luck!', Shari, Green Valley.
4, 'I knew you'd make it!', Pat, Blue Eyes.
5, 'Knock 'em dead!', Larry, Nurses.
6, You're a star!', Wayne, BMP.

Partners (No 36)

Sarah Thorson and her partner in Parkstown have been together two years longer than Vince Zaimis and his partner (clue 5), so not for 5 years or 6 years. Joe Murphy and his partner are the 6-year pair (clue 1), so Sarah Thorson and her partner aren't the 8-year pair and the 7-year pair work in Kingsland (clue 3), so they were together for 9 years. Thus Vince Zaimis and his partner are the 7-year Kingsland pair (clue 5). Andy Chen's partner is Angel Boncour (clue 6), so they aren't the 5-year pair, one of whom is Robyn Petrosian (clue 2) and we know they're not the 9-year pair, so they were partners for 8 years. Rick Salinas and his partner work in Stenburg (clue 1), so Sarah Thorson's partner in Parkstown is Floyd Gibowitz and, by elimination, Rick Salinas is Robyn Petrosian's 5-year partner. As the partners in West River have been together a shorter time than Erika Fahmy and her partner (clue 4), they must be Joe Murphy and his partner, the 6-year pair. Thus Erika Fahmy is Vince Zaimis' 7-year partner in Kingsland. By elimination, Joe Murphy's partner is Leah Kravchuk and Andy Chen and Angel Boncour work in Haven Point.

In summary:
Andy Chen, Angel Boncour, Haven Point, 8 years.
Floyd Gibowitz, Sarah Thorson, Parkstown, 9 years.
Joe Murphy, Leah Kravchuk, West River, 6 years.
Rick Salinas, Robyn Petrosian, Stenburg, 5 years.
Vince Zaimis, Erika Fahmy, Kingsland, 7 years.

Ardluck Stories (No 37)

One brother fled to Australia in 1888 (clue 5), so neither he nor the one who joined the Foreign Legion was Eustace, who was accused of forging cheques (clue 2). The one accused of murder fled to Canada (clue 1) and Cuthbert fled to Pingo-Pingo (clue 7), so Eustace the (alleged)

SOLUTIONS

forger fled to Tibet. He can't have done so in 1891 (clue 2), so fled in 1894 and Ambrose in 1900 (clue 4). Ambrose didn't join the Foreign Legion (clue 2), so he fled to Canada after being accused of murder. The brother who went to Australia in 1888 wasn't Desmond (clue 6), so he was Bernard. By elimination, Desmond joined the Foreign Legion. Since Eustace fled in 1894, Desmond joined the Legion in 1891 (clue 2) By elimination, 1897 was the year Cuthbert left for Pingo-Pingo. Now, from clue 6, it was Bernard who went to Oz in 1888 who was accused of cheating at cards. Desmond (clue 3) who fled to the Foreign Legion in 1891, wasn't accused of stealing a jewel, so he was accused of seducing a friend's wife and Cuthbert was accused of stealing the jewel.

In summary:
Ambrose, murder, Canada, 1900.
Bernard, cheating at cards, Australia, 1888.
Cuthbert, stealing jewel, Pingo-Pingo, 1897.
Desmond, seducing friend's wife, Foreign Legion, 1891.
Eustace, forging cheques, Tibet, 1894.

Revolutionary (No 38)
The President ousted on the 3rd, who wasn't an Air Force General (clue 2), fled to either Brazil, Switzerland or the USA (also clue 2). The former Admiral was assassinated (clue 5), so wasn't ousted on the 3rd. The ex-Cabinet Minister was ousted on the 11th (clue 4) and it wasn't the ex-diplomat who was ousted on the 3rd (clue 1), so it was the former Army General. Pablo Torcido was ousted on the 23rd (clue 4), so Kevin O'Malley was ousted on the 19th and the ex-diplomat on the 15th (clue 1). Kevin O'Malley wasn't the ex-Air Force General (clue 1), so he was the ex-Admiral and, by elimination, Pablo Torcido was ex-Air Force General. The former Army General wasn't Carlos Borracho (clue 2) or Jaime Indigno (clue 6), so he was Felipe Horrendo, who fled to Brazil. The ex-President who was imprisoned wasn't the ex-diplomat or the former Air Force General (clues 1 and 2), so was the ex-Cabinet Minister. The ex-diplomat didn't flee to Switzerland (clue 3), so to the USA and Pablo Torcida fled to Switzerland. Carlos Borracho also fled when ousted (clue 2), so he is the ex-diplomat. Jaime Indigno was the ex-Cabinet Minister and was imprisoned.

In summary:
Carlos Borracho, diplomat, 15th, fled to USA.
Felipe Horrendo, General (Army), 3rd, fled to Brazil.
Jaime Indigno, Cabinet Minister, 11th, imprisoned.
Kevin O'Malley, Admiral, 19th, assassinated.
Pablo Torcido, General (Air Force), 23rd, fled to Switzerland.

Sonia's Books (No 39)
Since book 2 is pink (clue 5) and book 4 is the maths book (clue 7), from clue 1, the history book is book number 5 and book 6 thus has a red cover. Book 7 cannot be devoted to English (clue 2), home economics (clue 3), or French (clue 6). Nor can it be her brown geography book (clue 4), so it's her science book. It isn't blue (clue 3), green (clue 4) or mauve (clue 6), so grey. The subject of book 6 is English (clue 2). From clue 6, her French book isn't number 1 or number 3, so it's number 2. Book 1 has the mauve cover (clue 6), so number 3 is brown and the subject of book 1 is home economics. From clue 6, the green book cannot be number 4, so it's book 5, leaving the maths book as that with a blue cover.

In summary:
1, Home economics, mauve.
2, French, pink.
3, Geography, brown.
4, Maths, blue.
5, History, green.
6, English, red.
7, Science, grey.

Picture Story (No 40)
Neither Adam (clue 1), nor Christopher and Karen (clue 3), went out on Wednesday, so Dean did so and his girlfriend is thus Jacqueline (clue 2), which leaves Adam's girl as Sophie. She didn't go out on Friday (clue 4), so they were the Thursday pair, leaving Christopher and Karen as the couple who went to the cinema on Friday. From clue 1, the film that Dean and Jacqueline saw on Wednesday was the space epic, and, from clue 3, it was Adam and Sophie who saw the romance on Thursday, leaving the action movie as the one seen by Christopher and Karen on Friday.

In summary:
Wednesday, Dean and Jacqueline, space epic,
Thursday, Adam and Sophie, romance.
Friday, Christopher and Karen, action movie.

On an Expedition (No 41)
Chris is 6 (clue 3). Adam isn't 5 (clue 1), so 7 and the 5-year-old with an apple drink (clue 2) is Billy. The boy with the strawberry drink and egg sandwich wasn't Adam (clue 1), so Chris and Adam had an orange drink. Billy's sandwich didn't contain ham (clue 2), so cheese. Adam's had ham.

In summary:
Adam, 7, orange, ham.
Billy, 5, apple, cheese.
Chris, 6, strawberry, egg.

SOLUTIONS

Farm Produce (No 42)

Hugh Holt of Chapel Farm didn't find the bowl (clue 2), the plate, which was found on Pond Farm (clue 1) or the cup, which was found by Ben Barns (clue 6), so he found the sword and the hoard of 30 coins (clue 5). Thus, from clue 2, the bowl was with the 40 coins and was thus found on Holly Farm (clue 4). By elimination, Ben Barns, who found the cup, must run Grove Farm. He didn't find 10 coins (clue 3), so he found 20 coins, and, by elimination, the 10 coins was found on Pond Farm, with the plate. The man who found them wasn't Sam Straw (clue 1), so he was Luke Lamb and Sam Straw was the farmer of Holly Farm who found the bowl and 40 coins.

In summary:
Ben Barns, Grove Farm, cup, 20 coins.
Hugh Holt, Chapel Farm, sword, 30 coins.
Luke Lamb, Pond Farm, plate, 10 coins.
Sam Straw, Holly farm, bowl, 40 coins.

The Four Sisters (No 43)

Marcia's surname is Sowright (clue 5). Miss Bluegrave, playing the invalid sister, isn't Esther (clue 4) or Cressida (clue 1), so she is Helen and the invalid sister is thus Anastasia (clue 3). Natasha's being played by Ms Duckson (clue 2). Ms Wyelor can't be playing Ludmilla (clue 1), so she is playing Feodosia, the actress (clue 4) and Ludmilla is Marcia Sowright's part. Natasha isn't the teacher sister (clue 2), who must thus be Ludmilla, leaving Natasha as the General's wife. Ms Wyelor, playing Feodosia, isn't forenamed Esther (clue 4), so she is Cressida, leaving Esther as Ms Duckson, who's playing Natasha.

In summary:
Anastasia, invalid, Helen Bluegrave.
Feodosia, actress, Cressida Wyelor.
Ludmilla, teacher, Marcia Sowright.
Natasha, General's wife, Esther Duckson.

Locomotives (No 44)

Moorcock belonged to the MWR (clue 3). Argus didn't belong to the EER (clue 1) or the LSWR (clue 5), so to the NBR and is thus chartreuse (clue 2). The ex-EER loco isn't Duncan (clue 1), so Granada; thus Duncan was owned by LSWR and is vermilion. Granada isn't the lavender loco coupled to the royal coach (clue 4), so Granada is russet. Thus Argus is hitched to a sleeping car (clue 5) and Moorcock is the lavender loco. Duncan isn't coupled to the restaurant car (clue 1), so to the 1st class carriage and the restaurant car is coupled to Granada.

In summary:
Argus, NBR, chartreuse, sleeping car.
Duncan, LSWR, vermilion, 1st class carriage.
Granada, EER, russet, restaurant car.
Moorcock, MWR, lavender, royal coach.

Back Lanes (No 45)

Anna cannot be in lanes 1, 2, 7 or 8 (clue 1) and Sally is in lane 3 (clue 7). Since Overton is in lane 6 (clue 5), clue 1 rules out lane 4 for Anna and clue 5 tells us Overton, in lane 6, isn't Anna, so Anna is in lane 5. Powell is in lane 7 (clue 1) and Edwards is Sally. Overton isn't Edwina (clue 4). Since Anna isn't in lane 8, Leeanne's surname is Calvert (clue 3). Overton isn't Chloë (clue 6) nor is she Briony. Since Powell is in lane 7, Overton isn't Delia (clue 2). Thus Overton is Vicky. Briony is Powell (clue 6). Leeanne is in Lane 8 (clue 3). We know Edwards is in lane 3, so Precious is in lane 5 and Delia in lane 4 (clue 2). She isn't Willis (clue 2) or Mavity (clue 8), so Burrows. Edwina is in lane 1 (clue 4), so Chloë is in lane 2. Chloë is Mavity (clue 2), so Edwina's surname is Willis.

In summary:
1, Edwina Willis. 2, Chloë Mavity.
3, Sally Edwards. 4, Delia Burrows.
5, Anna Precious. 6, Vicky Overton.
7, Briony Powell. 8, Leeanne Calvert.

Under the Hammer (No 46)

Lot 30 went for £1,250 (clue 5) and Lot 17 was bought by a man (clue 1), so the lot for which Rosa Mount paid £1,600, which was lower than 42, the number of the first edition (clue 3), was Lot 23. This wasn't the Art Deco bookcase, sold for £3,000 (clue 5), nor was it the Georgian table bought by Mr Upton-Pademoor (clue 6) and the porcelain figurine was acquired by a man (clue 1), so Rosa Mount bought the Victorian painting. Thus Job Lott bought Lot 30 (clue 4). This wasn't the table, so the figurine. By elimination, the table was Lot 17. Biddy Hyer bought Lot 42 (clue 2) and Warren I Pryce bought Lot 56. The bookcase sold for £3,000 wasn't Lot 17 (clue 1), so Lot 56. Mr Upton-Pademoor spent less than Biddy Hyer (clue 1), so £1,900 and Biddy Hyer spent £2,250.

In summary:
Lot 17, Mr Upton-Pademoor, Georgian table, £1,900.
Lot 23, Rosa Mount, Victorian painting, £1,600.
Lot 30, Job Lott, porcelain figurine, £1,250.
Lot 42, Biddy Hyer, first edition, £2,250.
Lot 56, Warren I Pryce, Art Deco bookcase, £3,000.

Little Arrows (No 47)

Jeff was in the pub (clue 4), so the boy struck at the fairground at 9.00, who wasn't Scott (clue 3), or Paul or Matt (clue 2), was Kevin and he fell for Natasha (clue 6). Gail wasn't love-struck at 8.30 or 8.40 (clue 3). We know that Natasha and Kevin became an item at 9 o'clock and since they were at the fairground, Gail wasn't targeted by Cupid at 9.10 (clue 3), so she and Matt fell in love at 8.50. Thus those at the cinema were targeted

SOLUTIONS

at 8.40 and Scott and his companion at 8.30 (clue 3). Jeff was in the pub, so Paul was in the cinema and (by elimination) Cupid struck in the pub at 9.10. We know that Scott wasn't in the restaurant (clue 1), so he was in the disco and fell for Elaine. This leaves Matt and Gail as the lovers in the restaurant. Gina wasn't in the cinema (clue 5), so she was with Jeff in the pub; and Paul and Liz were at the cinema.

In summary:
8.30, disco, Scott and Elaine.
8.40, cinema, Paul and Liz.
8.50, restaurant, Matt and Gail.
9.00, fairground, Kevin and Natasha.
9.10, pub, Jeff and Gina.

Hidden Talents (No 48)

Quentin became a sculptor (clue 2) and Franklyn started as a shoe salesperson (clue 6), so the man who left the insurance industry to become a jockey (clue 1) is Noel. Charmian's surname is Smith (clue 5). Nicholls, the former bank clerk, isn't Quentin (clue 2), so is Leonora. The fashion designer named Green (clue 7) is thus Franklyn. Noel isn't Minto (clue 4), so Davis and Quentin is Minto. Charmian didn't become an artist (clue 5), so she is the top model and Leonora is the artist. Charmian wasn't the postal worker (clue 3), so the cook; and Quentin was the postal worker.

In summary:
Charmian Smith, cook, top model.
Franklyn Green, shoe salesperson, fashion designer.
Leonora Nicholls, bank clerk, artist.
Noel Davis, insurance clerk, jockey.
Quentin Minto, postal worker, sculptor.

White Van Men (No 49)

The car parts aren't being delivered by Terry or Nigel (clue 2), Dean who is delivering food (clue 6), or Colin who is carrying either washing machines or TVs (clue 3), so the car parts are in Sam's Fiat van (clue 5). They aren't destined for St Albans (clue 2), Redhill (clue 5), Guildford, where the TVs are bound (clue 4), or Maidstone, where the Ford van is heading (clue 1), so Slough. The load of shoes isn't in the Ford or Leyland vans (clue 1), nor in the Mercedes carrying the washing machines (clue 4), so the Renault. As the TVs are bound for Guildford (clue 4), the Ford with the cargo of food is on its way to Maidstone, with Dean at the wheel. By elimination, the TVs are in the Leyland. Colin isn't driving the Leyland (clue 3), so the Mercedes. Terry isn't driving the Leyland (clue 2), so the Renault and he isn't heading for St Albans, so for Redhill. By elimination, the Leyland is driven by Nigel and Colin is going to St Albans.

In summary:
Colin, Mercedes, washing machines, St Albans.
Dean, Ford, food, Maidstone.
Nigel, Leyland, TVs, Guildford.
Sam, Fiat, car parts, Slough.
Terry, Renault, shoes, Redhill.

Carousel (No 50)

Keith owns No 3 (clue 5) and the Swansea resident owns case 5 (clue 7). The man who owns case 6 isn't from Lincoln (clue 3), Stoke (clue 1), Portsmouth (clue 2) or Carlisle (4), so Norwich. He isn't Dean (clue 8), so Ray. Holly is from Colchester (clue 6), thus owns case 7. Thus (clue 2) the Portsmouth resident owns case 1 and (clue 4) Keith is from Carlisle. Norma's is case 4 (clue 1) and the owner of case 2 is from Stoke (clue 1). This leaves Norma's home town as Lincoln. The owner of case 5 isn't Dean or Olga (clue 8), so Bernice. Olga is from Portsmouth (clue 2) and Dean from Stoke.

In summary:
1, Olga, Portsmouth.
2, Dean, Stoke.
3, Keith, Carlisle.
4, Norma, Lincoln.
5, Bernice, Swansea.
6, Ray, Norwich.
7, Holly, Colchester.

High-flyer (No 51)

Flight AA129 will be leaving on the 16th to a German destination (clue 2) and AA143 will leave from terminal 5 (clue 6), so the Stockholm flight from terminal 1, numbered more than 100 (clue 4) is AA182. The flight on the 10th will depart from terminal 2 (clue 1), so it isn't AA143, AA182, or AA84 (clue 1), so AA97. The flight on the 12th is to Milan (clue 2). We know that it isn't AA182 (clue 3), so that from terminal 4 cannot be on the 16th. Thus the flight from terminal 4 is AA84. As that on the 10th is AA97, the one from terminal 4 cannot be on the 14th (clue 3). The flight on the 16th is AA129, so the terminal 4 flight is leaving on the 18th. Thus AA182 is departing on the 14th (clue 3), leaving AA143 from terminal 5 as the departure on the 12th. Thus the Milan flight will depart from terminal 5. By elimination, the flight from terminal 3 will be AA129. This has a German destination, but isn't Frankfurt (clue 5), so Berlin. Terminal 2's flight isn't to Helsinki (clue 1), so Frankfurt, leaving the Helsinki flight as AA84.

In summary:
10th, Frankfurt, terminal 2, AA97.
12th, Milan, terminal 5, AA143.
14th, Stockholm, terminal 1, AA182.
16th, Berlin, terminal 3, AA129.
18th, Helsinki, terminal 4, AA84.

Nothing Like a Dame (No 52)

Cinderella starred Rory Lynes (clue 3) and Robin Hood was the 1999 production (clue 1). Bill Topper, who played the dame in the 2001 pantomime (clue 5) wasn't in Aladdin, nor (clue 6) Jack and the Beanstalk (clue 6), so Dick Whittington, for which 500 tickets were sold (clue 4). The panto in which Noel Season starred was seen by more people than Aladdin (clue 6), so wasn't staged in 1998, when 350 tickets were sold (clue 1), 2001 or 1997 (clue 6). Thus Noel played the dame in Robin Hood and the 1998 production was Jack and the Beanstalk. Jack's mother wasn't played by Will Hammett, who was seen by 450 people (clue 2), so by Phil Hall. By elimination, Will Hammett played the dame in Aladdin. Cinderella was seen by fewer than 500 (clue 3), so by 400 and 550 tickets were sold for Robin Hood. Aladdin wasn't in 1997 (clue 2), so 2000, leaving the 1997 panto as Cinderella.

In summary:
1997, Cinderella, Rory Lynes, 400.
1998, Jack and the Beanstalk, Phil Hall, 350.
1999, Robin Hood, Noel Season, 550.
2000, Aladdin, Will Hammett, 450.
2001, Dick Whittington, Bill Topper, 500.

Gone Fishing (No 53)

The Jenny is fishing for crabs (clue 2), so Capt Futtock, who is fishing for prawns in a boat with a name of five or six letters (clue 5) owns Marina, registered as SH18 (clue 1). Capt Bulwark owns Seagull (clue 1), so Capt Helm's SH60 with a six-letter or seven-letter name (clue 4) is Neptune. Ocean Queen isn't captained by Capt Windlass (clue 2), so Capt Binnacle, leaving Jenny as Capt Windlass's craft. Ocean Queen is neither fishing for mackerel (clue 2) nor lobsters (clue 3), so she is SH34, fishing for herring (clue 6). SH42's name has seven letters (clue 5), so is Seagull, leaving Jenny as SH56. Neptune isn't fishing for lobsters (clue 3), so mackerel and Seagull is the lobster boat.

In summary:
Jenny, SH56, Capt Windlass, crabs.
Marina, SH18, Capt Futtock, prawns.
Neptune, SH60, Capt Helm, mackerel.
Ocean Queen, SH34, Capt Binnacle, herring.
Seagull, SH42, Capt Bulwark, lobsters.

Drones Behaving... (No 54)

Mr Milton came from Dover (clue 6) and Mr Tripp was a CID officer (clue 2); the bookmaker from Runcorn wasn't Mr Fox or Mr Bell (clue 5), so, by elimination, he was Mr Westley. So, from clue 5, Edward Tanqueray was avoiding Mr Tripp the CID officer. We know that the bookmaker from Runcorn wasn't seeking Edward, nor could his quarry have been Archie, who was avoiding

the irate father (clue 1), or Gerald, who was avoiding Mr Fox (clue 3); Rupert was avoiding the man from Leeds (clue 7), so, by elimination, the Runcorn bookmaker was seeking Montague. We've matched Drones or home-towns with four out-of-towners, so, by elimination, the man from Leeds looking for Rupert was Mr Bell. Thus Mr Milton from Dover was the irate father seeking Archie. Gerald Huntington wasn't avoiding the journalist (clue 3), so Mr Fox was the solicitor, leaving the journalist as Mr Bell, who was seeking Rupert. Finally, from clue 4, Mr Fox wasn't from Bristol, so he was from Norwich, leaving the Bristolian as Edward's seeker, Mr Tripp of the CID.

In summary:
Archie Fotheringhay, Mr Milton, Dover, irate father.
Edward Tanqueray, Mr Tripp, Bristol, CID officer.
Gerald Huntington, Mr Fox, Norwich, solicitor.
Montague Ffolliott, Mr Westley, Runcorn, bookmaker.
Rupert de Grey, Mr Bell, Leeds, journalist.

Chief Constable's Awards (No 55)

PC French can't be officer F (clue 1), officer B or C (clue 2), officer D (clue 4) or officer A (clue 5), so is officer E. So, from clue 3, the award for charity work went to officer D. PC Abbot couldn't have received his award for winning the marathon (clue 2), arresting an armed man or records improvement (clue 4), foiling a robbery (clue 5) or rescuing a swimmer (clue 6), so got it for charity work. Thus the officer who arrested an armed man was PC Brennan and the one who improved the records PC Campbell (clue 4). PC Brennan can't be officer B (clue 1), C (clue 2) or A (clue 5), so F. Thus A is PC Campbell (clue 5) and PC Dodds foiled the robbery. PC Dodds is B (clue 2), C is PC Ellis and the marathon winner was PC French. By elimination, the swimmer was rescued by PC Ellis.

In summary:
Officer A, PC Campbell, records improvement.
Officer B, PC Dodds, foiling robbery.
Officer C, PC Ellis, rescuing swimmer.
Officer D, PC Abbot, charity work.
Officer E, PC French, winning marathon.
Officer F, PC Brennan, arresting armed man.

No Business Like It (No 56)

Ms Hayes wanted to be a pianist (clue 2) and Ms Miller's a chorus dancer (clue 6), so the would-be actress who became an usherette, not Ms Edison or Ms Oates (clue 3), is Ms Smith. Judy, who wanted to be a pop singer, isn't the chorus dancer or the stooge (clue 1) and the producer has an odd number of letters in her forename (clue 4), so Judy is the barmaid. Ms Edison's forename is Paula (clue 5), so Judy is Ms Oates. From clue 4, the producer isn't Ms Hayes, so she's Paula Edison and Ms Hayes is the stooge. Paula Edison didn't want to be a ballerina (clue 5), so her ambition was to be a comedienne, leaving the would-be ballerina as Ms Miller, the chorus dancer. From clue 6, she is Denise, Ms Hayes the stooge is Anita and Ms Smith the usherette is Gillian.

In summary:

Anita Hayes, pianist, stooge.
Denise Miller, ballerina, chorus dancer.
Gillian Smith, actress, usherette.
Judy Oates, pop singer, barmaid.
Paula Edison, comedienne, producer.

Guarding the Gates (No 57)

Gate 2 is Watergate (clue 5). Marketgate isn't gate 3 (clue 2), and since Jeremiah guards gate 4 (clue 3), clue 1 rules out gate 3 as Stonegate, so it's Castlegate. Thus (clue 4) Fletcher is guarding gate 1. Kettley is Moses (clue 6). Jeremiah isn't Lamb (clue 3), so he is Wise. Gate 4 isn't Stonegate (clue 1), so Marketgate, leaving Stonegate as gate 1. Thus (clue 1) Ezekiel is guarding gate 2. By elimination, Moses Kettley is guarding Castlegate, Ezekiel's surname is Lamb and Fletcher's first name is Nathaniel.

In summary:

Gate 1, Stonegate, Nathaniel Fletcher.
Gate 2, Watergate, Ezekiel Lamb.
Gate 3, Castlegate, Moses Kettley.
Gate 4, Marketgate, Jeremiah Wise.

Philip Phibbs (No 58)

Peter carried out Friday's count (clue 5) and Darren counted 96 lies (clue 6). The person who counted 87 lies on Wednesday wasn't Shaun (clue 1) or Desmond (clue 2), so Robert. The friend who counted 145 porkies did so on Thursday (clue 7) and (clue 5) Peter counted 138. Monday's total wasn't 101 (clue 4), so 96 and 101 were counted on Tuesday. Desmond counted 145 (clue 2) and is thus Philip's friend. This leaves Shaun as the person who totalled 101 lies. So (clue 1) Darren is Philip's brother and (clue 2) Peter is Philip's boss. Robert isn't his workmate (clue 3), so his father, leaving his workmate as Shaun.

In summary:

Monday, Darren, brother, 96.
Tuesday, Shaun, workmate, 101.
Wednesday, Robert, father, 87.
Thursday, Desmond, friend, 145.
Friday, Peter, boss, 138.

Chamber of Horrors (No 59)

Figure 1 can't be Arpad (clue 1), Istvan (clue 2) or Ferenc (clue 4), so is Laszlo Hederadam (clue 5). Figure 2 is Bardonyes (clue 3), so Wekesits, who isn't figure 3 (clue 1), is figure 4 and figure 3 is Szakanky. Now, from clue 1, Szakanky is Arpad and the werewolf is figure 2, Bardonyes. Figure 4, Wekesits, can't be the sorcerer (clue 2) or the vampire (clue 4), so is the murderer. Figure 3, Arpad Szakanky, isn't the sorcerer (clue 2), so he is the vampire, leaving the sorcerer as figure 1, Laszlo Hederadam. From clue 4, Ferenc is figure 4, Wekesits, leaving Bardonyes as Istvan.

In summary:

Figure 1, Laszlo Hederadam, sorcerer.
Figure 2, Istvan Bardonyes, werewolf.
Figure 3, Arpad Szakanky, vampire.
Figure 4, Ferenc Wekesits, murderer.

We Wuz Robbed (No 60)

Moanwell's team didn't score a goal on 25th January, when he blamed the state of the pitch (clue 3). This cannot have been the 0-2 defeat on 15th February (clue 5) and Moanwell blamed his goalkeeper for an error in the 0-1 defeat (clue 1), so they lost 0-4 on 25th January. Boxford United were not the opponents on 1st February, when Moanwell's team played Glumthorpe (clue 6), while clue 1 now rules out 18th January, 8th February and 15th February, so they were beaten by Moanwell' on 25th January. The 0-1 defeat (clue 1) was against Glumthorpe on 1st February. Dartlepool inflicted the 1-3 defeat (clue 7), so Hacklesfield, who didn't win 5-2 (clue 4), won 2-0 on 15th February, leaving the 5-2 winners as Dorquay, in a match where Moanwell blamed appalling refereeing (clue 2). He didn't blame injuries for the 0-2 defeat by Hacklesfield (clue 5), so intimidation and the Dartlepool defeat blamed on injuries. This match wasn't played on 8th February (clue 7), so on 18th January, leaving 8th February as the Dorquay match.

In summary:

18th January, Dartlepool, 1-3, injuries.
25th January, Boxford United, 0-4, state of pitch.
1st February, Glumthorpe, 0-1, goalkeeping error.
8th February, Dorquay, 2-5, appalling referee.
15th February, Hacklesfield, 0-2, intimidation.

Unlucky for Some (No 61)

From clue 5, the 1 cannot be in column 1 or column 5, and, since there are no two-digit numbers in columns 1 or 4 (clue 1), the 1 cannot be in column 2 or column 3 (clue 5), so it's in column 4. But it cannot be in B4 (clue 6), so it's in D4. So, from clue 5, the 12 is in C5 and the 10 in E3. The 8 is directly above the 13 (clue 7). This cannot be in column 1 or column 4 (clue 1),

SOLUTIONS

nor, since the 13 isn't in square D2 (clue 1), are they in column 2. Nor can the number 13 be in E5 (clue 4), which rules out column 5. Thus, from clue 7, the 8 is in A3 and the 13 in C3. So, from clue 4, square E5 must contain the 7. The 11 cannot be in column 1 or column 4 (clue 1), nor can it be in square A5 (clue 1), so it's in column 2. But it cannot be in D2 (clue 1), so it's in B2. The 9 isn't in a corner square (clue 2), which leaves only squares B4, C1 or D2. But it cannot be in B4 or D2 (clue 6), so it's in C1. Since the 6 is directly below the 2 (clue 3), it cannot be in D2, B4, A1 or A5, so it's in E1. The 2 is thus in A1 (clue 3). Remaining numbers are 3, 4 and 5; so (clue 6) the 5 is in B4 and the 3 in D2, which leaves the 4 in A5.

In summary:

	1	2	3	4	5
A	2		8		4
B		11		5	
C	9		13		12
D		3		1	
E	6		10		7

PIN Money (No 62)

Mrs Bradley is a Bank of East Anglia customer (clue 4) and the Lancashire Bank's customer has keyed in 3162 (clue 3), so Mr Mclean, whose number is 4630 and who isn't a Westshire customer (clue 1) and can't be the Mercia customer withdrawing £160 (clues 1 and 5), must bank with the Midminster. He isn't withdrawing £80 (clue 1), £20, for which the number 6757 is being used (clue 6), or £10 (clue 5), so £40. Thus £80 is being withdrawn from the Westshire Bank (clue 1). By elimination, the £20 is Mrs Bradley's withdrawal from the Bank of East Anglia and, by elimination, the withdrawal from the Lancashire Bank is £10. The number used by the Westshire customer isn't 4061 (clue 1), so it's 3989, leaving 4061 as the number entered by the Mercia Bank customer. The Lancashire customer isn't Mr Doyle (clue 3) or Miss Hanson (clue 2), as the amount being withdrawn is £10, so it's Mrs Kerr, whose number is 3162. As Miss Hanson's number isn't 3989 (clue 2), she is the person using number 4061 to withdraw £160 from the Mercia cash machine, leaving the Westshire customer entering 3989 to withdraw £80 as Mr Doyle.

In summary:
Bank of East Anglia, Mrs Bradley, 6757, £20.
Lancashire, Mrs Kerr, 3162, £10.
Mercia, Miss Hanson, 4061, £160.
Midminster, Mr Mclean, 4630, £40.
Westshire, Mr Doyle, 3989, £80.

Quick on the Draw (No 63)

Sally has been drawing for two years (clue 6). The person who drew four ponies, who has been drawing for only one year (clue 2), cannot be David (clue 1), or George (clue 5), or Mary, who drew just one pony (clue 3), so the most recent recruit to artistic pursuits is Jane. Sharpe took up drawing four years ago (clue 4). The contestant who has been drawing for five years cannot be Toobee (clue 1), Graffite (clue 5), or Lead who drew five ponies (clue 7), so it's Shading who has five years' experience. Jane isn't Toobee (clue 1). The number of ponies she drew rules her out as Lead and the number of years she has been drawing rule her out as Sharpe or Shading, so she is Graffite. From clue 1, David drew two ponies (clue 1) and Toobee drew three. We now know David isn't Lead, Toobee or Graffite, nor can he be Shading, who has been drawing a year longer than Sharpe (clue 1), so he is the latter, who has been drawing for four years. So, from clue 1, Toobee has been drawing for three years. By elimination, Sally drew five ponies, Toobee is George and Mary's has been drawing for five years. Clue 5 now reveals the prize winner as Jane Graffite, who drew four ponies.

In summary:
David Sharpe, 2 ponies, 4 years.
George Toobee, 3 ponies, 3 years.
Jane Graffite, 4 ponies, 1 year, winner.
Mary Shading, 1 pony, 5 years.
Sally Lead, 5 ponies, 2 years.

Bonanzah! (No 64)

10,000 gushas were paid out in 1998 (clue 4) and 15,000 was the reward for defending the oasis (clue 2), so (clue 5) the sheikh who won the camel Derby in the year 2000 was rewarded with 5,000 gushas. This wasn't Sheikh Yahand (clue 5), nor Sheikh Hays-el-rod who found water in the desert (clue 1). Sheikh Ratl-en-rol who received 12,500 gushas (clue 3), or Sheikh Adu-bel-sichs who won the 2001 gratuity (clue 6), so it was Sheikh Mahfist. The 2002 bounty wasn't 15,000 gushas (clue 1) and we know from his achievement that Sheikh Hays-el-rod didn't receive 15,000 gushas, so clue 1 also rules out 12,500 for the year 2002. Thus 7,500 gushas was paid out in 2002 and Sheikh Hays-el-rod was given 10,000. By elimination, the amount awarded to Sheikh Adu-bel-sichs in 2001 was 15,000 gushas, 1999 was the year Sheikh Ratl-en-rol was rewarded and it's Sheikh Yahand who was given a gratuity in 2002. The trainer of the Sheikh's racehorses wasn't Sheikh Ratl-en-rol (clue 3), so Sheikh Yahand and Sheikh Ratl-en-rol sank the oil well.

SOLUTIONS

In summary:

1998, S Hays-el-rod, 10,000 g, finding water.
1999, S Ratl-en-rol, 12,500 g, sinking oil well.
2000, S Mahfist, 5,000 g, winning camel Derby.
2001, S Adu-bel-sichs, 15,000 g, defending oasis.
2002, Sheikh Yahand, 7,500 g, training horses.

Soopergroop (No 65)

The Strolling Drones made three chart appearances (clue 6). The group with only one hit wasn't The Bleatles (clue 1), Dick's group, The Why (clue 2), or The Bluesy Moods (clue 3), so they were The Froggs, who were the keyboard player's former group (clue 5). The drummer achieved two chart placings (clue 7). The lead guitarist cannot have had four or five (clue 1) and we know he didn't have one, so he had three. So, from clue 1, The Bleatles had four, so they included Chick (clue 4) and Mick's group had five. The number of hits rules him out for three groups and we know Dick played with The Why, so Mick's group was The Bluesy Moods. Thus (clue 3) Chick provided The Bleatles' rhythm section. Mick wasn't the drummer, who had only two chart appearances, so he played bass guitar, leaving Dick on the drums. Since he had only two hits, from clue 2, Rick had one and played with The Froggs, which leaves Nick as the lead guitarist formerly with The Strolling Drones.

In summary:

Chick, rhythm guitar, The Bleatles, 4 hits.
Dick, drums, The Why, 2 hits.
Mick, bass guitar, The Bluesy Moods, 5 hits.
Nick, lead guitar, The Strolling Drones, 3 hits.
Rick, keyboard, The Froggs, 1 hit.

An America Raffles (No 66)

Annabelle's March victim wasn't Gus Stewart (clue 4) or Buck Wayne from Santa Fe (clue 2); Rusty Cooper was robbed in June or August (clue 1) and it wasn't March when Annabelle posed as a widow to rob Sam Autry (clue 5), so her March victim was Mason Hart. He wasn't the victim in Cheyenne, where she posed as an actress (clue 3) and Rusty Cooper's home-town had a two-word name (clue 1), so the Cheyenne victim was Gus Stewart. This wasn't in June (clue 3), so in September (clue 4) and Annabelle posed as a detective in August. She didn't pose as a singer when in Santa Fe robbing Buck Wayne (clue 2) or when robbing Rusty Cooper (1), so did so when robbing Mason Hart in March. Thus (clue 2) she robbed Buck Wayne in Santa Fe in May. We now know the month or the victim to go with four of Annabelle's rôles, so for the May crime in Santa Fe when Buck Wayne was the victim she posed as an heiress. By elimination, she posed as a widow to rob Sam Autry in June. Rusty Cooper was robbed in August but not in

Tombstone, nor (clue 6) in Dodge City (clue 6), so it was in El Paso. Finally, Tombstone wasn't where Annabelle robbed Sam Autry in June (clue 5), so was the location of the March crime, leaving June, when she posed as a widow to rob Sam Autry, as the month she was in Dodge City.

In summary:

March, Tombstone, singer, Mason Hart.
May, Santa Fe, heiress, Buck Wayne.
June, Dodge City, widow, Sam Autry.
August, El Paso, detective, Rusty Cooper.
September, Cheyenne, actress, Gus Stewart.

Camp Fire (No 67)

Figure 2 is Rizzo (clue 6). Figure 4 can't be Murray, aged 44 (clues 2 and 7), whose even-numbered position (clue 7) must thus be 6. He wasn't Henry, whose surname was Volker (clue 1), or Jim, who is figure 1 (clue 2); Levi was 24 (clue 5), so can't be figure 4, thus ruling out both himself and Bert from being figure 6 (clue 5). Clue 3 tells us figure 6, Murray, wasn't Dan, so, by elimination, he was Orrin. Thus, from clue 3, figure 5 is Redlaw. As we know Orrin Murray is figure 6, clue 3 rules out figure 1, Jim, from being Sutter and we know he wasn't Volker, so he was O'Carroll. We now know that Sutter is figure 3 or 4, so, from clue 3, Dan is either figure 2 or 3; in either case, Henry Volker can't be figure 3. We know he isn't figure 1, 2, 5 or 6, so he is figure 4 and Sutter is figure 3. Clue 1 now tells us figure 5 is the 19-year-old and clue 3 tells us that Dan is figure 2 and was thus Rizzo. We now know the forename or the date for five figures, so Levi, aged 24, is figure 3, Sutter. By elimination, Redlaw was Bert. Since figure 5, Bert Redlaw, was the 19-year-old, clue 2 tells us that figures 1 and 4 must each be either 31 or 38. Clue 4 tells us that Jim O'Carroll, figure 1, wasn't 38, so he was 31 and figure 4, Henry Volker, was 38. Finally, by elimination, figure 2, Dan Rizzo, was 17.

In summary:

1, Jim O'Carroll, 31.
2, Dan Rizzo, 17.
3, Levi Sutter, 24.
4, Henry Volker, 38.
5, Bert Redlaw, 19.
6, Orrin Murray, 44.

The Wild Geese (No 68)

Sheilah lives in Australia (clue 4). The Caseys living in the USA and Brazil are both male (clues 2 & 3), so Bridget, who doesn't live in Britain (clue 7), must live in Spain. The man in Brazil is a builder (clue 3), so can't be Declan, who's a priest (clue 6), nor is the builder Niall (clue 3), so he is Kevin. We now know the occupations of Declan and Kevin, so the soldier, who's also male (clue 5), is Niall. The police officer giving the jewellery isn't Bridget (clue 7), so is Sheilah, and, by elimination, Bridget is a folk-singer. The wine isn't being given by Kevin or Niall (clue 3) or Declan (clue 6), so is Bridget's gift. The American-based donor of the painting (clue 2) isn't Niall (clue 5), so is Declan the priest, and, by elimination, Niall must live in Britain. Finally, from clue 1, Niall's gift isn't the tea set, so it's the candlesticks, leaving the tea set as the gift of Kevin the builder from Brazil.

In summary:
Bridget, folk-singer, Spain, wine.
Declan, priest, USA, painting.
Kevin, builder, Brazil, tea set.
Niall, soldier, Britain, candlesticks.
Sheilah, police officer, Australia, jewellery.

Regimental Story (No 69)

Enoch Pitch missed his battle because he had gout (clue 5) and the Major-General because he was drunk (clue 1). The officer who missed Waterloo because he had fever, was never a general (clue 6), so Lieutenant-General Sidney Trow, who wasn't on leave (clue 4), was visiting HQ. Thus his missed battle wasn't El Alamein (clue 2), nor Bloemfontein (clue 4) and we know it wasn't Waterloo; it was Albert Bolt who missed Inkerman (clue 3), so Sidney Trow missed Cambrai. Albert Bolt's final rank wasn't Major-General (3), so he wasn't drunk and the battle he missed tells us he didn't have fever, so he was on leave. The Major-General who got drunk wasn't Oscar Ponto (clue 1), so was Joseph Knox. Thus, from clue 3, Albert Bolt was the Brigadier, and, by elimination, Oscar Ponto missed Waterloo because he had fever. Enoch Fitch wasn't the Colonel (clue 5), so was the Lieutenant-Colonel, leaving the Colonel as Oscar Ponto. Finally, Joseph Knox didn't miss El Alamein (clue 2), so missed Bloemfontein and it was Enoch Fitch who missed El Alamein.

In summary:
Albert Bolt, Brigadier, Inkerman, on leave.
Enoch Fitch, Lieutenant-Colonel, El Alamein, had gout.
Joseph Knox, Major-General, Bloemfontein, drunk.
Oscar Ponto, Colonel, Waterloo, had fever.
Sidney Trow, Lieutenant-General, Cambrai, visiting HQ.

A Korne Antiques (No 70)

Tuesday's buyers were the Fujitas (clue 1). Mrs Hofmann bought the tallboy (clue 5) and the Bergs were in the shop later than the buyers of the mirror (clue 2), so the wife who bought the lamp on Monday, who wasn't Mrs Yurkowitz, was Mrs McAndrew, whose husband bought

the musket (clue 3). Thus the music box, which was bought the day after the loving-cup (clue 2) wasn't sold on Tuesday or Thursday. The telescope was sold on Thursday (clue 4), so the music box wasn't sold on Friday and was sold on Saturday and the loving-cup was thus sold on Friday. As one couple bought the clock and the bust (clue 6), they weren't purchased on Thursday or Friday, so they were bought on Tuesday, by the Fujitas. Mrs Berg didn't buy the mirror (clue 2), so she bought the music box on Saturday, and, by elimination, the mirror was chosen by Mrs Yurkowitz and they were the Thursday buyers, with Mr Yurkowitz buying the telescope (clue 4). The man who bought the loving-cup on Friday was Mr Hofmann, whose wife bought the tallboy, leaving Mr Berg, as the Saturday shopper whose wife bought the music box, as the purchaser of the tantalus.

In summary:
Monday, musket, lamp, McAndrew.
Tuesday, clock, bust, Fujita.
Thursday, telescope, mirror, Yurkowitz.
Friday, loving-cup, tallboy, Hofmann.
Saturday, tantalus, music box, Berg.

Back to Back (No 71)

Eve rents house 5 (clue 7). The person in house 4 is 23 (clue 6), so (clue 1) Liam lives in either house 6 or 7 and a man five years his senior lives in 10 or 11 (clue 1). The resident of house 11 cannot be older than 22 (clue 8), so Liam's house is number 6 (clue 1) and the 29-year-old is in number 2. Douglas, who is 28 (clue 4), cannot live in house 1 (clue 8), so Gina cannot live in house 2 (clue 4), thus she lives in either 4 or 8 and Douglas in 3 or 7 (clue 4). If they lived in houses 3 and 4, from clue 2, Katie would live in 2 and Beverley in 1. We know the person in house 2 is 29. Since the person aged 23 is in house 4, the one in house 1 cannot be 20 (clue 8), and, since the person aged 25 is a woman (clue 5), Liam, in house 6, cannot be 20 either (clue 1), so, from clue 2, this cannot be the case. Thus Douglas is in 7 and Gina in 8 (clue 4). Katie cannot live in 1 or 4 (clue 2), so in 3 and Beverley's is number 2. Katie is 20 (clue 2), so (clue 7) Eve is 19. Harry lives in house 1 (clue 3) and Liam in house 6 is 22. The resident of house 10 is a man aged 27 (clue 1) and (clue 8) Harry is 24, so (clue 9) Claire lives in 4 and John in 9. The woman aged 25 doesn't live in house 11 (clue 8), so in 12 (clue 5) and (by elimination) she's Iris. Frank isn't in 9, nor can he be the man in house 10, who is 27 (clue 10), so he lives in 11, which leaves Angus in house 10. Frank isn't 26 (clue 8), nor, since Harry, in house 1, is 24, can Frank be 21 (clue 10), so he is 18. Thus John is 21, which leaves Gina's age as 26.

SOLUTIONS

In summary:

1, Harry, 24; 2; Beverley, 29; 3, Katie, 20; 4, Claire, 23

5, Eve, 19; 6, Liam, 22; 7, Douglas, 28; 8, Gina, 26

9, John, 21; 10, Angus, 27; 11, Frank, 18; 12, Iris, 25.

Expectant Drones (No 72)

Aunt Constance went out on Tuesday (clue 8). Since Montague was the Thursday escort (clue 6), from clue 2, Aunt Victoria cannot have been out on Friday, nor can that be the day Gerald and his Aunt Euphemia had an outing (clue 1). Clue 5 tells us the tapestry exhibition wasn't attended by Aunt Priscilla on Friday, so it was Aunt Millicent who went out that day. Her escort wasn't Archie (clue 4) and we know he wasn't Gerald or Montague and clue 2 rules out Friday for Rupert, so it was Edward who escorted Aunt Millicent, who thus went to the art exhibition (clue 3). Since Aunt Constance was escorted on Tuesday, clue 2 rules out Rupert for Monday escort duty and clue 4 rules out Archie. We know neither Edward nor Montague were on duty that day, so, by elimination, it was on Monday that Gerald escorted his Aunt Euphemia. This wasn't to the flower show (clue 1) and we know it wasn't to the art or tapestry exhibitions, while the opera outing was on Wednesday (clue 7), so Gerald and Aunt Euphemia went to the ballet. We now know Priscilla's tapestry exhibition wasn't on Monday, Tuesday, Wednesday or Friday, so it was attended by her and Montague on Thursday. By elimination, Aunt Constance went to the flower show on Tuesday and Aunt Victoria was escorted to the opera on Wednesday. So, from clue 2, Rupert took his Aunt Constance to the flower show on Tuesday, leaving Archie as Aunt Victoria's companion to the opera.

In summary:

Monday, Gerald Huntington, Aunt Euphemia, ballet.

Tuesday, Rupert de Grey, Aunt Constance, flower show.

Wednesday, Archie Fotheringhay, Aunt Victoria, opera.

Thursday, Montague Ffolliott, Aunt Priscilla, tapestry exhibition.

Friday, Edward Tanqueray, Aunt Millicent, art exhibition.

Freshers' Week (No 73)

Debbie joined the dramatic society (clue 6), so Jane is the girl (clue 1) from Croydon who joined the debating society. Luke who is studying architecture didn't join the music group (clue 4) and the photographic club was joined by the sociology student (clue 2), so Luke took up orienteering. Jane's subject isn't physics (clue 5)

and (clue 7) the classics student is from Ipswich, so Jane is reading French. Thus (clue 3) Debbie is from Bolton. The photography club member isn't Craig (clue 2), so Colin, thus Craig joined the music group and (by elimination) is from Ipswich, so Debbie studies physics. Colin isn't from Frome (clue 5), so Perth. Luke is from Frome.

In summary:

Colin, Perth, sociology, photography.

Craig, Ipswich, Classics, music.

Debbie, Bolton, physics, drama.

Jane, Croydon, French, debating.

Luke, Frome, architecture, orienteering.

Pride of Scotland (No 74)

The 2002 movie was Conspiracy (clue 3). The 2001 film in which Chisholm played a Saudi Arabian wasn't The Price (clue 4) or Nova, in which he played a Krysanian (clue 6); as he played a naval officer in the 2000 release (clue 5), clue 7 rules out Firecracker, which came out the year after the film in which Chisholm played a Swedish detective, as the 2001 release, which must thus have been Scorpion (clue 1), in which he played a secret agent. The 2003 film can't have featured Chisholm as an American (clue 1) or a Russian (clue 2), nor as the Swedish detective (clue 7); we know his 2003 rôle wasn't as a Saudi Arabian, so that was the year he played a Krysanian in Nova. We know he didn't play a Swedish detective in the 2000 or 2001 film and clue 7 rules out 2002 and 2003, so that was his 1999 rôle and from clue 7, Firecracker was the 2000 film in which he was a naval officer. Now, by elimination, the 1999 film was The Price. Clue 2 now tells us that the physician can't have been in the 2002 film Conspiracy, so was in 2003's Nova, leaving Chisholm's character in Conspiracy as a businessman. Finally, from clue 2, the businessman was Russian, leaving the naval officer in 2000's Firecracker as an American.

In summary:

1999, The Price, detective, Swedish.

2000, Firecracker, naval officer, American.

2001, Scorpion, secret agent, Saudi Arabian.

2002, Conspiracy, businessman, Russian.

2003, Nova, physician, Krysanian.

Ghosthunters (No 75)

Student 3's rôle is photography (clue 7). Student 6's rôle can't be interviews (clue 4), or site surveys, which are the speciality of the student from Pentecost (2); since student 5 is at St Magnus' (1), student 6 can't be the sound recordist, who is seated beside Peter Quist from Fairfax (clue 5), or Joanne Kaye the researcher, who's next to the Gladstone student (clue 3,) so (by elimination) he is the team leader. Sue Teague is student 1 (clue 8). Len Miller is student 2 (clue

5), so (clue 6) the sound-recordist isn't student 1, 2 or 4, so he is student 5 and, Peter Quist is student 6. Since student 3 is the photographer, he isn't Ben Coston (clue 2), so he is Mike Newman. Thus Joanne Kaye is student 4, and, from clue 3, the Gladstone student is student 3 who must, by elimination, be Ben Coston. So, from clue 2, Sue Teague is the Pentecost student who does site surveys, leaving student 2 as the interview specialist. He's not at Lyonesse (clue 4), so Carnegie and Joanne Kaye is at Lyonesse.

In summary:
1, Sue Teague, Pentecost, site surveys.
2, Len Miller, Carnegie, interviews.
3, Ben Coston, Gladstone, photography.
4, Joanne Kaye, Lyonesse, research.
5, Mike Newman, St Magnus', sound recording.
6, Peter Quist, Fairfax, team leader.

Knitting Needles (No 76)
The great-nephew's item was puce-coloured (clue 2), so the shocking pink item for a male relative (clue 7) was given to either the cousin or the nephew. Jemima's niece's item wasn't lime green (clue 1). October's work was for the cousin (clue 3) and the jersey was made in September (clue 5). Since the orange wool was used in July (clue 6), the lime green bootees (clue 1) were made in either August or October and the niece's item in either July or September. The wool used in September wasn't mauve (clue 5), so the niece's item cannot have been mauve; thus it was orange, so was made in July (clue 6). The bootees were made in August (clue 1) and (by elimination) were for the great-niece. The nephew was given the tie (clue 4), thus (by elimination) received his present in June and September's work was puce-coloured (great-nephew, clue 2). October's item wasn't gloves (clue 3), so socks and gloves were made in July. The tie wasn't shocking pink (7), so mauve. The socks were shocking pink.

In summary:
June, tie, mauve, nephew.
July, gloves, orange, niece.
August, bootees, lime green, great-niece.
September, jersey, puce, great-nephew.
October, socks, shocking pink, cousin.

Twins (No 77)
Nigel married Carol (clue 2). Tessa's surname was Haines (clue 3). David's bride, Miss McAlpine, wasn't Julie or Sarah (clue 1), so Karen. Peter's surname is Cammack (clue 3). Miss Cammack married Mr Purchan who isn't Keith (clue 4), who married David's sister, nor (clue 5) Simon, so Nigel and the former Miss

Cammack was thus Carol. We now know that neither David nor Nigel married Miss Purchan and since Nigel is her brother clue 4 rules out Keith. As Nigel Purchan married Carol Cammack, the intro tells us Peter Cammack can't have married Miss Purchan, so it was Simon who did so. We now know that Tessa Haines didn't marry David, Nigel or Simon, nor did she marry Peter Cammack (clue 3), so her husband was Keith. So, from clue 4, David, who married Karen McAlpine, is surnamed Haines, and, by elimination, Peter Cammack married Miss Tweedale. She isn't Sarah, who married Mr McAlpine (clue 1), so was Julie and Simon is Mr McAlpine. By elimination, Keith is Mr Tweedale.

In summary:
David Haines, Karen McAlpine.
Keith Tweedale, Tessa Haines.
Nigel Purchan, Carol Cammack.
Peter Cammack, Julie Tweedale.
Simon McAlpine, Sarah Purchan.

On the Rack (No 78)
The Five Points paper was in position 7 and the Star-Herald was in 5 (clue 4). The state for the Five Points paper wasn't Florida (clue 1), Ohio (clue 2) or Maine (clue 3). The Arizona paper was in 2 (clue 4) and the Texas community was Midway (clue 5); clue 6 rules out Pennsylvania for Five Points and clue 7 both Kentucky and Illinois, so Five Points is in Indiana, the paper in 7 was the Telegram (clue 5) and the one in 8 was from Pleasant Hill. We now know the paper in 1 wasn't from Arizona or Indiana; clue 1 rules out Florida (not in the top row), clue 2 rules out Ohio, clue 3 Maine, clue 5 Texas, clue 6 Pennsylvania and clue 7 Illinois, so the paper in 1 was from Kentucky. The Illinois paper was in 3 (clue 7). The paper in 9 wasn't from Florida (clue 1), Ohio (clue 2) Maine (clue 3) or Pennsylvania (clue 6), so Texas and (clue 5) the Globe was in 6. The paper in 3 wasn't from Pine Lake (clue 1), Riverside or Fairview (clue 3), Mount Lincoln (clue 6) or Centerville (clue 7), so Oak Grove and was thus the Recorder (clue 9). The Pine Lake paper wasn't in 1, 2, 4 or 6 (clue 1), so 5 and was thus the Star-Herald. The Journal was in 2 (clue 1) and the Florida paper in 4. The Riverside paper was in 6 (clue 3), the Maine paper in 5 and the Fairview paper in 1. The Mount Lincoln paper was in 4 (clue 6) and the Pennsylvania paper in 6. By elimination, the Pleasant Hill paper was from Ohio and the Journal from Centerville. The Midway paper was the Messenger (clue 6). The Enquirer was in 4 (clue 8) and the Chronicle in 1; so the paper in 8 was the Dispatch.

SOLUTIONS

In summary:
1, Fairview (Kentucky) Chronicle.
2, Centerville (Arizona) Journal.
3, Oak Grove (Illinois) Recorder.
4, Mount Lincoln (Florida) Enquirer.
5, Pine Lake (Maine) Star-Herald.
6, Riverside (Pennsylvania) Globe.
7, Five Points (Indiana) Telegram.
8, Pleasant Hill (Ohio) Dispatch.
9, Midway (Texas) Messenger.

Runners and Riders (No 79)
Declan rode on Wednesday (clue 3). Josh
didn't ride at Newcaster on Friday (clue 1), so
on Monday and Reggie raced on Friday. This
wasn't at Oldmarket (clue 2), so Mascott and his
horse was thus Black Cat (clue 4). Declan was
at Oldmarket. Four-leafed Clover wasn't ridden
by Josh (clue 1), so Declan. Josh rode Silver
Horseshoe.

In summary:
Declan, Wednesday, Four-leafed Clover,
Oldmarket.
Josh, Monday, Silver Horseshoe, Newcaster.
Reggie, Friday, Black Cat, Mascott.

Broad-based (No 80)
Widgeon is the Fishers' boat (clue 1). Daffodil
wasn't the Drakes' (clue 3), so the Nelsons' and
has a white hull (clue 2). The Drakes hired the
Jewel. The boat hired for 3 weeks wasn't the
Widgeon (clue 1) or the Daffodil (clue 2), so the
Jewel. Widgeon's hull isn't blue (clue 1), so green
and Jewel's is blue. The Widgeon was rented for
2 weeks (clue 1), so the Daffodil for 1 week.

In summary:
Daffodil, white, Nelson, 1 week.
Jewel, blue, Drake, 3 weeks.
Widgeon, green, Fisher, 2 weeks.

Four Guys Named Moe (No 81)
Moe Torway's forename is Montague (clue 5).
Moe Quette's forename isn't Morris or Moses
(clue 2), so it's Mortimer and Moe Quette is thus
the builder (clue 3) as well as the councillor (clue
2). Morris the scoutmaster isn't Moe Shunless
(clue 1), so is Moe Hare; thus Moe Shunless'
forename is Moses. The postman's forename isn't
Moses or Montague (clue 5), so it's Morris. As
Moe Shunless' full first name is Moses, he isn't
the publican (clue 3), so he is the farmhand and
also (clue 4) the lay reader. By elimination, Moe
Torway is the publican and the special constable.

In summary:
Moe Hare, Morris, postman, scoutmaster.
Moe Quette, Mortimer, builder, councillor.
Moe Shunless, Moses, farmhand, lay reader.
Moe Torway, Montague, publican, special
constable.

Sunday Sermons (No 82)
On May 4, Rev Keynes is speaking in Ricefield
(clue 5) and on May 18 his text is from Jubilees
(clue 2), so the sermon at Kerbstone using a
text from Reuben, which won't be on May 11
(clue 4), is on May 25, at St Rhea's (clue 1). Thus
the sermon at Heaviwater, which isn't on May
18 (clue 2), is on May 11 and it's at St Freya's in
Cherrypit (clue 3) that the Rev Keynes is going
to speak on May 18th on a text from Jubilees.
From the same clue, it's on May 11 that the text
is from 3 Corinthians, so, by elimination, Rev
Keynes' text on May 4, at Ricefield, will be from
Nicodemus. Finally, from clue 5, the church at
Ricefield isn't St Typhon's, so St Nudd's and St
Typhon's is where the Rev Keynes will speak
on May 11, at Heaviwater, on a text from 3
Corinthians.

In summary:
May 4, St Nudd's, Ricefield, Nicodemus.
May 11, St Typhon's, Heaviwater, 3 Corinthians.
May 18, St Freya's, Cherrypit, Jubilees.
May 25, St Rhea's, Kerbstone, Reuben.

For a Good Cause (No 83)
Pamela Rice works for Finch's (clue 2) and Fiona
Green gave the cheque for the swim (clue 5),
Andrew Bell gave the £600 cheque (clue 4), so
the person who gave the cheque from Grey and
Hick's quiz, who was the same gender as the one
who gave the £500 cheque from the mountain
climb (clue 3) can't have been Keith Lloyd and
must, by elimination, have been Andrew Bell. So,
from clue 3, the £500 from the mountain climb
was given by Keith Lloyd, and, by elimination,
Pamela Rice from Finch's gave the cheque from
the walk. The PennyCorp event made £800 (clue
1), so, by elimination, their cheque was given by
Fiona Green. Finally, by elimination, Pamela Rice
gave the £700 cheque and Keith Lloyd, who gave
the £500 cheque from the mountain climb, works
for JJL.

In summary:
Andrew Bell, Grey and Hick, quiz, £600.
Fiona Green, PennyCorp, swim, £800.
Keith Lloyd, JJL, mountain climb, £500.
Pamela Rice, Finch's, walk, £700.

Wizard Plot! (No 84)
Someone is studying fortune-telling at
Sowrash (clue 5) and Prof Squirrel teaches at
Gruntpimples, so Prof Deerkey, who teaches
wandwork and isn't a fellow of Hamboils or
Porkwens (clue 1) is at Boarpocks. His pupil
isn't Lottie Baxter (clue 2), Larry Lester, who

SOLUTIONS

attends Porkwens (clue 1), Barry Carter, who is taught by Prof Tumbledown (clue 3), or Carrie Foster, who is studying potions (clue 4), so Gary Dexter. Larry Lester isn't studying wandwork or potions, or invisibility, which is being studied at Gruntpimples. The Porkwens pupil isn't studying invisibility (clue 1), so Larry is studying flying there. His professor isn't McTavish (clue 2), so Snoop. Lottie Baxter isn't being taught by Prof McTavish (clue 2), so by Prof Squirrel. By elimination, Prof McTavish is teaching Carrie Foster about potions at Hamboils and the Sowrash pupil is Barry Carter. Thus Lottie Baxter is studying invisibility.

In summary:
L Baxter, Gruntpimples, invisibility, Prof Squirrel.
B Carter, Sowrash, fortune-telling, Prof Tumbledown.
G Dexter, Boarpocks, wandwork, Prof Deerkey.
C Foster, Hamboils, potions, Prof McTavish.
L Lester, Porkwens, flying, Prof Snoop.

Ms Fitt (No 85)

Lisa's class, for which Wanda wore a black leotard, is the day after that at the church hall (clue 6), which, not being in a proper gymnasium, can't be on Monday (clue 1), so Lisa's class can't be on Tuesday. As it's the day before the one at the community centre (clue 6), it can't be on Friday, nor can it be Wednesday, as Wanda wore a green leotard on that day last week (clue 4), so Lisa's class is on Thursday. Wednesday's is at the church hall (clue 6) and Friday's is at the community centre. Wanda wore a leotard for Kate's class (clue 3), which was thus pink. Thus Kate's class isn't on Monday (clue 2), so on Tuesday and Wanda wore her grey jogging suit on Monday. Neither Holly's class nor Beth's can be on Monday, since neither is held in a gymnasium (clue 1), so the Monday class is Heather's. It isn't at Starr's Gym (clue 2), so (clue 1) at the YWCA gym. The class at Starr's Gym isn't on Tuesday (clue 5), so on Thursday. By elimination, Kate's class is in the school hall and Wanda wore her blue jogging suit on Friday, at (clue 1) Holly's class, thus Beth's is at the church hall.

In summary:
Monday, Heather, YWCA gym, grey jogging suit.
Tuesday, Kate, school hall, pink leotard.
Wednesday, Beth, church hall, green leotard.
Thursday, Lisa, Starr's Gym, black leotard.
Friday, Holly, community centre, blue jogging suit.

Battleships (No 86)

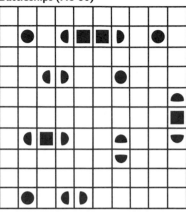

Logi-5 (No 87a)

B	A	E	C	D
E	C	A	D	B
D	E	C	B	A
C	B	D	A	E
A	D	B	E	C

ABC (No 87b)

C		A	B	
B		C	A	
	A		C	B
	C	B		A
A	B			C

But Is It Art? (No 88)

Sir Archie paid £10,000 for the pile of old car tyres (clue 4), so Ivan Rippov's stainless steel pyramid cost £20,000 (clue 1), the car tyres came from the Schamm Gallery and the Monty Banks's piece from the Foni Gallery was £5,000 (clue 2). The dustbin of cans cost more than the broken glass in the frame (clue 3), which was purchased from Fake Modern (clue 5), so the £5,000 piece was the yellow-painted kettle. The dustbin cost £25,000 (clue 3) and the broken glass £15,000. The Ivan Rippov piece wasn't from the Huddwinker Gallery (clue 1), so the Pinchbeck and the dustbin full of cans was the work from the Huddwinker. Artie Fishall's piece wasn't the car tyres or the dustbin (clue 4), so the broken glass. The Con Swindell piece cost £25,000 and the Esau Hoakes piece (clue 6) £10,000.

SOLUTIONS

In summary:

Fake Modern, Artie Fishall, broken glass in frame, £15,000.

Foni, Monty Banks, yellow-painted kettle, £5,000.

Huddwinker, Con Swindell, dustbin of old cans, £25,000.

Pinchbeck, Ivan Rippov, stainless steel pyramid, £20,000.

Schamm, Esau Hoakes, pile of old car tyres, £10,000.

The Tee-Vees (No 89)

The Tee-Vee who wears the apron does the cooking (clue 2), so the one who wears the top hat, who does not drive or do the laundry (clue 3) and isn't Dafi the cleaner (clue 5), is the gardener. The red Tee-Vee wears the waistcoat (clue 6), so the purple Tee-Vee, who does the laundry but doesn't wear the wellies (clue 4), must sport the sou'wester and is thus Bati (clue 6). Luni is yellow (clue 1), so Dipi, who is neither pink nor green (clue 1), is the red Tee-Vee with the waistcoat. Dipi does not do the cooking, gardening or laundry, so he is the driver. By elimination, Dafi wears the wellies. The green Tee-Vee isn't the gardener or the one who wears the apron, so it's Dafi. The Tee-Vee with the top hat isn't pink (clue 3), so yellow and Gaga is pink and wears the apron.

In summary:

Bati, purple, sou'wester, laundry.

Dafi, green, wellies, cleaning.

Dipi, red, waistcoat, driving.

Gaga, pink, apron, cooking.

Luni, yellow, top hat, gardening.

Place the Pooches (No 90)

The Labrador lives at number 6 (clue 4) and Butch at number 4 (clue 3). Ricky the Dalmatian isn't at number 8 (clue 1), so at number 2, and the Kennells live at number 4 and own Butch. The Doggetts' spaniel (clue 5) lives at number 8 and isn't Simba, so Jack. By elimination, the Labrador is Simba and Butch is the bulldog. The Barkers live at number 2 (clue 2), so the Yapps at number 6.

In summary:

2, Barker, Ricky, Dalmatian.

4, Kennell, Butch, bulldog.

6, Yapp, Simba, Labrador.

8, Doggett, Jack, spaniel.

The Passage of Time (No 91)

The clock on the library in Gregory Street cannot have been installed in 1953 (clue 4), while the 1735 clock is on the church (clue 3) and the 1897 clock is in Jubilee Road (clue 1), so the library clock was installed at the end of the war in 1918. So the library is building 2 (clue 5). The

1953 clock isn't on the school (clue 2), so it's on the bank, leaving the school as the building in Jubilee Road, whose clock dates from 1897. We now know the bank isn't in Gregory Street or Jubilee Road, nor is it in Spicer Street (clue 6), so it's in Long Lane, leaving the church in Spicer Street. From clue 4, building 1 is the bank, where the 1953 clock was installed. Thus, from clue 6, Spicer Street, where the church stands, is location 4, leaving the school in Jubilee Road as building 3.

In summary:

1, bank, 1953, Long Lane.

2, library, 1918, Gregory Street.

3, school, 1897, Jubilee Road.

4, church, 1735, Spicer Street.

Drones Will Be Drones (No 92)

Edward's birthday was in February (clue 5) and Rupert made a fool of himself in Piccadilly (clue 2). It wasn't Gerald who was involved in the June celebrations on the Embankment (clue 6), nor can it have been in June that Montague purloined the policeman's helmet (clue 3), so the June birthday is Archie's. He didn't sing (clue 6), while the swim took place in the Serpentine (clue 1) and the speech was made in August (clue 4). By elimination, Archie was debagged on the Embankment. So, from clue 1, the swim in the Serpentine took place in April. Montague's birthday was in October (clue 3). The location rules out Rupert for the April swim, which must thus have been taken by Gerald, leaving Rupert as the maker of the speech in August. By elimination, Edward sang on his birthday in February. This wasn't in the Strand (clue 5), so it was in Trafalgar Square, leaving the Strand as the location where Montague purloined the policeman's helmet.

In summary:

Archie Fotheringhay, June, debagged, Embankment.

Edward Tanqueray, February, sang, Trafalgar Square.

Gerald Huntington, April, swam, Serpentine.

Montague Ffolliott, October, purloined helmet, Strand.

Rupert de Grey, August, made speech, Piccadilly.

Evening Jobs (No 93)

Tom has just one child (clue 4). The father of five cannot be John, whose wife is the barmaid (clue 1), Nick (clue 3), or Ewan (clue 7), so he is Neville, whose wife is Delia (clue 3). So Nick is the father of four (clue 3). Since John's wife is the barmaid, he isn't the father of three children, whose mother is the fitness instructor (clue 6), so he has two, and, by elimination, the fitness instructor's husband is Ewan. John's wife isn't

Juliet (clue 1), or Andrea (clue 5). We know she isn't Delia, nor can she be Louise, who is the party plan sales organiser (clue 2), so she is Sally. Tom's wife, with just one child, isn't Juliet (clue 1), or Louise (clue 2), so Andrea. By elimination, Ewan's wife is Juliet and Nick's is Louise. Delia isn't the cleaner (clue 3), so she is the night-class teacher. Thus Andrea is the cleaner.

In summary:
Andrea, 1 child, cleaner, Tom.
Delia, 5 children, night-class teacher, Neville.
Juliet, 3 children, fitness instructor, Ewan.
Louise, 4 children, party plan salesperson, Nick.
Sally, 2 children, barmaid, John.

Good News, Bad News (No 94)

Tom Watson lives at No 12 (clue 4) and the income tax demand went to No 11 (clue 6), so, from clue 3, Annie Price, who was sent the reminder of an overdue library book, must live at No 4. No 4 received the gardening catalogue and isn't home to Debbie Blythe (clue 5), nor to Naomi Potts, who received the wedding invitation (clue 2), so Jack Brown. Thus (clue 1) the letter from the sister in Australia and the jury summons were both sent to No 5. So Naomi Potts cannot live there and must live at No 11, leaving Debbie Blythe as the resident of No 5. Tom Watson didn't receive the birthday card (clue 4), so his welcome letter was the premium bond prize, leaving the birthday card as Annie Price's. Jack's gardening catalogue wasn't delivered along with a begging letter from a student son (clue 5), so he received the gas bill, leaving Tom Watson as the father of the impecunious student.

In summary:
No 4, Jack Brown, gardening catalogue, gas bill.
No 5, Debbie Blythe, sister in Australia, jury summons.
No 11, Naomi Potts, wedding inv, tax demand.
No 12, Tom Watson, prem bond, begging letter.
No 14, Annie Price, birthday card, library rem.

On the Rigs (No 95)

Number 4 is Don (clue 5), so, from clue 4, the foreman cannot be in any of positions 3, 4 or 5. Number 2 is the chemist (clue 7), so the foreman is number 1. Thus, from clue 4, James, aged 28, is number 2, the chemist and Hoyle is number 3. The man aged 44 cannot be in either of positions 1 or 2 (clue 1), nor can he be number 5, who isn't as old as Jack (clue 3), and, since we know number 2 is the chemist, he cannot be number 3 (clue 1), so he is number 4, Don. So, from clue 1, the pilot is number 3, Hoyle and Barrell is number 2, James, the chemist. We now know the foreman, number 1, isn't Barrell or Hoyle, nor can he be Field, aged 36 (clue 2), while Sinker is

the rig worker (clue 6), so the foreman is Wells. This leaves Field, by elimination, as the engineer. Since he is 36, he cannot be Don, in position 4, so, by elimination, he is in position 5. This leaves Don as Sinker, the rig worker. Field, in position 5, isn't Nathan (clue 2), or Jack (clue 3), so he is Mervyn. Thus Jack isn't number 3 (clue 3) and is number 1, Wells, leaving Hoyle, the pilot, as Nathan. We know Jack isn't 44, so, from clue 3, he is 41, leaving Nathan Hoyle as the man aged 33.

In summary:
1, Jack Wells, foreman, 41.
2, James Barrell, chemist, 28.
3, Nathan Hoyle, pilot, 33.
4, Don Sinker, rig worker, 44.
5, Mervyn Field, engineer, 36.

Too Many Cooks (No 96)

The shaven-headed chef, whose restaurant is in Lambeth, isn't Jay Hammond-Eggz, Tim Sweet-Bredd or Dirk D'Essert (clue 2) or Perry Rasher, whose restaurant is in Chelsea (clue 6), so Angus Bannock, the Oriental cookery expert (clue 3). Jay has a pigtail (clue 5) and Perry has distinctive facial hair (clue 3). The chef in green isn't Tim (clue 1), so Dirk. As the cuisine nouveau chef has a goatee beard (clue 1) and the fish chef doesn't wear green (clue 1), neither is Dirk, nor is he the British traditional chef (clue 2), so Dirk is the vegetarian chef from Balham (clue 4). Jay's restaurant isn't in Hornsey (clue 5), so Islington and Tim's is in Hornsey. The fish chef isn't Tim (clue 1) or Perry (clue 6), so Jay. Tim's speciality isn't British traditional food (clue 7), so cuisine nouveau and (by elimination), Perry's is British traditional food and he has a walrus moustache.

In summary:
Angus Bannock, shaven head, Oriental, Lambeth.
Dirk D'Essert, dresses in green, vegetarian, Balham.
Jay Hammond-Eggz, pigtail, fish, Islington.
Perry Rasher, walrus moustache, British traditional, Chelsea.
Tim Sweet-Bredd, goatee beard, cuisine nouveau, Hornsey.

Me, Me, Me, Me, Me! (No 97)

Emma Starr's autobiography is priced at £18.99 (clue 6). The MP, whose book is priced at £15.99 (clue 4), isn't Hugh Jeago (clue 3), Ed Biggar (also clue 4), or Caleb Ritty, the footballer (clue 1), so it's Guy Fuller and the title of his autobiography is The Fuller Story (clue 1). Speaking Personally is priced at £16.99 (clue 2), so Talking of Me, written by the radio presenter (clue 3), is at least £17.99 and Hugh Jeago's book is more expensive still. It isn't £18.99 (clue 6), so is £19.99. Hugh Jeago isn't the pop singer (clue 2), so he is the opera singer. Speaking Personally isn't the autobiography of the opera singer or the pop singer (clue 2), so it's the footballer and is thus the £16.99 book by Caleb Ritty. By elimination, the £17.99 book is the one written by Ed Biggar. Quite a Life isn't the life-story of the pop singer (clue 2), so it's the opera singer's £19.99 volume. Finally, I Say! isn't priced at £17.99, so it's Emma Starr's £18.99 book, and, by elimination, she is the pop singer. Talking of Me is by Ed Biggar.

In summary:
The Fuller Story by Guy Fuller, £15.99, MP.
I Say! by Emma Starr, £18.99, pop singer.
Quite a Life by Hugh Jeago, £19.99, opera singer.
Speaking Personally by Caleb Ritty, £16.99, footballer.
Talking of Me by Ed Biggar, £17.99, radio presenter.

Detectives' Detectives (No 98)

Lucy Regan, the IAD officer, wasn't created by any of the police officers from Boston, Miami or New York (clue 1) and the Diamond Insurance investigator's creation is a Military Police officer (clue 6), so Lucy Regan is the creation of the Stern Agency investigator, John Kengo (clue 4). Dave Carey created the federal agent (clue 2), so the man who created the police chief (clue 5) is Saul Rossi. The New York cop is also male (clue 6); we know that he isn't John Kengo, nor is he Saul Rossi (clue 5), so he is Dave Carey. His federal agent isn't Andy Gomez (clue 5), Patsy-Ann Bowen (clue 2) or Maisie Hovik, who is Wendy Vance's creation (clue 3); we know that John Kengo created Lucy Regan, so the federal agent is Carl Van Damm. We know the creator's employers to go with three fictional detectives' occupations; the Miami cop's creation isn't a private eye (clue 4), so is the police chief created by Saul Rossi, who is thus the Miami cop, leaving the Boston cop as the creator of the private eye. We now know the employers of three real detectives; the Diamond Insurance investigator isn't Marion Penn (clue 6), so is Wendy Vance, creator of Maisie Hovik, leaving Marion Penn as the Boston cop who created the private eye. The private eye is female (clue 6), so is Patsy-Ann Bowen, leaving Andy Gomez as the police chief.

In summary:
Dave Carey, New York police, Carl Van Damm, federal agent.
John Kengo, Stern Agency, Lucy Regan, IAD officer.
Marion Penn, Boston police, Patsy-Ann Bowen, private eye.
Saul Rossi, Miami police, Andy Gomez, police chief.
Wendy Vance, Diamond Insurance, Maisie Hovik, Military Police officer.

Susie's Quilt (No 99)

The sun on a crimson background is on square C3 (clue 6). The rabbit cannot be in E3 (clue 1), so is in A3, A1 has a pale green background and square A1 a pale red one. The butterfly isn't in C5 (clue 4) and E5 depicts the fish (clue 8). Clue 5 tells us the butterfly cannot be in any of A1, A3, B2, C1, D4 or E1, so it's in either B4, D2 or E3. Since D4 has a brown background (clue 7), clue 5 tells us the apricot square, which is in line with the dark blue one, cannot be D2, which rules out E3 for the butterfly (clue 5). Similarly, the apricot square cannot be A3, depicting the rabbit, since we know the colours of both A1 and A5 (clues 1 and 5), which rules out B4 for the butterfly (clue 5), leaving only D2. So (clue 5) the apricot square is C1 and C5 is dark blue. From clue 9, the toadstool cannot be in column 1 or column 5, so it's in column 3. Thus it's in E3 and the beige square is A3. The grey square cannot be in rows D or E (clue 2) and we know it isn't in rows A or C, so it's in row B. The butterfly is in D2, which rules out B2 as the grey square (clue 2), which must thus be B4, with the bird in D4 (clue 2). Clue 3 now rules out the elephant for any of squares A1, A5, B2, B4, C1 or C5, so it's in E1 and D2 has a yellow background. Since the boat is somewhere in row B (clue 1), the ball, which is in the same row as the tree (clue 10), isn't in B2 or B4; nor (clue 10) in A5, C1 or C5, so it's in A1, the flower is in B2 and the tree in A5 and (clue 1) the boat is in B4. Clue 11 now rules out columns 1, 3, 4 and 5 for the pale blue square, which must thus be B2. So clue 11 places the doll in C1 and the cream square as E3. The lilac square is E5 (clue 3), depicting the fish, which leaves square E1 as dark green. By elimination, the house is in C5.

In summary:
A 1, ball, pale green; 3, rabbit, beige; 5, tree, pale red
B 2, flower, pale blue; 4, boat, grey.
C 1, doll, apricot; 3, sun, crimson; 5, house, dark blue.
D 2, butterfly, yellow; 4, bird, brown.
E 1, elephant, dark green; 3, toadstool, cream; 5, fish, lilac.

Beaux Afloat (No 100)

Matilda's father is the ambassador (clue 1) and Charlotte was a fellow guest of Beau Streate (clue 4). The admiral's daughter on the same cruise as Beau Legges wasn't Augusta or Caroline (clue 2), so Sophia who was on the 1817 cruise (clue 5). Caroline sailed in 1818 (clue 2) and is the earl's daughter (clue 6). Charlotte's father isn't the rich merchant (clue 4), so, the baronet and the merchant's daughter is Augusta. Charlotte wasn't aboard in 1816 or 1820 (clue

SOLUTIONS

4), so was a guest of Beau Spritt in 1819. Clue 1 rules out 1816 for Matilda's voyage, so she sailed with Beau Spritt in 1820, leaving Augusta on the 1816 trip. Matilda didn't sail with Beau Nydel (clue 1) or Beau Belles (clue 3), so Beau Tighe. Beau Belles didn't pursue Caroline in 1816 (clue 6), so he was Augusta's travelling companion, leaving Beau Nydel as the man who sailed with Caroline.

In summary:
1816, Beau Belles, Augusta, rich merchant.
1817, Beau Legges, Sophia, admiral.
1818, Beau Nydel, Caroline, earl.
1819, Beau Streate, Charlotte, baronet.
1820, Beau Tighe, Matilda, ambassador.

A Good Report (No 101)
Sophie got a B+ in French (clue 4). The subject awarded a C+ cannot have been Science (clue 2), or history (clue 5), nor was it given by Mr Fletcher for English (clue 7), so it was Sophie's maths grade. Thus, from clue 5, she received a B for history. This was from Mrs Jefferson (clue 6). The C+ in maths wasn't awarded by Miss Roberts (clue 5) and we know Sophie's maths teacher isn't Mr Fletcher or Mrs Jefferson, while clue 2 rules out Mr Dingle as the awarder of the C+, so Mrs Carter must teach maths. Her comment was 'A steady worker' (clue 3). Since Mr Dingle does not teach science (clue 2), he is Sophie's French teacher, who gave her the B+ and her science teacher is Miss Roberts. Clue 2 now reveals the comment 'intelligent' as the one accompanying the B grade in history, since we know it wasn't made for maths. The A grade was matched by the comment 'excellent' (clue 1), so the teacher who awarded the A- used either 'solid progress' or 'works hard'. But clue 1 rules out the latter, so 'solid progress' gone with the A-. Thus, from clue 7, it's Mr Fletcher who gave the A as his English assessment and that clue also tells us Miss Roberts gave the A- and commented 'solid progress' in science, which leaves 'works hard' as Mr Dingle's comment for French.

In summary:
English, A, Mr Fletcher, excellent.
French, B+, Mr Dingle, works hard.
History, B, Mrs Jefferson, intelligent.
Maths, C+, Mrs Carter, a steady worker.
Science, A-, Miss Roberts, solid progress.

Scots Wha Hae ... (No 102)
Hamish has a four-year record of success (clue 3). The three-year champion cannot be Iain (clue 2), Gregor, the hammer thrower (clue 4), or Alistair (clue 7), so he is Gordon McAlpine (clue 1), and, from that clue, the tossing the caber champion has a four-year reign and is thus Hamish. Gordon McAlpine's event isn't the mile

(clue 2), or the shot putt, which has been won by the same man for six years (clue 6) and we know it isn't the caber or the hammer, so it's the high jump. We now know the longest-standing champion isn't McAlpine, nor is he Bruce, who has won five years in a row (clue 5). Nor can he be Campbell (clue 4), or Stewart (clue 7), so he is Kennedy. The mile runner isn't Iain (clue 2), so he is Alistair, and Iain is the shot putter. Now, from clue 2, Alistair cannot be Kennedy, with a seven-year record, so his period as champion in the mile is five years and he is Bruce. This leaves Gregor as Kennedy, the seven-year champion, so, from clue 4, Campbell is Iain, with a six-year reign, leaving Hamish as Stewart.

In summary:
Alistair Bruce, mile, 5 years.
Gordon McAlpine, high jump, 3 years.
Gregor Kennedy, hammer, 7 years.
Hamish Stewart, caber, 4 years.
Iain Campbell, shot putt, 6 years.

Wanted! (No 103)
The reward on offer in White River is an even number of hundreds of dollars (clue 3), but $400 is the sum on the Little Pine posters (clue 2) and since the White River reward is $100 less than that for the murderer (also clue 3), it isn't $1,000, so it's $600 and thus the outlaw concerned is Link O'Reilly (clue 5). The reward for the murderer must thus be $700 (clue 3). The reward for Scotty McRae is $300 more than that for the cattle rustler (clue 1), but it isn't $1,000, since the reward for the murderer is $700. Thus, the reward offered in Harris Falls for Scotty McRae (clue 1) is $700 and the cattle rustler is wanted in Little Pine for $400. The 'Wanted' poster in White River isn't for the train robber Zack Monroe (clue 4), or the bank robber, wanted in Gibbsville (clue 6), so Link O'Reilly is wanted in White River for horse stealing. Thus, by elimination, the Yellow Creek poster is of Zack Monroe. The Gibbsville reward is $1,000 (clue 6) and $500 is being offered by Yellow Creek. The $400 isn't for the capture of Hank Gilmore (clue 2), so Baxter Gould. Hank Gilmore is wanted in Gibbsville.

In summary:
Gibbsville, Hank Gilmore, bank robbery, $1,000.
Harris Falls, Scotty McRae, murder, $700.
Little Pine, Baxter Gould, cattle rustling, $400.
White River, Link O'Reilly, horse stealing, $600.
Yellow Creek, Zack Monroe, train robbery, $500.

Sailor Sam (No 104)
Sam set out from Portsmouth in 1903 (clue 7), so (clue 1) he didn't land in Bordeaux in 1899, 1902 or 1903. In 1901 he ended up in Torquay (clue

5), so, by elimination, fetched up in Bordeaux in 1900 and (clue 1) started out from Brighton in 1901, ending up in Torquay and his 1899 destination was Gibraltar. We now know he didn't set out from Dover in 1901 or 1903 and clue 3 now rules out 1899 and 1902, so Dover is where he set sail in 1900, before reaching Bordeaux. So, from clue 3, he landed in Calais in 1899, when heading for Gibraltar. He had not set out from Worthing on that voyage (clue 4), so he started out from Southend, leaving Worthing as the starting point for his voyage in 1902. He didn't end up in Plymouth on that trip (clue 4), so he landed in Dunkirk and was thus heading for Algiers (clue 2). By elimination, in 1903 he landed in Plymouth after setting sail from Portsmouth. On that voyage he cannot have been aiming for Madeira or Tangier (clue 6), so he was intending to sail to Tunis. Clue 6 now tells us he was heading for Madeira in 1900 when he set out from Dover and Tangier when he set sail from Brighton in 1901.

In summary:
1899, Southend, Gibraltar, Calais.
1900, Dover, Madeira, Bordeaux.
1901, Brighton, Tangier, Torquay.
1902, Worthing, Algiers, Dunkirk.
1903, Portsmouth, Tunis, Plymouth.

Birthday Book (No 105)

Alma's uncle was born between February and June (clue 10), but not in March, when the birthday date is the 1st (clues 2 and 10), or June, which is Helen's birthday month (clue 8). Since Alma's son celebrates his birthday in April (clue 1), this rules out April and May (clue 10), so, by elimination, the uncle was born in February. Thus, grandma has a January birthday (clue 10). We now know the male relative born on 1st March (clue 2), isn't the uncle or the son, nor can he be the granddad, whose birthday fell on an even date (clue 6), or Alma's father, Henry, who was born in a month with only 30 days (clue 4). Clue 3 rules out the great-uncle, so, by elimination, it's a male cousin who was born on 1st March. Thus, from clue 9, the female cousin was born on 8th October. From clue 6, Melanie wasn't born in January, May, July or November. Clue 5 tells us a female connection has the July birthday, so clue 6 rules out August for Melanie; and clue 11 rules out December. So, by elimination, her birthday is on the 30th September and granddad was born in August (clue 6). We now know Alma's father, Henry, wasn't born in April, June or September, so, from clue 4, he a November birthday. Clue 3 rules out the great-uncle's birthday for May, June or July and we know it isn't in September. We

have identified a connection or a female name with seven other months, so he has a December birthday and Alma's aunt is thus Melanie, who was born on 30th September (clue 3). The goddaughter cannot have been born in May or June (clue 7), so, by elimination, her birthday is in July and Joyce's is thus in May (clue 7). Helen, born in June, isn't Alma's mother (clue 8), so she is her daughter, leaving her mother as Joyce. Clue 12 now tells us her birthday is on the 16th of May and that Derek is Alma's granddad, born in August. From clue 7, Rodney's birthday isn't in January, February, April, October or December and he cannot be the god-daughter born in July, so he is the male cousin born on 1st March and Valerie is Alma's grandma, whose birthday is thus on the 10th January (clue 7). Derek's August birthday isn't on the 8th, 10th, 16th or 30th and clue 12 rules out the 14th and the 22nd, so its even-numbered date (clue 6) is the 6th. From clue 13, Stanley's birthday isn't in February, April, July or October, so in December and he is Alma's great-uncle. Patricia is Alma's cousin (clue 13) born on 8th October and Henry's birthday is on 27th November. By elimination, Alma's god-daughter is Anne. From clue 12, Stanley's birthday is on 14th December. Anne's is on 31st July (clue 5) and Helen's on 11th June. Richard isn't Alma's uncle, (clue 10), so her son, leaving her uncle as George. George's birthday is on 22nd February (clue 10) and the former's on 23rd April.

In summary:
January 10th, Valerie, grandma.
February 22nd, George, uncle.
March 1st, Rodney, cousin.
April 23rd, Richard, son.
May 16th, Joyce, mother.
June 11th, Helen, daughter.
July 31st, Anne, god-daughter.
August 6th, Derek, granddad.
September 30th, Melanie, aunt.
October 8th, Patricia, cousin.
November 27th, Henry, father.
December 14th, Stanley, great-uncle.

Yesterday's Villains (No 106)

Sam Trevian's ancestor, the murderer, wasn't Yestin, whose descendant is a solicitor (clue 3), Ivo or Dewi, who was a smuggler (clue 5), or Wynn, who was Chris Davey's ancestor (clue 6), so was Sampson. Sam Trevian isn't the publican (clue 2) and we know he isn't the solicitor; the bus driver is Jack Kegwin (clue 4) and the ferryman's ancestor was a highwayman (clue 6), so Sam Trevian, descended from Sampson the murderer, is the hotelier. We now know the occupations for the descendants of two villains and the crime of a third, so the highwayman whose descendant is a ferryman, who wasn't Chris Davey's ancestor Wynn (clue 6), is Ivo. By elimination, Chris Davey is the publican, leaving Jack Kegwin as the descendant of Dewi the smuggler. Thus (clue 1) Alan Borlase is descended from Ivo the highwayman and is the ferryman; and Owen Pender is descended from Yestin, who wasn't a wrecker (clue 1) so was a forger, leaving the wrecker as Wynn.

In summary:
Alan Borlase, ferryman, Ivo, highwayman.
Chris Davey, publican, Wynn, wrecker.
Jack Kegwin, bus-driver, Dewi, smuggler.
Owen Pender, solicitor, Yestin, forger.
Sam Trevian, hotelier, Sampson, murderer.

Problem Problems (No 107)
Mr Tufto is from Malvern (clue 5), so his problem's unacceptable theme was neither cannibalism, which was in the problem from Norwich (clue 4), nor cruelty to animals (or, at least, animal products), which was in Miss Rugge's problem (clue 6). Mr Tufto's didn't involve a sport (clue 5), which rules out cricket and pankration, so it was sex and his character was thus James Link (clue 1). Ms Glump's problem featured the Knights (clue 3); neither Miss Rugge's nor Mr Lupin's featured the Beaus (clue 6), so Mrs Bleyes' did. Mr Lupin's problem wasn't the Drones one submitted from Walsall (clue 2), so it featured Miss Raffles and Miss Rugge lives in Walsall. Mr Lupin's problem didn't involve cannibalism or cricket (clue 4), so pankration. Thus Mr Lupin isn't from Runcorn (clue 8) and must live in Bristol. By elimination, the cricket problem come from Runcorn. It wasn't sent in by Mrs Bleys (clue 7), so it was Ms Glump's Knights problem, leaving Mrs Bleyes' Beaus problem as the one from Norwich which involved cannibalism.

In summary:
Mrs Bleyes, Norwich, Beaus, cannibalism.
Ms Glump, Runcorn, Knights, cricket.
Mr Lupin, Bristol, Miss Raffles, pankration.
Miss Rugge, Walsall, Drones, cruelty to animals.
Mr Tufto, Malvern, James Link, sex.

B&B and Evening Meal (No 108)
The meal at the village with standing stones was curry (clue 2). At The Willows it was fish and chips (clue 4). At Redgate, in the village with the hill fort, the meal wasn't pizza (clue 3) or burger and chips (clue 5), so pasty and chips. The holy well is at Rospentyr (clue 4); Polkear, where burgers and chips was served hasn't a stone circle (clue 5), so a castle. The village with

the hill fort and the B&B called Redgate isn't Polkear or Rospentyr, nor is it Mencarrow (clue 3), while the B&B at Henmelin is Camelot (clue 5), so Redgate is in Bosleven. Henmelin hasn't a stone circle (clue 5), so a standing stone and thus Camelot served the curry. As the meal at Haven House included chips (clue 1), it wasn't pizza, so Haven House is in Polkear and the B&B which served pizza was St Piran's. The B&B at Rospentyr isn't The Willows, where fish and chips was served (clue 4), so St Piran's and (by elimination) The Willows is in Mencarrow.

In summary:
Bosleven, hill fort, Redgate, pasty and chips.
Henmelin, standing stone, Camelot, curry.
Mencarrow, stone circle, The Willows, fish/chips.
Polkear, castle, Haven House, burger and chips.
Rospentyr, holy well, St Piran's, pizza.

At a Standstill (No 109)
Jill is in car 7 (clue 5), from clue 1, Sue cannot be in 1, 2, 3, 4, 5, 7, 9 or 11, and, since car 8 has a male driver (clue 5), Sue isn't in 8 or 12, thus in either 6 or 10 and (clue 1) Ruth is in either 2 or 6. In other words, the occupant of 6 is either Ruth or Sue. Don, who isn't in car 7 (clue 2) is the man in car 8 and Laura's is car 11. Car 1 is Leon's (clue 6). Car 9 has a female driver (clue 6), so Bill is in 5 (clue 1), so Sue is in 6 and Ruth in 2. Tina's odd-numbered vehicle isn't car 9 (clue 4), so 3. Mike is in 4 (clue 4) and Jack in 10. Mary is the woman in car 9 (clue 6), so Dick is in 12.

In summary:
1 Leon; 2 Ruth; 3 Tina; 4 Mike.
5 Bill; 6 Sue; 7 Jill; 8 Don.
9 Mary; 10 Jack; 11 Laura; 12 Dick.

Battleships (No 110)

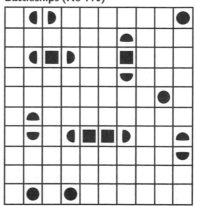

SOLUTIONS

Logi-5 (No 111a)

B	C	E	A	D
D	A	B	E	C
E	D	A	C	B
C	E	D	B	A
A	B	C	D	E

ABC (No 111b)

	C	B		A
A			C	B
B		A		C
	A	C	B	
C	B		A	

Something Special (No 112)

Rachel Shaw's reception will cost £2000 (clue 2) and the £2400 reception will be for Mark Lewis and his bride (clue 3), from clue 6, the reception for Alison Bell and Simon Ryder can't be costing £1400 or £1600, so it's costing £1800, and, from the same clue, Nick Murphy's is costing £1400. We now know the prices to go with three grooms; the £1600 reception is for the wedding at the stately home (clue 5), so Jon Ireton's reception at the football ground (clue 1) is costing £2000 and his bride is thus Rachel Shaw. From the same clue, Liz Monk's reception is costing £2400 and she is thus marrying Mark Lewis. By elimination, the stately home wedding and £1600 reception is Daniel Clark's. As Clare Dane will be marrying on the lake shore (clue 4), her reception isn't costing £1600, so it's costing £1400 and she's thus marrying Nick Murphy, leaving Emma Finch as Daniel Clark's bride who's having the £1600 reception. Finally, Liz Monk and Mark Lewis aren't marrying in a hot-air balloon (clue 3), so they booked a Tudor chapel and the hot-air balloon is where Alison Bell and Simon Ryder are marrying before their £1800 reception.

In summary:
Alison Bell, Simon Ryder, hot-air balloon, £1800.
Clare Dane, Nick Murphy, lake shore, £1400.
Emma Finch, Daniel Clark, stately home, £1600.
Liz Monk, Mark Lewis, Tudor chapel, £2400.
Rachel Shaw, Jon Ireton, football ground, £2000.

Music and ... (No 113)

John was in coach C (clue 4). The passenger in B was reading a textbook (clue 5). Bach was the favourite composer of the coach D passenger (clue 6). Julia with the financial report wasn't in A or E (clue 1), so in D and was listening to Bach. Thus (clue 1) John favours Mozart. Martin's prefers Haydn (clue 2). Bella isn't the magazine reader listening to Beethoven (clue 3), so her composer is Handel, and Beethoven is Carole's choice. John wasn't reading the newspaper (clue 4), so a novel. Martin wasn't in B (clue 2), so he read the newspaper and Bella had the textbook. Carole was in A (clue 3), so Martin was in E.

In summary:
Bella, coach B, textbook, Handel.
Carole, coach A, magazine, Beethoven.
John, coach C, novel, Mozart.
Julia, coach D, financial report, Bach.
Martin, coach E, newspaper, Haydn.

... Meals on Wheels (No 114)

Julia in coach D drank coffee (clue 3). John was second in the queue in the buffet car (clue 4) and Martin ordered the ham and tomato sandwich (clue 6). The person with a ham salad sandwich and orange juice wasn't from coaches B or C (clue 1), so is Carole, from A, who was first in the queue. John ordered lager (clue 2), so Martin is the man referred to in clue 5. By elimination, Bella drank shandy, and, since Martin and at least one other passenger were behind her in the queue (clue 5), she was third and Martin was fourth, so Julia was fifth. Julia had the cheese salad sandwich (clue 5). John ate cheese and tomato (clue 2) and Bella had the chicken salad sandwich. By elimination, Martin ordered tea.

In summary:
Bella, third, chicken salad, shandy.
Carole, first, ham salad, orange juice.
John, second, cheese and tomato, lager.
Julia, fifth, cheese salad, coffee.
Martin, fourth, ham and tomato, tea.

Literary Associations (No 115)

The 1776 pub is associated with Ian Fleming (clue 3) and the 1612 pub is in Leman Street (clue 5). E M Forster's favourite in Market Place wasn't built in 1689 or 1740 (clue 4), so 1824 and is thus the Old Ship (clue 6). The 1612 pub isn't associated with Charles Dickens (clue 2) or J R R Tolkien (clue 5), so is Ms Sayers' favourite, the Royal Dragoon (clue 1). The Devil and Boot is older than the pub associated with Charles Dickens (clue 2), so is associated with J R R Tolkien and dates from 1689 and the one associated with Charles Dickens is from 1740. The Hawk and Hound is in Dog Lane (clue 2). The Jack O'Lantern isn't in Queen's Road (clue 7), so Rose Street and the Devil and Boot is in Queen's Road. The 1740 pub isn't in Rose Street (clue 7), so Dog Lane. The Jack O'Lantern is in Rose Street.

In summary:
Devil and Boot, Queen's Road, 1689, J R R Tolkien.
Hawk and Hound, Dog Lane, 1740, C Dickens.
Jack O'Lantern, Rose Street, 1776, I Fleming.
Old Ship, Market Place, 1824, E M Forster.
Royal Dragoon, Leman Street, 1612, D L Sayers.

April Foolery (No 116)

The biology teacher tricked by Jimmy is female (clue 1) and Mr Green wasn't fooled by Tommy (clue 4), so he was Danny's victim. His subject isn't English (clue 4), so maths and Danny is Catcher (clue 3). Tommy tricked the English teacher, not Miss Jones (clue 4), so Mrs Baker and Tommy is thus Diddler (clue 2). Thus Jimmy's surname is Kidham and his biology teacher is Miss Jones.

In summary:
Danny Catcher, Mr Green, maths.
Jimmy Kidham, Miss Jones, biology.
Tommy Diddler, Mrs Baker, English.

Logi-5 (No 117a)

E	C	B	D	A
B	A	C	E	D
A	E	D	C	B
D	B	E	A	C
C	D	A	B	E

ABC (No 117b)

	A		C	B
C		B	A	
A	B	C		
	C		B	A
B		A		C

Pile Up (No 118)

From the top: F, D, B, C, A, E.

Back to School (No 119)

The English teacher captained the swimming team (clue 3). The rugby captain doesn't teach biology (clue 4), so geography and the biology teacher's sport is cricket. The geography teacher was captain in 1975 (clue 4), so (clue 1) Bruce Otway was captain in 1980. The biology teacher wasn't

captain in 1970 (clue 2), so 1980. The swimmer was captain in 1970. He isn't Clive Price (clue 3), so Alan Newton and Clive teaches geography.

In summary:
Alan Newton, English, swimming, 1970.
Bruce Otway, biology, cricket, 1980.
Clive Price, geography, rugby, 1975.

All the As (No 120)

Anton the Abominable was married to Anastasie (clue 2) and Anton the Amiable died of alcohol (clue 4), so Astrud's husband who died in an ambush, whose nickname wasn't 'the Arrogant' (clue 5), was Anton the Asinine. Anton II was Agathe's husband (3). Anton the Asinine wasn't Anton I (clue 1) or Anton IV (clue 1), so Anton III. Anton the Abominable didn't die of apoplexy (clue 2), so arsenic. Anton the Arrogant died of apoplexy. Adamante's spouse didn't die of alcohol (clue 4), so apoplexy, thus Agathe's was Anton the Amiable. Anton the Arrogant wasn't Anton IV (clue 5), so Anton I. Anton IV was Anastasie's husband.

In summary:
Anton I, the Arrogant, Adamante, apoplexy.
Anton II, the Amiable, Agathe, alcohol.
Anton III, the Asinine, Astrud, ambush.
Anton IV, the Abominable, Anastasie, arsenic.

Batswomen (No 121)

The Essex player is pregnant (clue 3), so Carol, who has been arrested and who doesn't play for Hampshire or Cheshire (clue 2), plays for Durham. Her surname isn't Wicket or Ball (clue 1) and Ms Field got engaged (clue 4), so Carol's surname is De Clare. Sarah is Ms Ball (clue 1). Ms Field isn't Lucy (clue 4), so Ellen; thus Lucy is Ms Wicket of Cheshire (clue 1). By elimination, Lucy is retiring, Ellen plays for Hampshire and Sarah is pregnant.

In summary:
Carol De Clare, Durham, arrested.
Ellen Field, Hampshire, engagement.
Lucy Wicket, Cheshire, retirement.
Sarah Ball, Essex, pregnancy.

Synchronise Your Watches... (No 122)

One agent will set off for Shed B at 23.01 hours (clue 1). Shed D is the objective for 'Eagle' (clue 4) and C is a later objective than the one 'Hawk' must enter (clue 3), so 'Raven', who will go at 23.00, but not to A (clue 1) is heading for E to (clue 6) disable vehicles. 'Condor', who is to move 1 minute after someone goes to plant explosives (clue 2), isn't waiting for either 23.01 or 23.03. The agent who is to knock out the

SOLUTIONS

generator is to move at 23.03, so 'Condor' is going at 23.05 and (clue 2) the agent planting explosives is going at 23.04. 'Falcon' will create a diversion (clue 5), so will go at 23.01. The agent going to C isn't 'Hawk' (clue 3), so 'Condor'. 'Hawk' will thus head for A at (clue 1) 23.03, so 'Eagle' will go at 23.04 and building D will be mined, leaving the agent who is to destroy the enemy radio as 'Condor'.

In summary:
23.00, 'Raven' to disable vehicles in Shed E.
23.01, 'Falcon' to create diversion at Shed B.
23.03, 'Hawk' to knock out generator in Shed A.
23.04, 'Eagle' to plant explosives in Shed D.
23.05, 'Condor' to destroy enemy radio in Shed C.

Celebrity Pets (No 123)

Fido is a rabbit (clue 1). Anna Bell owns Prince (clue 4). Jay Jaye's guinea pig isn't Rover (clue 5), so Tigger. The budgie has a headache (clue 2) and Vicki White's pet has a sore foot (clue 6). Tigger hasn't depression (clue 3), so indigestion. Phil Rubio's pet isn't depressed (clue 3), so he owns the budgie which (by elimination) is called Rover. By elimination, Prince is a tree frog, suffering from depression and Vikki White's pet is Fido.

In summary:
Anna Bell, tree frog, Prince, depression.
Jay Jaye, guinea pig, Tigger, indigestion.
Phil Rubio, budgie, Rover, headache.
Vikki White, rabbit, Fido, sore foot.

Dinner Ladies (No 124)

Shelley is in year 8 (clue 2). The year 7 pupil is served by Mavis (clue 3) and Nicky is in year 9. Lee has fish fingers (clue 5). The year 10 child being served peas isn't Rosie (clue 4), so Matthew, being served by Wendy (clue 6). Annie is serving the beans (clue 1) and Kay, who isn't serving either the pies or potatoes, is serving Lee. By elimination, Lee is in year 11 and Mavis is serving Rosie. The potatoes aren't Nicky's or Shelley's (clue 2), so Rosie's. Nicky hasn't the pie (clue 3), so beans. Hazel is serving the pie to Shelley.

In summary:
Annie, beans, Nicky, year 9.
Hazel, pie, Shelley, year 8.
Kay, fish fingers, Lee, year 11.
Mavis, potatoes, Rosie, year 7.
Wendy, peas, Matthew, year 10.

Battleships (No 125)

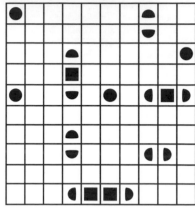

Logi-5 (No 126a)

D	A	C	E	B
E	C	B	D	A
A	B	D	C	E
C	E	A	B	D
B	D	E	A	C

ABC (No 126b)

	B	A		C
A	C		B	
	A	B	C	
B		C		A
C			A	B

What the Butler Saw (No 127)

Bickerstaffe's sighting was in the library (clue 5). Viscount Drummond was in the billiard room (clue 7), so the interior location of Howe-Green's sighting of Lord Portington (clue 1) was the landing cupboard. Masters saw the chambermaid (clue 6). The governess was seen in the summerhouse but not by Walcott (clue 2), so by Groombridge. Thus (clue 4) Howe-Green saw the kitchen-maid. The chambermaid wasn't in the arboretum (clue 6), so in the billiard room; thus the arboretum was where Walcott saw something. The Hon Augustus Rimmington and Lady Violet weren't seen by Bickerstaffe (clue 5), so by Walcott. The governess wasn't with Sir Jeremy Catkin (clue 3), so with the Hon Freddie Wythenshawe; and Bickerstaff saw Sir J Catkin with (by elimination) Lady Antonia.

SOLUTIONS

In summary:
Bickerstaffe, Sir J Catkin, Lady Antonia, library.
Groombridge, Hon F Wythenshawe, governess, summerhouse.
Howe-Green, Lord Portington, kitchen-maid, landing cupboard.
Masters, Viscount Drummond, chambermaid, billiard room.
Walcott, Hon A Rimmington, Lady Violet, arboretum.

Friends at Court (No 128)
The two officers referred to in clue 4, who are both males are James and Barry. Since James was assigned the mugger (clue 5), Barry dealt with the offender guilty of assault and the mugger is Christian (clue 4). Martin dealt with the shoplifter (clue 3) and isn't Nathan. Rachel's surname is Atkins (clue 2), so Martin's forename is Pamela. Farouk wasn't the mugger, and, since his officer's surname is Lowther (clue 6), he wasn't the shoplifter, nor did he commit the public disorder offence. Since Jonathan was convicted of taking without consent (clue 1), Farouk was found guilty of assault, so Lowther is Barry's surname. James's surname isn't Holloway (clue 5), so Berryman and Nathan's is Holloway. Rachel, who didn't deal with the public disorder offender (clue 2), saw Jonathan. Thus Nathan Holloway dealt with the public disorder offender. Since Marlon wasn't the shoplifter (clue 3), Pamela's client was Craig, leaving Marlon as the public disorder offender allocated to Nathan Holloway.

In summary:
Christian, mugging, James Berryman.
Craig, shoplifting, Pamela Martin.
Farouk, assault, Barry Lowther.
Jonathan, taking without consent, Rachel Atkins.
Marlon, public disorder, Nathan Holloway.

Cute Quads (No 129)
The third quad to be born cannot be number 1 (clue 1), or number 4, since Andrew is in position 3 (clues 1 and 4). The fourth to arrive has a blue shirt (clue 2), so Andrew wasn't born third (clue 4), thus quad 2 was third. Kevin is number 1 (clue 1). The fourth to be born isn't number 1 (clue 2) or number 3 (clue 4), so number 4. Stuart is number 2 (clue 2), so Mervin is number 4. Kevin wasn't born first (clue 3), so second and Andrew was first. Kevin's shirt is yellow (clue 4). Stuart's is red (clue 3), so Andrew is in green.

In summary:
1, Kevin, yellow, second.
2, Stuart, red, third.
3, Andrew, green, first.
4, Mervin, blue, fourth.

On Call (No 130)
The sheepdog was seen on Monday (clue 4), so (clue 1) Plowman's farm wasn't visited on Monday or Tuesday. Farm 1 received Wednesday's visit (clues 1 and 2), so Plowman called in the vet on Thursday. Thus (clue 1) the sick cow was treated on Wednesday and Plowman is on farm 2. His sick animals weren't chickens (clue 3), so pigs. By elimination, the chickens were seen on Tuesday. The sick sheepdog wasn't at farm 4 (clue 4), so farm 3; and the chickens were at farm 4. Field called in the vet on Tuesday (clue 3). Farm 3 doesn't belong to Hayes (clue 4), so Herd; thus Hayes owns farm 1.

In summary:
1, Hayes, cow, Wednesday.
2, Plowman, pigs, Thursday.
3, Herd, sheepdog, Monday.
4, Field, chickens, Tuesday.

A Driving Ambition (No 131)
Wheeler was the bus-driver (clue 1) and Niven's first name was Arthur (clue 5). Wilfred, the train driver, wasn't Rogers (clue 3) or Pascoe (clue 2), so Oakman, who started in 1932 (clue 6). Rogers achieved his ambition in 1931 (clue 3). Eric, who started in 1934 (clue 7), wasn't Wheeler (clue 1), or Pascoe. Wheeler didn't start in 1935 (clue 1), so in 1933 and Arthur Niven began in 1935. Wheeler wasn't Herbert (clue 7), so George, leaving Herbert as Rogers. Clue 4 now tell us the underground driver was Eric Pascoe, who started work in 1934. Arthur wasn't the taxi-driver (clue 5), so he was the tram driver, leaving the taxi-driver as Herbert Rogers.
Arthur Niven, tram, 1935.
Eric Pascoe, underground, 1934.
George Wheeler, bus, 1933.
Herbert Rogers, taxi, 1931.
Wilfred Oakman, train, 1932.

Crime in the Streets (No 132)
The car from Herring Street was burned out (clue 3) and Mr Mason's car was repainted (clue 7). His car wasn't the Ford stolen from Spice Street (clue 1), nor did he keep it in York Street or Barracks Street (clue 7), so in Myrtle Street and the Ford was found abandoned. Mr Kennedy owned the Toyota (clue 2) and the BMW was dismantled (clue 6). Mr Mason's car wasn't the Renault (clue 4), so the Volvo. Mr Green's car from Barracks Street wasn't crashed (clue 5), so had been dismantled, thus the car from York Street was crashed. It wasn't the Renault (clue 4), so the Toyota and the Renault was from Herring Street. Mrs Robins didn't own the Renault (clue 4), so the Ford and Ms Wells owned the Renault.

In summary:

Barracks Street, BMW, Mr Green, dismantled.
Herring Street, Renault, Ms Wells, burned out.
Myrtle Street, Volvo, Mr Mason, repainted.
Spice Street, Ford, Mrs Robins, abandoned.
York Street, Toyota, Mr Kennedy, crashed.

Daily Dozen (No 133)

The 12 is in square B2 (clue 1). Since neither the 2 nor the 1 is in column 1 (clue 5), neither can be one of the factors of 12 referred to in clue 1. Nor is the 4 in column 1 (clue 4), so the two numbers in question are 3 and 6. Since the 6 is next to the 10 in the same horizontal row (clue 2), it cannot be in B1, so, from clue 1, the 6 is in C1 and the 10 in C2 (clue 2), while, from clue 1, the 3 is in B1, and, from clue 2, the 8 is in A1. We have placed the 3 and the 10, so, from clue 3, the number in C3 cannot be 2 or 3, nor can it be 4 (clue 7), so, since the highest number in the layout is 12, from clue 3, the 1 is in C3 and the 9 thus in C4. Clue 4 now places the 7 in B4, the 4 in A4 and the 5 in B3. The 2 is in A2 (clue 5) and the 11 in A3.

In summary:

	1	2	3	4
A	8	2	11	4
B	3	12	5	7
C	6	10	1	9

The Moltons of Molton (No 134)

Anthony's parish was Molton St John (clue 1). Matthew was born in 1809 (clue 6) and Greville was born two years after the rector of Castle Molton (clue 3). The rector of Great Molton born in 1805 wasn't Dominic (clue 2), so Quentin, the writer of commentaries (clue 5). The rector of Molton St John wrote either novels or ghost stories (clue 1), the man at Molton St Mary wrote only his diary (clue 6) and the one at Castle Molton was born before Greville (clue 2), so the hymn-writer born in 1813 (clue 4) was rector of Little Molton. Matthew wasn't rector of Molton St Mary (clue 6), so of Castle Molton. He didn't write novels (clue 3), so ghost stories, and Anthony was the novelist. Greville was born in 1811 (clue 3), so was rector of Molton St Mary. By elimination, Anthony was born in 1807 and Dominic was born in 1813.

In summary:

Anthony, 1807, Molton St John, novels.
Dominic, 1813, Little Molton, hymns.
Greville, 1811, Molton St Mary, diary.
Matthew, 1809, Castle Molton, ghost stories.
Quentin, 1805, Great Molton, commentaries.

Just Rambling (No 135)

Barbie Wyre is eating eggs (clue 6) and Una P Hill is by the wall (clue 3). The chicken sandwich eater by the stream isn't Flo Wingbrook (clue 5) or Donna Dale (clue 1), so is Hy Styles in (clue 7) the brown fleece. The woman in amber has a ham roll (clue 4). The tuna sandwich eater isn't in blue (clue 2), or green (clue 1), so red. She isn't Donna Dale (clue 1) or Flo Wingbrook (clue 5), so is Una P Hill. The woman by the gate has the green fleece (clue 1), so the woman in the amber fleece is by the tree (clue 4) and the woman in blue is by the rock. Barbie Wyre isn't by the gate (clue 6), so by the rock; and (by elimination) the woman in green has soup. She isn't Donna Dale (clue 1), so Flo Wingbrook. Donna Dale is the woman in the amber fleece.

In summary:

Barbie Wyre, blue, eggs, by rock.
Donna Dale, amber, ham roll, by tree.
Flo Wingbrook, green, soup, by gate.
Hy Styles, brown, chicken sandwich, by stream.
Una P Hill, red, tuna sandwich, by wall.

The Nominations Are... (No 136)

The film for which Rachel Morris has been nominated was released in November and has a two-word title (clue 1) and Miranda Kemp has been nominated as Best Actress, so the female director of The Marked Man (clue 2) is Imogen Penn. The May release has been nominated for its special effects (clue 3), but not by Hugh Talbot. Rachel Morris' film was released in November, so the nominee for the May film is Duncan McKee. Queen of Manhattan was released in July (clue 6), so (clue 4) since its nominee isn't Imogen Penn, the costume design nomination isn't for the November film. Thus the costume designer is Hugh Talbot. His nomination isn't for the September film (clue 4), so for the January film. Thus The Marked Man, with its nominated director Imogen Penn, was released in September (clue 4), leaving Miranda Kemp as the nominated leading actress in Queen of Manhattan. By elimination, Rachel Morris wrote the nominated score for a film with a two-word title (clue 1), not Desert Ice (clue 5), so Funny Business. The film released in May wasn't One Rainy Day (clue 3), so Desert Ice, and One Rainy Day was released in January.

In summary:

May, Desert Ice, special effects, Duncan McKee.
July, Queen of Manhattan, leading actress, Miranda Kemp.
September, The Marked Man, director, Imogen Penn.
November, Funny Business, score, Rachel Morris.
January, One Rainy Day, costume design, Hugh Talbot.

SOLUTIONS

A Day at the Seaside (No 137)

Eve Flynn lives in Croydon (clue 2) and Peter Rowe in Guildford (clue 6), so Toby Wells and Gail Hope, who aren't from South London or West London (clue 7), are from Maidstone and were thus arrested (clue 5). Dan Gibbon and his girlfriend broke up (clue 3) and Lynne Lee and her boyfriend had a good time (clue 1). Lynne wasn't with John Maple, whose girlfriend's first name and surname initials differ (clue 4), nor did John fall into the sea (clue 4), so he got engaged. Lynne Lee's boyfriend isn't Alan Blake (clue 1), so Peter Rowe and Alan Blake fell into the sea. John Maple's girlfriend isn't Jane Joad (clue 4), and, since he and his girlfriend got engaged, she can't be Pam Scott (clue 2), so was Eve Flynn. The girl with whom Dan Gibbon broke up wasn't Jane Joad (clue 3), so Pam Scott and Jane Joad fell into the sea with Alan Blake. The couple from South London aren't Dan Gibbon and Pam Scott (clue 2), so Alan Blake and Jane Joad; thus Dan Gibbon and Pam Scott are from West London.

In summary:
Alan Blake, Jane Joad, South London, fell in sea.
Dan Gibbon, Pam Scott, West London, broke up.
John Maple, Eve Flynn, Croydon, got engaged.
Peter Rowe, Lynne Lee, Guildford, had good time.
Toby Wells, Gail Hope, Maidstone, arrested.

Working Titles (No 138)

The thriller is based on a bestseller (clue 2), one film has a great script but is a remake (clue 3) and Deep Water, which has a hot director, doesn't involve an ex-boyfriend (clue 1). The war film whose producer is an ex-boyfriend is being made entirely in the studio (clue 4) so can hardly have great locations and doesn't have a superb script; thus has a hot co-star. It isn't Road Hog (clue 2), Blue Devil, which is science fiction (clue 3), or Night Watch, which has nude scenes (clue 5), so it's Wild Wings. Deep Water hasn't an ex-boyfriend as director, so has a low budget. It isn't the horror (clue 1) or science fiction film (clue 3), so it's the comedy. As the movie with the great script isn't Blue Devil (clue 3), it's the horror, and Blue Devil has great locations. Night Watch hasn't a great script, so it's the thriller. By elimination, the movie with the great script is Road Hog and Blue Devil has an ex-boyfriend as director.

In summary:
Blue Devil, science fiction, locations, ex- directs.
Deep Water, comedy, hot director, low budget.
Night Watch, thriller, based on bestseller, nude scenes.
Road Hog, horror, great script, remake.
Wild Wings, war, hot co-star, ex- produces.

Safe Harbour (No 139)

Ship B is Pole Star (clue 7), so ship A isn't the privateer commanded by Bower (clue 1) or the merchantman (clue 4). Clue 6 rules out the island trader and clue 3 the packet boat, so, as the frigate is ship D (clue 5) and A is the brig. Thus, from clue 3, the packet boat is B, Pole Star. Lee is captain of C (clue 2). The captain of A isn't Hatch (clue 3), Moor (clue 4) or Wake (clues 7 and 8), so Fay. Ship A is thus the Rainbow (clue 6) and C is the island trader. F isn't the merchantman (clue 4), so the privateer and E is the merchantman. The merchantman is Jane Cary (clue 1) and (clue 4) the privateer is Merlin. Wake's ship isn't the merchantman or packet boat (clue 8), so is the frigate. The Sceptre isn't C (clue 4), so is D and C is the Dolphin. The captain of E is Moor (clue 4), so the captain of B is Hatch.

In summary:
A, Rainbow, brig, Fay.
B, Pole Star, packet boat, Hatch.
C, Dolphin, island trader, Lee.
D, Sceptre, frigate, Wake.
E, Jane Cary, merchantman, Moor.
F, Merlin, privateer, Bower.

Night Court (No 140)

Zeke Weiss's case is being dealt with by the 4th Precinct cop (clue 1) and Gus Herero is testifying against Benny Capone (clue 4). Ross Trani from the 16th Precinct isn't testifying against Ed Dillinger (clue 6) and didn't arrest Vic Torrio, so is appearing against Mary O'Brian, who is charged with assaulting an officer (clue 5). Joe Keegan is testifying in the shoplifting case (clue 3), so the cop in the drunk-driving case, not Noah Penny (clue 2) or Bill Adler (clue 7), is Gus Herero. He isn't from the 7th Precinct (clue 7), while the 9th Precinct cop dealt with the stealing case (clue 2), so Gus Herero is from the 12th Precinct. The 9th Precinct cop isn't Noah Penny (clue 2), so Bill Adler, and Noah Penny's case is the vandalism charge. The 4th Precinct cop is Joe Keegan (clue 1) and Zeke Weiss is charged with shoplifting. By elimination, Noah Penny is from the 7th Precinct, so (clue 6) he is testifying against Vic Torrio and Bill Adler against Ed Dillinger.

In summary:
B Adler, Ninth, Ed Dillinger, stealing.
G Herero, Twelfth, Benny Capone, drunk-driving.
J Keegan, Fourth, Zeke Weiss, shoplifting.
N Penny, Seventh, Vic Torrio, vandalism.
R Trani, Sixteenth, Mary O'Brian, assaulting officer.

Knightly Ailments (No 141)

Sir Timid was examined on Thursday (clue 6), the potion was prescribed on Tuesday (clue 3) and flavostriatus was diagnosed on Wednesday

SOLUTIONS

(clue 7), so, from clue 1, Sir Spyneless cannot have been seen on Monday, Tuesday, Thursday or Friday and was the Wednesday patient. So, from clue 1, pills were prescribed on Thursday for Sir Timid to tackle his pavidus rigidus. The lozenges weren't prescribed on Friday or Wednesday (clue 4), so on Monday. Thus, from clue 4, gallinacardia was the Tuesday ailment treated with a potion. Sir Sorely was suffering from dracophobia (clue 2) and Sir Poltroon was given some liniment (clue 5), so Sir Coward was prescribed the potion. By elimination, Sir Sorely was given lozenges and Sir Poltroon was seen on Friday, so Sir Poltroon was suffering from alba penna syndrome and Sir Spyneless was given ointment.

In summary:
Sir C de Custarde, Tuesday, gallinacardia, potion.
Sir P à Ghaste, Friday, alba p syndrome, liniment.
Sir S à Frayde, Monday, dracophobia, lozenges.
Sir S de Feete, Wednesday, flavostriatus, ointment.
Sir T de Shayke, Thursday, pavidus rigidus, pills.

Mountain Rescue (No 142)

The party of six climbers was being assisted by Cliff Ledge and his team (clue 6), so the two in difficulty in Glen Tarvie (clue 2), who weren't helped by Miles Trudge or Ben Peake (clue 2), or Alan Slyde (clue 3), were helped by Will Findham and his Kilcarn team (clue 5). Cliff Ledge and his team assisted the group of six, so the climbers stuck at Meall Lodge numbered three (clue 3) and Alan Slyde helped the group of five. The three climbers weren't rescued by Miles Trudge's team (clue 2), so it was Ben Peake and, by elimination, the leader of the Gordonburn team, assisting the four climbers (clue 4), is Miles Trudge. He wasn't heading for Culmor Crags (clue 2), or Craigmore, which was the Achnadubh team (clue 1), so it was Crask Forest. The Glenmoine team isn't led by Ben Peake (clue 1), so didn't assist the group of three and as the Glenmoine team's party was smaller than that sought by the Achnadubh team (also clue 1), it wasn't six so five and the team leader was Alan Slyde. Thus the Achnadubh rescue team was looking for the party of six on Craigmore (clue 1). By elimination, Ben Peake leads the Strathness team and the Glenmoine team was going to the aid of the group of five climbers on Culmor Crags.

In summary:
Achnadubh, Cliff Ledge, six on Craigmore.
Glenmoine, Alan Slyde, five on Culmor Crags.
Gordonburn, Miles Trudge, four in Crask Forest.
Kilcarn, Will Findham, two in Glen Tarvie.
Strathness, Ben Peake, three at Meall Lodge.

Pile Up (No 143)

From the top: C, E, D, B, A, F

Battleships (No 144)

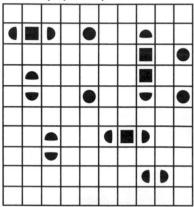

Up, Up and Away (No 145)

David was terrified (clue 3) and Ronald landed on the roundabout (clue 5), so, from clue 1, the man who landed among the grazing cows after feeling airsick is John. The birthday tripper landed in a pond (clue 7), which rules out John and Ronald, nor was this passenger Pauline (clue 7). Mary had passed her A-levels (clue 4), so, by elimination, it was David's birthday. Thus, the person who landed in the garden is Mary or Pauline, so, from clue 2, one of these two remained calm and serene. Ronald didn't enjoy his trip excitedly (clue 5), so he is the one who couldn't look down and was thus celebrating a job promotion (clue 6). So John was celebrating his ruby wedding (clue 4) and Pauline had retired. She didn't land in the garden (clue 2), so the beach and Mary's landing place was the garden. Pauline remained calm and serene (clue 2) and Mary enjoyed her trip excitedly.

In summary:
David, birthday, terrified, pond.
John, ruby wedding, airsick, herd of cows.
Mary, passing A-levels, enjoyed excitedly, garden.
Pauline, retirement, calm and serene, beach.
Ronald, job promotion, couldn't look down, roundabout.

Good Nights – and Bad (No 146)

Seven Pillars is in Menmellick (clue 2) and Acapulco Lodge was 'pretty bad' (clue 6), so the B&B in Pendowgan which was 'acceptable' and had a two-word name (clue 4), was Eagle's Nest. Wednesday night was spent at Grasmere (clue 5), so the B&B in Looe wasn't the 'disappointing' one used on Monday (clues 1 and 3), which wasn't in Tredew or Menmellick (clues 3 and

SOLUTIONS

2), so in St Orgo, and, by elimination, was called Versailles. Seven Pillars in Menmellick wasn't 'great!' (clue 2), so was 'poor', leaving the 'great' B&B as Grasmere, where Wednesday night was spent. From clue 2, Seven Pillars was Thursday's B&B, so the Cuthberts were in Looe on Wednesday, and at the 'acceptable' Eagle's Nest on Friday. Thus Tuesday's stay was at Acapulco Lodge in Tredew.

In summary:
Monday, Versailles, St Orgo, 'disappointing'.
Tuesday, Acapulco Lodge, Tredew, 'pretty bad'.
Wednesday, Grasmere, Looe, 'great!'.
Thursday, Seven Pillars, Menmellick, 'poor'.
Friday, Eagle's Nest, Pendowgan, 'acceptable'.

Musical Boxes (No 147)

The box with the gold and red cover had a 24-page booklet (clue 3), so, from clue 5, the box containing the 22-page booklet was gold and blue. So it cannot have been produced in 1998 (clue 4), or 2002 (clue 5). Clue 6 tells us The Thrilling 30s set issued in 2000 didn't have a 22-page booklet and clues 5 and 6 together rule out 1999, so it appeared in 2001. From clue 5, the 2002 set was named The Fighting 40s. The Fabulous 50s set wasn't issued in 1998 (clue 7) and its 28 pages rule it out for 2001, so, by elimination, it was the set produced in 1999. From clue 7, The Swinging 60s was the 1998 set, leaving 2001 for The Sizzling 70s. From clue 1, The Fighting 40s didn't have the 26-page booklet; nor, since it had silver printing on its box, can it have had the 24-page booklet – thus it had the 30-page booklet. Since we now know the 1998 set was The Swinging 60s and it wasn't in the silver and red box (clue 7), from clue 4, it was in the gold and red box. By elimination, The Thrilling 30s had the 26-page booklet. From clue 7, the silver and red box didn't house the 28- or 30-page booklets, so it contained the 26-page one. Since the 2001 set had a booklet of 22 pages, the silver and green box didn't have the 30-page booklet (clue 2), so it housed the 1999 set, the 1998 set had the 24-page booklet, and the cover of the 2002 box is silver and blue.

In summary:
1998, The Swinging 60s, gold and red, 24 pages.
1999, The Fabulous 50s, silver and green, 28 pages.
2000, The Thrilling 30s, silver and red, 26 pages.
2001, The Sizzling 70s, gold and blue, 22 pages.
2002, The Fighting 40s, silver and blue, 30 pages.

On the Clock (No 148)

Since no car's first digit on the display is a zero (clue 6) and none has reached 50,000 miles (clue 2) and no digit appears in the same position on more than one display (clue 1), the four first digits are 1, 2, 3 and 4. The first digit of car 3 is 1 or 2 and that of car 1 is 3 or 4 (clue 3). The fourth number on its clock is 4 (clue 7), so its first cannot be (clue 1), thus it begins with a 3 and that of car 3 starts with 1 (clue 3). So, from clue 2, car 2's display must start with a 2, leaving the first digit on car 4's clock as 4. So this vehicle is blue and car 3 is the Fiat (clue 4). We know car 1's fourth digit's 4, so this car cannot be the black Volvo, whose last three digits are 735 (clue 8). We know this vehicle isn't number 3 or number 4, so it's number 2. So, from clue 5, car 4's display ends in a 7. So this car cannot be the Audi (clue 9), which must, by elimination, be car 1, leaving car 4 as the Ford. The Audi's final digit's a 1 (clue 9), so this cannot be the car with a zero in that position (clue 6). We know the last digits on the clocks of car 2 and car 4, so it's car 3's display which ends in 0. So, from clue 6, 0 is the third digit on car 1's clock and (clue 3) its second is an 8. So this car isn't red (clue 4) and is green, leaving car 3, the Fiat, as the red vehicle, whose second digit's a 9 (clue 4). We can now see, from clue 10, that 6 and 5 is in third and fourth position on either car 3 or car 4, as must 9 and 8. But the display on car 3 already has a 9, so, from clue 1, its full display is 19650 and that of car 4 must end with 987 (clue 10). One 2 and one 6 still remain to be assigned (clue 1). The 2 cannot be on car 2, since its display starts with that digit (clue 1), so it's the second digit on car 4's clock, leaving the 6 in that position on the clock of car 2.

In summary:
1, green Audi, 38041.
2, black Volvo, 26735.
3, red Fiat, 19650.
4, blue Ford, 42987.

Battleships (No 149)

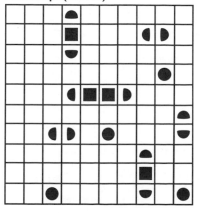

SOLUTIONS

Logi-5 (No 150a)

A	B	E	C	D
D	A	B	E	C
C	D	A	B	E
E	C	D	A	B
B	E	C	D	A

ABC (No 150b)

C			A	B
	B	C		A
A		B		C
	C	A	B	
B	A		C	

Romeos and Juliets (No 151)

The Last Goodbye appeared in 1998 (clue 3). Rupert featured in the 2000 romance (clue 5) and Josephine in the one published in 2002 (clue 7). The book featuring Raymond and Jeannette wasn't published in 1998 or 1999 (clue 1), so in 2001, and Amour No More was the 2000 title. The man who featured with Josephine wasn't Roland or Roger (clue 4), so Rory. From clue 4, Roger was the hero of The Last Goodbye and Roland appeared in the 1999 novel. The Loneliest Nights was published in 2001 (clue 6). A Heavy Heart wasn't published in 2002 (clue 2), so in 1999, leaving 2002 as the publication date of A Fond Farewell. The Last Goodbye featured Julia (clue 2), so Rupert, whose female friend wasn't Jayne (clue 5), appeared with Jacqueline in Amour No More, and Jayne was in A Heavy Heart.

In summary:
1998, The Last Goodbye, Roger, Julia.
1999, A Heavy Heart, Roland, Jayne.
2000, Amour No More, Rupert, Jacqueline.
2001, The Loneliest Nights, Raymond, Jeanette.
2002, A Fond Farewell, Rory, Josephine.

On the Level (No 152)

Five vehicles queued at 10.15 (clue 6) and a goods train passed at 10.00, so the express passenger train, which held up eight vehicles at the level crossing earlier in the morning than when the gates were closed for 4 minutes at 10.23 (clue 2), passed at 10.10. The gates were not then closed for 4 minutes or 5 minutes, when 14 vehicles waited (clue 1), nor was it 6 minutes, which was for the up goods (clue 1).

The 3-minute closure was for a goods train (clue 3), so the gates remained closed for 2 minutes for the express. Fourteen vehicles were held up for 5 minutes, but not at 10.00 (clue 3), so at 10.31. Thus the down goods caused delay to five vehicles at 10.15 (clues 1 and 6) thus for 3 minutes. By elimination, the up goods passed at 10.00, when the gates closed for 6 minutes. From clue 4, the local passenger train went through at 10.23 and the coal train at 10.31. Eleven vehicles were held up by the goods train (clue 3) and twelve by the local passenger train.

In summary:
10.00, up goods, 6 minutes, 11 vehicles.
10.10, express passenger, 2 minutes, 8 vehicles.
10.15, down goods, 3 minutes, 5 vehicles.
10.23, local passenger, 4 minutes, 12 vehicles.
10.31, coal, 5 minutes, 14 vehicles.

Holiday Reading (No 153)

Sunbeam, set in Los Angeles, wasn't about a car racing team (clue 5), nor, from the number of letters in the title, wasn't Lucy Keats's book about an auction house (clue 4). Kingwood was about a hospital (clue 1) and the book about a TV studio was set in Manchester (clue 2), so Sunbeam was about a restaurant. Ruth Pound's book wasn't set in Britain (clue 1), nor was it about the restaurant in Los Angeles (clue 1), so was set in Sydney. This tells us it wasn't about a restaurant or a TV studio and we know that Lucy Keats wrote about the auction house; clue 1 rules out Kingwood, the hospital story, so Ruth Pound's book was about a car racing team. From the title or the writer's name, Castaways by Gail Frost (clue 3) can't have been about a restaurant, a hospital, an auction house or a car racing team, so it was about a TV studio in Manchester. The book set in Sydney wasn't Glow Worm (clue 6) and can't have been Kingwood (clue 1), so it was Whirlwind, and, by elimination, Glow Worm was Lucy Keats' book about an auction house. Thus, from clue 4, Zena Wilde's book was Sunbeam. By elimination, Kingwood was by Emma Donne. This wasn't the book set in Edinburgh (clue 2), so was set in Bristol, leaving Edinburgh as the setting for Glow Worm by Lucy Keats.

In summary:
Castaways, Gail Frost, TV studio, Manchester.
Glow Worm, Lucy Keats, auction house, Edinburgh.
Kingwood, Emma Donne, hospital, Bristol.
Sunbeam, Zena Wilde, restaurant, Los Angeles.
Whirlwind, Ruth Pound, car racing team, Sydney.

Pile Up (No 154)

From the top: A, B, C, D, E, F.

SOLUTIONS

Logi-5 (No 155a)

D	E	C	B	A
E	A	D	C	B
C	B	A	E	D
A	C	B	D	E
B	D	E	A	C

ABC (No 155b)

A	B	C		
		A	B	C
C		B		A
	A		C	B
B	C		A	

Cuckoo (No 156)

James is the vicar (clue 1), so Millicent, who isn't the nurse (clue 2), is the librarian, leaving the nurse as Norah. Her claim wasn't for the 16th (clue 2), or the 17th (clue 3), so it was for the 18th April. So, from clue 2, James claimed to have heard his cuckoo on the 17th, leaving the 16th for Millicent. So she is Bird (clue 1). Norah isn't Clutch (clue 2), so she is Nest, leaving James is Clutch.

In summary:
James Clutch, vicar, 17th April.
Millicent Bird, librarian, 16th April.
Norah Nest, nurse, 18th April.

Meet the Family (No 157)

Ernie is Mickey's brother (clue 3), so Andy, who isn't his cousin (clue 2), is his nephew, who he's meeting at the bus station (clue 1). By elimination, Jack is the cousin. He's not being picked up at the airport (clue 2), so Mickey is meeting him at the rail station, at 10.00am (clue 4). By elimination, Ernie is arriving at the airport. Andy is being picked up at 9.00am (clue 2), leaving Ernie as Mickey's 11.00am pick-up.

In summary:
Andy, nephew, 9.00am, bus station.
Ernie, brother, 11.00am, airport.
Jack, cousin, 10.00am, rail station.

A Moving Story (No 158)

Rookov played the second game (clue 2), so, from clue 4, Bishopnik played in the third, Rookov was Ivan and the man from Corki played in the fourth game. Piotr, the first player, wasn't Pawnchev (clue 3), so he was Knightovich and Pawnchev was the fourth opponent. We now

know the surname or home city of Queenie's opponent in three games, so Boris from Gorki (clue 1) was the third game opponent, Bishopnik, and, by elimination, Queenie's fourth opponent, Pawnchev, was Yuri. Finally, the second challenger, Ivan Rookov, wasn't from Yorki (clue 2), so was from Porki, leaving the man from Yorki as the first game opponent Piotr Knightovich.

In summary:
First, Piotr Knightovich, Yorki.
Second, Ivan Rookov, Porki.
Third, Boris Bishopnik, Gorki.
Fourth, Yuri Pawnchev, Corki.

VIP(ictures) (No 159)

The sailor's appointment is at 12.00 noon (clue 2). Jean Keeler, who has the 10.00am appointment, isn't the barrister (clue 4), nor can she be the MEP (clue 3), so she is the novelist. Amanda Barker's appointment is on Tuesday (clue 1). The Thursday appointment isn't Jean Keeler's (clue 4) or Rebecca Say's (clue 2), so is Martina Nash's. Her appointment isn't at 4.00pm (clue 3), nor is the 4.00pm appointment Rebecca Say's (clue 2) and we know that Jean Keeler's due at 10.00am, so 4.00pm is the time of Amanda Barker's Tuesday appointment. We know that the sailor's 12.00 noon appointment isn't on Tuesday, nor can it be on Monday (clue 2); as Rebecca Say's appointment isn't on Tuesday, clue 2 tells us the sailor's can't be on Wednesday, so it's on Thursday and the sailor is Martina Nash. Thus, from clue 2, the Wednesday appointment is Rebecca Say's and, by elimination, Jean Keeler's is on Monday. From clue 3, the MEP has the 2.00pm appointment, and, by elimination, is Rebecca Say. The barrister is Amanda Barker.

In summary:
Monday, 10.00am, Jean Keeler, novelist.
Tuesday, 4.00pm, Amanda Barker, barrister.
Wednesday, 2.00pm, Rebecca Say, MEP.
Thursday, 12 noon, Martina Nash, sailor.

Doing Their Bits (No 160)

Dr Naruda is raising money for a community hospital (clue 1), so the doctor raising money for the orphanage, whose name is listed between those of the Saxon Road GP who's supporting the nursing school and the parachute jumper, is Dr Harwood (clue 3); thus the Saxon Road GP is Dr Adams and the parachute jumper is Dr Naruda. By elimination, Dr Wood is raising funds for a maternity clinic. The cycle rider's surname is shorter than the one immediately preceding it in the alphabetical list (clue 2), so can't be Adams or Harwood. We know Dr Naruda's doing a parachute jump, so the cycle rider is Dr Wood. He doesn't work at Milton House (clue 2) and we know he's not at Saxon Road; clue 4 tells us he can't work at The Beeches, so he is at the Piper Centre surgery. From clue 2, Dr Naruda can't be at Milton House, so The Beeches and it's Dr Harwood who works at Milton House. Since Dr Naruda's surname is longer than that of the doctor doing the canoe trip (clue 4), he or she can't be Dr Harwood and is Dr Adams, leaving Dr Harwood's sponsored event as a marathon.

In summary:
Dr Adams, Saxon Road, canoe trip, nursing school.
Dr Harwood, Milton House, marathon, orphanage.
Dr Naruda, The Beeches, parachute jump, community hospital.
Dr Wood, Piper Centre, cycle ride, maternity clinic.

Idol Thoughts (No 161)
Luaho was worshipped in spring (clue 2), so the god represented by an eagle, worshipped in summer, who a name of five or six letters (clue 4), was Pangul, god of mountains (clue 1). Knualei took the shape of a lizard (clue 1), so the river god, who took the form of a fish and had a name of six or seven letters (clue 5), was Jagradi. Bahamatotl wasn't represented by a monkey (clue 3), so a dragon, leaving Luaho as the monkey god. Bahamatotl was neither worshipped in autumn (clue 3) nor winter (clue 2), so he was the sun god worshipped on midsummer day (clue 6). From clue 4, the god of forests has a seven-letter name, so is Knualei, leaving Luaho as the god of dance. Jagradi wasn't worshipped in the winter (clue 2), so autumn and Knualei was the god worshipped in the winter.

In summary:
Bahamatotl, sun, dragon, midsummer day.
Jagradi, river, fish, autumn.
Knualei, forests, lizard, winter.
Luaho, dance, monkey, spring.
Pangul, mountains, eagle, summer.

Gentlemen of the Road (No 162)
The rider of Grey Mist, who operated at Witch Wood, wasn't Hateful Dan (clue 7), nor can he have been Handsome Hal (clue 1), while Happy Tom lurked at Crow's Corner (clue 3) and Hairy Jem rode Midnight (clue 4), so Hardhearted Jack rode Grey Mist. He was the ostler (clue 6). The rider of Black Shadow cannot have been the brother who was a flour miller and held up travellers at Devil's Dyke (clue 1), nor was he the tailor (clue 2). The blacksmith rode Flyer (clue 5), so Black Shadow was the cobbler's horse. We know this man wasn't Hardhearted Jack or Hairy Jem, nor was he Hateful Dan (clue 7) or Handsome Hal (clue 1), so Happy Tom. The

blacksmith didn't operate at Gibbet Hill (clue 5), so at Dead Oak Dell. Fleetfoot's rider didn't use Gibbet Hill (clue 5), so he lurked by Devil's Dyke and Hairy Jem was the tailor and the location for his evil trade was Gibbet Hill. The flour miller wasn't Handsome Hal (clue 1), so Hateful Dan. Handsome Hal was the blacksmith.

In summary:
Hateful Dan, flour miller, Fleetfoot, Devil's Dyke.
Handsome Hal, blacksmith, Flyer, Dead Oak Dell.
Hardhearted Jack, ostler, Grey Mist, Witch Wood.
Hairy Jem, tailor, Midnight, Gibbet Hill.
Happy Tom, cobbler, Black Shadow, Crow's Corner.

A Matter of Taste (No 163)
Farrell Brothers was rated at 40% (clue 1), so the Drake River wine which wasn't given a rating of 50% or 70% (clue 3) and couldn't have been 100%, was 60% and was thus the sparkling wine (clue 2). The German wine must thus have been given a rating of 70% (clue 3). The Black Knight dessert wine's rating was 30% higher than the Californian wine (clue 5), so it received 70% and the Californian wine was rated at 40%. The Drake River isn't the white South African wine (clue 6) or the French Chateau de Lisle (clue 4), so is a sparkling Australian wine. By elimination, Clay Hill is the South African white. The Chateau de Lisle wasn't rated at 50% (clue 4), so 100%, leaving the 50% wine as the Clay Hill. The Farrell Brothers' wine isn't the rosé (clue 1), so is the red, leaving the rosé as the Chateau de Lisle wine.

In summary:
Black Knight, dessert, Germany, 70%.
Chateau de Lisle, rosé, France, 100%.
Clay Hill, white, South Africa, 50%.
Drake River, sparkling, Australia, 60%.
Farrell Brothers, red, California, 40%.

Knights of the Theatre (No 164)
Sir Sorely appeared in the fourth production (clue 5), so (clue 1) the man playing Theseus, who tripped over the dead Minotaur, wasn't in the fifth. The third debutante shivered and shook (clue 6). The knight in the fifth production didn't dry up (clue 2), or develop a stammer (clue 4), so he was Sir Poltroon, who fainted on stage (clue 7). Since the third knight shivered and shook, Sir Timid cannot have been in the second production (clue 1), nor was Sir Coward, who played Apollo (clue 3), so, by elimination, Sir Spyneless was in the second play. Thus, from clue 2, the first knight dried up while he was playing Hercules (clue 8). This rôle rules him out as Sir Coward, so he was Sir Timid, leaving Sir Coward playing Apollo in the third play. From clue 1, Theseus

SOLUTIONS

was played by Sir Spyneless, who appeared second, and, by elimination, Sir Sorely developed a stammer. So, from clue 4, Sir Poltroon was playing Ajax when he fainted, leaving Hector as Sir Sorely's rôle.

In summary:
First, Sir Timid de Shayke, Hercules, dried up.
Second, Sir Spyneless de Feete, Theseus, tripped.
Third, Sir Coward de Custarde, Apollo, shivered.
Fourth, Sir Sorely à Frayde, Hector, developed a stammer.
Fifth, Sir Poltroon à Ghaste, Ajax, fainted.

On the Ropes (No 165)
Soldier 3 is from Berkshire (clue 4). Number 1 isn't Brett from Dorset (clue 1), or Gunn from Cheshire (clue 5), so is from Suffolk and (clue 3) number 2 is Bullett, who (by elimination) is from Dorset. This leaves Gunn as number 4; so (clue 5) Pete is number 3. Thus (clue 1) Squaddey is from Suffolk. He isn't Sandy (clue 2), so he is Dave and Sandy as Gunn. Thus Pete is March.

In summary:
1, Dave Squaddey, Suffolk.
2, Brett Bullett, Dorset.
3, Pete March, Berkshire.
4, Sandy Gunn, Cheshire.

Making Their Mark (No 166)
Charlie is in chair 3 (clue 4) and the customer in chair 1 had the eagle tattoo (clue 3). Warren who had his chest tattooed isn't in 2 (clue 1), so 4 and Charlie had the dragon tattoo. Andrew isn't in chair 1 (clue 3), so 2 and James is in 1. Thus Andrew had the butterfly tattoo (clue 2) and Warren had a heart. Andrew's tattoo isn't on his shoulder (clue 2) or back (clue 4), so his forearm. James's isn't on his shoulder (clue 2), so his back, and Charlie's is on his shoulder.

In summary:
1, James, eagle, back.
2, Andrew, butterfly, forearm.
3, Charlie, dragon, shoulder.
4, Warren, heart, chest.

Chamber of Horrors (No 167)
Marcus Brand is to be tortured with hot irons (clue 6), alleged sorcerer Watt Payne is booked after 9 o'clock (clue 4) and Edward Brake's is booked for either 10.30 or 10.50 (clue 1). The person booked for 9 o'clock on the rack isn't Angus Hyghe (clue 2), so Will Yeald. The mutineer to be subjected to the thumbscrews at least 70 minutes before Watt Payne's appointment (clue 4) isn't Edward Brake, whose appointment is after 10 o'clock (clue 1), so is Angus Hyghe whose appointment isn't 8 o'clock (clue 2), so at 9.20am. This is more than 70 minutes before Watt's, so Watt's is at 10.50am

and Edward's at 10.30am. By elimination, Marcus Brand's is scheduled for 8 o'clock. The thief whose appointment is before 9.20am (clue 2) isn't Will Yeald (clue 3), so Marcus Brand. Edward isn't being tortured as a traitor (clue 1), so a blasphemer and Will is the traitor. Edward isn't to be lashed (clue 5), so he is due for the 'iron maiden' and Watt Payne will be lashed.

In summary:
8.00, Marcus Brand, theft, hot irons.
9.00, Will Yeald, treason, rack.
9.20am, Angus Hyghe, mutiny, thumbscrews.
10.30am, Edward Brake, blasphemy, 'iron maiden'.
10.50am, Watt Payne, sorcery, lashing.

Red Faces at the Fête (No 168)
The head teacher's ticket 245 (clue 2) can't have won the hamper, which went to the police officer (clue 5). Since ticket 110 won the holiday (clue 6), clue 5 also rules out the DVD player as ticket 245's prize and the head teacher didn't win Champagne (clue 2), so the portable TV. Thus Judy Iverson can't have won her DVD player with a ticket numbered below 482, which was the number of Sam Ratcliff's ticket (clue 4), so Judy's was number 599. Thus Sam is the police officer who won a hamper (clue 5). By elimination, ticket number 367 won Champagne. Carol Brooke is Chair of the PC (clue 3). The head teacher isn't Harry Gadway (clue 2), so is Nigel Moore. Harry won the holiday (clue 2) and Carol won Champagne. Mr Gadway is the publican (clue 1) and the parish clerk is Judy Iverson.

In summary:
110, holiday, Harry Gadway, publican.
245, portable TV, Nigel Moore, Head Teacher.
367, Champagne, Carol Brooke, Chair of PC.
482, hamper, Sam Ratcliff, police officer.
599, DVD player, Judy Iverson, parish clerk.

Battleships (No 169)

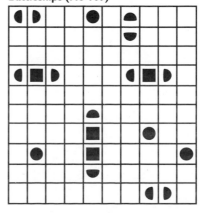

SOLUTIONS

Logi-5 (No 170a)

C	B	D	E	A
B	A	E	D	C
E	D	A	C	B
A	E	C	B	D
D	C	B	A	E

ABC (No 170b)

B		A	C	
	C	B		A
A		C		B
C	B		A	
	A		B	C

The Merry Month (No 171)

Since LILY is in B4 (clue 3), the 5-letter word in A4 (clue 6) isn't APPLE (clue 1), so QUEEN. TIME is in A2 (clue 5) and (clue 4) TREE is in C2. If FAIR is in C3 (clue 7), APPLE could not be in B3 (clue 1). Clue 1 already rules out squares A1, A3, B1, B2 C1, C3 or C4 for APPLE, so FAIR is in C4 (clue 7) and APPLE is in B3. BUG is in B2 (clue 1) and BLOSSOM in C3. FLY is in A3 (clue 2), FLOWER in A1, POLE in B1 and DAY in C1.

In summary:

	1	2	3	4
A	Flower	Time	Fly	Queen
B	Poke	Bug	Apple	Lily
C	Day	Tree	Blossom	Fair

Students at War (No 172)

The history student came from Oxford (5). The Sheffield-born student who went to Washington had a four-letter surname (clue 2), so Colin Finch, the law student, who wasn't from North London or West London (clue 1), was from Dover. He didn't go to Berlin (clue 6) and we know he didn't go to Washington; the engineering student went to Liverpool (clue 4) and Ann Dale to Paris (clue 3), so Colin Finch went to Bletchley Park. Eric Hay didn't go to Washington (clue 2) and he wasn't the engineering student who went to Liverpool (clue 4), so he went to Berlin. His subject wasn't history (clue 5) and we know it wasn't law or engineering; the art student had a four-letter surname (clue 7), so Eric Hay was studying chemistry. He was a Londoner (clue

1), but not from North London (clue 4), so he was from West London. We know that the student from Sheffield who went to Washington wasn't studying history, law, or chemistry, nor engineering (clue 4), so he or she studied art. By elimination, the engineering student who went to Liverpool was from North London and the history student from Oxford was Ann Dale, who went to Paris. Clue 7 now tells us that it was Julia Moor who came from Sheffield, studied art and went to Washington and Paul Shaw who came from North London, studied engineering and went to Liverpool.

In summary:

Ann Dale, Oxford, history, Paris.
Colin Finch, Dover, law, Bletchley Park.
Eric Hay, West London, chemistry, Berlin.
Julia Moor, Sheffield, art, Washington.
Paul Shaw, North London, engineering, Liverpool.

Mine's a Cornet (No 173)

Steve visited the shop on Tuesday (clue 6). Karen, who took only 25 minutes to choose, wasn't there on Thursday (clue 2) or Wednesday (clue 1). The Friday customer took 30 minutes (clue 3), so, by elimination, Karen was there on Monday. So her instrument wasn't the double-bass (clue 3), or the cornet (clue 7), while clue 4 rules out the electric guitar for Monday. The acoustic guitar took 45 minutes to choose (clue 5), so Karen bought the saxophone. Wednesday's purchases wasn't of either guitar (clue 1), nor of the cornet (clues 6 and 7), so it was the double-bass. So, from clue 3, Steve took 50 minutes. By elimination, the acoustic guitar was bought on Thursday. Steve didn't buy the cornet (clue 7), so the electric guitar, leaving the cornet as the Friday purchase. Nick's purchase was on Thursday (clue 7), so Wednesday's took 40 minutes. Wednesday's buyer wasn't Greg (clue 1), so Rose, and Greg bought the cornet.

In summary:

Greg, cornet, Friday, 30 minutes.
Karen, saxophone, Monday, 25 minutes.
Nick, acoustic guitar, Thursday, 45 minutes.
Rose, double-bass, Wednesday, 40 minutes.
Steve, electric guitar, Tuesday, 50 minutes.

Field Trip (No 174)

Lord Duncraig won the Battle of Forton (clue 2) and the Duke of Radnor's exploits were commemorated by the planting of a wood (clue 4), so the obelisk marking the site of the Battle of Pressholme, which wasn't won by the Earl of Ashby or the Earl of Kenilworth (clue 5), was for Prince Cuthbert. The Earl of Ashby won his battle in 1435 (clue 6), so the Battle of Rowtingham wasn't the 1294 clash marked today by a chapel (clue 3); nor was the 1294 battle

Gorfield (clue 1) or Pressholme, so it was Killin. By elimination, the victor at this battle was the Earl of Kenilworth. The battlefield of Forton isn't marked by a tower (clue 2) so it's the museum, leaving the tower as marking the Earl of Ashby's 1435 victory. From clue 3, the museum cannot commemorate the battle in 1372, or 1640, so must deal with the 1509 battle, thus the Battle of Rowtingham took place in 1435 and the obelisk must commemorate the 1640 battle (clue 3). By elimination, the wood commemorates the Duke of Radnor's victory at Gorfield in 1372.

In summary:
1294, Killin, Earl of Kenilworth, chapel.
1372, Gorfield, Duke of Radnor, wood.
1435, Rowtingham, Earl of Ashby, tower.
1509, Forton, Lord Duncraig, museum.
1640, Pressholme, Prince Cuthbert, obelisk.

Deadwinter Deaths (No 175)
The doctor was the fourth victim of the murderer (clue 2) and the gardener was poisoned (clue 5), so the first victim, who was shot (clue 1) and who wasn't the farmer (clue 4) or the publican (clue 1), was the actress, Donna Waywith (clue 6). Di Carnidge was the second victim (clue 1), so Hugh Dunnett, who was stabbed (clue 4), was at least the third victim. Thus the farmer was either the fourth or fifth victim. He or she wasn't fourth (clue 2), so was fifth. The farmer wasn't cudgelled (clue 3), so blown up with explosives. Di Carnidge, the second victim, wasn't killed with the cudgel (clue 1), so was poisoned and she was thus the gardener. By elimination, the third victim was the publican. Guy Slade wasn't cudgelled (clue 3), so he was the farmer. Finally, Celia Fayte wasn't the third victim (clue 2), so was the doctor, killed fourth with, by elimination, the cudgel, leaving Hugh Dunnett as the publican, the murderer's third victim.

In summary:
Di Carnidge, gardener, second, poison.
Hugh Dunnett, publican, third, knife.
Celia Fayte, doctor, fourth, cudgel.
Guy Slade, farmer, fifth, explosives.
Donna Waywith, actress, first, gun.

To Meet the Queen (No 176)
Samantha is in one of positions 1, 3 or 4 in the line. Clue 4 rules out position 1, since Simmons could not then be the same distance from her as from the producer. If she were 3, Simmons could not be any of numbers 4, 5 or 6, since he would then be further from the producer than from her, nor could he be 1 or 2, since he would then be next to either the producer or Samantha, but not both (clue 4). Thus Samantha is 4 in the line and (clue 4) Simmons is 2. Melinda is immediately

to the left of Bradley (clue 6), so she's 1 and Bradley is 2. The remaining woman, in 3, is Julia. Angus is neither the producer nor number 6 (clue 2), so he is in position 5. Rick is either the producer or number 6. In either case, from clue 3, Meade is Julia. Samantha is either Brand or Goodman (clue 2), so the woman named Arnold (clue 5) is Melinda. The producer isn't Clifford (clue 5), so is Rick, leaving Clifford in 6. He isn't Goodman (clue 2), so Brand and Goodman is Samantha (clue 2). Mathers is Angus (clue 1) in 5 and Watson is Rick, the producer.

In summary:
Producer, Rick Watson.
1, Melinda Arnold.
2, Bradley Simmons.
3, Julia Meade.
4, Samantha Goodman.
5, Angus Mathers.
6, Clifford Brand.

Sought and Bold (No 177)
Garth and Samantha were engaged in 1999 (clue 7) and the test pilot proposed in 2000 (clue 5). Gerard, the jockey, didn't buy her a ring in 2002 (clue 2), nor can he be the man who proposed in 2001, aged 25 (clues 2 and 3), so he became Sam's fiancé in 1998. Garth's predecessor was Gerard, so he isn't the rally driver (clue 1) and he wasn't the commando (clue 2), so he was the footballer. He wasn't 26 (clue 4) and we know he wasn't 25. Nor, since he succeeded Gerard in Sam's affections, can Garth have been 28 (clue 2) and Dennis was 27 (clue 6), so Garth was 24. So Gerard was 26 (clue 2). Now clue 1 tells us the rally driver was 25. So he was the 2001 fiancé, leaving the man engaged to Sam in 2002 as the commando. From clue 1, Bruce was the test pilot who proposed to Sam in 2000. The rally driver's age rules him out as Dennis, so he was Darren, leaving Dennis, aged 27, as the commando, which leaves Bruce as the fiancé aged 28.

In summary:
1998, Gerard, jockey, 26.
1999, Garth, footballer, 24.
2000, Bruce, test pilot, 28.
2001, Darren, rally driver, 25.
2002, Dennis, commando, 27.

Truckers ... (No 178)
Fletcher drove 207 miles (clue 5) and Treadwell is 220 miles from the depot (clue 2), so Slingsby, who drove to Kidborough (clue 1), cannot have had a longer journey than 193 miles. So Andy drove either 158 or 186 miles (clue 1). But it was Vinnie who drove 186 miles (clue 7), so Andy made the shortest run of 158 miles. We now know Lewis Patterson (clue 3) didn't drive

158, 186 or 207 miles and clue 3 rules out 220, so he travelled 193 miles that day. So, from clue 3, Worlington, which we know isn't 220 miles from the depot, is 207, so Fletcher drove there. We now know Patterson's destination wasn't Kidborough, Treadwell or Worlington, nor was it Stonemarket (clue 4), so it was Ashfield. Kidborough cannot be 158 miles away (clue 1), so Slingsby is Vinnie, who drove 186 miles, which leaves Andy's destination as Stonemarket. His surname cannot be Warren (clue 6), so it's Burley, leaving Warren as the man who drove to Treadwell. His first name isn't Clyde (clue 6), so it's Mel, leaving Clyde as Fletcher.

In summary:
Andy Burley, Stonemarket, 158 miles.
Clyde Fletcher, Worlington, 207 miles.
Lewis Patterson, Ashfield, 193 miles.
Mel Warren, Treadwell, 220 miles.
Vinnie Slingsby, Kidborough, 186 miles.

... Tuck In (No 179)
The driver who stopped at 1.15 had Irish stew (clue 5). From clue 1, the beef pie cannot have been ordered at 12.15 or 12.30, so it was the choice at either 12.45 or 1.00. But it was Andy who ate at 12.30 (clue 3), not Clyde, who was heading for Worlington, so clue 1 rules out 12.45 for the beef pie, which was eaten at 1.00. So, from clue 1, Clyde ate at 12.45 and Andy, who ate at 12.30, dined at Luigi's. Dan's Diner is where the mixed grill was ordered (clue 4), but Clyde didn't eat there (clue 4). We know the meals chosen at 1.00 and 1.15 and the café visited at 12.30, so, by elimination, the mixed grill was ordered at Dan's Diner at 12.15. We know Mel didn't eat at 12.30 or 12.45 and clue 6 rules him out for 1.00 or 1.15, so he ate at 12.15. From clue 6, fish and chips was Andy's choice at Luigi's, leaving Clyde as the driver who ordered curry. Lewis ate at Meals-R-Us (clue 2), but not at 1.15 (clue 5), so he stopped for lunch at 1.00 and had the beef pie. This leaves Vinnie as the man who stopped for Irish stew at 1.15. Clyde drove 207 miles, so he cannot have eaten his curry at the Cosy Café (clue 7) and was in Eataway, leaving the Cosy Café as the establishment where Vinnie ate his Irish stew.

In summary:
Andy, 12.30, Luigi's, fish and chips.
Clyde, 12.45, Eataway, curry.
Lewis, 1.00, Meals-R-Us, beef pie.
Mel, 12.15, Dan's Diner, mixed grill.
Vinnie, 1.15, Cosy Café, Irish stew.

Pile Up (No 180)
From the top: C, E, A, D, B, F

Battleships (No 181)

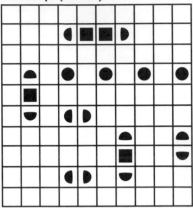

Because It's There (No 182)
Victor was the 2001 companion (clue 3) and Peake went in 2000 (clue 7). Armand Piton cannot have been on the 2002 climb (clue 1), and, since the 1999 expedition was to the Alps (clue 5), clue 1 also rules out 1998 for Armand, who must thus have climbed with Will in the Alps in 1999. Thus, from clue 1, Peake accompanied Will in the Scottish Highlands for the 2000 climb. Julian climbed with him in the Rockies, but not in 2002 (clue 6), so in 1998. The trip to the Himalayas wasn't in 2001 (clue 2), so in 2002 and that to the Andes was in 2001 with (by elimination) Victor Scales. Julian isn't Boulder (clue 6), so Cleft and Boulder was the climber in 2002. Clarence is Peake (clue 4), so Timothy is Boulder.

In summary:
1998, Rockies, Julian Cleft.
1999, Alps, Armand Piton.
2000, Scottish Highlands, Clarence Peake.
2001, Andes, Victor Scales.
2002, Himalayas, Timothy Boulder.

Nightmares (No 183)
Medusa was the leader in the Tuesday dream (clue 6). The Thursday dream's leader can't have been Darth Vader (clue 1), nor Count Dracula, who led the vampires (clue 5); clue 3 rules out Anne Robinson as the Thursday leader, who must thus have been The Mummy, who chased me round the deserted city (clue 2). His monsters weren't orcs (clue 2) and we know they weren't vampires; the giant rats were in the sewers (clue 4) and clue 1 tells us the zombies weren't in the Thursday dream, so The Mummy's monsters were giant spiders. The zombies can't have featured in the Tuesday dream (clue 1), so weren't led by Medusa, nor by Darth Vader (clue 1), thus by Anne Robinson. Thus they weren't

in the Friday dream (clue 3) and clue 1 rules out Monday; we know they weren't in the dream on Thursday, so they were in the Wednesday one. Now, from clue 1, Darth Vader was the leader in the Monday dream, and, by elimination, Dracula and his vampires were in the Friday dream. From clue 7, the zombies were in the Gothic castle, and, from clue 3, the caves was the location for the Friday dream with Count Dracula and his vampires. Since Medusa wasn't the leader in the forest (clue 6), she led the giant rats in the sewers. By elimination, the forest was the location for the Monday dream, in which Darth Vader led the orcs.

In summary:
Monday, forest, orcs, Darth Vader.
Tuesday, sewers, giant rats, Medusa.
Wednesday, Gothic castle, zombies, Anne Robinson.
Thursday, deserted city, giant spiders, The Mummy.
Friday, caves, vampires, Count Dracula.

Spoilt for Choice (No 184)

Since the Red Lion is pub number 5 (clue 4) and the Cheshire Cheese cannot be number 9 (clue 2), clue 2 tells us Alan cannot be the landlord of pub 1. Nor can Marion (clue 1), Terence (clue 2), Wilf (clue 3), Sandra (clue 5), Malcolm, landlord of the Cat and Fiddle (clue 7), or Graham (clue 7), while Lorna runs pub 6 (clue 6), so, by elimination, pub 1 is Trixie's. Graham's even-numbered pub cannot be 2 or 4 (clue 7), so it's 8. So, from clue 7, Malcolm cannot run pub 9. We already know this pub isn't Graham's, Lorna's or Trixie's, nor can it be run by Marion (clue 1), Alan (clue 2), Wilf (clue 3), or Sandra (clue 5), so its landlord is Terence. Its name cannot be the Galloping Major or the Wallingfen Arms (clue 1), the Cheshire Cheese (clue 2), the White Horse (clue 3), the Three Tuns (clue 5), the Cat and Fiddle or the Green Dragon (clue 7) and we know it isn't the Red Lion, so it's the Blue Boar. We know Malcolm's Cat and Fiddle isn't in locations 5 or 6, 8 or 9, so, from clue 7, it's 2 or 3 and the Green Dragon is 1 or 2. So we know pub 7 is none of the Blue Boar, Cat and Fiddle, Green Dragon or Red Lion. Nor can it be the Galloping Major or the Wallingfen Arms (clue 1), the Cheshire Cheese (clue 2) or the Three Tuns (clue 5), so it's the White Horse. We have seen that both the Cat and Fiddle and the Green Dragon are in the northernmost row, so, from clue 1, the Galloping Major and the Wallingfen Arms, which cannot be in the southernmost, are in the middle row. So the Galloping Major is pub 4 and the Wallingfen Arms pub 6, run by Lorna and Marion is the licensee of pub 7, the White Horse (clue 1). The Cheshire Cheese cannot be

in the northernmost street (clue 2), so it's pub 8, run by Graham, and, from clue 2, Alan is the landlord of pub 4, the Galloping Major. So, from clue 5, the Three Tuns cannot be pub 1 or pub 2, and, by elimination, is pub 3. Now, from clue 7, Malcolm's Cat and Fiddle is pub 2 and the Green Dragon pub 1, leaving Wilf as landlord of pub 3.

In summary:
1, Green Dragon, Trixie.
2, Cat and Fiddle, Malcolm.
3, Three Tuns, Wilf.
4, Galloping Major, Alan.
5, Red Lion, Sandra.
6, Wallingfen Arms, Lorna.
7, White Horse, Marion.
8, Cheshire Cheese, Graham.
9, Blue Boar, Terence.

Brightbourne Weekend (No 185)

Montague's girlfriend's father was Admiral Tagg (clue 7) and Daphne's was General Drew (clue 5), so, from clue 1, Archie's girlfriend Angela, whose father wasn't Lord Hartopp or Lord St Simon, was Sir Guy Graeme's daughter and Archie thus spent the weekend at the Links Hotel (clue 4). The girlfriend who took her Drone to the Grand Hotel wasn't Angela and clue 3 tells us she wasn't Daphne or Melanie; Hannah took her Drone to the Normandie (clue 6), so, by elimination, it was Phyllis who went to the Grand. So, from clue 3, Melanie was Lord Hartopp's daughter. She didn't go to the Esplanade (clue 1), so she to the Marine and her Drone was thus Edward (clue 2). By elimination, Daphne went to the Esplanade. Lord St Simon's daughter wasn't Gerald's girlfriend (clue 5), who was thus Daphne, and Lord St Simon's daughter was Rupert's girlfriend. She wasn't Phyllis (clue 5), so was Hannah, leaving Phyllis as Montague's girlfriend.

In summary:
Archie Fotheringhay, Angela, Links, Sir Guy Graeme.
Edward Tanqueray, Melanie, Marine, Lord Hartopp.
Gerald Huntington, Daphne, Esplanade, General Drew.
Montague Ffolliott, Phyllis, Grand, Admiral Tagg.
Rupert de Grey, Hannah, Normandie, Lord St Simon.

All-Day Breakfast (No 186)

The man who had a burger added wasn't Nelson (clue 2), Brian, Gary or Ray (clue 5), so Jonathan, who omitted tomato (clue 3). Nelson drank white coffee (clue 2), the orange juice drinker omitted beans (clue 4) and the tea-drinker added mushrooms (clue 6). Jonathan didn't drink black coffee (clue 5), so cola. The man who had tea and added mushrooms didn't omit toast (6) or the sausage, omitted by the man who added scrambled egg (clue 4), so he omitted fried egg. He wasn't Brian (clue 1), or Ray (clue 5), so Gary. Brian didn't drink black coffee (clue 1), so had orange juice, and, by elimination, Ray had black coffee. Neither he nor Nelson added poached egg (clues 5 and 2), so Brian did so. We know it was the man who omitted the sausage who added the scrambled egg, so, by elimination, it was the one who omitted toast who added black pudding. This can't have been Nelson (clue 2), so was Ray, leaving Nelson as the man who omitted the sausage and added scrambled egg.

In summary:
Brian, orange juice, beans, poached egg.
Gary, tea, fried egg, mushrooms.
Jonathan, cola, tomato, burger.
Nelson, white coffee, sausage, scrambled egg.
Ray, black coffee, toast, black pudding.

Hanover Captains (No 187)

The 14th Precinct area has a two-word name (clue 3). It can't be Oak Glen (clue 4), so is South Ridge. So Captain De Torres must command the 11th Precinct (clue 5). From clue 3, Captain Callaghan's precinct is in Oak Glen. Wesley Seaborg can't be captain of the 14th Precinct (clue 1), nor can the captain of the 14th be Callaghan from Oak Glen, De Torres of the 11th or Negretti (clue 3), so he or she is surnamed Kreisky. Kreisky can't be Martin (clue 4), Colleen or Rosina (clue 2), so is Abraham. Thus Lancaster is the 11th Precinct (clue 3). Wesley Seaborg's precinct can't be in Jamestown (clue 1), so is in Middlewood and Negretti's precinct must, by elimination, be in Jamestown. Rosina isn't De Torres nor, as she's not in command in Oak Glen, Callaghan (clue 4), so she is Negretti. Since Callaghan is male (clue 2), Colleen is De Torres, and, by elimination, Martin is Callaghan. From clue 4, his precinct is the 8th, and Wesley's Middlewood the 2nd, leaving Rosina as captain of the 5th.

In summary:
Abraham Kreisky, 14th, South Ridge.
Colleen De Torres, 11th, Lancaster.
Martin Callaghan, 8th, Oak Glen.
Rosina Negretti, 5th, Jamestown.
Wesley Seaborg, 2nd, Middlewood.

Team De Ronda (No 188)

Mary Garth was co-driver of the Romola (clue 3) and Martin Poyser drove the Melema (clue 6), so the car crewed by Jim Salt and Esther Lyon, which wasn't the Zarca GT or the Zarca GTi (clue 1), was the Bardo, the engine of which blew up (clue 4). Dinah Morris, the only female driver, ran her car into a tree (clue 2), so can't

have been driving the Zarca GT (clue 5). So the female member of the Zarca GT's crew referred to in clue 5 is the co-driver Celia Brooke. The car Stephen Guest co-drove lost a wheel (clue 2); since the Zarca GT co-driven by Celia Brooke can't have hit a tree or a wall (clue 5) and we know that its engine didn't blow up, its gearbox jammed. Martin Poyser's co-driver wasn't Don Silva (clue 6), so Stephen Guest and the Melema thus lost a wheel. By elimination, Don Silva co-drove the Zarca GTi. From clue 3, William Dane didn't drive the Romola or Zarca GT, so he was with Don Silva in the Zarca GTi. As Dinah Morris' car hit a tree, it was the Romola. By elimination, Godfrey Cass drove the Zarca GT and the Zarca GTi hit a wall.

In summary:
Dinah Morris, Mary Garth, Romola, hit tree.
Godfrey Cass, Celia Brooke, Zarca GT, gearbox jammed.
Jim Salt, Esther Lyon, Bardo, blew up engine.
Martin Poyser, Stephen Guest, Melema, lost wheel.
William Dane, Don Silva, Zarca GTi, hit wall.

One to Go (No 189)

Bob holds four Kings (clue 6). The man with four Jacks isn't John (clue 1), nor can he be Frank, whose required card is an 8 (clues 1 and 4), or Mike (no picture cards, clue 3), so he is Kevin. The card he wants isn't a 4 (clue 5), so (clue 1) a Queen and the Queen is thus John's unwanted card. The man with all four 3s, who has an unwanted 2 (clue 7) isn't Bob, John or Kevin, nor Mike (clue 3), so Frank. The man with four 5s cannot be John (clue 6), so he is Mike, leaving John with four 9s. So his pair are not 6s (clue 8), nor can they be 4s, since the player holding those has an unwanted 7 (clue 2), so John has a pair of Aces. Bob's unwanted card bears an even number of pips (clue 3), so he cannot be the player with an unwanted 7, who requires a 4 (clue 2), so the latter is Mike, leaving Bob requiring a 6 to go out. Clue 3 now tells us Bob's unwanted card is the 4, leaving Kevin with the unwanted 10.

In summary:
Bob, four Kings, pair of 6s, unwanted 4.
Frank, four 3s, pair of 8s, unwanted 2.
John, four 9s, pair of Aces, unwanted Queen.
Kevin, four Jacks, pair of Queens, unwanted 10.
Mike, four 5s, pair of 4s, unwanted 7.

Two's Company (No 190)

The bakers' business started next after Egg's (clue 5), so, since Agg was one of the fourth pair to start up (clue 3), the bakers cannot have been the fifth. Nor were the shoemakers (clue 4), or the furriers (clue 7), while the third couple were fishmongers (clue 6), so the fifth pair was the

SOLUTIONS

wheelwrights. Thus, from clue 2, one of these two was Clogg and Jigg was Agg's partner in the fourth enterprise. Clogg's partner in the fifth cannot have been Ogg (clue 1) and we know he wasn't Agg. Clue 5 rules out Egg and Ugg's partner was Kegg (clue 7), so, by elimination, it was Igg who went into the wheel-making business with Clogg. So, from clue 4, Agg and Jigg were shoemakers. The bakers' business wasn't the first to be launched (clue 5), so, by elimination, it was the second, and, from clue 5, Egg was one of the first pair, who, by elimination, were furriers. So, from clue 7, Ugg and Kegg were the second pair, who became bakers. This leaves Ogg as a fishmonger. Egg's partner wasn't Flagg (clue 5), so he was Lugg, which leaves Flagg as Ogg's partner in the fishmongers' business.

In summary:
First, Egg and Lugg, furriers.
Second, Ugg and Kegg, bakers.
Third, Ogg and Flagg, fishmongers.
Fourth, Agg and Jigg, shoemakers.
Fifth, Igg and Clogg, wheelwrights.

Small Craft (No 191)

Seagull, the fishing boat (clue 1), can't have been captained by Dave Lewis, whose boat was either Melanie or Prudence (clue 5), John Briggs, whose boat was Dolphin (clue 2) or Sam Watson, whose boat was the foot ferry (clue 7); since Seagull was neither Melanie nor the crabbing boat, it can't have been the one captained by Tom Platt and crewed by 'Spud' (clues 3 and 6), so its captain was Nick Bady. His crewman wasn't Jack (clue 1), 'Ginger' or Terry, who worked on the sightseeing boat (clue 4), so Seagull's crewman was Mike. We now know that the crewman on Sam Watson's foot ferry wasn't Mike, 'Spud' or Terry; clue 7 rules out 'Ginger', so he was Jack. Melanie's crewman was 'Ginger' or 'Spud' (clue 6), so Melanie can't have been the foot ferry or the sightseeing boat; nor was she the crabbing boat (clue 6), so she was the diving boat. Thus her captain wasn't Dave Lewis (clue 5), who must have captained Prudence. Thus Melanie was captained by Tom Platt. This leaves Sam Watson's foot ferry as Hercules and the crabbing boat's crewman as 'Ginger'. The crabbing boat was the Dolphin (clue 7) and Prudence was the sightseeing boat.

In summary:
Dolphin, crabbing, John Briggs, 'Ginger'.
Hercules, foot ferry, Sam Watson, Jack.
Melanie, diving, Tom Platt, 'Spud'.
Prudence, sightseeing, Dave Lewis, Terry.
Seagull, fishing, Nick Bady, Mike.

Pile Up (No 192)

From the top: F, D, A, B, C, E.

Logi-5 (No 193a)

C	A	D	E	B
A	B	E	D	C
B	D	A	C	E
E	C	B	A	D
D	E	C	B	A

ABC (No 193b)

		C	B	A
A	C	B		
B			A	C
	A		C	B
C	B	A		

Weekend Walks (No 194)

It was overcast in the Yorkshire Dales (clue 4), so in the Peak District, which wasn't where Esther met the drizzle (clue 3), it was sunny and Esther was walking on Exmoor. Edward was in the Peak District (clue 1). Esther's companion wasn't Charles (clue 2), so Stuart. Thus Charles was in the Yorkshire Dales, not with Naomi (clue 2), so Joyce. Naomi was with Edward.

In summary:
Charles, Joyce, Yorkshire Dales, overcast.
Edward, Naomi, Peak District, sunny.
Stuart, Esther, Exmoor, drizzle.

Survivors (No 195)

The bosun wasn't shipwrecked in 1810 (clue 1) and neither was the third mate (clue 2), so that was the year the cook was shipwrecked. Sam Thole was shipwrecked in 1750 (clue 4); Ben Cable can't have been shipwrecked in 1690 (clue 2), so he was the cook stranded in 1810 and Hugh Keel was stranded in 1690. The bosun's ship was the Sturgeon (clue 1). He wasn't Sam Thole (clue 4), so was Hugh Keel. By elimination, Sam Thole was the third mate. Ben Cable wasn't on the Pole Star (clue 2), so was the cook of the Rose leaving Sam Thole aboard the Pole Star.

In summary:
Ben Cable, cook, Rose, 1810.
Hugh Keel, bosun, Sturgeon, 1690.
Sam Thole, third mate, Pole Star, 1750.

Is That a Folk Song? (No 196)

A man whose surname begins with a vowel sings with Carol Dodds and the other sings American songs with Jane Kenny, so, since it can't be Steven Thorp who sings with Sue Rogers (clue

5), it's Hans Gruber and the duo thus perform English songs (clue 1), and, by elimination, Steven Thorp sings with Nancy O'Hara, as Rose and Thorn (clue 2). The man in the duo who sing their own compositions (clue 5) is Peter Owen and the duo is thus the Starr Twins (clue 4). Since they sing American songs, Jane Kenny's partner, whose surname begins with a vowel (clue 3), is Ben Ashby and Peter Owen sings with Carol Dodds. By elimination, Rose and Thorn sings Irish songs. Ben Ashby and Jane Kenny aren't the Merlyns (clue 4), so Dirk and Daisy. Hans Gruber and Sue Rogers perform as the Merlyns.

In summary:
Ben Ashby, Jane Kenny, Dirk and Daisy, American.
Hans Gruber, Sue Rogers, Merlyns, English.
Peter Owen, Carol Dodds, Starr Twins, own compositions.
Steven Thorp, Nancy O'Hara, Rose and Thorn, Irish.

Sports Writers (No 197)

Emma Ford's book is Winning and Losing (clue 4), so (clues 1 and 4) Lifetime Ambition is by Amanda Bourn. It's a satire on her sport (clue 3), which isn't tennis (clue 1), golf (clue 2) or fencing (clue 3), so motor racing. Thus (clue 2) Katie Lloyd wrote Championship, so (by elimination) Sally Tate's book is Top of the World. From clue 2, her sport is golf and her book is thus a history. Emma Ford's sport isn't tennis (clue 4) so fencing and Kate is the tennis star. Emma's book isn't a whodunnit (clue 4), so an autobiography and the whodunnit is Championship.

In summary:
A Bourn, motor racing, Lifetime Ambition, satire.
E Ford, fencing, Winning and Losing, autobiography.
K Lloyd, tennis, Championship, whodunnit.
S Tate, golf, Top of the World, history.

Haunted Houstead (No 198)

'Old John' haunts the Norman house (clue 2) and 'Wicked Peter' was an alchemist (clue 4), so the Early Tudor building haunted by the murder victim, who isn't 'Little Tam' (clue 1), is haunted by 'Grey Susan'. So the Early Tudor house isn't Okehurst (clue 3), nor, from clue 1, can it be Ashepound or Helm Grange, so it's Martyn's. Thus (clue 1) 'Little Tam' haunts Ashepound. We know that 'Old John' at the Norman house isn't an alchemist or a murder victim, nor is he the dog (clue 2), so he is the suicide, and, by elimination, 'Little Tam', is the dog. Ashepound isn't the Saxon house (clue 3) so, by elimination, it's Late Tudor and the Saxon house is haunted by 'Wicked Peter'. Finally, from clue 5, 'Old John'

doesn't haunt Helm Grange, so Okehurst and Helm Grange is the Saxon house.

In summary:
Ashepound, Late Tudor, 'Little Tam', dog.
Helm Grange, Saxon, 'Wicked Peter', alchemist.
Martyn's, Early Tudor, 'Grey Susan', murder victim.
Okehurst, Norman, 'Old John', suicide.

Sects and the City (No 199)

One sect was founded in Cardiff in 1871 (clue 6) and the Grisinians were founded in 1875 (clue 4), so the Pakorians who were founded in Manchester but not in 1860 or 1865 (clue 1), was established in 1884. Amos Strangefellow founded his sect in 1860 (clue 2), but not in Cardiff, Manchester, London (clue 2) or Birmingham, where Ellen Brimstone's sect was established (clue 5), so it was Glasgow. The Waitists were founded by Evan Waites (clue 3). The Pakorians weren't founded by Saul Bunkham (clue 1), so by Connor Swindell. Amos Strangefellow didn't found the Grisinians or the Sennonists (clue 2), so the Marsillians. The foundation date of the Waitists wasn't 1865 (clue 3) so 1871. The Sennonists weren't established in London (clue 2), so Birmingham in (by elimination) 1865. Thus the Grisinians were founded by Saul Bunkham in London.

In summary:
Grisinians, London, 1875, Saul Bunkham.
Marsillians, Glasgow, 1860, Amos Strangefellow.
Pakorians, Manchester, 1884, Connor Swindell.
Sennonists, Birmingham, 1865, Ellen Brimstone.
Waitists, Cardiff, 1871, Evan Waites.

Jacks of All Trades (No 200)

The Plummers live in Brick Road (clue 1) and Jack Gardner works in Locksmith Lane (clue 4), so (clue 2) The Joyners live in Tyler Street. The sweep is working for the Bakers (clue 5). The carpet-layer in Cobblers Drive isn't employed by the Butchers (clue 3), so he is Jack Painter, working for the Pipers (clue 6). Jack Glaser is an electrician (clue 6), so (clue 1) Jack Naylor is the sweep working (by elimination) in Millers Way. Thus Jack Gardner is working for the Butchers. The builder isn't working for the Joyners or the Plummers (clue 1), so for the Butchers. The Joyners are not emploving the decorator (clue 2), so the electrician and, by elimination, the decorator is Jack Carpenter, who is working for the Plummers.

In summary:
Jack Carpenter, decorator, Plummer, Brick Road.
Jack Gardner, builder, Butcher, Locksmith Lane.
Jack Glaser, electrician, Joyner, Tyler Street.
Jack Naylor, sweep, Baker, Millers Way.
Jack Painter, carpet-layer, Piper, Cobblers Drive.

SOLUTIONS

Battleships (No 201)

Logi-5 (No 202a)

B	D	C	A	E
E	A	D	C	B
A	C	E	B	D
D	B	A	E	C
C	E	B	D	A

ABC (No 202b)

A		B		C
	C	A		B
B			C	A
C	B		A	
	A	C	B	

Lord Preserve Us (No 203)

Jane has produced 10 lbs of preserve (clue 3), so she cannot be Mrs Jamieson, who made the lemon curd (clue 1), while the raspberry jam is from Phyllis (clue 6) and 7 lbs of plum jam has been donated (clue 4). Clue 7 rules out strawberry jam as Jane's preserve, so she made the bramble jelly. Betty is Mrs Storton and Jane cannot be Mrs Banks (clue 5). We know she isn't Mrs Jamieson and Mrs Potterton's offering weighed 8 lbs (clue 2), so, by elimination, Jane is Mrs Fraser. We know Mrs Jamieson, who made lemon curd, isn't Phyllis, nor is she Mildred (clue 1), so she is Fenella. We know she has not made 7, 8 or 10 lbs of lemon curd and clue 1 rules out 9 lbs, so she made 6 lbs. Mildred thus made 7 lbs of plum jam (clue 1), so, by elimination, Betty

Storton made strawberry jam for the fair. We know she didn't make 6, 7, 8 or 10 lbs, so she produced 9 lbs, leaving Phyllis as Mrs Potterton, who thus made 8 lbs of raspberry jam. This leaves Mildred's surname as Banks.

In summary:
Betty Storton, 9 lbs, strawberry jam.
Fenella Jamieson, 6 lbs, lemon curd.
Jane Fraser, 10 lbs, bramble jelly.
Mildred Banks, 7 lbs, plum jam.
Phyllis Potterton, 8 lbs, raspberry jam.

The Sixth Passenger (No 204)

Ernest Finch, the jeweller, was sure the sixth passenger was male (clue 4); it was Norton Oates who described him as a foreign man (clue 1) and the MP who said he was a tall man (clue 6), so Ernest Finch described him as a young man. We now know that the bodyguard who said the sixth passenger wore a brown cloak (clue 1) didn't describe him as a young man or a tall man, nor did he say he was a foreign man (clue 1); the young woman was described as wearing a black waterproof (clue 3), so the bodyguard said the traveller was a motherly woman. We know that Joseph Kilne didn't describe the sixth passenger as a foreign man or a young man and since he said the mystery traveller was wearing a grey duster (clue 2), he can't have been referring to the motherly woman or the young woman, whose clothes we know, so called him a tall man and was thus the MP. Albert Busby didn't describe the sixth traveller as a motherly woman (clue 5), so used the description a young woman and Percy Ruskin was the bodyguard who thought the sixth passenger was a motherly woman in a brown cloak. We know that Albert Busby wasn't the jeweller, his bodyguard or the MP; nor was he the factory owner (clue 5), so he was a bank manager. By elimination, the factory owner was Norton Oates. He didn't describe the sixth passenger as wearing an Inverness (clue 5), so said he wore a blue coat, leaving the Inverness worn by the young man jeweller Ernest Finch thought he saw.

In summary:
Albert Busby, bank manager, young woman, black waterproof.
Ernest Finch, jeweller, young man, Inverness.
Joseph Kilne, MP, tall man, grey duster.
Norton Oates, factory owner, foreign man, blue coat.
Percy Ruskin, bodyguard, motherly woman, brown cloak.

The Great Escape (No 205)

Goodhart is number 2 in the tunnel (clue 3). Number 4 cannot be Marshall (clue 1), or Bottle (clue 4), so he is Valliant, of the Royal Navy (clue

SOLUTIONS

2) and 'Kipper' is in position 3. Valliant cannot be 'Biggles', who is in the RAF (clue 1), nor can 'Jingo' be in position 4 (clue 5), so Valliant is 'Puffer'. From clue 4, 'Kipper' is Bottle. By elimination, the escaper in position 1 is Marshall. He isn't 'Biggles' (clue 1), so he is 'Jingo', which leaves Goodhart as 'Biggles' of the RAF. 'Jingo' isn't from the Artillery regiment (clue 5), so he is a Royal Marine, leaving the Artillery officer as 'Kipper' Bottle.

In summary:
1, 'Jingo' Marshall, Royal Marines.
2, 'Biggles' Goodhart, RAF.
3, 'Kipper' Bottle, Artillery.
4, 'Puffer' Valliant, Royal Navy.

In Orbit (No 206)

Maz'k is Technician of satellite 4 (clue 2), so, from clue 3 and the introduction, the Lamorakian Technician on satellite 2, the Sentinel, is Lo'Bu. From the introduction, D'Poj, Administrator of the Watchman, can't be on satellite 2 or 4, nor is he on satellite 1 (clue 4), so he is on satellite 3 and B'Kap is the Administrator on satellite 1. Satellite 1's Technician isn't Thomas (clue 4), who must thus be Technician on satellite 3, Watchman, with Administrator D'Poj and the Technician on Satellite 1 is Brown. Thus, from clue 1, Smith can't be the Administrator on satellite 2, the Sentinel, so Technician Lo'bu's partner on that satellite is Administrator Jones and Administrator Smith is on satellite 4 with technician Maz'k. Satellite 4 isn't the Custodian (clue 2), so is the Guardian, leaving Custodian as satellite 1, crewed by Administrator B'Kap and Technician Brown.

In summary:
1, Custodian, B'Kap, Brown.
2, Sentinel, Jones, Lo'Bu.
3, Watchman, D'Poj, Thomas.
4, Guardian, Smith, Maz'k.

Logi-Path (No 207)

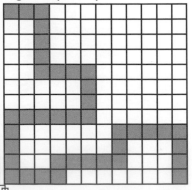

Domino Search (No 208)

2	4	1	3	1	6	5	4
5	0	6	3	0	5	5	3
6	6	3	4	4	0	2	5
0	1	0	4	4	1	2	6
2	5	3	1	2	6	6	5
4	1	1	4	3	2	3	3
2	5	0	6	2	0	0	1

Stor Detectives (No 209)

Jack Lowe made his find on Bluegate Farm (clue 5). Eddie Green's find was made in Glemsfield, not on a farm (clue 6), so it came from The Rectory or Turkey Bridge. Turkey Bridge is in Boxstone (clue 1), so Eddie Green made his find at Glemsfield Rectory. Bob Dean found the Russian medal (clue 4). The whaling harpoon was found at Chapel Farm (clue 2), so can't have been discovered by Eddie Green or Jack Lowe, nor was it found by Mick O'Leary (clue 2), so it was Paul Ray's find. Chapel Farm, where he found it, isn't in Lavenstead (clue 2). It was the Inca helmet that was found in Waldleigh, so the whaling harpoon was found in Mellingford. As the location of the discovery in Waldleigh wasn't Hazel Farm (clue 3), it was Bluegate Farm and the Inca helmet was thus found by Jack Lowe. By elimination, Hazel Farm is in Lavenstead. The Japanese sword wasn't found at The Rectory (clue 4), so wasn't Eddie Green's discovery and was Mick O'Leary's, leaving Eddie Green's find as the Arab dagger. Finally, since Bob Dean made his find on a farm (clue 4), he discovered it at Hazel Farm, Lavenstead and Mick O'Leary made his find at Turkey Bridge, Boxstone.

In summary:
Bob Dean, Russian medal, Hazel Farm, Lavenstead.
Eddie Green, Arab dagger, The Rectory, Glemsfield.
Jack Lowe, Inca helmet, Bluegate Farm, Waldleigh.
Mick O'Leary, Japanese sword, Turkey Bridge. Boxstone.
Paul Ray, whaling harpoon, Chapel Farm, Mellingford.

Dishonourable Members (No 210)

Sir Ivor Vyce is MP for Blotton (clue 6) and Lou Smorrells is member for a constituency beginning with the letter C (clue 3), so the member for Giltley, who isn't Ben de Rooles or Will Fiddle (clue 2), is LibDem Phil Pocket (clue 1). His misdemeanour isn't his underworld connections

SOLUTIONS

(clue 2), undeclared earnings (clue 1), cash for questions, which is the MP for Chiselham (clue 4), or having an affair, which is the Conservative (clue 1), so he is accused of insider dealing. The Tainton MP isn't a member of the Conservative or Labour parties (clue 1), nor is he the LibDem member for Giltley or the Scottish National member for Crooklow (clue 5), so he's the Independent member. By elimination, the Conservative having the affair is the Blotton MP and Chiselham has a Labour MP. This isn't Lou Smorrells (clue 3), so he is the MP for Crooklow and a member of the Scottish National party. Ben de Rooles isn't a Labour MP (clue 2), so he is the Independent member for Tainton and as he does not have underworld connections, he is accused of having undeclared earnings. By elimination, the Labour MP is Will Fiddle and Lou Smorrells is the member for Crooklow whose underworld connections have been exposed.

In summary:
Will Fiddle, Labour, Chiselham, cash for questions.
Phil Pocket, LibDem, Giltley, insider dealing.
Ben de Rooles, Independent, Tainton, undeclared earnings.
Lou Smorrells, Scottish National, Crooklow, underworld connections.
Sir Ivor Vyce, Conservative, Blotton, affair.

Passing the Test (No 211)
Chester is number 3 at turnstile B (clue 4). Salim cannot head line A (clue 2), so (clue 1) he is number 3 and Edward is number 5. So, from clue 7, Faisal is number 5 in line B. Clue 7 now tells us Keith is either 1 or 2 in that line and thus Michael is 1 or 2 in the other. But clue 2 rules him out as number 1 in line A, so he is number 2 and Keith is number 2 in line B. Whichever line Owen and Johnny are in, their respective positions (clue 5) are 4 and 6, but clue 6 rules out Owen as number 4 in line A, so they are in line B. We have now named five men in that queue, so, from clue 3, Ravi and Denzil are in line A and Farouk thus is number 1 in line B, the only vacant position. Ravi cannot be number 1 or number 4 (clues 3 and 6), so he is number 6 in line A and Denzil, who cannot be number 1 (clue 3), is number 4, leaving Gareth at the head of that line.

In summary:

Turnstile A	Turnstile B
1 Gareth	1 Farouk
2 Michael	2 Keith
3 Salim	3 Chester
4 Denzil	4 Owen
5 Edward	5 Faisal
6 Ravi	6 Johnny

End of the Year (No 212)
Amanda, whose tutor is Dr Nurse, wasn't given the 'favourable' assessment (clue 1), nor can her work have been described as 'competent' at 4pm (clues 1 and 5). Caroline's was rated 'excellent' (clue 8) and Mr Moldham used the term 'promising' (clue 7), so, by elimination, Amanda was rated 'adequate'. So she wasn't seen at 10am (clue 2) and we have already ruled out 4pm. Prof Groom conducted the 11am interview (clue 6) and Damien was seen at 3pm (clue 3), so Dr Nurse saw Amanda at 2pm. We know the person rated 'competent' at 4pm wasn't Damien or Caroline and clue 2 rules out Tara, so James was seen at that time. So his tutor wasn't Prof Groom or Mr Moldham, nor was he seen by Mrs Cram (clue 4), so his tutor is Miss Foster. We know her 4pm comment was 'competent', so, from clue 1, the 'favourable' assessment was made at 3pm and thus referred to Damien's work. This leaves Mr Moldham's student as Tara who (by elimination) was interviewed at 10am. The time of his interview rules out Damien's tutor as Prof Groom, so he was seen by Mrs Cram at 3pm, thus Caroline saw Prof Groom at 11am.

In summary:
Amanda, Dr Nurse, 2pm, 'adequate'.
Caroline, Prof Groom, 11am, 'excellent'.
Damien, Mrs Cram, 3pm, 'favourable'.
James, Miss Foster, 4pm, 'competent'.
Tara, Mr Moldham, 10am, 'promising'.

Lambs to the Slauta (No 213)
Tuesday's charge was being indecently dressed (clue 4) and at the temple ruins the charge was spying (clue 2). Jake, charged with picking a flower, didn't offend on Wednesday or Thursday (clue 5), so the Lamb arrested at the fishing port on Thursday, who wasn't charged with theft (clue 3) insulted the flag. This wasn't Andrew (clue 6), Gemma, who was arrested at the vineyard (clue 1), or Dave (clue 3), so was Carol. The vineyard wasn't visited on Monday or Tuesday (clue 1), so Gemma wasn't accused of being indecently dressed (clue 4), so was charged with theft. The indecent-dressing charge wasn't made at the villa ruins (clue 4), so at the village market, leaving the villa ruins as the place where Jake was arrested. The Lamb charged with indecent dressing wasn't Andrew (clue 6), so was Dave, leaving Andrew as the one charged with spying. Jake's arrest at wasn't on Wednesday (clue 5), nor were the villa ruins visited on Monday (clue 4), so Jake was charged on Friday. Gemma wasn't arrested on Monday or Tuesday (clue 1), so was charged on Wednesday, leaving Monday as the day Andrew was accused of spying.

SOLUTIONS

In summary:
Monday, temple ruins, Andrew, spying.
Tuesday, village market, Dave, indecently dressed.
Wednesday, vineyard, Gemma, theft.
Thursday, fishing port, Carol, insulting flag.
Friday, villa ruins, Jake, picking flower.

Off Course on Course (No 214)
Edward, whose total was 108, didn't have his mishap at the seventeenth hole (clue 2), nor was he the man stuck in the bunker at the thirteenth, whose total was an odd number of strokes (clue 1). The Drone whose bad experience was at the eighth finished in 101 (clue 5), and it was Gerald who had a problem at the tenth (clue 7), so, by elimination, Edward must have suffered his mishap at the third. We know he didn't linger in the bunker, nor did he lose his monocle in the rough (clue 2), while the Drone whose ball was lost down the hollow tree finished with 96 (clue 3), and it was Montague who tore his plus-fours on the brambles (clue 6), so Edward's ball was taken by a squirrel. So, from clue 4, it must be Archie who scored 101 after a mishap at the eighth. His score rules him out for the hollow tree incident, and the hole rules him out for the bunker, so he must have lost his monocle in the deep rough. We have now matched four holes with a name or a mishap, so it was at the seventeenth that Montague tore his plus-fours. This leaves Gerald as the Drone who lost his ball down a hollow tree, but scored 96, and Rupert spent twenty minutes in the bunker. From clue 6, he must have taken 115 strokes to complete his round, and Montague must have gone round in 99.

In summary:
Archie Fotheringhay, lost monocle in rough, 8th, 101.
Edward Tanqueray, ball taken by squirrel, 3rd, 108.
Gerald Huntington, lost ball in hollow tree, 10th, 96.
Montague Ffolliott, tore plus-fours, 17th, 99.
Rupert de Grey, spent 20 minutes in bunker, 13th, 115.

Knights on the Cards (No 215)
Sir Spyneless was the subject of card 48 (clue 3), and the favourite food mentioned on card 50 was junket (clue 7). Since dragons were the pet hate on card 40 (clue 6), Sir Coward, who liked custard, cannot have appeared on card 40 or card 42 (clue 1), so he was featured on card 45. So, from clue 1, jousting was the pet hate mentioned on card 42. We have now matched four series numbers with a knight or a pet hate, so Sir Poltroon, whose pet hate was mice (clue

5), must have appeared on card 50, and thus liked junket. Sir Timid cannot have been on card 40 (clue 2), so he must be the knight who hated jousting featured on card 42, leaving Sir Sorely on card 40. Clue 2 tells us jelly was the favourite food mentioned with his pet hate, dragons. Since Sir Spyneless didn't express a hatred of ugly ogres (clue 3), he gave polishing armour as his pet hate, leaving ugly ogres as Sir Coward's. Sir Spyneless didn't express a liking for trifle (clue 4), so blancmange, and trifle was Sir Timid's choice.

In summary:
Card 40, Sir Sorely à Frayde, dragons, jelly.
Card 42, Sir Timid de Shayke, jousting, trifle.
Card 45, Sir C de Custarde, ugly ogres, custard.
Card 48, Sir Spyneless de Feete, polishing armour, blancmange.
Card 50, Sir Poltroon à Ghaste, mice, junket.

In the Round (No 216)
Since the 1 in neither ring A nor ring B can be in circle 1 (clue 1), clue 3 tells us the digit in that circle in ring A cannot be 1, 2, 3, 5 or 7, so it must be one of 4, 6 or 8. Thus circle 1 of ring B must contain one of 2, 3 or 4 (clue 3). But the 2 is in circle 5 (clue 2), and the 4 cannot be in circle 1 (clue 4), so the number in circle 1 must be 3. Thus circle 1 in ring A must contain the 6 (clue 3). So, from clue 6, circle 7 of ring A must contain the 3, and circle 5 the 1. So the 1 in ring B must be in circle 7 (clue 7). Also, from clue 5, the 8 must be in circle 2 of ring B. So the 8 in ring A cannot be in circles 2 or 8 (clue 1), nor in circle 3, which is opposite the 3 (clue 4). We have inserted digits in circles 1, 5 and 7, so the 8 must be in 4 or 6. So the 4 in ring A is in circles 2 or 8 (clue 4). But clue 4 tells us it cannot be in 8, so it must be in 2, and the 8 must be in circle 6 (clue 4). We now know the 7 in ring A isn't in any of circles 1, 2, 5, 6 or 7, so it must be in one of 3, 4 or 8. Thus the one in ring B must be in one of circles 2, 3 or 7 (clue 8). But we know the numbers in 2 and 7, so the 7 must be in circle 3. Thus the 7 in ring A must be in circle 4 (clue 8). From clue 9, the 5 must be in circle 3 of ring A, and the 2 in circle 8. Also, from clue 9, the 5 in ring B cannot be in circle 4 or circle 6, so it must be in circle 8. From clue 1, the 4 in ring B must be in circle 6, and the 6 in circle 4.

In summary:
Ring A	Ring B
1, 6.	1, 3.
2, 4.	2, 8.
3, 5.	3, 7.
4, 7.	4, 6.
5, 1.	5, 2.
6, 8.	6, 4.
7, 3.	7, 1.
8, 2.	8, 5.

Ghost Stories (No 217)

Mr Wayne, who called the ghost Lily, isn't the publican or the librarian (3); the postmistress is Miss Duke (clue 2), and the parish councillor called the ghost Valerie (clue 5), so Mr Wayne must be the local historian. We now know that the person who called the ghost Abigail wasn't the local historian or the parish councillor; as this person was male (clue 6), he can't have been the postmistress, Miss Duke, and, as he described Abigail as a murdered maid (clue 6), he can't have been the librarian, who identified the ghost as the seduced governess (clue 4), so he was the publican. We know that he isn't Mr Wayne, and he can't be Miss Duke or Mrs Selby; Mr Price described the ghost as a bride (clue 1), so the publican who spoke of Abigail the murdered maid was Mr Jarvis. We now know the descriptions of the persons who gave three names for the ghost; the one who named her as Harriet wasn't the librarian who identified her as the seduced governess (clue 4), so was Miss Duke the postmistress, and the librarian's seduced governess was called Phyllis. From clue 1, Mr Price can't have identified the ghost as Phyllis the seduced governess, so the librarian must be Mrs Selby, and Mr Price is the parish councillor who called the ghost Valerie. From clue 1, he didn't describe her as the heartbroken housekeeper, nor was that the description of Mr Wayne's nomination Lily (clue 5), so the heartbroken housekeeper was Harriet, Miss Duke's ghost. Mr Wayne's Lily wasn't the cursed bride (clue 3), so was the jilted bride, thus the cursed bride is Valerie, identified by Mr Price.

In summary:
Abigail, murdered maid, Mr Jarvis, publican.
Harriet, heartbroken housekeeper, Miss Duke, postmistress.
Lily, jilted bride, Mr Wayne, local historian.
Phyllis, seduced governess, Mrs Selby, librarian.
Valerie, cursed bride, Mr Price, parish councillor.

Spun Off (No 218)

Kenny Young studied archaeology (clue 6) and in his new series George Todd dies and becomes a ghost (clue 2), so the theology student, who gets a job in TV and who is also male (clue 3) must be Ian Vickers. We know that in her new series Brenda Owen doesn't die and become a ghost or get a job in TV; as it's called Pinkies (clue 5), she can't move to London, which is the premise of City Lights (clue 1) or inherit a title, the premise of a series with a number in its title (clue 7), so she must marry a politician. She wasn't the drama student (clue 8) or the engineering student, whose new series is Room 102 (clue 4), so Brenda Owen studied medicine. The series in which Ian Vickers gets a job in TV isn't Number 7 (clue 3), and, as he studied theology, it can't be Room 102; so Ian Vickers' new job must feature in Hard Times. We now know the subjects studied by three students; George Todd's subject wasn't drama (clue 8), so was engineering, and his new series, in which he becomes a ghost, is thus Room 102. By elimination, Esther Reid must have studied drama. Thus her new series isn't Number 7 (clue 8) and must be City Lights, in which she moves to London. Finally, it must be Kenny Young who will appear in Number 7, in which, by elimination, he must inherit a title.

In summary:
Brenda Owen, medicine, Pinkies, marries politician.
Esther Reid, drama, City Lights, moves to London.
George Todd, engineering, Room 102, dies and becomes ghost.
Ian Vickers, theology, Hard Times, gets job in TV.
Kenny Young, archaeology, Number 7, inherits title.

Ask an Acquaintance (No 219)

Sharon was a contestant's sister (clue 4), and Annie tried to help with the 'Atlas' question (clue 5), so the answer 'Liverpool' which was suggested by a neighbour who wasn't Gary or Charlie (clue 2), was offered by Terry. He wasn't attempting to help Dave (clue 3), Graham, who asked Charlie (clue 1), or Linda who needed help with the 'Elizabeth I' question or Scott who asked a workmate (clue 6), so it was Kirsty. We know that Charlie, who aided Graham, wasn't the neighbour or workmate. He wasn't the college friend (clue 1), so he was the cousin. Thus Graham wasn't seeking help with the 'Liverpool', 'Elizabeth I' or 'Atlas' questions. Nor was it the 'Pink' question (clue 3), so it was the one to which the answer was 'Rhododendron'. Dave wasn't trying to decide on the answer 'Pink' (clue 3), so he must have asked Annie about the 'Atlas' question. By elimination, the 'Pink' question was the one for which Scott asked for help from his workmate. By elimination, this was Gary. Thus Sharon is Linda's sister, and helped her with the 'Elizabeth I' question, and Dave must have asked Annie, his college friend, if the answer to his question was 'Atlas'.

In summary:
Dave, Annie, college friend, 'Atlas'.
Graham, Charlie, cousin, 'Rhododendron'.
Kirsty, Terry, neighbour, 'Liverpool'.
Linda, Sharon, sister, 'Elizabeth I'.
Scott, Gary, workmate, 'Pink'.

Pile Up (No 220)

From the top: D, B, E, A, F, C.

SOLUTIONS

Battleships (No 221)

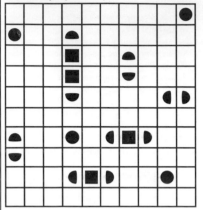

A Card from Sandra (No 222)

Cathy's surname is Smith (clue 8). Julie's message was 'Hotel excellent' (clue 7), so she cannot be Evans, who was told 'Wish you were here' (clue 5), nor can she be Jones, who must be either Adam or Mary (clue 3). She isn't Green (clue 7), so, by elimination, she must be Parker, whose card depicted the pier (clue 3). So clue 3 now tells us Green must be Mary. Thus, from clue 3, Jones must be Adam, leaving Harry as Evans. Mary Green's card showed the smugglers' cave (clue 6). Adam wasn't told Sandra was 'Having a great time' (clue 4), or that she was 'Getting quite brown' (clue 1), so he must have received the card depicting the lighthouse, and stating 'Weather good' (clue 2). So clue 1 tells us Harry's card showed the abbey ruins. This leaves Cathy Smith as the recipient of the card depicting the floral clock. So she didn't receive the 'Getting quite brown' message (clue 1), and was told 'Having a great time', leaving Mary Green as the recipient of the 'Getting quite brown' message.

In summary:
Adam Jones, lighthouse, 'Weather good'.
Cathy Smith, floral clock, 'Having a great time'.
Harry Evans, abbey ruins, 'Wish you were here'.
Julie Parker, pier, 'Hotel excellent'.
Mary Green, smugglers' cave, 'Getting quite brown'.

Happy Couples (No 223)

The May honeymoon was in Rome (clue 5). The one in August cannot have been in Paris (clue 1), Florida, where Paul spent his honeymoon (clue 3), or Barbados (clue 4), so it was the one in New York enjoyed by Susan (clue 6). We now know the April bride wasn't Susan, nor can she have been Sheila (clue 1), or Sarah, who married Patrick on the 31st (clue 2). Clue 3 rules out

Sally, so, by elimination, Samantha had the April wedding. Since the Rome honeymoon was in May, clue 1 rules out Sheila as the June bride, and clue 2 rules out Sarah. We know she wasn't Samantha or Susan, so she's Sally. So, from clue 3, Paul's Florida honeymoon, which we know wasn't in May, was in April, and his bride was thus Samantha. Now, from clue 1, Sheila cannot have married in May, so she was the July bride, leaving the woman married in May as Sarah, who married Patrick. Sheila didn't honeymoon in Paris (clue 1), so she must have gone to Barbados in July, leaving Paris as Sally's June honeymoon location. Now, from clue 4, Perry must have married Susan in August. Sheila didn't marry Peter (clue 1), so her new husband must be Philip, leaving Peter as Sally's bridegroom.

In summary:
April, Paul, Samantha, Florida.
May, Patrick, Sarah, Rome.
June, Peter, Sally, Paris.
July, Philip, Sheila, Barbados.
August, Perry, Susan, New York.

Photo-Finish (No 224)

Mr Golden was number 5 (clue 6), so, from clue 7, Red Rag wasn't number 7. The same clue tells us that it wasn't number 3, 4 or 8, so Red Rag was number 6, and was thus ridden by Colin Archer (clue 1). From clue 7, number 4 was Thunder Away. We now know that Proud Dancer wasn't number 4, 5 or 6, and clue 4 tells us it wasn't number 3 or number 8, so Proud Dancer, which finished second (clue 4), was number 7 and Ed Scott rode number 5. Dandy Hill, Jack Carson's mount, wasn't number 8 (clue 6), so was number 3 and number 8 was Bold Venture. From clue 5, horse number 3, Dandy Hill didn't win or come second, so must have come fifth or sixth, with Bold venture third or fourth. From clues 3 and 5, Bold Venture's rider was Geoff Watts. He didn't finish third (clue 2), so must have come fourth and Dandy Hill must have finished in sixth place. We now know the positions of the horses numbered 3, 7 and 8. Colin Archer's Red Rag, number 6, didn't win (clue 1), or come second or third (clue 2), so must have finished fifth. From clue 7, Mark Buckle's mount was number 7 and, by elimination, Phil Richards' third-place horse was Thunder Away, leaving Ed Scott on Mr Golden as the winner.

In summary:
1st, 5, Mr Golden, Ed Scott.
2nd, 7, Proud Dancer, Mark Buckle.
3rd, 4, Thunder Away, Phil Richards.
4th, 8, Bold Venture, Geoff Watts.
5th, 6, Red Rag, Colin Archer.
6th, 3, Dandy Hill, Jack Carson.

SOLUTIONS

Lighthouse Family (No 225)

The 110-year-old lighthouse overlooks the Irish Sea (clue 5). The 70-year-old lighthouse looked after by Eddie Stone (clue 2) isn't on the Atlantic or the English Channel (clue 2) or the North Sea (clue 3), so it must be in the Orkneys, and thus is at Mull of Dounsay (clue 6). The 110-year-old lighthouse is on the Irish Sea, so (clue 3) the North Sea one is 100 and that kept by Des O'Lett is 80 years old. The latter isn't on the Atlantic (clue 2), so on the English Channel and, by elimination, 90-year-old West Nab lighthouse (clue 4) is on the Atlantic coast. Its keeper isn't Harry Mote (clue 2) or St Mary's Point's Don C Fowkes (clue 1), so is Ray Beames. Flint Head isn't on the English Channel (clue 1) and isn't 80 years old, it is younger than St Mary's Point (clue 1), so it isn't 110 years old – thus it's 100 years old. Thus St Mary's Point is 110 (clue 1) and must be guarding the Irish Sea. By elimination, the English Channel lighthouse must be Highburgh, and Flint Head is the 100-year-old lighthouse looked after by Harry Mote.

In summary:
Flint Head, North Sea, 100, Harry Mote.
Highburgh, English Channel, 80, Des O'Lett.
Mull of Dounsay, Orkneys, 70, Eddie Stone.
St Mary's Point, Irish Sea, 110, Don C Fowkes.
West Nab, Atlantic, 90, Ray Beames.

Holiday Reading (No 226)

Audrey recommended the book by Kate Lovel (clue 1), so the one recommended by Zoe, which isn't by Lucy Mowiss (clue 2), Coral Carey or Saul Snape (clue 4), is by Greta Hallaby. Its one-word title (clue 3) isn't be Constantinople (clue 2), so Empress and Patsy recommended Constantinople, which (clue 2) is the Lucy Mowiss book, which Fran thought pornographic (clue 1). The book recommended by Dawn isn't by Coral Carey (clue 5), so by Saul Snape and Jane recommended the Coral Carey. Passion Fruit wasn't recommended by Jane or Audrey (clue 3), so by Dawn. Audrey didn't recommend Rupert's Woman (clue 1), so Lord of Eagles and Jane recommended Rupert's Woman, which Fran thought boring, (clue 1). Fran didn't think Empress infantile (clue 2) or mildly amusing (clue 4), so badly researched. The infantile book was thus Dawn's recommendation (clue 2) and Fran thought Lord of Eagles mildly amusing.

In summary:
Audrey, Lord of Eagles, Kate Lovel, mildly amusing.
Dawn, Passion Fruit, Saul Snape, infantile.
Jane, Rupert's Woman, Coral Carey, boring.
Patsy, Constantinople, Lucy Mowiss, pornographic.
Zoe, Empress, Greta Hallaby, badly researched.

Elegant Victims (No 227)

The March crime took place in Cheapside (clue 4) and Beau Belles was robbed in May (clue 6). Beau Tighe wasn't attacked by Temple Bar in January or September (clue 1), so in July, and was thus robbed of a purse full of guineas (clue 5) and (clue 1) the gold watch was taken in September. Beau Nydel wasn't robbed in January or September (clue 3), so in March and the top hat was stolen in January on Ludgate Hill. Aldgate was thus the scene of the May robbery (clue 2), and the Strand was that of the September affair. The watch stolen in the Strand wasn't Beau Streate's (clue 2), so Beau Legges', and Beau Streate's hat was stolen. Beau Belles wasn't the owner of the stolen gloves (clue 6), so it was his silver-topped cane which was stolen in Aldgate; thus Beau Nydel lost his gloves.

In summary:
Beau Belles, May, Aldgate, silver-topped cane.
Beau Legges, September, Strand, gold watch.
Beau Nydel, March, Cheapside, gloves.
Beau Streate, January, Ludgate Hill, top hat.
Beau Tighe, July, Temple Bar, purse of guineas.

Pooled Resources (No 228)

Prentice is number 5 (clue 5). From clue 1, Myers cannot be 1, 4, 7, 8 or 9, nor can she be Harriet, in position 6 (clue 7) and Myers isn't number 3, so she must be in position 2. Thus Alicia is Prentice, in position 5, and number 4 is Jordan (clue 1). From clue 4, Cassandra Orton cannot be 3, 7, 8 or 9, so she must be in position 1. Lawson is number 3 (clue 4). Harriet is Ryan (clue 7) and Diane is either 7 or 8 (clue 3). From names already placed, Beverley and Ines cannot be at either end of the front or middle rows, so they are in the back row, and Quigley is number 8 (clue 2). From clue 3, Diane must be in position 8. Clue 8 now tells us Frances must be Jordan in position 4, and Gill must be Myers. By elimination, number 3 is Eve. Thus (clue 2) Ines is number 7, so number 9 is Beverley. Beverley is Kettley (clue 6), so Ines is Nolan.

In summary:
1, Cassandra Orton.   2, Gill Myers.
3, Eve Lawson.   4, Frances Jordan.
5, Alicia Prentice.   6, Harriet Ryan.
7, Ines Nolan.   8, Diane Quigley.
9, Beverley Kettley.

SOLUTIONS

Battleships (No 229)

Logi-5 (No 230a)

E	B	A	D	C
A	D	C	E	B
D	C	B	A	E
C	A	E	B	D
B	E	D	C	A

ABC (No 230b)

		C	A	B
		B	C	A
C	B	A		
A	C		B	
B	A			C

Crop Swap (No 231)

Rampleigh changed tack seven years ago (clue 1). Clue 4 tells us the decision to stop growing oats was the most recent, so that from potatoes to rapeseed was made ten years ago and (clue 2) Linton made his switch twelve years ago. Vereker, who used to grow wheat (clue 5) ceased to do so five years back; and the man who changed to linseed did so three years ago, thus used to grow oats. He isn't Corbyn (clue 6), so Grant and Corbyn changed from potatoes to rapeseed. Linton's former crop wasn't beans (clue 3), so alfalfa, leaving beans as Rampleigh's former crop. The man who turned to pig farming was Linton (clue 3). Chickens replaced beans on Rampleigh's farm (clue 6), so Vereker has turkeys.

In summary:
Corbyn, potatoes, rapeseed, 10 years.
Grant, oats, linseed, 3 years.
Linton, alfalfa, pigs, 12 years.
Rampleigh, beans, chickens, 7 years.
Vereker, wheat, turkeys, 5 years.

Celebrity Household (No 232)

The former MP was voted out first (clue 2). The eventual winner wasn't the TV personality (clue 1), or the retired athlete (clue 4), and clue 5 rules out the gossip columnist, so the winner was the male radio presenter (clue 3). He isn't Clyde Crowe (clue 1), or Max, who was voted out second (clue 6), so he's Steve. The third to go wasn't the gossip columnist (clue 5), and clue 1 rules out the TV personality, who departed next after Clyde Crowe, so the retired athlete was third. Pushey, who wasn't the winner, was voted out fourth (clue 4). This person isn't Linda (clue 4), so is Adrienne. Steve, the winner, isn't Headstrong (clue 7) or Boast (clue 3), so Loudleigh. Adrienne isn't the gossip columnist (clue 7), so the TV personality. Thus (clue 1) Clyde Crowe was expelled third, and Linda is the MP. She isn't Headstrong (clue 2), so Boast, and Headstrong as Max, who is a gossip columnist.

In summary:
Adrienne Pushey, TV personality, fourth.
Clyde Crowe, retired athlete, third.
Linda Boast, former MP, first.
Max Headstrong, gossip columnist, second.
Steve Loudleigh, radio presenter, winner.

Summer Seasons (No 233)

Andrew was in Hooray for Holidays in 2002 (clue 5), so (clue 1) wasn't in Fun in the Sun in Brightbourne in 1998, 2001 or 2003, thus in 2000 and in 2001 he was at the Galleon in Summer Stars. In 2000, he wasn't at The Neptune in Swanmouth (clue 2), the Marine Pier or Pierhead; so the Anchorage. The Havensands theatre isn't the Marine Pier or the Pierhead (clue 3), so the Galleon. He wasn't at the Neptune in 1998 or 2003 (clue 2), so in 2002 and was at the Marine Pier in 2003, leaving the theatre in 1998 as the Pierhead. It isn't in Dingle-on-Sea (clue 4), so Marcliff and Dingle-on-Sea is the location of the Marine Pier which (clue 4) didn't show Seaside Sensation, so Song of Summer was the 1998 show. Seaside Sensation was the 1998 show.

In summary:
1998, Marcliff, Pierhead, Seaside Sensation!
2000, Brightbourne, Anchorage, Fun in the Sun!
2001, Havensands, Galleon, Summer Stars!
2002, Swanmouth, Neptune, Hooray for Holidays!
2003, Dingle-on-Sea, Marine Pier, Song of Summer!

For the Love of Melanie (No 234)

The owner of the country manor joined the navy rather than marrying a widow (clue 3) and the hotelier lived in a seaside hotel (clue 5), so the stockbroker who married the widow and didn't have a penthouse flat or townhouse (clue 1) had a country cottage. Ambrose Boulby was a racing driver (clue 2), Lambert Moodie became a monk (clue 4) and Meredith Nyman had a townhouse (clue 6). The stockbroker wasn't Peregrine Quex (clue 1), so Bruce Coggesby. Meredith Nyman wasn't the solicitor (clue 6), so the man-about-town. He didn't emigrate (clue 7), so he married Melanie. The solicitor hadn't a penthouse flat (clue 6), so a country manor. By elimination, the penthouse flat was occupied by Ambrose Boulby who emigrated, Lambert Moodie was the hotelier and Peregrine Quex was the solicitor.

In summary:
A Boulby, racing driver, p'house flat, emigrated.
B Coggesby, s'broker, cottage, married widow.
L Moodie, hotelier, seaside hotel, became monk.
M Nyman, man-a'-town, t'house, married Melanie.
P Quex, solicitor, country manor, joined navy.

Pile Up (No 235)

From the top: B, A, C, D, E, F

Logi-5 (No 236a)

E	A	D	C	B
C	B	E	D	A
B	E	C	A	D
A	D	B	E	C
D	C	A	B	E

ABC (No 236b)

C		A	B	
	B		C	A
B	A			C
	C	A	B	
A	C	B		

Taking Flight (No 237)

Newton was bound for Seattle (clue 4). Faraday, who was on the 9.20 flight (clue 3) wasn't going to Melbourne (clue 1), so Bangkok, thus Melbourne was Fleming's destination. The person who took off at 9.40 wasn't Alicia (clue 1) or Glenda (clue 2), so Cicely. She wasn't going to Seattle (clue 4), so Melbourne, leaving Newton's take-off time as 9.30. Alicia is Newton (clue 1), so Glenda is Faraday.

In summary:
Alicia Newton, Seattle, 9.30.
Cicely Fleming, Melbourne, 9.40.
Glenda Faraday, Bangkok, 9.20.

Star Sports Stars (No 238)

A man will open a shop on Monday (clue 1), so Dawn Pearce will open a shop on Wednesday and the Friday opening is in St Albans. Barry Noble isn't doing the Monday opening (clue 3), so the Friday one, leaving Fergus Ross doing the Monday one. Dawn Pearce isn't going to Maidstone (clue 4), so Guildford; thus her sport is judo (clue 2) and (by elimination) Fergus Ross is going to Maidstone. Barry Noble doesn't play golf (clue 3), so his sport is tennis and Fergus Ross plays golf.

In summary:
Barry Noble, tennis, Friday, St Albans.
Dawn Pearce, judo, Wednesday, Guildford.
Fergus Ross, golf, Monday, Maidstone.

Dig This (No 239)

The University of New York expedition is to excavate the temple (clue 2) and the one from Arizona is sending its expedition to China (clue 4). The expedition to the pyramid in Egypt won't be from Berlin (clue 5), so Miami. The Arizona expedition isn't to the villa (clue 4), so the fort, leaving the villa as the target for the Berlin expedition led by Prof Voelkner (clue 5). Prof Azimovic is going to Peru (clue 1). The Arizona expedition isn't being led by Prof Katsouris (clue 3), so Prof Partington. As the pyramid is in Egypt, it isn't Prof Azimovic's dig, so is Prof Katsouris' and Prof Azimovic's is to the temple and (by elimination) is from New York. Thus Prof Voelkner will be going to Scotland.

In summary:
Professor Azimovic, New York, temple, Peru.
Professor Katsouris, Miami, pyramid, Egypt.
Professor Partington, Arizona, fort, China.
Professor Voelkner, Berlin, villa, Scotland.

Monsieur Le Duc (No 240)

The Berlin wedding took place in 1936 (clue 2). The banking heiress married the Duc in 1938, but not in Athens (clue 1) or Monte Carlo (clue 3), so Paris and the bride was thus Drusilla Camden (clue 5). Regina Stamford married in 1934 (clue 4). Mabelle Oakland's wedding wasn't in 1932 (clue 3), so in 1936; thus Horatia Hampton, the oil heiress was married in 1932 (clue 1). Regina Stamford's family fortune wasn't from automobiles (clue 4), so mining and Mabelle Oakland's was from automobiles. Horatia's wedding wasn't in Athens (clue 1), so Monte Carlo. Regina married in Athens.

SOLUTIONS

In summary:
Drusilla Camden, banking, Paris, 1938.
Horatia Hampton, oil, Monte Carlo, 1932.
Mabelle Oakland, automobiles, Berlin, 1936.
Regina Stamford, mining, Athens, 1934.

Teachers' Little Secrets (No 241)
Mr Green's nickname is Slime and the history teacher's is Thumper (clue 2). Blondie is the ex-pop singer (clue 3), so the female maths teacher who is an ex-astronaut (clue 4) is nicknamed The Dragon. She isn't Miss Ashby (clue 1), so Mrs Polton. Miss Ashby is the ex-tennis star (clue 1), so Mr Green is the ex-naval officer, who doesn't teach physics (clue 5), so English. By elimination, Miss Ashby is Thumper and Blondie is Mr King, who teaches physics.

In summary:
Miss Ashby, Thumper, history, ex-tennis star.
Mr Green, Slime, English, ex-naval officer.
Mr King, Blondie, physics, ex-pop singer.
Mrs Polton, The Dragon, maths, ex-astronaut.

Movie Mayhem (No 242)
Clark Bagel starred in the 1939 picture (clue 3) and the gangster film was made in 1941 (clue 5). The brawl on set was in 1940 (clue 6), so Betty Garble who giggled constantly (clue 1) starred in the 1941 film and the screwball comedy was made in 1940. The failure to show up wasn't in 1938 or 1942 (clue 4), so 1939 and the Western during which lines were not learned was made in 1938. Rita Worthless starred in the French Revolution film (clue 2).The Western's star wasn't Cary Grunt (clue 4), so Greta Garbage. By elimination, Rita Worthless appeared in the 1942 film and threw tantrums. This leaves the 1939 film as the murder mystery; and Cary Grunt was in the screwball comedy.

In summary:
1938, Greta Garbage, Western, hadn't learned lines.
1939, Clark Bagel, murder mystery, failed to show up on set.
1940, Cary Grunt, screwball comedy, brawled with co-star.
1941, Betty Garble, gangster movie, giggled constantly.
1942, Rita Worthless, French Revolution tale, threw tantrums.

Been Runners (No 243)
The 1500m winner in 1962 was a woman (clue 1) and the 800m race was in Paris (clue 6), so Miles Farster's London win which wasn't in a hurdles race (clue 3) was in the 200m. The 1953 win was in Edinburgh but not in the 200m (clue 2), so the Berlin event didn't take place in 1962 (clue 4). Thus the Berlin meeting wasn't remembered for

the 1500m race, so the 400m hurdles. It wasn't in 1959 (clue 4), so in 1965 and Miles Farster's was in 1959. By elimination, the 1500m race was in Milan. The winning woman (clue 1) wasn't Wanda Gold (clue 5), so Enya Marks. Aled Field's event wasn't in Edinburgh (clue 2), so Berlin. Wanda Gold's was the 100m hurdles in Edinburgh.

In summary:
1953, Wanda Gold, Edinburgh, 100m hurdles.
1956, Vic Torrius, Paris, 800m.
1959, Miles Farster, London, 200m.
1962, Enya Marks, Milan, 1500m.
1965, Aled Field, Berlin, 400m hurdles.

The Army Name (No 244)
The regiment of Foot received its nickname in the 1730s (clue 4). The regiment of Lancers didn't gain its nickname in either the 1760s or the 1810s (clue 2), nor was it the 1780s, when the Cheesemongers were so called (clue 3), so in the 1830s. The '2nd' regiment gained its nickname in the 1760s (clue 3), so it isn't a regiment of Foot or Lancers, nor is it the 11th Hussars (clue 5) or the Life Guards (clue 3), so it must be the Queen's Bays, the 2nd Dragoon Guards (clue 6). Bingham's Dandies is the nickname of the 17th regiment (clue 1). The Cherry-Pickers do not bear the number 1st or 4th (also clue 1), so they must be the 11th Hussars and, by elimination, were nicknamed in the 1810s. By elimination, the Cheesemongers must be a regiment of Life Guards. Since the '1st' regiment isn't the Lancers nicknamed in the 1830s, or the regiment of Foot (clue 2), it must be the 1st Life Guards, nicknamed the Cheesemongers. The Lancers are not the 4th (clue 2), so they must be Bingham's Dandies, the 17th Lancers, and, by elimination, Barrell's Blues must be the 4th Foot, so-called from the 1730s.

In summary:
Barrell's Blues, 4th Foot, 1730s.
Bingham's Dandies, 17th Lancers, 1830s.
Cheesemongers, 1st Life Guards, 1780s.
Cherry-Pickers, 11th Hussars, 1810s.
Queen's Bays, 2nd Dragoon Guards, 1760s.

Away From It All (No 245)
David and Mary (clue 2) cannot have been away in May or December (clue 6), and clue 2 also rules out April and September, since the July holiday location cannot have been Jamaica (clue 6). So they must have gone away in July. Thus, from clue 2, the holiday in Jamaica must have taken place in May. John and his wife cannot have had the April holiday (clue 4), nor can John have gone to Jamaica in May (clue 6). We know he didn't go in July (which clue 6 rules out anyway), and clue 1 rules out December, so they must have gone in September. So, from clue 1, Sally

SOLUTIONS

went on the December holiday. We now know John's wife isn't Mary or Sally, nor can she be Julia (clue 6), and clue 4 rules out Deborah, so he must be Angela's husband. Alan's holiday cannot have been in April (clue 6), and clue 3 rules out December, so he must have taken the May holiday to Jamaica. Sally's husband cannot be Simon (clue 6), so Martin accompanied her on the December holiday, which leaves Simon as one of the pair who went away in April. No one went to Australia in July (clue 5), nor can they have done so in April (clue 6), or in May, when Alan went away, or September, when Angela did so (also clue 6), so Martin and Sally must have gone there in December. The woman who went to Jamaica with Alan wasn't Julia (clue 6), so Deborah, leaving Julia as the wife of Simon. They didn't go to Malta (clue 5), nor can David and Mary have done so (clue 6), so the couple who went are John and Angela. Simon and Julia didn't go to Spain (clue 6), so to Denmark, which leaves Spain as the holiday choice of David and Mary in July.

In summary:
April, Simon, Julia, Denmark.
May, Alan, Deborah, Jamaica.
July, David, Mary, Spain.
September, John, Angela, Malta.
December, Martin, Sally, Australia.

Hole in the Wall (No 246)
Number 4 in the line isn't Graham (clue 1), Reg (clue 2), or Tom (clue 4), so he must be Liam, who is withdrawing £100 (clue 3). The man drawing out £50 cannot be number 1 or number 2 (clue 1), so he must be number 3. Nor is number 2 drawing out £30 (clue 5), so he must be taking out £80, leaving £30 for number 1. The latter cannot be the soldier (clue 2), the plumber (clue 4), or the taxi-driver (clue 5), so he must be the student, and, from clue 1, Graham must be number 2. He cannot be the soldier, since he is drawing out £80 (clue 2), so Reg cannot be the student currently using the machine in position 1 (clue 2), who must thus be Tom, leaving Reg as number 3. Now, from clue 2, Liam must be the soldier, and, from clue 4, Graham must be the plumber, leaving Reg as the taxi-driver.

In summary:
1, Tom, student, £30.
2, Graham, plumber, £80.
3, Reg, taxi-driver, £50.
4, Liam, soldier, £100.

A Troubled Coach (No 247)
The woman in seat 7 complained at 9.07 (clue 5). The woman who complained at 9.12 wasn't in seat 20 (clue 3) or seat 34 (clue 5). Nor was the 9.12 complainant Mrs Simpkins in seat 13 (clue

4), thus the woman in seat 25 complained at 9.12. The passenger who left her handbag complained at 9.10 (clue 6). The 9.03 complaint was from the woman who wanted a window seat (clue 1). Mrs Clooney complained of being too far back in the coach (clue 2), and wasn't in seat 7 (nearest the front, intro), thus didn't complain at 9.07, so at either 9.05 or 9.12. Mrs Rogers complained at either 9.03 or 9.10 (clue 2). The woman in seat 7 wasn't Mrs Bowyer (clue 5), so Mrs Harper. The request for a toilet stop was made at 9.05 (clue 3) and the woman in seat 20 made the 9.03 complaint. By elimination, the woman who felt travel sick complained at 9.07 and the one who complained about being too far back did so at 9.12. Mrs Rogers complained at 9.10 (clue 2). By elimination, Mrs Simpkins in seat 13 requested the toilet stop, Mrs Bowyer complained at 9.03 and Mrs Rogers occupied seat 34.

In summary:
9.03, Mrs Bowyer, seat 20, wanted window seat.
9.05, Mrs Simpkins, seat 13, requested toilet stop.
9.07, Mrs Harper, seat 7, felt travel sick.
9.10, Mrs Rogers, seat 34, left handbag behind.
9.12, Mrs Clooney, seat 25, too far back in coach.

Off the Peg (No 248)
From clue 2, the sexes split 3-1 in both row A and row C, so they must split 2-2 in row B. Both Shelley, who has peg C1 (clue 7) and Lucy (clue 5) have pegs in row C, so that's the one with three girls and one boy (clue 2). Both Tom and Robert must have pegs in row B (clue 5), so (above) no other boy has a peg in that row. Dean's peg isn't in row A (clue 3), so row C. Its number cannot be 3 or 4 (clue 3), and we know it isn't C1, so it must be C2. So the only girl in row A must have peg A2 (clue 2). We know this isn't Shelley or Lucy, nor can it be Annette (clue 1), while Kylie and Josie have pegs in the same row (clue 6), which must be row B, since it cannot be row A (clue 2), and we have already named one boy and two girls in row C. So, by elimination, the girl with peg A2 must be Candice, and from clue 4, Owen must have peg A4. From clues 2 and 3, a girl with a four-letter name must have peg C4, so this can only be Lucy. We have named all four children who have row B pegs, so Annette, who cannot be in row A (clues 1 and 2) must have peg C3. So Barry, who isn't one of the four in row B, must have peg A3 (clue 1). So, by elimination, Neil, who is in row A (clue 5), must have peg A1. Since Lucy has peg C4, clue 5 now tells us Tom's peg must be B2 and Robert's B3, since neither can have the same number as Neil or Lucy. So clue 6 now reveals Kylie's peg as B1, and Josie's as B4.

In summary:
Row A: 1, Neil; 2, Candice; 3, Barry; 4, Owen.
Row B: 1, Kylie; 2, Tom; 3, Robert; 4, Josie.
Row C: 1, Shelley; 2, Dean; 3, Annette; 4, Lucy.

Ferry Tales (No 249)

Braemar operates from the island of Kilgarry (clue 2) and Maid of Mull operates to Dunsay (clue 2), so the ferry from Corray to Ballinch, which isn't the Western Countess (clue 1), or Kinloch Castle (clues 1 and 5), must be Lady Moira. The Kinloch Castle operates 16 times a week (clue 5), so, from clue 1, Lady Moira cannot sail eight times. The ferry to Ardray goes twice a week (clue 6), so Lady Moira, which sails more than once (clue 4), operates four times a week. Thus Western Countess operates her route eight times a week (clue 1). Maid of Mull goes to Dunsay, so the twice-a-week service to Ardray must be the Braemar from Kilgarry, and, by elimination, the ferry to Dunsay operates just once a week. Western Countess does not sail to Glenholm (clue 1), so it must go to Scalnish, leaving Kinloch Castle as the Glenholm ferry. Maid of Mull does not operate from Dunsay as that's where it goes (clue 2) or Sheillin (clue 3), as it sails just once a week, so it must ply between Orinsay and Dunsay. The ferry from Sheillin does not go to Scalnish (clue 3), so it must be the Kinloch Castle, plying between Sheillin and Glenholm 16 times a week, leaving the starting point of the Scalnish ferry, the Western Countess, as Dunsay.

In summary:
Braemar, Kilgarry-Ardray, twice.
Kinloch Castle, Sheillin-Glenholm, 16 times.
Lady Moira, Corray-Ballinch, four times.
Maid of Mull, Orinsay-Dunsay, once.
Western Countess, Dunsay-Scalnish, eight times.

Mush! (No 250)

Sledge 1 isn't occupied by Jasmine (clue 1), Adam (clue 2), or Henry (clue 4), so Katie must be on it. Thus, from clue 5, Kevin must be pulling sledge 2. Brendan isn't pulling sledge 3 or sledge 4 (clue 1), so he must be the father of Katie, on sledge 1. Tony isn't pulling sledge 4 (clue 3), so Noel must be, and Tony must be in charge of sledge 3. So Noel's boy, Adam (clue 2), on sledge 4, must be four years old (clue 3). Katie cannot be three or five (clue 1), so she must be six. Thus Henry is on sledge 3 (clue 4) and Jasmine is three years old and is on sledge 2. By elimination, Henry is five.

In summary:
1, Brendan, Katie, 6.
2, Kevin, Jasmine, 3.
3, Tony, Henry, 5.
4, Noel, Adam, 4.

Dutiful Drones (No 251)

Cousin Griselda's request was carried out on Tuesday (clue 4), and Montague obliged his cousin Ariadne (clue 2). That clue also tells us Aunt Sophia, who wanted a package collecting from the jewellers, cannot have given this task to Edward, who carried out his commission on Monday (clue 7), nor was the latter obliging his sister Hermione (clue 7), so he must have done something for his Aunt Ermintrude. We know this task wasn't to collect the package, nor can it have been to tell a fellow Drone his feelings were not reciprocated (clue 3), while it was Archie who was asked to deliver the letter to the insurance salesman (clue 1), and the risqué novel was purchased on Wednesday (clue 6), so Edward placed the bet on a horse. Wednesday's purchase of the risqué novel cannot have been for sister Hermione (clue 5), nor, from the day, was it for cousin Griselda. Thus, by elimination, it was for cousin Ariadne, and was bought by Montague. So, from clue 2, Aunt Sophia's package was collected on Thursday, which leaves the Friday commission as the one performed for sister Hermione. Clue 3 tells us, since Edward obliged a relative on Monday, that the brush-off message cannot have been delivered on Tuesday on behalf of cousin Griselda, so, by elimination, it was initiated by sister Hermione, which leaves cousin Griselda's request as the delivery of the letter to the insurance salesman, which we know was carried out by Archie. Finally, clue 3 tells us Rupert cannot have obliged Hermione on Friday, so he must have collected the package from the jewellers for his Aunt Sophia on Thursday, leaving Gerald as the brother of Hermione.

In summary:
Archie Fotheringhay, cousin Griseld, deliver letter, Tuesday.
Edward Tanqueray, Aunt Ermintrude, put money on horse, Monday.
Gerald Huntington, sister Hermione, tell of feelings, Friday.
Montague Ffolliott, cousin Ariadne, buy risqué novel, Wednesday.
Rupert de Grey, Aunt Sophia, collect package, Thursday.

Number One (No 252)

Agnew who chose the film 1984 is female (clue 2), but cannot be Stella (clue 1), while Marcia named 101 Dalmatians (clue 7), so Agnew is Charlotte. The television gardener cannot be Charlotte, Stella or Marcia (clues 1 and 7), while Tony is the union leader (clue 3), so, by elimination, he must be Adam. Thus the tennis-player who selected The Thirty-Nine Steps (clue 6) is Stella. Adam cannot have chosen The Magnificent Seven (clue 5), so chose Catch-22, and Jefferson chose The Magnificent Seven, so (by elimination) he is Tony. Stella isn't Henson (clue 1), or Wignall (clue 6), so Briggs. From clue 1, Adam cannot be Henson, so he's Wignall, leaving Henson as Marcia's surname. Marcia is the ballet-dancer (clue 4), so Charlotte is the novelist.

In summary:
Adam Wignall, television gardener, Catch-22.
Charlotte Agnew, novelist, 1984.
Marcia Henson, ballet-dancer, 101 Dalmatians.
Stella Briggs, tennis-player, The Thirty-Nine Steps.
Tony Jefferson, union leader, The Magnificent Seven.

Lunch in Acapulco (No 253)
Kent's surname is Tyler (clue 6) and figure 3's surname is Grant (clue 7), so, from clue 6, Natasha can't be figure 1, 5 or 6. Figure 5 is Candy (clue 3), clue 6 rules out Natasha as figure 3 and figure 2 is male (clue 2), so Natasha must be figure 4, thus works for the Bank of Ohio (clue 7). Kent Tyler is figure 6 (clue 6). Munroe from the Hammett Agency (clue 8) is figure 2, and is thus male (clue 2). Russ is with the Ohio State Police (clue 1), so Munroe must be Nick. Adams, also at the left-hand table (clue 5) is figure 1. From clue 1, Miss Van Buren can't be Candy, so she's Natasha and Russ is figure 3, surnamed Grant, This leaves Adams as Lauren, and, by elimination, Candy's surname must be Lincoln. So neither she nor Kent works for Eagle Insurance (clue 4), whose agent must thus be Lauren Adams. From clue 6, Kent Tyler, who isn't the thief, must be from the FBI, leaving Candy Lincoln as the thief.

In summary:
Figure 1, Lauren Adams, Eagle Insurance.
Figure 2, Nick Munroe, Hammett Agency.
Figure 3, Russ Grant, Ohio State Police.
Figure 4, Natasha Van Buren, Bank of Ohio.
Figure 5, Candy Lincoln, thief.
Figure 6, Kent Tyler, FBI.

County Line (No 254)
Since Zebra-4's roadblock 3 isn't at a bridge (clue 6), from clue 2 the car assigned to roadblock 1, with a call sign two lower than that of the car at Cactus River Bridge, can't be Zebra-2, Zebra-6 or Zebra-7, and the same clue also rules out Zebra-5. Clue 1 rules out Zebra-1, so the car that is must be Zebra-3, and roadblock 1 is thus Eagle Creek Bridge (clue 4). Thus, from clue 2, the car at Fort Clark must be Zebra-4, and Fort Clark is roadblock 3 and Zebra-5 must be at Cactus River Bridge. From clue 1, the Gold River Bridge roadblock can't be numbered higher

than 3, and we've already identified the sites of roadblocks 1 and 3, so Gold River Bridge must be roadblock 2. So Buffalo Canyon must be roadblock 4 or 5 and Zebra-1 is at roadblock 6 or 7. But roadblock 6 at Murphy's Diner is assigned to a car with a call sign higher than Zebra-3's (clue 4), so Zebra-1 is at roadblock 7, and, from clue 1, Buffalo Canyon must be roadblock 5. We now have a site name or a car call sign for six roadblocks, so, by elimination, roadblock 4 must be the Cactus River Bridge blocked by Zebra-5. Also by elimination, Zebra-1's roadblock 7 must be at Comanche Butte. Thus, from clue 5, the car at roadblock 5, Buffalo Canyon, must be Zebra-2. Finally, from clue 3, Zebra-6 isn't at roadblock 2, Gold River Bridge, so must be at roadblock 6, Murphy's Diner, leaving the car at roadblock 2 as Zebra-7.

In summary:
1, Eagle Creek Bridge, Zebra-3.
2, Gold River Bridge, Zebra-7.
3, Fort Clark, Zebra-4.
4, Cactus River Bridge, Zebra-5.
5, Buffalo Canyon, Zebra-2.
6, Murphy's Diner, Zebra-6.
7, Comanche Butte, Zebra-1.

Jam Sales (No 255)
The 17 jars of jam were made by the lady from Pickwell WI (clue 4) and the raspberry jam came from Hedgeley (clue 3), so the eight jars of blackcurrant jam (clue 3), which were not from Bramblewood (clue 2) or Canefield (clue 3), must have come from Great Punnett WI, and thus the maker was Miss Pecktin (clue 6). Mrs Jarritt made ten jars of jam (clue 1), so Miss Setwell must have made at least 15 jars of her gooseberry jam (clue 2). Thus the Bramblewood member must have made more than that. It wasn't 17 jars (clue 4), so 18. This wasn't blackberry and apple jam (clue 1), so it was strawberry. Mrs Jarritt's ten jars didn't contain strawberry or blackberry and apple jam (clue 1), so it was raspberry, and she must be a member of Hedgeley WI. By elimination, the 15 jars of jam was made by the Canefield member. Mrs Boyle didn't make the blackberry and apple jam (clue 1), so hers was strawberry. Finally, Mrs Potts didn't bring the 15 jars (clue 5), so 17 and she is a member of Pickwell WI. By elimination, she made the blackberry and apple jam. This leaves Miss Setwell as the Canefield WI member who made 15 jars of gooseberry jam.

In summary:
Mrs Boyle, Bramblewood, 18, strawberry.
Mrs Jarritt, Hedgeley, 10, raspberry.
Miss Pecktin, Great Punnett, 8, blackcurrant.
Mrs Potts, Pickwell, 17, blackberry and apple.
Miss Setwell, Canefield, 15, gooseberry.

SOLUTIONS

Inspectors All (No 256)

The school inspector at number 68 isn't Robin (clue 7), or Charlie, who is a ticket inspector on the buses (clue 2). Harry's house is number 103 (clue 6), so, from clue 2, Edward, who lives at a lower number than Charlie, cannot live at number 68 either. It must thus be the home of Lindsay Naylor (clue 1). So Mr Dobbs, at number 22, who isn't the building inspector (clue 4), cannot be the police inspector (clue 1), while the tax inspector's surname is Priestley (clue 3). By elimination, Dobbs is Charlie, so (clue 2) Edward lives at number 7, which leaves Robin at number 51. Carson isn't Edward or Harry (clue 5), so he's Robin. Edward isn't Thompson (clue 3), so Priestley and Harry is Thompson. The police inspector isn't Harry (clue 1), so Robin; and Harry is the building inspector.

In summary:
7, Edward Priestley, tax inspector.
22, Charlie Dobbs, ticket inspector.
51, Robin Carson, police inspector.
68, Lindsay Naylor, school inspector.
103, Harry Thompson, building inspector.

Health Workers (No 257)

Eddie Ford is the porter (clue 1) so, from clue 2, Ann Barratt, who has taken up swimming (clue 4), must be the clerk. She isn't giving up smoking (clue 2), getting drunk, which is being given up by the person taking up jogging (clue 3), or takeaway meals (clue 4), so must be giving up chocolate. Thus, from clue 3, Nina O'Toole must be the security officer and, by elimination, Tom Usher must be a cleaner. From clue 3, he's giving up getting drunk and taking up jogging. Thus, from clue 2, Nina O'Toole is giving up smoking, and, by elimination, Eddie Ford must be giving up takeaway meals. He's not taking up aerobics (clue 1), so must be taking up cycling, and it must be Nina O'Toole who's taking up aerobics.

In summary:
Ann Barratt, clerk, chocolate, swimming.
Eddie Ford, porter, takeaway meals, cycling.
Nina O'Toole, security officer, smoking, aerobics.
Tom Usher, cleaner, getting drunk, jogging.

Winnington Winners (No 258)

Donald is the taxi-driver (clue 1), so Martin must be the policeman. Julie won the world cruise (clue 2) and Pyke won the car (clue 3), so Angela Strong, who didn't win £2.4 million (clue 4) won the house. Thus, from clue 1, Donald is Benton, who (by elimination) won £2.4 million. By elimination, Martin won the car and Julie's surname is Cobb. Julie is the saleswoman (clue 5) and the waitress is Angela Strong.

In summary:
Angela Strong, waitress, house.
Donald Benton, taxi-driver, £2.4 million.
Julie Cobb, saleswoman, world cruise.
Martin Pyke, policeman, car.

Missing in Action (No 259)

The Private lost his boots (clue 2). The Sergeant is neither Mike Gordon nor Buller (clue 3), so the man who lost his rifle can't be the Corporal or the Sergeant (clue 3), thus he's the Lance-Corporal. Thus, from clue 3, Buller, who lost his mess kit, is the Corporal and Mike Gordon is the Private who lost his boots. By elimination, the Sergeant lost his sleeping bag, so (clue 1) Steve is Buller and David is the Lance-Corporal. David isn't Moore (clue 4), so Woolfe and Geoff is Moore, the Sergeant.

In summary:
Private Mike Gordon, boots.
Lance-Corporal David Wolfe, rifle.
Corporal Steve Buller, mess kit.
Sergeant Geoff Moore, sleeping bag.

Not So Stately (No 260)

Tatham Manor was built in 1767 (clue 6). The house built in 1579 can't have been Pincot House, Lord Casby's home built in the same century as another house (clue 1), Hugby House (clue 2) or Fermin Place (clue 7), so was Bevil House, whose site is now occupied by a school (clue 2). The building now replaced by a park was 18th century (clue 3), so can't have been the Earl of Pyke's home, which dated from 1685 (clue 5), and which hasn't been replaced by an industrial estate either (clue 5). Sir Hugh Fern's home has a zoo on its site (clue 8), so the Earl of Pyke's was replaced by a housing estate. Thus, from clue 1, Lord Casby's Pincot House was finished in 1634. We know it hasn't been replaced by a housing estate, a school or a zoo, and clue 3 rules out the park, so Pincot House's site must be an industrial estate. Lord Gowan's house can't have dated from the 18th century (clue 7), and we know it wasn't built in the 17th century, so it was Bevil House. Thus, from clue 7, Fermin Place was the Earl of Pyke's 1685 home, leaving 1723 as the date of Hugby House. This wasn't built by Lord Quale (clue 4), so was Sir Hugh Fern's home, now replaced by a zoo. So Tatham Manor was Lord Quale's home, and is now a park.

In summary:
Bevil House. Lord Gowan, 1579, school.
Fermin Place, Earl of Pyke, 1685, housing estate.
Hugby House, Sir Hugh Fern, 1723, zoo.
Pincot House, Lord Casby, 1634, industrial estate.
Tatham Manor. Lord Quale, 1767, public park.

SOLUTIONS

Head of the Queue (No 261)

The third shopper is going to spend £10 (clue 6). The person who wants the TV set for £40 isn't fourth (clue 1), nor, since Becky Quilp is second (clue 4), first (clue 1), so it must be Becky Quilp wants the TV and (clue 1) Karen Brass is in third place, planning to spend £10. The fourth shopper isn't Sharon Jarley (clue 5), so Donna Nubbles, who wants a coat (clue 2). By elimination, Sharon Jarley is first. She plans to spend £30 (clue 5), and Donna Nubbles £20. Thus Sharon Jarley isn't queuing for the washing machine (clue 3), so a tea set, and Karen Brass wants the washing machine.

In summary:
First, Sharon Jarley, tea set, £30.
Second, Becky Quilp, TV set, £40.
Third, Karen Brass, washing machine, £10.
Fourth, Donna Nubbles, coat, £20.

First Birthdays (No 262)

Maxine's surname is Cooper (clue 2) and Esther works in Sales (clue 6), so Ms Forbes of Administration (clue 4), must be Pamela. Donald was born in 1963 (clue 5), so Thorne isn't the Customer Service manager, who was born in 1943 (clues 1 and 3) nor is the manager's surname Kent (clue 3) or Cooper (clue 2), so it must be Green and, by elimination, he must be Rodney. Maxine Cooper doesn't work in Accounts (clue 2), so she must be in Transport, leaving the Accounts worker as Donald, born in 1963. From clue 2, Maxine Cooper was born in 1973, so Thorne was born in 1963 and Pamela Forbes of Administration in 1983 (clue 1). Thus Thorne must be Donald from Accounts, and, by elimination, Esther of Sales must be Kent and have been born in 1953.

In summary:
1943, Rodney Green, Customer Service.
1953, Esther Kent, Sales.
1963, Donald Thorne. Accounts.
1973, Maxine Cooper, Transport.
1983, Pamela Forbes, Administration.

With a View to Purchase (No 263)

Since Claire showed the Bakers round at 2.30 (clue 7), her appointment in Birch Street was at 11.30 (clue 3), and she saw the Moodys at 10.30. So, (clue 1) Jason wasn't in Chestnut Close at 10.30. He was in Maple Drive at 3.30 (clue 6), and clues 1 and 7 rule him out for Chestnut Close at 2.30, so he was there at 11.30, with (clue 8) the Smythes. Thus (clue 1) Claire was with the Olivers in Birch Street 11.30. The McCoys weren't Claire's 3.30 appointment (clue 2), so they were shown round by Jason. This wasn't at 10.30 (clue 2), so 3.30, thus the Littles were Jason's 2.30 clients, and Claire was

in Sycamore Crescent at 3.30. By elimination, the Clarkes, who visited the property in Lime Avenue (clue 4), were there with Jason at 10.30. This leaves the couple in Sycamore Crescent as the Taylors. Claire was in Hawthorn Road at 10.30 (clue 5) but not in Oak Lane at 2.30; thus she was in Poplar View at 2.30, and Jason was in Oak Lane at 2.30.

In summary:
Claire: 10.30, Moody, Hawthorne Road.
Jason: 10.30, Clarke, Lime Avenue.
Claire: 11.30, Oliver, Birch Street.
Jason: 11.30, Smythe, Chestnut Close.
Claire: 2.30, Baker, Poplar View.
Jason: 2.30, Little, Oak Lane.
Claire: 3.30, Taylor, Sycamore Crescent.
Jason: 3.30, McCoy, Maple Drive.

First Past the Post (No 264)

Les Waite won the 3.15 race (clue 6). Phil Sadler won the race after Sparkler won at 10-1 (clue 5), so it wasn't the 2.15. The 2.15 was also not won by Miles Littler on his 3-1 mount (clue 2), and Guy Smallhouse won the race after Harve Pynte (clue 3), so the winner of the 2.15 was Harve Pynte on Red Tape, and Guy Smallhouse won the 2.45. As the winner of the 3.45 came in at 7-2 (clue 4), the 4.15 winner was Miles Littler. By elimination, the winner of the 3.45 was ridden by Phil Sadler, so Sparkler's 10-1 victory was in the 3.15 (clue 5). Impetus didn't win the 2.45 or the 3.45 (clue 1), so it must been Miles' 4.15 mount. The 7-2 winner wasn't Red Tape or Micko, since the name of the 5-4 winner is shorter than that of the 7-2 horse (clue 4), so it was Gaelic Boy. Thus Micko was ridden by Guy Smallhouse in the 2.45. Micko's odds were 5-4 (clue 1) and Red Tape's were 5-1.

In summary:
2.15, Harve Pynte, Red Tape, 5-1.
2.45, Guy Smallhouse, Micko, 5-4.
3.15, Les Waite, Sparkler, 10-1.
3.45, Phil Saddler, Gaelic Boy, 7-2.
4.15, Miles Littler, Impetus, 3-1.

Dear Sir ... (No 265)

The 130-word letter was published on Thursday in an evening paper (clue 3), and that about the one-way system had 120 words (clue 6), so the letter about litter in the Morning Clarion, of more than 100 words (clue 4) had 115. The letter about the pavements was published on Monday and hadn't 80 words (clue 2), so 90. One letter was published in Tuesday's Daily Courier (clue 1) and hadn't 115 words, so that about vandalism didn't appear in Thursday's paper. Thus the vandalism letter had 80 words. It wasn't published on Tuesday or Wednesday (clue 1), so Friday and the 115-word letter in the Morning Clarion was in Wednesday's edition (clue 1), leaving the 120-word letter in Tuesday's. By elimination, the letter about the bus service had 130 words. It was in an evening paper (clue 3), not the Evening Bugle (clue 5), so the Evening Herald. The letter in the Daily Reporter wasn't about the pavements (clue 2), so vandalism and the one about the pavements was in the Evening Bugle.

In summary:
Monday, Evening Bugle, pavements, 90 words.
Tuesday, Daily Courier, one-way system, 120 words.
Wednesday, Morning Clarion, litter, 115 words.
Thursday, Evening Herald, bus service, 130 words.
Friday, Daily Reporter, vandalism, 80 words.

In the Nick (No 266)

Palmer is in cell 1 (clue 4) and Crippen is Mike (clue 6). The Detective-Sergeant is in cell 3 (clue 2), so Joanne in cell 4 (clue 1) can't be Maybrick, whose cell is numbered immediately above that of Susan the housewife (clue 3). Nor, from her cell number, can Joanne be Armstrong (clue 5), so her surname must be Seddon. Now, from clue 3, the person in cell 5 can't be Maybrick, nor can he or she be Armstrong (clue 5), so cell 5 must be Mike Crippen's, and thus Joanne Seddon in cell 4 is the sailor and the one real prisoner (clue 6). The Detective-Sergeant in cell 3, who isn't Vince (clue 2), must be Brian. His surname isn't Armstrong (clue 5), so it's Maybrick. From clue 3, Susan the housewife was in cell 2 and, by elimination, her surname is Armstrong. By elimination, Palmer in cell 1 is Vince. He isn't the police surgeon (clue 4), so a van driver, leaving the police surgeon as Mike Crippen in cell 5.

In summary:
Brian Maybrick, cell 3, Detective-Sergeant.
Joanne Seddon, cell 4, sailor.
Mike Crippen, cell 5, police surgeon.
Susan Armstrong, cell 2, housewife.
Vince Palmer, cell 1, van driver.

Outlook Fair (No 267)

Jane is at the stand run by the bank (clue 4), and the discussion at the computer company's stand has only lasted 5 minutes (clue 7), so Stella's 10-minute discussion, which isn't at the stand run by the FE college or the university (clue 1), is at the department store's stand. The intending FE student is 19 (clue 5), so Nick, who is 21, but does not intend to go to university (clue 6), is at the computer company's stand. The 19-year-old isn't Lisa (clue 5), so Rob and (clue 2) Stella is 17. By elimination, Lisa is at the university stand. Jane isn't 18 (clue 4), so 20, and is thus a participant in the 12-minute discussion (clue 3). This leaves

Lisa's age as 18. Rob has not been talking for 18 minutes (clue 5), so for 15 minutes, leaving 18 minutes as the length of Lisa's discussion.

In summary:
Jane, 20, bank, 12 minutes.
Lisa, 18, university, 18 minutes.
Nick, 21, computer company, 5 minutes.
Rob, 19, FE college, 15 minutes.
Stella, 17, department store, 10 minutes.

Oh Yes They Did! (No 268)

Ann-Marie was taken to see Robinson Crusoe (clue 1), and Cinderella was on at the Empire (clue 2). The show Damien saw at the Grand wasn't Babes in the Wood (clue 5), and one of the girls was taken to see Dick Whittington (clue 3), so Damien must have seen Aladdin, which was on in Petershill (clue 7). That clue now tells us it was Desmond who was taken to the Palace, which is thus in Waterburn (clue 4). We know Dick Whittington wasn't playing at the Grand or the Empire, and clue 3 rules out both the Civic and the Palace, since it was a girl who saw it, so it was performed at the New Theatre in Kingsford (clue 6). By elimination, the panto at the Palace was Babes in the Wood, and Robinson Crusoe was staged at the Civic theatre. It wasn't Janine who saw Dick Whittington at the New Theatre in Kingsford (clue 6), and we know it wasn't Ann-Marie, so it was Laura (clue 3), and, by elimination, Janine was taken to see Cinderella at the Empire. Clue 3 tells us the Civic isn't in Northwold, so it must be in Greenwell, leaving Northwold as the home of the Empire.

In summary:
Ann-Marie, Greenwell, Civic, Robinson Crusoe.
Damien, Petershill, Grand, Aladdin.
Desmond, Waterburn, Palace, Babes in the Wood.
Janine, Northwold, Empire, Cinderella.
Laura, Kingsford, New Theatre, Dick Whittington.

Arms and the Men (No 269)

The cross-keys device isn't found on the crest of Earl Stones (clue 1), Viscount Vickers (clue 2), the Dukes of Ellington, whose device is the castle (clue 2), or Lord Knowes, who has a kind of plant on his family's arms (clue 1), so the cross-keys must appear with the eagle on the arms of the Meyer family (clue 4). Their motto isn't 'Fear none' (clue 1), 'Strong of arm' (clue 4), 'Truth and honour', which is on the same crest as the rose (clue 5), or 'Unity in faith', which appears with the boar (clue 3), so 'Always loyal'. The sword isn't part of the same crest as the boar or dragon (clue 3) or the lion, which appears with the oak tree (clue 6), so its companion is the stag. 'Truth and honour' is the motto of the

SOLUTIONS

family with the rose on their crest, so the boar and 'Unity in faith' motto accompanies the castle. By elimination, the rose and dragon form part of one coats of arms. It isn't that of Lord Knowes (clue 1), so his crest features the oak tree and the lion. Earl Stones' arms don't include a dragon (clue 1), so the stag and the sword, and as his motto isn't 'Fear none' (clue 1), it's 'Strong of arm'. Thus the dragon appears on the arms of Viscount Vickers, and the Knowes family arms has the motto 'Fear none'.

In summary:
Dukes of Ellington, boar and castle, 'Unity in faith'.
Earl Stones, stag and sword, 'Strong of arm'.
Lord Knowes, lion and oak tree, 'Fear none'.
Lord Meyer, eagle and cross-keys, 'Always loyal'.
Viscount Vickers, dragon and rose, 'Truth and honour'.

Footballers' Wives (No 270)
Danny Tyler's wife is becoming a film actress (clue 1) and Vangi who isn't Mrs Duffy is becoming a couturier (clue 4). Jay Duffy's wife isn't becoming a pop singer or a TV presenter (clue 2), so a model. Rick Broom plays for Langwood (clue 5). The Hillby United player whose wife is becoming a TV presenter (clue 3) isn't Heinz Lammer, so Nico Solti, who is married to Daffodil (clue 6). Maribelle's husband plays for Riverton (clue 6). Billi-Jo's doesn't play for Newdale or Oxham Town (clue 1), so Langwood. By elimination, Billi-Jo will be a pop singer and Vangi's husband is Heinz Lammer. The Newdale player isn't Danny Tyler (clue 1) or Jay Duffy (clue 2), so Heinz Lammer. Jay Duffy doesn't play for Oxham Town (clue 2), so Riverton and Danny Tyler plays for Oxham Town and is married to Shannon.

In summary:
Billi-Jo, Rick Broom, Langwood, pop singer.
Daffodil, Nico Solti, Hillby United, TV presenter.
Maribelle, Jay Duffy, Riverton, model.
Shannon, Danny Tyler, Oxham Town, film actress.
Vangi, Heinz Lammer, Newdale, couturier.

Storbury Books (No 271)
The travel book is D (clue 1), so (clue 3) the autobiography is C, Over the Water is B, and Simon Talbot's book is A. Georgian Storbury, the local history book (clue 2), is thus A. Carol Dillon's whodunnit (clue 4) is B. The travel book isn't The Trumpeter (clue 1), so Going West, leaving The Trumpeter as the autobiography. Book D isn't by John Keene (clue 5), so by Martin North, and John Keene is the author of book C.

In summary:
A, Georgian Storbury, Simon Talbot, local history.
B, Over the Water, Carol Dillon, whodunnit.
C, The Trumpeter, John Keene, autobiography.
D, Going West, Martin North, travel.

As I Was Going To … (No 272)
Sarah does the garden (clue 2), wife number 2 washes the clothes (clue 3) and Lucy is number 3 (clue 5). Wife 1 isn't Kate (clue 1), Sarah or Jill (clue 2), Valerie (clue 4) or Annie (clue 6), so she's Marjorie. She doesn't groom the cats (clue 1), cook (clue 4), sew (clue 6) or clean the house (clue 7), so she feeds the cats and (clue 1) wife 4 grooms them. Wife 2 isn't Kate (clue 1), Jill (clue 2) or Annie (clue 6), so Valerie. Wife 3 does the cooking (clue 4). Wife 4 isn't Kate (clue 1), Sarah (clue 2) or Annie (clue 6), so Jill. Sarah is wife 6 (clue 2). Wife 5 isn't Annie (clue 6), so Kate and Annie is wife 7. Kate sews and mends (clue 6), so Annie cleans the house.

In summary:
1, Marjorie, feeds cats.
2, Valerie, washes clothes.
3, Lucy, cooks.
4, Jill, grooms cats.
5, Kate, sews.
6, Sarah, does garden.
7, Annie, cleans house.

Heads and Tails (No 273)
The donkey's head was targeted by the third player to take part (clue 4), so, from clue 6, the cousin, who went immediately before Samantha, who pinned the tail to the back leg (clue 6), cannot have gone second or fifth. Helen went fourth (clue 5), so clue 6 also rules out the first and third turns for the cousin, so the latter must be Helen, who had the fourth go. So, from clue 6, Samantha went fifth. We know the first player did not pin the tail to the back leg or the head. Clue 1 rules out the front leg, and clue 2 the shoulder, so, by elimination, the first player must have pinned the tail to the donkey's back. From clue 2, since the birthday girl did not make the first attempt, the shoulder cannot have been adorned with a tail by the second player, who must thus have pinned it to the donkey's front leg, leaving the shoulder as Helen's target on the fourth go. Clue 1 now reveals the first player as Kevin, the birthday girl's brother, and clue 2 identifies the third player as the birthday girl. She is not Madeleine (clue 4), so she must be Agnes, leaving Madeleine as the maker of the second attempt. From clue 3, she must be the sister, and Samantha the friend of the birthday girl.

SOLUTIONS

In summary:
First, Kevin, brother, back.
Second, Madeleine, sister, front leg.
Third, Agnes, birthday girl, head.
Fourth, Helen, cousin, shoulder.
Fifth, Samantha, friend, back leg.

Everyday Story of ... (No 274)
The programme for which Sheila provided the climax cannot have been on Thursday or Friday (clue 4), while Wednesday's ending featured Brian (clue 1). Since the bar attendant was spotlighted on Thursday (clue 2), clue 4 rules out Tuesday for the programme featuring Sheila, which was two days before the one centred on the vet, so she was involved in the ending to Monday's programme. So (clue 4) the marriage proposal was made on Tuesday, and the vet featured in Wednesday's climax. We now know the doctor's decision to retire (clue 6), was not made on Tuesday, Wednesday or Thursday, and clue 6 rules out Friday, so it was Sheila's Monday denouement. Thus Stan featured in the ending to Tuesday's programme (clue 6). We now know a name or description to match four days, so Brenda, the shopkeeper (clue 5) featured at the end of Friday's broadcast. By elimination, the bar attendant is Laura, and Stan must be the farmer. From clue 5 Laura is the person expecting a baby, and clue 3 finally tells us the long-lost brother must have visited Brian on Wednesday, leaving Brenda's Friday storyline as the lottery win.

In summary:
Monday, Sheila, doctor, announced retirement.
Tuesday, Stan, farmer, proposal of marriage.
Wednesday, Brian, vet, visit of long-lost brother.
Thursday, Laura, bar attendant, baby expected.
Friday, Brenda, shopkeeper, win on lottery.

Trick or Treat (No 275)
Tim the ghost must have knocked on the door of either No 3 or No 11 (clue 2). But the witch, not the skeleton, called at No 5 (clue 5), so Tim must have visited No 11, and the skeleton was at No 13. Thus the child in the skeleton costume was Zoe (clue 3), and Tim must have received toffees (clue 6). Since Belinda was given fruit jellies (clue 1), she was not the child dressed as Dracula who received chocolate buttons (clue 1), and Holly was not dressed as Dracula (clue 1 again), so that was James. Zoe was not given a chocolate bar (clue 3), so she was the skeleton with the chews, leaving Holly as the child with the chocolate bar. 'Dracula' James did not knock at No 8 (clue 4), so at No 3, leaving Frankenstein as the character at No 8. Since Belinda's house number was lower than Holly's (clue 1), Belinda was the witch at No 5 and Holly dressed as Frankenstein's monster and called at No 8.

In summary:
No 3, James, Dracula, chocolate buttons.
No 5, Belinda, witch, fruit jellies.
No 8, Holly, Frankenstein, chocolate bar.
No 11, Tim, ghost, toffees.
No 13, Zoe, skeleton, chews.

Santa's Little Elves (No 276)
Elf D is 'Nasty' (clue 4). From the same clue, elf F isn't 'Spotty', while clue 1 tells us he or she isn't 'Fusty' and clue 3 rules out 'Droopy'; as Penny is wearing orange (clue 2), she can't be elf E, who is wearing yellow (clue 5), so, from clue 2, 'Grotty' can't be elf F, who is 'Grimy' and is thus wearing pale blue (clue 6). From the same clue, Steve is elf D, 'Nasty'. We know that elf A isn't wearing pale blue or yellow, nor is he or she in pale green (clue 5); he or she can't be wearing lilac (clue 1) or pink (clue 3), so she is the elf in orange, Penny. Thus, from clue 2, 'Grotty' is elf B. Since elf C is Dilly (clue 7), elf B can't be wearing lilac (clue 1), nor can he or she be in pink (clue 3), and we know he or she isn't in orange, pale blue or yellow, so he or she is in pale green. We know Steve is elf D, so, from clue 1, the elf in lilac can't be elf C and is elf D, leaving elf C, Dilly, clad in pink. Now, from clue 1, elf E is Jo and elf C is 'Fusty'. Finally, from clue 7, Nicci, who isn't elf B, is elf F, leaving Frank as elf B. Now, from clue 3, Penny is 'Droopy' and Jo is 'Spotty'.

In summary:
A, Penny, orange, 'Droopy'.
B, Frank, pale green, 'Grotty'.
C, Dilly, pink, 'Fusty'.
D, Steve, lilac, 'Nasty'.
E, Jo, yellow, 'Spotty'.
F, Nicci, pale blue, 'Grimy'.

Schoolreunion.com (No 277)
Ruth's old friend was from 1974 (clue 1), so Paul, who hadn't been in touch with the person who contacted him since an even-numbered year but not 1980 (clue 4), has been estranged since 1976, and was thus contacted by Neil Murphy (clue 5). The old school-friend from 3A must thus have been a name from 1977 (clue 4). Now, since Mark hadn't heard from Steve Dale since three years more recently than another subscriber had been in touch with the school-friend from 5B (clue 3), they cannot have been in touch since 1977. Thus the friend from 5B was the person Ruth hadn't heard from since 1974. Paul's contact Neil Murphy was not Tracey Evans from 4B (clue 6), while Vanessa had known her old friend in 2A (clue 2), so Paul must have known Neil in 3C. Thus, by elimination, Robert was contacted by his old friend Tracey Evans from 4B. As it was not 1975 since Vanessa had heard from her old friend (clue 2), it was 1980, leaving 1975 as the year

when Robert last saw Tracey. Ruth's friend from 1974 wasn't John Gibson (clue 1), so Pamela Clifford. John Gibson was thus in class 2A.

In summary:
Mark, Steve Dale, 3A, 1977.
Paul, Neil Murphy, 3C, 1976.
Robert, Tracey Evans, 4B, 1975.
Ruth, Pamela Clifford, 5B, 1974.
Vanessa, John Gibson, 2A, 1980.

On the Fiddle (No 278)

Anna plays the cello (clue 4) and the first violin is played by the Pole (clue 6), so Elena from Bulgaria, who doesn't play the viola (clue 1) is the ensemble's second violin. Anna isn't from the Czech Republic (clue 3) or the Ukraine (clue 4), so Russia. Maria is 28 (clue 3). Anna isn't 27 (clue 2), 30 or 31 (clue 4), so 25. The first violinist isn't Maria (clue 3) or Katarina (clue 6), so Basia and since she's the immediate senior of Katarina (clue 6), she isn't 27 or 30, so 31. Katarina is 30 (clue 6), so Elena is 27. From clue 3, Katarina is from the Czech Republic and Maria from the Ukraine, and both play the viola, thus (clue 5) Katarina plays first viola and Maria plays second viola.

In summary:
Anna, Russia, 25, cello.
Basia, Poland, 31, first violin.
Elena, Bulgaria, 27, second violin.
Katarina, Czech Republic, 30, first viola.
Maria, Ukraine, 28, second viola.

Legionaries (No 279)

Donald is 82 (clue 4), so the man who was in the Fleet Air Arm isn't 80 (clue 1). The 80-year-old wasn't in the RAF (clue 2), Eighth Army (clue 3) or Royal Navy (clue 5), so the Royal Marines. Thus (clue 6) he's Johnstone and Abbot is 81. Abbot was in the Royal Navy (clue 5) and isn't Thomas (clue 1), James (Coates, clue 2) or William (clue 5), so Walter. The man in the Fleet Air Arm is 82 (clue 1) and Thomas is 84. James's surname is Coates (clue 2), so (by elimination) Mr Johnstone is William and James is 83. Thomas was thus (clue 2) in the RAF. His surname isn't Graham (clue 3), so Markham. By elimination, Donald is Mr Graham and James was in the Eighth Army.

In summary:
Donald Graham, 82, Fleet Air Arm.
James Coates, 83, Eighth Army.
Thomas Markham, 84, RAF.
Walter Abbott, 81, Royal Navy.
William Johnstone, 80, Royal Marines.

Zeroing In (No 280)

The 19 in B3 is row 3's only two-digit number (clue 2), so the 9 cannot be in any of rows 1, 3 or 4 (clue 3), while the only single-digit number in

row 2 is the 7 (clue 2), so the 9 must be in row 5, but not in square E5 (clue 3). Since the 11 is in row 4 (clue 6), clue 5 rules out the 16 for A4, so the 9 cannot be in A5. Nor can it be in C5 (clue 8). Since the 17 is in column D (clue 7), clue 5 rules out the 12 for E5, so, from clue 3, the 9 cannot be in D5, and, by elimination, must be in square B5. Therefore, from clue 3, the 16 must be in B4, and the 12 in C5. There must be exactly one zero in each row and each column (clue 1). We know the one in row 5 is not in B5 or C5, nor can it be in D5 (clue 7), or E5 (clue 5), so it must be in A5. The 1 in row 5 (clue 9) cannot be in E5, since the 6 is in row 1 (clues 5 and 9), so, by elimination, it must be in D5. The 17 in column D cannot be in D1 or D4 (clue 7), and clue 2 rules out D3. Therefore it must be in D2, and D1 therefore contains a zero (clue 7). The zero in row 3 cannot be in A3, C3 or D3 (clue 1), and we know it is not in B3, so it must be in E3. Clue 1 now rules out A4, D4 and E4 for the zero in row 4, which therefore must be in C4. The one in column B cannot be in B1 (clue 1), so it must be in B2. Clue 6 now places the 11 in E4, and the 5 in D4, so, from clue 7, the 8 must be in D3. The number in E5 cannot be any of 16 to 20 (clue 5), nor is it 1, 5, 6 (clue 9), 7 (clue 2), 8, 9, 11 or 12, so it's one of 2, 3, 4, 10, 13, 14 or 15. Clue 5 rules out 3, 4 and 14, since we have placed 8, 9 and 19, and also rules out 2, 10 or 13, since we know none of 1, 9 or 12 is in C2, so 15 must be in E5, and (clue 5) 20 is in A4 and 14 in C2. Since the numbers in column E total 45 (clue 4), those in E1 and E2 total 19. Thus, since we have placed the 12, the 7 isn't in E2, so is in A2 (clue 2). The 13 is in E2 (clue 4) and E1 contains the 6. The 3 isn't in C3 (clue 8), so (clue 10) it's in A3 and the 10 in A1. The 18 is not in C1 or C3 (clue 8), so in B1. Clue 6 now places the 2 in C1, and the 4 in C3.

In summary:

	A	B	C	D	E
1	10	18	2	0	6
2	7	0	14	17	13
3	3	19	4	8	0
4	20	16	0	5	11
5	0	9	12	1	15

Copycats (No 281)

The records department's employee used the machine fourth (clue 6). Sarah, who was fifth in line (clue 5), doesn't work in accounts (clue 1), planning (clue 2), or personnel (clue 3), so in customer services. Thus she didn't need 24 copies (clue 3), nor 10 (clue 5), while 12 were required by the person from planning (clue 2), and 15 by the second user of the machine (clue 7), so Sarah made 20 copies. The 24 copies weren't made by the person from personnel (clue 3), so from the records department, whose representative used the machine fourth. The person who used the photocopier first wasn't Nick (clue 5), Jayne (clue 1), or James (clue 2), so Claire. She didn't make 12 copies (clue 4), so doesn't work in planning. Thus the person in planning used the photocopier third. By elimination, Claire made 10 copies. James used the machine fourth (clue 2). Clue 1 now reveals that Jayne cannot have been the third user, since her predecessor from accounts needed fewer copies, and the second user made 15, so Jayne used the photocopier second, thus Nick used it third. Claire is from accounts (clue 1), so Jayne is from personnel.

In summary:
First, Claire, accounts, 10 copies.
Second, Jayne, personnel, 15 copies.
Third, Nick, planning, 12 copies.
Fourth, James, records, 24 copies.
Fifth, Sarah, customer services, 20 copies.

Box Numbers (No 282)
The box emptied at 5.20 yielded 30 letters (clue 4), and the 5.00 collection was not made in a Street (clue 1), so the collection of 43 items from the Rose Street box made earlier than the 5.30 collection from the box in the shop wall (clue 2) must be made at 5.10. The box in Rose Street is neither in the shop wall nor the one in the supermarket that held 68 items (clue 5), nor is it the metal pillar-box in Market Close (clue 6), and the brick pillar-box is not in a Street (clue 1), so the box in Rose Street must be attached to a telegraph pole. The box in the supermarket contained 68 items, but it is not emptied at 5.00 (clue 1), so it must be 5.40. Thus (clue 3) the Victoria Road box contained 30 items and (by elimination is the brick one. By elimination, the Market Close box must be the metal pillar-box emptied at 5.00. We therefore know that the Mill Street box must be emptied at 5.30 (clue 2), and the Highgate one with 68 items at 5.40. Since the amount of post in the Market Close box was less than in the Mill Street box (clue 1), it must have been 51 items, and the box in the shop wall in Mill Street must have contained 62 items.

In summary:
5.00, Market Close, metal pillar-box, 51 items.
5.10, Rose Street, on telegraph pole, 43 items.
5.20, Victoria Road, brick pillar-box, 30 items.
5.30, Mill Street, in shop wall, 62 items.
5.40, Highgate, inside supermarket, 68 items.

Ahoy! (No 283)
Telescope 2 is focused on the seabirds (clue 3) and John is watching the motorboat but not from telescope 4 (clue 4). Viewer 4 isn't looking at the cruise ship (clue 1), so the surfer. Viewer 3 is from Hull (clue 2). Richard is from Sheffield (clue 1). Viewer 1 isn't from Sheffield (clue 1) or Rotherham (clue 4), so Halifax. Telescope 2 is being used by Marcus or Simon (clue 3), so Richard is using telescope 4. John isn't from Hull (clue 4), so Halifax. By elimination, the man from Hull is watching the cruise ship. He isn't Simon (clue 2), so Marcus and Simon viewer 2 from Rotherham.

In summary:
1, John, Halifax, motorboat.
2, Simon, Rotherham, seabirds.
3, Marcus, Hull, cruise ship.
4, Richard, Sheffield, surfer.

Reading Matters (No 284)
Maeve McCarthy wrote Dusty Death (clue 2) and Jenny Royle's novel was 'too long' (clue 6). Rosie Jones which was hilarious wasn't written by Brian Maxwell or Leo Tanner (clue 5), so by Anne Gavin. Leo Tanner was the June author (clue 4). The author of April's 'gripping' work (clue 1) was (by elimination) Brian Maxwell. Dusty Death wasn't 'gripping' or 'trashy' (clue 2), so 'unputdownable'. It's publication wasn't in May (clue 2), so in July (clue 3). Leo Tanner's book was thus Daybreak (clue 3) and considered 'trashy' (clue 2). Also from clue 3, Rosie Jones's book came out in August. April's 'gripping' novel wasn't Dark Guest (clue 1), so King's Park, leaving Dark Guest as Jenny's 'too long' tome.

In summary:
April, King's Park, Brian Maxwell, 'gripping'.
May, Dark Guest, Jenny Royle, 'too long'.
June, Daybreak, Leo Tanner, 'trashy'.
July, Dusty Death, Maeve McCarthy, 'unputdownable'.
August, Rosie Jones, Anne Gavin, 'hilarious'.

Coupling (No 285)
We're going to cook boeuf bourguignon on the 10th (clue 4), while the main course when Margaret and Jim come will be roast lamb (clue 5), and paella will be on the menu later than when Sue and Tony are here (clue 3), so when Jane and Paul come, and the dish won't be poached salmon (clue 1), we are preparing pheasant, so the second couple are Jan and Andy (clue 6). Thus Heather and Alan, who are coming the week after Pat and Ray (clue 2), will not be our guests on the 10th or the 24th. Annie and Tom are coming on the 24th (clue 1), so

SOLUTIONS

Heather and Alan won't be with us on the 31st either, so they are coming on the 7th. Thus Pat and Ray are coming on the 31st. As Sheila and Peter and Jane and Richard are coming on the same evening (clue 2), it is neither the 24th nor the 31st, so the 10th, when we'll be serving the boeuf bourguignon. We won't be serving paella to Heather and Alan and, by elimination, we'll be doing the poached salmon for Sue and Tony. This reveals that they'll be sharing our dinner table with Annie and Tom on the 24th, and Pat and Ray on the 31st will be enjoying roast lamb with Margaret and Jim, leaving Elaine and Robert as the second couple with Heather and Alan on the 7th.

In summary:
3rd, Jane and Paul, Jan and Andy, pheasant.
10th, Sheila and Peter, Jane and Richard, boeuf bourguignon.
24th, Sue and Tony, Annie and Tom, poached salmon.
31st, Margaret and Jim, Pat and Ray, roast lamb.
7th, Heather and Alan, Elaine and Robert, paella.

On the Piste (No 286)
The Lonsdales leave on the 18th, but not for Norway (clue 6). Clue 1 rules them out for Austria, and clue 2 for Italy, and the Nevilles are heading for France (clue 6), so the Lonsdales are skiing in Switzerland. The family who go away on the 16th for seven days (clue 4) are not the Nevilles (clue 6). The Robinsons have booked a nine-day holiday (clue 5), and we know the holiday in Norway does not begin on the 18th, so clue 3 rules out the Bentleys for a start on the 16th. So the family in question are the Terrys. So, from clue 1, the Austrian holiday begins on the 14th, and lasts eight days, so (by elimination) it's the Bentleys' holiday. The one in Italy begins on the 12th (clue 2), so the Nevilles leave on the 10th; thus the Robinsons will go on the 12th and the Terrys are heading for Norway. The Lonsdales' holiday isn't for six days (clue 6), so ten and the Nevilles are going for six days.

In summary:
Bentley, Austria, 14th January, 8 days.
Lonsdale, Switzerland, 18th January, 10 days.
Neville, France, 10th January, 6 days.
Robinson, Italy, 12th January, 9 days.
Terry, Norway, 16th January, 7 days.

Hat Parade (No 287)
Lucy has seat 6 (clue 4), and lady 8 has the black hat (clue 6), clue 1 rules out seats 6 or 7 for Madge, who, having two immediate neighbours, is thus in either seat 2 or 3. From clue 1, those in the pink and brown hats are in the pew to the

left of the aisle, as are also both Polly and the lady in the yellow hat (clue 2). Lucy's hat isn't blue or green (clue 4). The beige hat is Sarah's (clue 5), so white. The lady in the brown hat is in position 3 (clue 1), Madge is in position 2, and the lady in the pink hat in position 1. The hats of the women to the left of the aisle are yellow, green, brown and pink (above), so Sarah is to the right of the aisle. She's next to Winifred, thus her odd-numbered position isn't 5 (clue 5), so 7 and Winifred is in position 8. The blue hat belongs to lady 5 (clue 4). We know this is not Polly (clue 2), or Ellen (clue 4), nor can it be Dorothy, who has a lower-numbered position than Joyce (clue 3). So Joyce is in position 5. Polly isn't in position 1 (clue 3), so Madge's hat is green (clue 2), the lady with the yellow hat is in position 4 and Polly is in position 3. Ellen is in position 1 (clue 4), so Dorothy is in position 4.

In summary:
1, Ellen, pink hat.
2, Madge, green hat.
3, Polly, brown hat.
4, Dorothy, yellow hat.
5, Joyce, blue hat.
6, Lucy, white hat.
7, Sarah, beige hat.
8, Winifred, black hat.

Battleships (No 288)

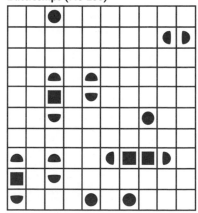

Logi-5 (No 289a)

C	E	A	B	D
B	D	E	C	A
E	A	B	D	C
D	B	C	A	E
A	C	D	E	B

SOLUTIONS

ABC (No 289b)

C			A	B
	B	C		A
A			B	C
B	C	A		
	A	B	C	

Joint Operations (No 290)

Ivan Bykov's MCIS-7 partner in Operation TOGA (clue 7) can't be Jeff Bruce, who's on BARD (clue 1), John Blake, who's on NOMAD or SALVO (clue 4), or Jack Booth, whose partner is Yuri Sidrov (clue 6), nor, since the two operations based in Europe are NOMAD and the one involving Olga Kozlova (clue 5), can Ivan Bykov's partner in TOGA be Justin Bell, who's based in Budapest (clue 2), so he's Jeremy Bray. TOGA's not based in Havana (clue 7), and clue 5 rules out Budapest and Oslo. The CVRS agent in Manila is Vera Luvina (clue 3), so TOGA must be based in Tokyo. We now know that Jack Booth and Yuri Sidrov aren't based in Budapest, Manila or Tokyo, and clue 6 rules out Oslo, so they must be based in Havana. NOMAD must be based in Budapest or Oslo (clue 5), so can't involve Vera Luvina or Yuri Sidrov, and we know it doesn't involve Ivan Bykov; nor is the CVRS agent involved Olga Kozlova (clue 5), so he's Boris Monokov. His MCIS-7 partner isn't John Blake (clue 4), so, from the same clue, John Blake must be involved in SALVO. We now know the MCIS-7 agents for three operations, and a fourth agent with his CVRS partner, so Operation NOMAD, which involves Boris Monokov, must also involve Justin Bell and is thus based in Budapest. This leaves Jack Booth and Yuri Sidrov working on Operation ICON, and Olga Kozlova based in Oslo. Thus she isn't working on SALVO with John Blake (clue 6), and must be on BARD with Jeff Bruce, leaving John Blake's SALVO partner as Vera Luvina and their base thus as Manila.

In summary:
BARD, Jeff Bruce, Olga Kozlova, Oslo.
ICON, Jack Booth, Yuri Sidrov, Havana.
NOMAD, Justin Bell, Boris Monokov, Budapest.
SALVO, John Blake, Vera Luvina, Manila.
TOGA, Jeremy Bray, Ivan Bykov, Tokyo.

Stately Gardens (No 291)

The gardens at Fullwell House were embellished in 2000 (clue 7). The new feature at Wilton Towers wasn't opened in 2001 or 2002 (clue 1). Since Lord Underdale can't have commissioned the Japanese garden completed in 2001 (clue 6), from clue 1, the feature at Wilton Towers wasn't introduced in 1999, so it was completed in 1998; and Lord Underdale is the owner of Fullwell House, where the new feature was opened in 2000. The waterlily lake at Sunbury Castle wasn't built for Sir Jeremy Wilson (clue 4), while the knot garden was Lord Gleneaton's brainchild (clue 2), and the Marquess of Dunroamin owns Tinkerton Hall (clue 3). Thus Viscount Fetlocke lives at Sunbury Castle. His waterlily lake there wasn't opened in 2002 (clue 5), so in 1999 and the cascades were built for Lord Underdale. Tinkerton Hall's feature didn't open in 2002 (clue 3), so the Japanese garden opened there in 2001 and the 2002 novelty was the orangery, which, by elimination, was at Moatbridge Manor. Also by elimination, the knot garden commissioned by Lord Gleneaton was introduced in 1998 at Wilton Towers, which leaves the owner of Moatbridge Manor as Sir Jeremy Wilson.

In summary:
Fullwell House, Lord Underdale, cascades, 2000.
Moatbridge Manor, Sir Jeremy Wilson, orangery, 2002.
Sunbury Castle, Viscount Fetlocke, waterlily lake, 1999.
Tinkerton Hall, Marquess of Dunroamin, Japanese garden, 2001.
Wilton Towers, Lord Gleneaton, knot garden, 1998.

Lucky Winners (No 292)

A blue ticket won the fourth prize (clue 7), and the number on the green ticket was 293 (clue 2). The third winning number, 508, wasn't on a pink ticket (clue 4), and, since Mr Marchant had ticket 615 (clue 3), clue 1 rules out 508 for the yellow ticket, which bore a number lower than Mr Vernon's, so it was Mrs Evans' white ticket (clue 5) which won the third prize. From clues 1 and 2, Mr Vernon's ticket can't have been numbered 293 or 337, and we know it wasn't 508 or 615, so it was 472. Thus, from clue 1, the yellow ticket was numbered 337. The blue ticket, which won the fourth prize, can't have been number 615 (clue 7), so it was Mr Vernon's one numbered 472, leaving the number on the pink ticket as 615, so that was Mr Marchant's. We now know Mr Vernon won fourth prize, so, from clue 1, the yellow ticket numbered 337 was drawn fifth. From clue 7, it was Mr Marchant's pink ticket bearing the number 615 which won the first prize, leaving 293 on the green ticket as the second prize winner. Miss Ryder didn't win the fifth prize with the yellow ticket (clue 6), so she held green ticket 293, and won the second prize, leaving the yellow ticket as the one bought by Mrs Harkness.

In summary:
First, Mr Marchant, pink, 615.
Second, Miss Ryder, green, 293.
Third, Mrs Evans, white, 508.
Fourth, Mr Vernon, blue, 472.
Fifth, Mrs Harkness, yellow, 337.

Jack the Lad (No 293)

Paula was with Jack when he spotted Annabel (clue 6). Since he crossed the road to avoid Wendy (clue 5), he can't have been with Annabel, with whom he dashed into the pub (clue 2), nor was he with Stella (clue 5), so the girl he was with was Caroline. This wasn't on Monday (clue 1), nor can it have been on Tuesday or Saturday (clue 3). On Thursday he darted into a shop (clue 7), so it was on Friday that he was with Caroline and saw Wendy. From clue 3, he took evasive action on seeing Caroline on Saturday. We now know he wasn't with Annabel on Friday, and clue 2 rules out Tuesday and Saturday, and, since it was Stella he saw approaching the following day (clue 2), he wasn't with Annabel on Thursday, since he saw Wendy coming on Friday, so he was with Annabel on Monday, and dashed into the pub. Thus on Tuesday he avoided Stella (clue 2). By elimination, when he was with Annabel, he didn't catch sight of Stella or Wendy, and the day rules out Caroline, so he saw Paula. We know when he saw Stella on Tuesday he wasn't with Annabel, Caroline or Paula, so he was with Wendy. Thus he was with Stella on the day he avoided Caroline. He didn't do a swift about turn (clue 4), the day rules out the dash into a shop, so when he was with Stella he leapt on to a bus. By elimination, he was with Paula on Thursday when he darted into a shop to avoid Annabel, and he did a swift about turn on Tuesday.

In summary:
Monday, with Annabel, saw Paula, dashed in pub.
Tuesday, with Wendy, saw Stella, swift about turn.
Thursday, with Paula, saw Annabel, darted in shop.
Friday, with Caroline, saw Wendy, crossed road.
Saturday, with Stella, saw Caroline, leapt on to bus.

November Night Out (No 294)

Since the 8.00pm display was in Tresham Walk (clue 2), from clue 4 the football club display can't have started at 7.30am, 8.30pm or 9.00pm, while the Cubs display began at 7.00pm (clue 6), so the football club display was the Tresham Walk one which began at 8.00pm. So, from clue 4, the Bates Lane display began at 8.30pm, and Joey Keene went to the one that started at 9.00pm. We now know that the display in Winter Hill attended by Wayne York (clue 5) didn't start at 8.00pm, 8.30pm or 9.00pm. The King's Head display didn't begin at 8.00pm, so (clue 5) Wayne York went to the one that began at 7.00pm, run by the Cubs. So, from clue 5, the 7.30pm display was at the King's Head. Thus the display at Alan Bush's family home (clue 1) began at 8.30pm, in Bates Lane. This leaves the display Joey Keene attended, which began at 9.00pm, as the one at the Community Centre. This wasn't in Catesby Road (clue 3), so was in Percy Drive, leaving Catesby Road as the address of the King's Head. Since it began at 7.30pm, the boy who attended it wasn't Chris Day (clue 7), so Ricky Salt, leaving Chris Day as the one who attended the football club display.

In summary:
Alan Bush, home, Bates Lane, 8.30pm.
Chris Day, football club, Tresham Walk, 8.00pm.
Joey Keene, Community Centre, Percy Drive, 9.00pm.
Ricky Salt, King's Head, Catesby Road, 7.30pm.
Wayne York, Cubs, Winter Hill, 7.00pm.

On Screen (No 295)

The child aged 9 is watching a video (clue 4). The one watching a TV film in room 3 isn't 15 (clue 5), nor can this be Jennifer, aged 13, who has an even-numbered room (clue 3), so the child in room 3 is 11. Tim is 15 (clue 5). Since the 11-year-old is watching the TV film, clue 2 tells us Marcus can't be 9, so he's 11, and has room 3, which leaves the youngest child as Alicia. From clue 2, Jennifer is surfing the internet, which leaves Tim watching TV sport. Alicia isn't in room 1 (clue 6), nor can Jennifer be (clue 3), so that must be Tim's room. So, from clue 1, Alicia is in room 2, so room 4 is Jennifer's.

In summary:
1, Tim, 15, TV sport.
2, Alicia, 9, video.
3, Marcus, 11, TV film.
4, Jennifer, 13, internet.

Cover Girls (No 296)

Caroline was on the April cover (clue 3), so the traffic warden, whose picture featured in the same half of the year as Louise (clue 1), wasn't on the January cover. Nor was she on the July cover (clue 1), and the October cover shows the charity worker (clue 3), so the traffic warden was on the April cover and is thus Caroline, and Louise appeared on the January cover and is Ms Sharp (clue 2). From clue 4, the January cover didn't feature the Mayoress, who was thus on the July cover, and the January cover shows the teacher. The charity worker isn't Julia (clue 4), so she's Helen, and Julia was the Mayoress on the July cover. Her surname isn't Crabtree (clue 1), and neither is that of the charity worker,

SOLUTIONS

which is one letter shorter than Caroline's (clue 3). We know that Ms Sharp was on the January cover, so the April one shows Ms Crabtree, the October one shows Ms Marsden (clue 3) and, by elimination, the July one shows Ms Forman.

In summary:
January, Louise Sharp, teacher.
April, Caroline Crabtree, traffic warden.
July, Julia Forman, Mayoress.
October, Helen Marsden, charity worker.

Looks Familiar (No 297)

Liza Minnelli's engagement was at 2.30 (clue 6), so the 12.30 lookalike celebrity opening the football match, who wasn't Madonna or Baroness Thatcher (clue 2) or Marilyn Monroe (clue 4), was Prince Charles and the impersonator was thus Arthur Fishall (clue 5). Liza Minnelli appeared at 2.30, so, from clue 4, Marilyn Monroe appeared at 2 o'clock, and the village hall was opened at 1 o'clock. The opening wasn't performed by Madonna (clue 3), so was Baroness Thatcher. By elimination, Isla Fakenham's engagement at 1.30 (clue 5) was in the guise of Madonna. She wasn't opening the supermarket (clue 3) or the village fête, which was Imogen Spitton (clue 1), so it was the sports shop. Bess Mimwick doesn't look like Baroness Thatcher (clue 2), so her engagement wasn't at 1 o'clock and, as her appearance was earlier than Imogen Spitton's (clue 1), it wasn't at 2.30, so at 2 o'clock, and Bess is thus the Marilyn Monroe lookalike. Thus Imogen Spitton opened the village fête at 2.30 (clue 1), and did so in the guise of Liza Minnelli. By elimination, Carrie Cature is the Baroness Thatcher lookalike, and Bess Mimwick opened the supermarket at 2 o'clock.

In summary:
Arthur Fishall, Prince Charles, 12.30, charity football match.
Bess Mimwick, Marilyn Monroe, 2.00, supermarket.
Carrie Cature, Baroness Thatcher, 1.00, village hall.
Imogen Spitton, Liza Minnelli, 2.30, village fête.
Isla Fakenham, Madonna, 1.30, sports shop.

Transports of Delight (No 298)

The Hertford-built exhibit dates from 1881 (clue 1), so Unity, the narrowboat, which was built seven years after the exhibit built in Doncaster (clue 2), can't have been built before 1895. However, it was the locomotive that was built in 1895 (clue 5) and Galahad that was built in 1909 (clue 6), so Unity was built in 1902, and from clue 2 the 1895 locomotive was built in Doncaster. Thus Minerva, built in Ipswich (clue 3) dates

from 1888. The fishing boat was built in Brixham (clue 4), so in 1909. By elimination, Unity was built in Nantwich. The traction engine was built in Hertford and isn't Unity (clue 1), so Unity is the horse-bus, and the traction engine is the Minerva. The locomotive isn't Pegasus (clue 5), so Amazon, leaving Pegasus as the horse-bus.

In summary:
Amazon, locomotive, Doncaster, 1895.
Galahad, fishing boat, Brixham, 1909.
Minerva, traction engine, Ipswich, 1888.
Pegasus, horse-bus, Hertford, 1881.
Unity, narrowboat, Nantwich, 1902.

Theatrical Digs (No 299)

The five-week run is at the Hippodrome (clue 5) and the variety show is on at the Albion (clue 6), so the two-week run of the J B Priestley play, which isn't on at the Palace (clue 4) or the Queen's (clue 1) must be at the Empire, and thus features Barnes Tormer (clue 3). Bill Topper is staying for three weeks (clue 2), so Kirton Cawles' comedy play (clue 1) must be running for at least four and the play at the Queen's Theatre must be on for longer than that (clue 1); however, it isn't five weeks (clue 5), so six. The production isn't the whodunnit (clue 2), so the Shakespeare. Bill Topper's three-week run isn't the Shakespeare or the whodunnit (clue 2), so it must be the variety show, and is thus at the Albion Theatre for three weeks. By elimination, the four-week run must be at the Palace Theatre. Treadwell Boards isn't appearing in the whodunnit (clue 2), so it must be the six-week Shakespeare season. Finally, Will Hammett isn't staying at Mrs Drarmer's for four weeks (clue 3), so it must be the five weeks of the Hippodrome production, which, by elimination, must be the whodunnit. This leaves Kirton Cawles as the actor appearing for four weeks at the Palace Theatre.

In summary:
Barnes Tormer, Empire, two weeks, J B Priestley.
Bill Topper, Albion, three weeks, variety.
Kirton Cawles, Palace, four weeks, comedy.
Treadwell Boards, Queen's, six weeks, Shakespeare.
Will Hammett, Hippodrome, five weeks, whodunnit.

A Crop of Pimpernels (No 300)

The Chevalier de Sauverne was saved in Lille and the Marquis de St Menard by the Hon Jack Hallam (clue 6), so the aristocrat rescued in Falaise by Lord Bidmore, who wasn't the Comte de la Roche or the Comte de Passy (clue 3), was the Vicomtesse d'Elbes. The aristovrat rescued in

SOLUTIONS

Amiens by an old lady (clue 6) wasn't the Comte de Passy, who was saved by an army officer (clue 5), nor did this happen in Rennes (clue 5), so the Comte de Passy was saved in Paris. The Marquis de St Menard wasn't rescued in Amiens (clue 6), so in Rennes, and the aristocrat saved in Amiens by an old lady was the Comte de la Roche. This leaves the Chevalier de Sauverne as the aristocrat saved by a drunken tramp who was really Lord Geraldin (clue 2). As the Comte de Passy's rescuer in Paris wasn't Sir John Merton (clue 1), he was Sir Simon Bolt, and Sir John Merton saved the Comte de la Roche in Amiens. Lord Bidmore wasn't disguised as a labourer (clue 4), so as a chimney sweep, and the labourer was the Hon Jack Hallam.

In summary:
Chevalier de Sauverne, Lille, drunken tramp, Lord Geraldin.
Comte de la Roche, Amiens, old lady, Sir John Merton.
Comte de Passy, Paris, army officer, Sir Simon Bolt.
Marquis de St Menard, Rennes, labourer, Hon Jack Hallam.
Vicomtesse d'Elbes, Falaise, chimney sweep, Lord Bidmore.

Folk Club (No 301)

Ralph Oakes took the stage third (clue 2). The first performer wasn't Jake Field (clue 6), Willy Hedges (clue 5) or Danny Lane with his accordion (clue 1), so he was Toby Straw playing Heloise the Milkmaid (also clue 5) followed by Willy second, Ralph third and the pianist fourth (clue 2). By elimination, Danny was fifth, the pianist was Jake and Bridget be Mine on the Irish bagpipes was the third piece (clue 6). Sweet Susannah wasn't the second piece (clue 1), so the fifth. Jake didn't accompany Lady Sarah (clue 2), so Willy did so, leaving Lady Guinevere as Jake's effort. Willy didn't play the tin whistle (clue 4), so Toby Straw did so, leaving Willy as the guitarist.

In summary:
First, Toby Straw, Heloise the Milkmaid, tin whistle.
Second, Willy Hedges, Lady Sarah, guitar.
Third, Ralph Oakes, Bridget Be Mine, Irish bagpipes.
Fourth, Jake Field, Queen Guinevere, piano.
Fifth, Danny Lane, Sweet Susannah, accordion.

Calling All Cars (No 302)

The call at 02.20 was to Queen Square (clue 3). PC Cawtion answered the 03.00 call (clue 4). PC Cuffham was called to Station Street, but not at 00.30 or 01.20 (clue 5), so at 04.30. Blackbird Lane was the scene of the break-in (clue 6). The traffic accident at 00.30 wasn't in Parkway (clue 1), so London Road. PC Custerdy dealt with the assault (clue 2). The Station Street incident wasn't a domestic dispute (clue 5), so a disturbance. The traffic accident wasn't attended by PC Collarfield (clue 1), so PC Coppall. PC Custerdy's incident wasn't at 01.20 (clue 2), so at 02.20. PC Collarfield wasn't called to Parkway (clue 1), so Blackbird Lane at 01.20. Thus PC Cawtion went to a domestic dispute at Parkway.

In summary:
PC Cawtion, Parkway, 03.00, domestic.
PC Collarfield, Blackbird Lane, 01.20, break-in.
PC Coppall, London Road, 00.30, traffic accident.
PC Cuffham, Station Street, 4.30, disturbance.
PC Custerdy, Queen Square, 02.20, assault.

Logi-Path (No 303)

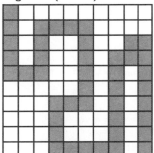

Making the Grades (No 304)

One student will read philosophy at Lernham (clue 1). The English student won't be attending Traynham or Reedmoor Universities or Knolledge University, where Helen is going (clue 2), so Studiard University. The BBC grades are required for modern languages (clue 5). The Reedmoor student whose grades are BCC grades isn't reading physics (clue 3), so music and she's Cathy (clue 6). Zoe got her BBB grades (clue 4). Liz didn't require ABB or CCC (clue 1), so BBC. By elimination, Liz is going to Traynham and Helen is reading physics. The ABB grades weren't for philosophy or English (clue 1), so physics. By elimination, Zoe will read English and Samantha got CCC and will read philosophy.

In summary:
Cathy, BCC, Music, Reedmoor.
Helen, ABB, Physics, Knolledge.
Liz, BBC, Modern languages, Traynham.
Samantha, CCC, Philosophy, Lernham.
Zoe, BBB, English, Studiard.

SOLUTIONS

Pile Up (No 305)
From the top: D, A, E, B, C, F.

Friends and Neighbours (No 306)
House 4 isn't in Chestnut Road (clue 1), or Union Street, where Mrs Adams lives (clue 2), while house 2 is in Nelson Street (clue 4), so house 4 is in Melbourne Avenue. House 3 isn't in Chestnut Avenue (clue 1), so the woman at house 4 isn't Joan. Nor is she Marion (clue 3), or Lily (clue 4), so she's Chloë. The woman in house 2 isn't Marion (clue 3) or Lily (clue 4), so she's Joan. House 1 isn't in Chestnut Road (clue 1), so house 3 is in Union Street. Chloë is Mrs Green (clue 2). Joan in house 2 is Mrs Skinner (clue 3), so Mrs Gilbert is in house 1. She isn't Marion (clue 3), so she's Lily. Marion is Mrs Adams.

In summary:
1, Lily Gilbert, Chestnut Road.
2, Joan Skinner, Nelson Street.
3, Marion Adams, Union Street.
4, Chloë Green, Melbourne Avenue.

QED (No 307)
The Derby firm has six directors (clue 5). The four-man board of the machine tools company (clue 3), cannot sit in Stockport (clue 1), or Mansfield (clue 4), and the Cardiff company produces farm equipment (clue 2), so they must be in Walsall. Their firm is not VRC (clue 3), nor can it be HJK (clue 1), or QLH (clue 6), while MDE has an eight-member board (clue 7), so BGN must be based in Walsall. The company which has twelve directors cannot make textiles (clue 1), earthmovers (clue 4), or chemicals (clue 6), and we know they are not in charge of the machine tools company, so they must run the farm equipment company in Cardiff. The six-man board cannot run HJK (clue 1), or QLH (clue 6), and we know their firm is not MDE or BGN, so it must be VRC. The textiles firm cannot have ten directors (clue 1), nor can the earthmover makers (clue 4). We know the number running the machine tools and farm equipment firms, so it must be the chemicals company which has a ten-man board. So, from clue 6, QLH must make farm equipment in Cardiff. This leaves the chemicals company as HJK. It is not based in Stockport (clue 1), so it must be the Mansfield firm, leaving MDE in Stockport. They do not make textiles (clue 1), so they must make the earthmovers, leaving textiles as the product of VRC in Derby.

In summary:
BGN, Walsall, machine tools, 4.
HJK, Mansfield, chemicals, 10.
MDE, Stockport, earthmovers, 8.
QLH, Cardiff, farm equipment, 12.
VRC, Derby, textiles, 6.

Invasion Cancelled (No 308)
Qdh'adv took over Richard Frazier (clue 2) and Knp'eoc's victim was a bus-driver (clue 3). The traffic warden wasn't taken over by Bdr'aal, Ghl'uik or Qdh'adv (all clue 2), so was Xpj'ioz's victim in Solihull (clue 1). Estate agent Seymour Griffiths wasn't taken over by Ghl'uik (clue 4), so was Bdr'aal's victim. Diane Sims is from Port Talbot (clue 1). Richard Frazier isn't a fast food cook and isn't from Wimbledon (clue 5), so he's the civil servant and is from Gateshead. By elimination, Ghl'uik's victim is a fast food cook. The bus-driver taken over by Knp'eoc is male (clue 3), so is Paul Metcalfe. By elimination, Diane Sims was Ghl'uik's victim, the fast food cook; and Xpj'ioz's victim was Karen Wainwright. Bdr'aal wasn't in Wimbledon (clue 2), so in Oldham, and Knp'eoc was in Wimbledon.

In summary:
Bdr'aal, Oldham, Seymour Griffiths, estate agent.
Ghl'uik, Port Talbot, Diane Sims, fast food cook.
Knp'eoc, Wimbledon, Paul Metcalfe, bus-driver.
Qdh'adv, Gateshead, Richard Frazier, civil servant.
Xpj'ioz, Solihull, Karen Wainwright, traffic warden.

Day-trippers (No 309)
Trip 1 went to Verkeerhoven (clue 5), trip 7 to the barge museum (clue 7) and trip 5 to another museum (clue 6). Thus the odd-numbered trip to Slechtfoort's craft market (clue 1) was number 3. Since number 1 was to Verkeerhoven, the trip to the zoo (clue 4) wasn't number 1 or number 2. Also from clue 4, as the trip to Bochtingen was numbered 2 or higher, the zoo trip wasn't number 6. The zoo trip wasn't number 5 (clue 6), so was number 4. Number 2 was to Bochtingen (clue 4) and number 6 was to Bushalteborg. Trip 7 went to the barge museum, so (clue 3) that to Houdenwijk wasn't number 5 or number 7, so it was trip 4 and number 6 was to the shopping centre. Trip 5 wasn't to Rijdendoorn (clue 6), so to Zachteveld, thus Rijdendoorn was trip 7. Zachteveld isn't the location of the windmill museum (clue 2), or botanical gardens (clue 6), so features the cheese museum. The botanical gardens aren't in Verkeerhoven (clue 5), so in Bochtingen. By elimination, Verkeerhoven is the location of the windmill museum.

In summary:
1, Verkeerhoven, windmill museum.
2, Bochtingen, botanical gardens.
3, Slechtfoort, craft market.
4, Houdenwijk, zoo.
5, Zachteveld, cheese museum.
6, Bushalteborg, shopping centre.
7, Rijdendoorn, barge museum.